THE RULE OF OUR WARFARE

THE RULE OF OUR WARFARE

JOHN HENRY NEWMAN
AND THE TRUE CHRISTIAN LIFE

A Reader

EDITED BY JOHN HULSMAN

Scepter

THE RULE OF OUR WARFARE: JOHN HENRY NEWMAN AND
THE TRUE CHRISTIAN LIFE
Introduction and annotations copyright © John Hulsman 2003

Published by Scepter Publishers, Inc.
New York, N.Y.
www.scepterpublishers.org
ALL RIGHTS RESERVED

ISBN 1-889334-83-9

Composed in Monotype Baskerville
PRINTED IN THE UNITED STATES OF AMERICA

S UCH is the rule of our warfare. We advance by yielding; we rise by falling; we conquer by suffering; we persuade by silence; we become rich by bountifulness; we inherit the earth through meekness; we gain comfort through mourning; we earn glory by penitence and prayer. Heaven and earth shall sooner fall than this rule be reversed; it is the law of Christ's kingdom, and nothing can reverse it but sin.

—*Sermons Bearing on Subjects of the Day*, no. 162,
"Joshua a Type of Christ and His Followers"

*I am indebted to Beverly Maximonis
for her cheerful and generous assistance*

*and to my good friend Eloise Goreau,
whose guidance was, as always, invaluable.*

JOHN HULSMAN

OCTOBER 2002
LAWRENCEVILLE, NEW JERSEY

CONTENTS

INTRODUCTION

The idea for this reader arose out of the wish to introduce my undergraduate Victorian seminar to a fresh John Henry Newman to complement the Newman represented in standard selections from the literary anthologies, usually passages from the erudite *Apologia Pro Vita Sua*, in which Newman recounts the steps toward his famous conversion, or from the satirical *Tamworth Reading Room*, in which Newman skewers liberal views of religion, or perhaps from a lecture in *Idea of a University*, where Newman redefines utilitarian education or gives his famous description of an educated man. More specifically, since a lecture on the "Oxford Movement" is part of my seminar, I wanted my students to hear, behind the dry description of this early nineteenth-century attempt at doctrinal reform of the Anglican Church, what Ian Ker, Newman's fine biographer, calls "the most potent spiritual force behind the Oxford Movement"; that is, Newman's brilliant sermons of the period, collected as *Parochial and Plain Sermons*. It is Newman the famous nineteenth-century preacher who gives a richer, more balanced picture of his genius, because in his sermons Newman is especially personal and concrete—"heart speaks to heart" (*Cor ad cor loquitor*), to use the motto chosen when he became a cardinal. Here we also find in the form of moral and spiritual guidance many ideas that Newman develops in later discursive writing. Newman's thought was remarkably all of a piece, despite a conversion, decades of controversy, and long development through a varied course of writing. He had the most comprehensive and unified view of life—what he called "the Providential system of the world"—of any of the great Victorian writers, so his writing on spirituality gives ready insight into his later and more famous works.

In the course of making this selection, I have tried, too, to provide a guide—one of many possible, given the extraordinary number and variety of the sermons within the grand organic unity of the *Parochial and Plain Sermons*—to one of the fundamental missions of Newman's life and work as theologian, preacher, educator, controversialist, and priest: the restoration of holiness to the Christian life, that of both individuals and the Church. No picture of Newman's work should leave this mission out, though the image of Newman as Victorian "sage" tends to obscure it, just as the historical treatment of nineteenth-century religious life tends to conceal the living tissue of faith in the lives of ordinary Victorians, who consumed sermons as avidly as they did the great entertainment of the age—novels. History foregrounds the great disturbance of traditional Christian faith occasioned by an array of new, concerted secular forces, among them the utilitarian material philosophy reshaping national institutions and a liberal, sceptical spirit of the age, challenging orthodoxies, particularly the doctrinal foundation of Christianity. The latter is displayed in Victorian "crises of faith" precipitated by "Higher Criticism," the beginning of the long-running attempt by scholars to historicize Scripture and strip it of divine authority, and the Darwinian revolution, which, for many, called into question not only the authority of Scripture but the very definition of man as a special creation in the image and likeness of God. So powerful was the Enlightenment heritage of doubt in the nineteenth century, despite the counter-balancing forces of Romanticism, that Newman, later, as a Catholic, would come to believe that only Catholicism or scepticism could prevail in the contemporary world. If the Victorians looked to their "sages," or public intellectuals—chief among them Thomas Carlyle, Matthew Arnold, John Stuart Mill, John Ruskin, and John Henry Newman—to guide them through the thicket of social debate to an understanding of their fractured Christian world, they looked to their preachers to guide them in the duties of daily Christian life. Newman was uniquely suited to the task of combining the roles of sage and shepherd. Threaded throughout his Anglican and Catholic writings composed over many decades—his sermons, treatises, lectures, autobiography, devotions, and letters—is a profound attempt to relate learning and inquiry, even into the great mysteries of Redemption, to the most humble duties of daily Christian life.

Newman's life at Oxford over twenty-five years (1817–1842),

as undergraduate, fellow, and public tutor, but also as curate, vicar, and preacher was, accordingly, two lives running parallel: thinker and pastoral minister. Newman, the student of logic, tutor at Oriel College, church historian, and ecclesiastical reformer, came to be the motive force behind the Oxford Movement. Through a series of scholarly tracts, Newman, John Keble, E. B. Pusey, and others attempted to reform the Anglican Church, which these critics had come to see as no more than an appendage of the state, increasingly subject to liberal political designs, and thoroughly at home in the world. Later, as a Catholic, Newman described graphically his frustration with the Established Church:

> If it be life to impart a tone to the court and houses of parliament . . . to be a principle of order . . . and an organ of benevolence . . . to make men decent, respectable, and sensible . . . to shed a gloss over avarice and ambition,—if indeed it is the life of religion to be the first jewel in the queen's crown, and the highest step of her throne, then doubtless the National Church is replete, it overflows with life; but . . . Life of what kind? Is the Establishment's life merely national life, or is it something more? Is it Catholic life as well? Is it supernatural life? [1]

Through the Tracts, which were disbursed widely, the Tractarians wished to reconnect the Anglican Church to its catholic roots in the Primitive Church and to shore up Anglican doctrine weakened by sectarian controversy, neglect, and the influence of "private judgement"—even at the great risk of arguing for "Romish" views on contested ground such as "justification by faith alone" and sacramentalism. Importantly, they also labored to return the Established Church to a higher standard of sanctity, personal holiness, and reverence before the divine mystery. In their efforts they offended, by turns, the High Church Establishment, the Broad Church "latitudinarian" liberals, and the Evangelicals,

---

[1] *The Difficulties of Anglicans*, in *The Works of Cardinal Newman*, vol. 1 (London: Longmans, Green, and Co., 1910), p. 47.

among others. Finally, the Tractarians came under strong censure from the university and the bishops when Newman published his famous Tract 90 in 1841, arguing essentially that the Anglican credo, the Forty-nine Articles, was really aimed at the abuses of Rome and did not substantially alter its doctrines, which were the universal doctrines Anglicanism shared with Roman Catholicism. After attempts to establish a historical foundation for an Anglo-Catholic Church ended by finding Anglicanism a "paper church" that had never actually existed, Newman moved slowly but inexorably toward Rome. He took with him many Oxford converts, especially among younger men who had come under his influence. In this, by many accounts, his personal sanctity, great empathy, and uncompromising call to holiness in the sermons played as great a part as the Tractarian attack on the Established Church, even greater.

His severance from Oxford and retreat to the nearby village of Littlemore, reception into the Catholic Church in 1845, the national scandal it occasioned, his life as a Catholic priest and head of the English Oratorian Movement are recorded in the *Apologia* and treated in detail by his biographers, but it is in Newman's Anglican years and in his other life at Oxford that he establishes the view of the Christian life that underpins his life and works. Newman came from a Bible-reading Church of England family. His father was a London banker. Newman was converted, or "born again," at fifteen under the influence of an Evangelical teacher. He wavered almost unconsciously when exposed to philosophic scepticism as an undergraduate at Oxford; but then, after setbacks in his academic ambitions and a serious illness while travelling in Sicily, he settled into the personal habits of holiness—he had already decided on celibacy at age fifteen—that he would retain for the rest of his life. And now he began to pursue his unique intellectual mission of reintroducing the religion of the apostles, martyrs, and saints to the age of "progress," the "cash nexus," and "respectability."

The direction that Newman took as a young man in his duties at Oxford is in keeping with the message of the sermons that for the Christian one's religion and work are inseparable. When assigned curate at St. Clement's Church in Oxford, having been ordained deacon in 1824, he came to see in often difficult pastoral duties among working people the limitation of Protestant "saving faith," when faith was so clearly joined to "works." Faith realized in action, not merely words and feelings, became a cardinal truth to him. Likewise, Newman wanted the Christian life to be more integrated with undergraduate life, but was rebuffed when he proposed to reform the tutorial system at Oriel by creating much greater contact, and thus the possibility of healthy personal influence, between tutors and undergraduates. But it was chiefly in the preparation of his Sunday sermons that Newman worked out his spirituality. Part of his duty as Fellow was to serve as vicar of St Mary the Virgin, the university parish church, preaching at the 4:00 service on Sundays and Holy Days. Here, while studying the Church Fathers and conducting, through the Tracts, often arcane theological debates in an atmosphere of political and religious controversy, Newman was able through his preaching to exert extraordinary influence on the daily lives of his parishioners and a widening circle of visitors. Yet he succeeded not by aiming at social "relevance" in the manner of the Evangelical preachers of the day, but by using lively and abundant scriptural quotation, showing the real relation of Christians living in a dangerous and perplexing world to the mystery of revelation and bringing the great catholic doctrines to bear on the ordinary problems of Christians in the world: strong faith, obedience, and discipline, prayer and self-denial, avoiding the snares of a disbelieving and pharisaical world. His very first sermon sets the tone: "Holiness Necessary for Future Blessedness."

There are many accounts by those who heard Newman's sermons, which were carefully drafted and read in a low voice—the preacher rarely looking up—with occasional pauses for emphasis. His mixed audience of the parishioners of St. Mary's was mostly local tradesmen and their families, and undergraduates, though Newman gathered an audience of outsiders, many distinguished, as his reputation grew. Matthew Arnold gives the most famous description of Newman's presence:

> Who could resist the charm of that spiritual apparition, gliding through the dim afternoon light through the

aisles of St. Mary's, rising into the pulpit, and then in the most entrancing of voices, breaking the silence with words and thoughts which were religious music—subtle, sweet, mournful?[2]

Not so well known but even more impressive is a comment by the historian James Anthony Froude. As an undergraduate, he heard Newman preach his sermon "The Incarnate Son, a Sufferer and a Sacrifice." Years later, he described the effect Newman had on his listeners:

Newman described closely some of the incidents of our Lord's Passion; he then paused. For a few minutes there was breathless silence. Then in a cold clear voice, of which the faintest vibration was audible in the farthest corner of St. Mary's, he said, "Now I bid you recollect that He to whom these things were done was Almighty God." It was as if an electric stroke had gone through the church, as if every person present understood for the first time the meaning of what he had all his life been saying. I suppose it was an epoch in the mental history of more than one of my contemporaries.[3]

On the page, these plain sermons represent a brilliant use of the English conversational style. They are never conventional, forced, or ornamental, but stylistically transparent. They are concrete, focused, and alive to the needs of a specific audience, answering to Newman's own description of the art of sermon writing in a later essay, "University Preaching":

Definiteness is the life of preaching. A definite hearer, not the whole world. A definite topic, not the whole evangelical tradition; and in like manner, a definite speaker. Nothing that is anonymous will preach; nothing that is

[2] *The Complete Prose Works of Matthew Arnold*, ed. Daniel Super, vol. 10 (Ann Arbor: University of Michigan Press, 1974), p. 165.

[3] *Short Studies on Great Subjects*, vol. 4 (New York: Charles Scribner's Sons, 1886), p. 88.

dead and gone; nothing even which is of yesterday, however religious in itself and useful. Thought and word are one in the Eternal Logos, and must not be separate in those who are his shadow on earth. They must issue fresh and fresh, as from the preacher's mouth, so from his breast, if they are to be "spirit and life" to the hearts of his hearers.[4]

Newman's sister Jemima has the final word. Though speaking of the collected *Oxford University Sermons*, she could as easily be describing the *Parochial and Plain Sermons*: "It makes deep things so very simple."[5]

Unfortunately, excerpting these sermons sacrifices perhaps their most pronounced feature, scriptural lessons so rich in detail, so alive, surprising, and subtle that it is impossible not to hear these Biblical texts anew. Generally, a reading involving a passage or parable, feast or mystery, Biblical incident or character is used to probe deeply into a virtue of or danger to the Christian life— earnestness or equanimity, conscience, or the temptation of worldly advantages—illuminating its many facets by a uniquely Newmanesque circling of the subject. Newman likes to develop his theme through a whole range of ideas, testing it again and again in relation to differing standards and perceptions—the light of Scripture, the mandate of conscience, the authority of doctrine, and then in contrast, perhaps the power of custom and evidence of common sense, the fashions of the world, and the prism of often-deceiving "private judgement"—cutting away the grounds of rationalization, self-delusion, and denial. Newman has the singular ability to present the great complexity of life and the paradoxes of Christian warfare in the world while keeping us ever aware of the one Truth behind it all. Error is always renewing itself, but truth is always the same. The Christian who lives by faith not sight and is steadfast in the disciplines of holiness will be led to a deeper understanding of the Truth. Obedience and active faith in a world of "excitements" and temptations is the means to developing "spiritual discernment," a life-long conversion in

[4] *Idea of a University*, in *The Works of Cardinal Newman*, vol ??, p. 426.
[5] *Letters and Correspondence of John Henry Newman*, ed. Anne Mozley, vol. 2 (London: Longmans, Green, and Co., 1970), p. 367.

contrast to the single emotional conversion of the evangels that Newman had long suspected. Newman's spirituality, especially in the sermons, reflects the two sayings of Thomas Scott of Aston Sandford, whom Newman read in his youth, which are mentioned in the *Apologia* as deeply influential: "Holiness rather than peace" and "Growth, the only evidence of life." [6]

These lessons are not mere exhibitions or arguments but, to use Newman's language, "realizations" of the subject in which the reader, engaged wholly, finds himself obliged to examine his life. "Real Assent," as Newman argued in his *Oxford University Sermons* and later in the *Essay in Aid of a Grammar of Assent*, requires not abstract argument but vivid particular images. Religious truth, which we are bound by conscience to seek, eludes scientific demonstration. It is an accumulation of probabilities "sufficient for certitude." Repeated exposure to the multivalent truth of revelation through Newman's evocative sermons is a concrete embodiment, a realization, of his grammar of assent.

Readers who have in mind the urbane author of the *Apologia* or the brilliant expositor of the relationship of faith and reason or the formulator of the mission of education in a secularizing world are surprised by the uncompromising severity of the sermons. For Newman, "beauty and severity" are the inseparable attributes of religion. Some scholars attribute this to Newman's youthful exposure to Calvinism, but Newman found ample justification in his society to use these sermons to attack what he sees as the apostasy of the age, which the lax, worldly "religion of the day" has no resources to counter. Too often, the latter has identified itself with this world as if religion were no different from decent behavior, philanthropic attitudes, and improvement in sanitation. Moreover, Newman was perfectly aware that traditional religious practice, with its creeds and disciplines, was a weariness to most men and for others violated "private judgement," democratic individualism, or the "cheerfulness" of those already saved by their experience of faith. He had no illusion that his view of holiness as the standard for all Christians, not simply clergy, was a novel ideal to many and at sharp variance with the attitudes of an enlightened

[6] *Apologia Pro Vita Sua*, ed. Martin Svaglic (Oxford: Clarendon Press, 1967), p. 19.

and progressive age. Those whose principles conflicted with his own were, he wrote in 1850, "on the best terms with queen and statesmen, and practical men, and country gentlemen, and respectable tradesmen, fathers and mothers, schoolmasters, churchwardens, vestries, public societies, newspapers, and their readers in the lower classes." [7]

Thus Newman holds before his age and ours the picture of the faith of the Apostolic Age, the presence of the Invisible Church and the power of the Indwelling Spirit. He warns the educated that faith can be destroyed by the corrosive power of the untempered critical reason; that Christianity is a system, the suppression of any part of which invites disobedience and falsehood; that conscience is God in man and must be followed at any cost; that the world is the same idol that it has always been, despite "progress." The true Christian must, with much effort, develop consistent habits of obedience, reverence, and self-denial if he is to overcome the deeply ingrained habit of sin and reach a higher level of spiritual discernment afforded by grace. He must live a life "hidden in Christ," watching and waiting, as enjoined by Revelation.

Newman created a highly developed and consistent discourse on the Christian life in his Anglican sermons, one which threads throughout his numerous works, but since almost all of his writing is for occasions—in answer to "divine calls"—he did not write a systematic spiritual theology per se, although Vincent Blehl and Ian Ker have examined the parts lucidly and demonstrated their living unity. [8]

My purpose in these selections has not been to systematize Newman—although Newman's whole view of the moral and spiritual life of man combined with his insistence on balance and consistency in both religious discourse and Christian living should be a caution to any anthologist—but to give an introductory sampling, particularly of the formidable bulk of the hundred and ninety-one densely written *Parochial and Plain Sermons*, that might serve as a

[7] *Difficulties of Anglicans*, in *The Works of Cardinal Newman*, vol. 1, p. 13.

[8] See Vincent Blehl, *The White Stone* (Petersham, Mass.: St. Bede's Publications, 1993); and Ian Ker, *Newman on Being a Christian* (Notre Dame: University of Notre Dame Press, 1990), particularly chap. 7, "Christian Life." See also Ker's introduction to *John Henry Newman: Selected Sermons* (New York: Paulist Press, 1994).

guide or daily reader. For the sake of variety and breadth, the selections from these sermons delivered by Newman at St. Mary's between 1828 and 1843 are leavened by passages on the Christian life from other works, both Anglican and Catholic, including *Sermons bearing on Subjects of the Day, Oxford University Sermons, Sermons Preached on Various Occasions, Lectures on Certain Difficulties Felt by Anglicans, The Idea of a University, An Essay in Aid of a Grammar of Assent, Discussions and Arguments,* etc. However, it is those fifteen years of *Parochial and Plain Sermons* that form the monument of Newman's spirituality and set the tone for his many later investigations of the Christian life.

The divisions I have marked out—Faith, The True Christian Life, Temptation, The World, Doubt, and Mysteries—are, as the reader will see, a simple arrangement of Newman's view of Christian development, one with highly permeable membranes, for Newman is always in his sermons constructing a picture of the whole Christian life, nor can he speak long about faith without introducing temptation, the world, and doubt. The Christian mysteries—Newman's study of the Church Fathers profoundly affected his theology—are ever-present in his thought, so we are continually made aware that the individual soul is wedded to the Church Invisible. I also hope to capture both the elegant prose and the profound lessons of the other Newman, whose great contribution to our understanding of the spiritual life is the ballast to his more public career as Victorian thinker and controversialist. Having taken note of Newman's remarkable contribution to the nineteenth-century debate over faith and reason, Pope John Paul II ends a recent papal letter on the second centenary of Newman's birth with the hope that "the time will soon come when the Church can officially and publicly proclaim the exemplary holiness of Cardinal John Henry Newman, one of the most distinguished and versatile champions of English spirituality." [9]

John Hulsman
RIDER UNIVERSITY

[9] "Papal Letter on Cardinal John Henry Newman on Occasion of Second Centenary of His Birth," Feb. 27, 2001.

Newman's works are collected in a 36-volume uniform edition of 1868–1881. He continued to make minor changes in individual volumes until his death in 1890. All references in the reader are to volumes in the uniform edition published by Longmans, Green, and Co. after 1890. I have retained Newman's puncuation but moved his biblical citations from footnotes to parenthetical entries in the text.

ABBREVIATIONS

DA   *Discussions and Arguments on Various Subjects*

Diff.   *Certain Difficulties Felt by Anglicans in Catholic Teaching* (2 vols.)

Ess.   *Essays Critical and Historical* (2 vols.)

GA   *An Essay in Aid of a Grammar of Assent*

HS   *Historical Sketches* (3 vols.)

Idea   *Idea of a University*

Jfc   *Lectures on the Doctrine of Justification*

LG   *Loss and Gain: The Story of a Convert*

OS   *Sermons Preached on Various Occasions*

PS   *Parochial and Plain Sermons* (8 vols.)

SD   *Sermons Bearing on Subjects of the Day*

US   *Fifteen Sermons Preached before the University of Oxford*

John Henry Newman by J. A. Vinter after Maria Giberne. NPG.

BY COURTESY OF THE NATIONAL PORTRAIT GALLERY, LONDON

FAITH

1. Private Judgement and Divine Voice

[T]he very staple of the sacred narrative, from beginning to end, is a call on all men to believe what is not proved, not plain, to them on the warrant of divine messengers; because the very form of our Lord's teaching is to substitute authority for argument; because the very principle of His grave earnestness, the very key to His regenerative mission, is the intimate connexion of faith with salvation. Faith is not simply trust in His legislation, as the writer says; it is definitely trust in His word, whether that word be about heavenly things or earthly; whether it is spoken by His own mouth, or through His ministers. The angel who announced the Baptist's birth, said, "Thou shalt be dumb, because thou believest not my words." The Baptist's mother said of Mary, "Blessed is she that believed." The Baptist himself said, "He that believeth on the Son hath everlasting life: and he that believeth not the Son shall not see life, but the wrath of God abideth on him.". . .

How is it possible to deny that our Lord, both in the text and in the context of these and other passages, made faith in a message, on the warrant of the messenger, to be a condition of salvation, and enforced it by the great grant of power which He emphatically conferred on His representatives? "Whosoever shall not receive you," He says, "nor hear your words, when ye depart, shake off the dust of your feet." "It is not ye that speak, but the Spirit of your Father.". . . "I will give unto thee the keys of the kingdom of heaven; and whatsoever thou shalt bind on earth shall be bound in heaven, and whatsoever thou shalt loose on earth shall be loosed in heaven.". . .

. . . Our Lord rested His teaching, not on the concurrence and testimony of His hearers, but on His own authority. He imposed upon them the declarations of a Divine Voice. . . . No revelation then is conceivable, which does not involve, almost in its very idea as being something new, a collision with the human intellect, and demands accordingly, if it is to be accepted, a sacrifice of private judgement on the part of those to whom it is addressed. If a revelation be necessary then also in consequence is that sacrifice necessary. One man will have to make a sacrifice in one respect, another in another, all men in some.

We say, then, to men of the day, Take Christianity, or leave it; do not practise upon it; to do so is as unphilosophical as it is dangerous. Do not attempt to halve a spiritual unit. You are apt to call it a dishonesty in us to refuse to follow our reasonings, when faith stands in the way; is there no intellectual dishonesty in your self-trust? . . . You either accept Christianity, or you do not: if you do, do not garble and patch it; if you do not, suffer others to submit to it ungarbled.

(DA 395–98, "An Internal Argument for Christianity")

2. The Cross of Christ

Now, let me ask, what *is* the real key, what is the Christian interpretation of this world? What is given us by revelation to estimate and measure this world by? . . .

It is the death of the Eternal Word of God made flesh, which is our great lesson how to think and how to speak of this world. His Cross has put its due value upon every thing which we see, upon all fortunes, all advantages, all ranks, all dignities, all pleasure; upon the lust of the flesh, and the lust of the eyes, and the pride of life. It has set a price upon the excitements, the rivalries, the hopes, the fears, the desires, the efforts, the triumphs of mortal man. It has given a meaning to the various, shifting course, the trials, the temptations, the sufferings, of his earthly state. It has brought together and made consistent all that seemed discordant and aimless. It has taught us how to live, how to use this world, what to expect, what to desire, what to hope. It is the tone into which all the strains of this world's music are ultimately to be resolved. . . .

But it will be said, that the view which the Cross of Christ imparts to us of human life and of the world, is not that which we should take, if left to ourselves; that it is not an obvious view. . . . The world seems made for the enjoyment of just such a being as man, and man is put into it. He has the *capacity* of enjoyment, and the world supplies the *means*. How natural this, what a simple as well as pleasant philosophy, yet how different from that of the Cross! The doctrine of the Cross, it may be said, disarranges two parts of a system which seem made for each other; it severs the fruit from the eater, the enjoyment from the enjoyer. How does this solve a problem? Does it not rather itself create one? . . .

. . . [I]t is but a superficial view of things to say that this life is made for pleasure and happiness. To those who look under the surface, it tells a very different tale. The doctrine of the Cross does but teach, though infinitely more forcibly, still after all it does but teach the very same lesson which this world teaches to those who live long in it, who have much experience in it, who know it. The world is sweet to the lips, but bitter to the taste. It pleases at first, but not at last. . . . Therefore the doctrine of the Cross of Christ does but anticipate for us our experience of the world. It is true, it bids us grieve for our sins in the midst of all that smiles and glitters around us; but if we will not heed it, we shall at length be forced to grieve for them from undergoing their fearful punishment. . . .

And as the doctrine of the Cross, though it be the true interpretation of this world, is not prominently manifested in it, upon its surface, but is concealed; so again, when received into the faithful heart, there it abides as a living principle, but deep, and hidden from observation. . . .

. . . [T]he great and awful doctrine of the Cross of Christ, which we now commemorate, may fitly be called, in the language of figure, the *heart* of religion. The heart may be considered as the seat of life; it is the principle of motion, heat and activity; from it the blood goes to and fro to the extreme parts of the body. It sustains the man in his powers and faculties; it enables the brain to think; and when it is touched, man dies. And in like manner the sacred doctrine of Christ's Atoning Sacrifice is the vital principle on which the Christian lies, and without which Christianity is not. Without it no other doctrine is held profitable; to believe in

Christ's Divinity, or in His manhood, or in the Holy Trinity, or in a judgement to come, or in the resurrection of the dead, is an untrue belief, not Christian faith, unless we receive also the doctrine of Christ's sacrifice. On the other hand, to receive it presupposes the reception of other high truths of the Gospel besides; it involves the belief in Christ's true divinity, in His true incarnation and in man's sinful state by nature; and it prepares the way to belief in the sacred Eucharistic feast, in which He who was once crucified is ever given to our souls and bodies, verily and indeed, in His body and in His Blood. But again, the heart is hidden from view; it is carefully and securely guarded; it is not like the eye set in the forehead, commanding all, and seen of all: and so in like manner the sacred doctrine of the Atoning Sacrifice is not one to be talked of, but to be lived upon; not to be put forth irreverently, but to be adored secretly; not to be used as a necessary instrument in the conversion of the ungodly, or for the satisfaction of reasoners of this world, but to be unfolded to the docile and obedient; to young children, whom the world has not corrupted; to the sorrowful, who need comfort; to the sincere and earnest, who need a rule of life; to the innocent, who need warning; and to the established, who have earned the knowledge of it.

(PS 6:84–90, "The Cross of Christ: The Measure of the World")

3. Living Faith

We know Scripture tells us that God accepts those who have faith in Him. Now the question is, What *is* faith, and how can a man tell that he *has* faith? Some persons answer at once and without hesitation, that "to have faith is to feel oneself to be nothing, and God every thing; it is to be convinced of sin, to be conscious one cannot save oneself, and to wish to be saved by Christ our Lord; and that it is, moreover, to have the love of Him warm in one's heart, and to rejoice in Him, to desire His glory, and to resolve to live to Him and not to the world." But I will answer with all due seriousness, as speaking on a serious subject, that this is *not* faith. Not that it is not necessary (it is very necessary) to be convinced that we are laden with infirmity and sin, and without health in us, and to look for salvation solely to Christ's blessed sacrifice on the cross; and we may well be thankful if we are thus minded; but that a man may feel all this that I have described, vividly, and still not yet possess one particle of true religious faith. Why? Because there is an immeasurable distance between feeling right and doing right. A man may have all these good thoughts and emotions, yet (if he has not yet hazarded them to the experiment of practice) he cannot promise himself that he has any sound and permanent principle at all. If he has not yet acted upon them, we have no voucher, barely on *account* of them, to believe that they are any thing but words. Though a man spoke like an angel, I would not believe him, on the mere ground of his speaking. Nay, till he acts upon them, he has not even evidence to himself that he has true living faith. . . . He who does one little deed of obedience, whether he denies himself some comfort to relieve the sick and needy, or curbs his temper, or forgives an enemy, or asks forgiveness for an offence committed by him, or resists the clamour or ridicule of the world—such an one (as far as we are given to judge) evinces more true faith than could be shown by the most fluent religious conversation, the most intimate knowledge of Scripture doctrine, or the most remarkable agitation and change of religious sentiments. Yet how many are there who sit still with folded hands, dreaming, doing nothing at all, thinking they have done every thing, or need do nothing, when they merely have had these good *thoughts*, which will save no one!

(PS 1:170–72, "Promising without Doing")

4. Faith and Fear

Whole societies called Christian make it almost a first principle to disown the duty of reverence; and we ourselves, to whom as children of the Church reverence is as a special inheritance, have very little of it, and do not feel the want of it. Those who, in spite of themselves, are influenced by God's holy fear, too often are ashamed of it, consider it even as a mark of weakness of mind, hide their feelings as much as they can, and, when ridiculed or censured for it, cannot defend it to themselves on intelligible grounds. They wish indeed to maintain reverence in their mode of speaking and acting, in relation to sacred things, but they are at a loss how to answer objections, or how to resist received customs and fashions; and at length they begin to be suspicious and afraid of their own instinctive feelings. . . .

. . . [C]an anything be clearer than that the *want* of fear is nothing else but *want* of faith, and that in consequence we in this age are approaching in religious temper that evil day of which it is said, "When the Son of Man cometh, shall He find faith on the earth?" (Lk 18: 8) Is it wonderful that we have no fear in our words and mutual intercourse, when we exercise no *acts* of faith? What, you will ask, are acts of faith? Such as these—to come often to prayer, is an act of faith; to kneel down instead of sitting, is an act of faith; to strive to attend to your prayers, is an act of faith; to behave in God's House otherwise than you would in a common room, is an act of faith; to come to it on week-days as well as Sundays, is an act of faith; to come often to the most Holy Sacrament, is an act of faith; and to be still and reverent during that sacred service, is an act of faith. These are all acts of faith, because they all are acts such as we should perform, if we saw and heard Him who *is* present though with our bodily eyes we see and hear Him *not*. But "blessed are they who have not seen, and yet have believed;" for, be sure, if we thus act, we shall, through God's grace, be gradually endued with the spirit of His holy fear. We shall in time, in our mode of talking and acting, in our religious services and our daily conduct, manifest, not with constraint and effort, but spontaneously and naturally, that we fear Him while we love Him.

(PS 5:14–15, 27–28, "Reverence, a Belief in God's Presence")

5. Faith Leading to Truth

A subtle infidel might soon perplex any one of us. Of course he might. Our very state and warfare is one of faith. Let us aim at, let us reach after and (as it were) catch at the things of the next world. There is a voice within us, which assures us that there is something higher than earth. We cannot analyze, define, contemplate what it is that thus whispers to us. It has no shape or material form. There is that in our hearts which prompts us to religion, and which condemns and chastises sin. And this yearning of our nature is met and sustained, it finds an object to rest upon, when it hears of the existence of an All-powerful, All-gracious Creator. It incites us to a noble faith in what we cannot see.

Let us exercise a similar faith, as regards the Mysteries of Revelation also. Here is the true use of Scripture in leading us to the truth. If we read it humbly and inquire teachably, we shall find; we shall have a deep impression on our minds that the doctrines of the Creed are there, though we may not be able to put our hands upon particular texts, and say how much of it is contained here and how much there. But, on the other hand, if we read in order to *prove* those doctrines, in a critical, argumentative way, then all traces of them will disappear from Scripture as if they were not there. They will fade away insensibly like hues at sunset, and we shall be left in darkness. We shall come to the conclusion that they are not in Scripture, and shall, perhaps, boldly call them unscriptural. Religious convictions cannot be forced; nor is Divine truth ours to summon at will. If we *determine* that we will find it out, we shall find nothing. Faith and humility are the only spells which conjure up the image of heavenly things into the letter of inspiration; and faith and humility consist, not in going about to prove, but in the outset confiding on the testimony of others. . . . Be sure, the highest reason is not to reason on system, or by rules of argument, but in a natural way; not with formal intent to draw out proofs, but trusting to God's blessing that you may gain a right impression from what you read. If your reasoning powers are weak, using argumentative forms will not make them stronger. They will enable you to dispute acutely and to hit objections, but not to discover truth. There is nothing creative, nothing progressive in exhibitions of argument. The utmost they do is to enable us to state well what we have already discovered by the tranquil exercise of our reason. Faith and obedience are the main things; believe and do, and pray to God for light, and you will reason well without knowing it.

Let us not then seek for signs and wonders; for clear, or strong, or compact, or original arguments; but let us *believe*; evidence will come after faith as its reward, better than before it as its ground-work. Faith soars aloft; it listens for the notes of heaven, the faint voices or echoes which scarcely reach the earth, and it thinks them worth all the louder sounds of cities or of schools of men. It is foolishness in the eyes of the world; but it is a foolishness of God wiser than the world's wisdom. Let us embrace the sacred Mystery of the Trinity in Unity, which, as the Creed tells us, is the ground of the Catholic religion. Let us think it enough, let us think it far too great a privilege, for sinners such as we are, for a fallen people in a degenerate age, to inherit the faith once delivered to the Saints; let us accept it thankfully; let us guard it watchfully; let us transmit it faithfully to those who come after us.

(PS 6:339–42, "Faith without Demonstration")

6. Saving Grace

In a word, the state of the multitude of men is this,—their hearts are going the wrong way; and their real quarrel with religion, if they know themselves, is not that it is strict, or engrossing, or imperative, not that it goes too far, but that it *is* religion. It is religion itself which we all by nature dislike, not the excess merely. Nature tends towards the earth, and God is in heaven. If I want to travel north, and all the roads are cut to the east, of course I shall complain of the roads. I shall find nothing but obstacles; I shall have to surmount walls, and cross rivers, and go round about, and after all fail of my end. Such is the conduct of those who are not bold enough to give up a profession of religion, yet wish to serve the world. They try to reach Babylon by roads which run to Mount Sion. Do you not see that they necessarily must meet with thwartings, crossings, disappointments, and failure? They go mile after mile, watching in vain for the turrets of the city of Vanity, because they are on the wrong road; and, unwilling to own what they are really seeking, they find fault with the road as circuitous and wearisome. They accuse religion of interfering with what they consider their innocent pleasures and wishes. But religion is a bondage only to those who have not the heart to like it, who are not cast into its mould.

We Christians are indeed under the law as other men, but, as I have already said, it is the new law, the law of the Spirit of Christ. We are under grace. That law, which to nature is a grievous bondage, is to those who live under the power of God's presence, what it was meant to be, a rejoicing. When then we feel reluctant to serve God, when thoughts rise within us as if He were a hard Master, and that His promises are not attractive enough to balance the strictness of His commandments, let us recollect that we, as being Christians, are not in the flesh, but in the Spirit, and let us act upon the conviction of it. Let us go to Him for grace. . . . They who pray for His saving help to change their likings and dislikings, their tastes, their views, their will, their hearts, do not indeed all at once gain what they seek;—they do not gain it as once asking;—they do not *perceive* they gain it while they gain it,— but if they come continually day by day to Him,—if they come humbly,—if they come in faith,—if they come, not as a trial how they shall like God's service, but throwing (as far as may be) their whole hearts and souls into their duty as a sacrifice to Him,—if they come, not seeking a sign, but determined to go on seeking Him, honouring Him, serving Him, trusting Him, whether they see light, or feel comfort, or discern their growth, or no,—such men *will* gain, though they know it not; they will find, even while they are still seeking; before they call, He will answer them, and they will in the end find themselves saved wondrously, to their surprise, how they know not, and when their crown seemed at a distance. . . .

(PS 4:14, 16–17, "The Strictness of the Law of Christ")

7. A Lifelong Act

[I] am speaking of [Faith's] relation to works, and I say that, viewed as justifying, it lives in them. It is not (as it were) a shadow or phantom, which flits about without voice or power, but it is faith developed into height and depth and breadth, as if in a bodily form, not as a picture but as an image, with a right side and a left, a without and within; not a mere impression or sudden gleam of light upon the soul, not knowledge, or emotion, or conviction which ends with itself, but the beginning of that which is eternal, the operation of the Indwelling Power which acts from within us outwards and round about us, works in us mightily, so intimately with our will as to be in a true sense one with it; pours itself out into our whole mind, runs over into our thoughts, desires, feelings, purposes, attempts, and works, combines them all together into one, makes the whole man its one instrument, and justifies him into one holy and gracious ministry, one embodied lifelong act of faith, one "sacrifice, holy, acceptable to God, which is his reasonable service." Such is faith, springing up out of the immortal seed of love, and ever budding forth in new blossoms and maturing new fruit, existing indeed in feelings but passing on into acts, into victories of whatever kind over self, being the power of the will over the whole soul for Christ's sake, constraining the reason to accept mysteries, the heart to acquiesce in suffering, the hand to work, the feet to run, the voice to bear witness, as the case may be. These acts we sometimes call labours, sometimes endurances, sometimes confessions, sometimes devotions, sometimes services; but they are all instances of self-command, arising from Faith seeing the invisible world, and Love choosing it.

(JFC 302-03, "Faith Viewed Relatively to Rites and Works")

8. Continual Conversion

That religion is true which has power, and so far as it has power; nothing but what is divine can renew the heart. And this is the secret reason *why* religious men believe, whether they are adequately conscious of it or no, whether they can put it into words or no; viz. their past experience that the doctrine which they hold is a reality in their minds, not a mere opinion, and has come to them, "not in word, but in power." And in this sense the presence of religion in us is its own evidence. . . . [We] rest upon our logical proofs only when we get perplexed with objections, or are in doubt, or otherwise troubled in mind; or, again, we betake ourselves to the external evidence, or to argumentative process, not as a matter of personal interest, but from a desire to gaze upon God's great work more intently, and to adore God's wisdom more worthily. . . .

I suppose a religious man is conscious that God has been with him, and given him whatever he has of good within him. He knows quite enough of himself to know how fallen he is from original righteousness, and he has a conviction, which nothing can shake, that without the aid of his Lord and Saviour, he can do nothing aright. I do not say he need recollect any definite season when he turned to God and gave up the service of sin and Satan; but in one sense every season, every year is such a time of turning. I mean, he ever has experience, just as if he had hitherto been living to the world, of a continual conversion; he is ever taking advantage of holy seasons and new providences, and beginning again. The elements of sin are still alive within him; they still tempt and influence him, and threaten when they do no more; and it is only by a continual fight against them that he prevails; and what shall persuade him that his power to fight is his own, and not from above? And this conviction of a Divine Presence with him is stronger according to the length of time during which he has served God, and to his advance in holiness. The multitude of men—nay, a great number of those who think themselves religious—do not aim at holiness, and do not advance in holiness; but consider what a great evidence it is that God is with us, so far as we have it. Religious men, really such, cannot but recollect in the course of years, that they have become very different from what they were. I say "in the course of years": this it is, among other things, which makes young persons less settled in their religion. They have not given it a trial; they have not had time to do so; but in the course of years a religious person finds that a mysterious unseen influence has been upon him and has changed him. He is indeed very different from what he was. His tastes, his views, his judgements are different. You will say that time changes a man as a matter of course; advancing age, outward circumstances, trials, experience of life. It is true; and yet I think a religious man would feel it little less than sacrilege, and almost blasphemy, to impute the improvement in his heart and conduct, in his moral being, with which he has been favoured in a certain sufficient period, to outward or merely natural causes. He will be unable to force himself to do so: that is to say, he has a conviction, which it is a point of religion with him not to doubt, which it is a sin to deny, that

God has been with him. And this is of course a ground of hope to him that God will be with him still; and if he, at any time, fall into religious perplexity, it may serve to comfort him to think of it.

(SD 346, 348–50, "Grounds for Steadfastness in Our Religious Profession")

9. Filling the Void Within

Man is not sufficient for his own happiness; he is not happy except the Presence of God be with him. When he was created, God breathed into him that supernatural life of the Spirit which is his true happiness: and when he fell, he lost the divine gift, and with it his happiness also. Ever since he has been unhappy; ever since he has a void within him which needs filling, and he knows not how to fill it. He scarcely realizes his own need: only his actions show that he feels it, for he is ever restless when he is not dull and insensible, seeking in one thing or another that blessing which he has lost. Multitudes, indeed, there are, whose minds have never been opened; and multitudes who stupify and deaden their minds, till they lose their natural hunger and thirst: but, whether aware of their need or not, whether made restless by it or not, still all men have it, and the Gospel supplies it; and then, even if they did not recognize their want by nature, they at length learn it by its supply. This, then, is the secret of the triumph of Christ's Kingdom. Soldiers of this world receive their bounty-money on enlisting. They take it, and become the servants of an earthly prince: shall not they, much more, be faithful, yea, unto the death, who have received the earnest of the true riches, who have been fed with the hidden manna, who have "tasted the good word of God, and the powers of the world to come," and "the graciousness of the Lord," and "the peace which passeth all understanding?" . . . Others marvel; others try to analyze what it is which does the work; they imagine all manner of human causes, because they cannot see, and do not feel, and will not believe the inward influence; and they impute to some caprice or waywardness of mind, or to the force of novelty, or to some mysterious insidious persuasives, or to some concealed enemy, or to some dark and subtle plotting, and they view with alarm, and they fain would baffle, what is really the keen, vivid, constraining glance of Christ's countenance. "The Lord turned and looked upon Peter;" and "as the lightning cometh out of the east, and shineth even unto the west, so also is the Presence of the Son of man." It is come, it is gone, it has done its work, its abiding work, before men see it. . . .

. . . [I]f you have gained any good thing, not merely in, but through your Church; if you have come to Service, and been favoured with the peace or the illumination you needed; or if you can recollect times when you visited holy places, and certainly gained there a manifestation such as the world could not give; or if sermons have come to you with power, and have been blessed to your spiritual good; or if your soul has been, as it were, transfig-ured within you, when you came to the Most Holy Sacrament. . . . [O]r if strange providences, and almost supernatural coincidences have hung about the Church's Ordinances; if mercies or judge-ments have descended through them upon yourselves, or upon those about you; or if you have experience of death-beds, and know how full of hope the children of our Church can die; O! pause ere you doubt that we have a Divine Presence among us still. . . . . [W]hy should not we enjoy the hidden Kingdom of Christ, though others may not have faith to see it? And we will cling to the Church in which we are, not for its own sake, but because we humbly trust that Christ is in it; and while He is in it, we will abide in it. . . .

(SD 312–13, 321–23, "Invisible Presence of Christ")

10. Holiness through Infirmity

True faith is not shown here below in peace, but rather in conflict; and it is no proof that a man is not in a state of grace that he continually sins, provided such sins do not remain on him as what I may call ultimate results, but are ever passing on into something beyond and unlike themselves, into truth and righteousness. As we gain happiness through suffering, so do we arrive at holiness through infirmity, because man's very condition is a fallen one, and in passing out of the country of sin, he necessarily passes through it. . . .

. . . The soul of man is intended to be a well-ordered polity, in which there are many powers and faculties, and each has its due place; and for these to exceed their limits is sin; yet they cannot be kept within those limits except by being governed, and we are unequal to this task of governing ourselves except after long habit. While we are learning to govern ourselves, we are constantly exposed to the risk, or rather to the occurrence, of numberless failures. We have failures by the way, though we triumph in the end; and thus, as I just now implied, the process of learning to obey God is, in one sense, a process of sinning, from the nature of the case. We have much to be forgiven; nay, we have the more to be forgiven the more we attempt. The higher our aims, the greater our risks. They who venture much with their talents, gain much, and in the end they hear the words, "Well done, good and faithful servant;" but they have so many losses in trading by the way, that to themselves they seem to do nothing but fail. They cannot believe that they are making any progress; and though they do, yet surely they have much to be forgiven in all their services. They are like David, men of blood; they fight the good fight of faith, but they are polluted with the contest. . . .

We indeed have not knowledge such as His; were we ever so high in God's favour, a certainty of our justification would not belong to us. Yet, even to know only thus much, that infirmities are no necessary mark of reprobation, that God's elect have infirmities, and that our own sins may possibly be no more than infirmities, this surely, by itself, is a consolation. And to reflect that at least God continues us visibly in His Church; that He does not withdraw from us the ordinances of grace; that He gives us means of instruction, patterns of holiness, religious guidance, good books; that He allows us to frequent His house, and to present ourselves before Him in prayer and Holy Communion; that He gives us opportunities of private prayer; that He has given us a care for our souls; and anxiety to secure our salvation; a desire to be more strict and conscientious, more simple in faith, more full of love than we are; all this will tend to soothe and encourage us, when the sense of our infirmities makes us afraid. And if further, God seems to be making us His instruments for any purpose of His, for teaching, warning, guiding, or comforting others, resisting error, spreading the knowledge of the truth, or edifying His Church, this too will create in us the belief, not that God is certainly pleased with us, for knowledge of mysteries may be separated from love, but that He has not utterly forsaken us in spite of our sins, that He still remembers us, and knows us by name, and desires our salvation. And further, if, for all our infirmities, we can point to some occasions on which we have sacrificed anything for God's service, or to any habit of sin or evil tendency of nature which we have more or less overcome, or to any habitual self-denial which we practice, or to any work which we have accomplished to God's honour and glory; this perchance may fill us with the humble hope that God is working in us, and therefore is at peace with us. And, lastly, if we have, through God's mercy, an inward sense of our own sincerity and integrity, if we feel that we can appeal to God with St. Peter, that we love Him only, and desire to please Him in all things, in proportion as we feel this, or at such times as we feel it, we have an assurance shed abroad on our hearts, that we are at present in His favour, and are in training for the inheritance of His eternal kingdom.

(PS 5:210, 213–14, 219–21, "Sins of Infirmity")

11. Divine Calls

For in truth we are not called once only, but many times; all through our life Christ is calling us. He called us first in Baptism; but afterwards also; whether we obey His voice or not, He graciously calls us still. If we fall from our Baptism, He calls us to repent; if we are striving to fulfil our calling, He calls us on from grace to grace, and from holiness to holiness, while life is given us. Abraham was called from his home, Peter from his nets, Matthew from his office, Elisha from his farm, Nathanael from his retreat; we are all in course of calling, on and on, from one thing to another, having no resting-place, but mounting towards our eternal rest, and obeying one command only to have another put upon us. He calls us again and again, in order to justify us again and again,—and again—and again, and more and more, to sanctify and glorify us.

It were well if we understood this; but we are slow to master the great truth, that Christ is, as it were, walking among us, and by His hand, or eye, or voice, bidding us follow Him. We do not understand that His call is a thing which takes place now. We think it took place in the Apostles' days; but we do not believe in it, we do not look out for it in our own case. . . .

Now what I mean is this: that they who are living religiously, have from time to time truths they did not know before, or had no need to consider, brought before them forcibly; truths which involve duties, which are in fact precepts, and claim obedience. In this and such-like ways Christ calls us now. There is nothing miraculous or extraordinary in His dealings with us. He works through our natural faculties and circumstances of life. Still what happens to us in providence is in all essential respects what His voice was to those whom He addressed when on earth: whether He commands by a visible presence, or by a voice, or by our consciences, it matters not, so that we feel it to be a command. If it is a command, it may be obeyed or disobeyed; it may be accepted as Samuel or St. Paul accepted it, or put aside after the manner of the young man who had great possessions.

And these Divine calls are commonly, from the nature of the case, sudden now, and as indefinite and obscure in their consequences as in former times. The accidents and events of life are, as is obvious, one special way in which the calls I speak of come to us; and they, as we all know, are in their very nature, and as the word accident implies, sudden and unexpected. A man is going on as usual; he comes home one day, and finds a letter or a message, or a person, whereby a sudden trial comes on him which, if met religiously, will be the means of advancing him to a higher state of religious excellence, which at present he as little comprehends as the unspeakable words heard by St. Paul in paradise. By a trial we commonly mean, a something which if encountered well, will confirm a man in his present way; but I am speaking of something more than this; of what will not only confirm him, but raise him into a high state of knowledge and holiness. . . .

Or again, perhaps something occurs to force us to take a part for God or against Him. The world requires of us some sacrifice which we see we ought not to grant to it. Some tempting offer is made us; or some reproach or discredit threatened us; or we have to determine and avow what is truth and what is error. We are enabled to act as God would have us act; and we do so in much fear and perplexity. We do not see our way clearly; we do not see what is to follow from what we have done, and how it bears upon our general conduct and opinions: yet perhaps it has the most important bearings. That little deed, suddenly exacted of us, almost suddenly resolved on and executed, may be as though a gate into the second or third heaven—an entrance into a higher state of holiness, and into a truer view of things than we have hitherto taken. . . .

Once more, it may so happen that we find ourselves, how or why we cannot tell, much more able to obey God in certain respects than heretofore. Our minds are so strangely constituted, it is impossible to say whether it is from the growth of habit suddenly showing itself, or from an unusual gift of Divine grace poured into our hearts, but so it is; let our temptation be to sloth, or irresolution, or worldly anxiety or pride, or to other more base and miserable sins, we may suddenly find ourselves possessed of a power of self-command which we had not before. Or again, we may have a resolution grow on us to serve God more strictly in His house and in private than heretofore. This is a call to higher things; let us beware lest we receive the grace of God in vain. Let us beware of lapsing back; let us avoid temptation. Let us strive by quietness and caution to cherish the feeble flame, and shelter it from the storms of this world. God may be bringing us into a higher world of religious truth; let us work with Him.

(PS 8:23–25, 28–30, "Divine Calls")

12. The Tranquil Christian Course

This spiritual plant of God is placed by the running waters; it is nourished and recruited by the never-failing, the perpetual, the daily and hourly supply of their wholesome influences. It grows up gradually, silently, without observation; and in proportion as it rises aloft, so do its roots, with still less observation, strike deep into the earth. Thus it determinately takes up its habitation in one place, from which death alone shall part it. Year after year it grows more and more into the hope and the posture of a glorious immobility and unchangeableness. What it has been that it shall be; if it changes, it is as growing into fruitfulness, and maturing in its fruit's abundance and perfection. Nor is that fruit lost; it neither withers upon the branches nor decays upon the ground. Angels unseen gather crop after crop from the unwearied never-failing parent, and carefully store them up in heavenly treasure-houses. Its very leaf remains green to the end; not only its fruit, which is profitable for eternal life, but its very foliage, the ordinary dress in which it meets our senses, its beautiful colouring, its rich yet delicate fulness of proportion, the graceful waving of its boughs, the musical whispers and rustlings of its leaves, the fragrance which it exhales, the refreshment which it spreads around it,—all testify to that majestic, serene beneficence which is its very nature, and to a mysterious depth of life which enables it ever to give out virtue, yet never to have less of it within.

Such is the holy servant of God, considered in that condition which is both his special reward and his ordinary lot. There are those, indeed, who, for the good of their brethren, and according to the will of God, are exercised by extraordinary trials, and pass their lives amid turbulence and change. There are others, again, who are wonderfully called out of error or of sin, and have experience of much conflict within or without them before they reach the heavenly river, and the groves which line its banks. Certainly history speaks much more of martyrdom and confessorship on the one hand, and of inquiry and conversion, of sin and repentance, on the other, than of the tranquil Christian course; but history does but give the surface of what actually takes place in the heavenly kingdom. If we would really bring before us what is both the highest blessedness in God's service, and also in fact the ordinary portion of good men, we shall find it to consist in what from its very nature cannot make much show in history;—in a life barren of great events, and rich in small ones; in a life of routine duties, of happy obscurity and inward peace, of an orderly dispensing of good to others who come within their influence, morning and evening, of a growth and blossoming and bearing fruit in the house of God, and of a blessed death in the presence of their brethren.

Such has been the round of days of many a pastor up and down Christendom, as even history has recorded, of many a missioner, of many a monk, of many a religious woman, of many a father or mother of a family, of many a student in sacred or profane literature,—each the centre of his own circle, and the teacher of his own people, though more or less unknown to the world. . . .

(OS 245–47, "The Tree beside the Water")

13. The Ventures of Faith

As regards individuals, then, it is quite true that all of us must for certain make ventures for heaven, yet without the certainty of success through them. This, indeed, is the very meaning of the word "venture;" for that is a strange venture which has nothing in it of fear, risk, danger, anxiety, uncertainty. Yes; so it certainly is; and in this consists the excellence and nobleness of *faith*; this is the very reason why *faith* is singled out from other graces, and honoured as the especial means of our justification, because its presence implies that we have the heart to make a venture. . . .

If then faith be the essence of a Christian life, and if it be what I have now described, it follows that our duty lies in risking upon Christ's word what we have, for what we have not; and doing so in a noble, generous way, not indeed rashly or lightly, still without knowing accurately what we are doing, not knowing either what we give up, nor again what we shall gain; uncertain about our reward, uncertain about our extent of sacrifice, in all respects leaning, waiting upon Him, trusting in Him to fulfil His promise, trusting in Him to enable us to fulfil our own vows, and so in all respects proceeding without carefulness or anxiety about the future. . . .

. . . This is the question, what have *we* ventured? I really fear, when we come to examine, it will be found that there is nothing we resolve, nothing we do, nothing we do not do, nothing we avoid, nothing we choose, nothing we give up, nothing we pursue, which we should not resolve, and do, and not do, and avoid, and choose, and give up, and pursue, if Christ had not died, and heaven were not promised us. I really fear that most men called Christians, whatever they may profess, whatever they may think they feel, whatever warmth and illumination and love they may claim as their own, yet would go on almost as they do, neither much better nor much worse; if they believed Christianity to be a fable. When young, they indulge their lusts, or at least pursue the world's vanities; as time goes on, they get into a fair way of business, or other mode of making money; then they marry and settle; and their interest coinciding with their duty, they seem to be, and think themselves, respectable and religious men; they grow attached to things as they are; they begin to have a zeal against vice and error; and they follow after peace with all men. Such conduct indeed, as far as it goes, is right and praiseworthy. Only I say, it has not necessarily any thing to do with religion at all; there is nothing in it which is any proof of the presence of religious principle in those who adopt it; there is nothing they would not do still though they had nothing to gain from it, except what they gain from it now: they do gain something now, they do gratify their present wishes, they are quiet and orderly, because it is their interest and taste to be so; but they *venture* nothing, they risk, they sacrifice, they abandon nothing on the faith of Christ's word. . . .

How is it that we are so contented with things as they are,—that we are so willing to be let alone, and to enjoy this life,—that we make such excuses, if any one presses on us the necessity of something higher, the duty of bearing the Cross, if we would earn the Crown, of the Lord Jesus Christ?

I repeat it; what are our ventures and risks upon the truth of His word? for He says expressly, "Every one that hath forsaken houses, or brethren, or sister, or father, or mother, or wife, or children, or lands, for My Name's sake, shall receive an hundredfold, and shall inherit everlasting life. But many that are first shall be last; and the last shall be first." (Mt 19: 29, 30)

(PS 4:296, 299, 301–302, 306, "The Ventures of Faith")

14. Preparing for Happiness

I call resignation a more blessed frame of mind than sanguine hope of present success, because it is the truer, and the more consistent with our fallen state of being, and the more improving to our hearts; and because it is that for which the most eminent servants of God have been conspicuous. . . . It is a far nobler frame of mind, to labour, not with the hope of seeing the fruit of our labour, but for conscience' sake, as matter of duty; and again, in faith, trusting good *will* be done, though we see it not. Look through the Bible, and you will find God's servants, even though they began with success, end with disappointment; not that God's purposes or His instruments fail, but that the time for reaping what we have sown is hereafter, not here; that here there is no great visible fruit in any one man's lifetime. . . . Even in the successes of the first Christian teachers, the apostles, the same rule is observed. After all the great works God enabled them to accomplish, they confessed before their death that what they experienced, and what they saw before them, was reverse and calamity, and that the fruit of their labour would not be seen, till Christ came to open the books and collect His saints from the four corners of the earth. . . .

. . . The truth is (though it is so difficult for us to admit it heartily), our nature is not at first in a state to enjoy happiness, even if we had it offered to us. We seek for it, and we feel we need it; but (strange though it is to say, still so it is) we are not fitted to be happy. If then at once we rush forward to seek enjoyment, it will be like a child's attempting to walk before his strength is come. If we would gain true bliss, we must cease to seek it as an end; we must postpone the prospect of enjoying it. For we are by nature in an unnatural state; we must be changed from what we are when born, before we can receive our greatest good. . . . Should *he* shrink from low notions of himself, and sharp pain, and mortification of natural wishes, whose guilt called down the Son of God from heaven to die upon the cross for him? May he live in pleasure here, and call this world his home, while he reads in the Gospel of his Saviour's lifelong affliction and disappointment?

. . . Give not over your attempts to serve God, though you see nothing come of them. Watch and pray, and obey your conscience, though you cannot perceive your own progress in holiness. Go on, and you cannot but go forward; believe it, though you do not see it. Do the duties of your calling, though they are distasteful to you. Educate your children carefully in the good way, though you cannot tell how far God's grace has touched their hearts. Let your light shine before men, and praise God by a consistent life, even though others do not seem to glorify their Father on account of it, or to be benefited by your example. "Cast your bread upon the waters, for you shall find it after many days. . . . In the morning sow your seed, in the evening withhold not your hand; for you know not whether shall prosper, either this or that; or whether they both shall be alike good." (Eccles 11: 1, 6) Persevere in the narrow way. The Prophets went through sufferings to which ours are mere trifles; violence and craft combined to turn them aside, but they kept right on, and are at rest.

. . . You must begin on faith: you cannot see at first whether He is leading you, and how light will rise out of the darkness. You must begin by denying yourselves your natural wishes, a painful work; by refraining from sin, by rousing from sloth, by preserving your tongue from insincere words, and your hands from deceitful dealings, and your eyes from beholding vanity; by watching against the first rising of anger, pride, impurity, obstinacy, jealousy; by learning to endure the laugh of irreligious men for Christ's sake; by forcing your minds to follow seriously the words of prayer, though it be difficult to you, and by keeping before you the thought of God all through the day. These things you will be able to do if you do but seek the mighty help of God the Holy spirit which is given you. . . .

(PS 8:129–30, 136–40, "Jeremiah, A Lesson for the Disappointed")

THE TRUE
CHRISTIAN LIFE

15. The Scriptural Picture of the True Christian Life

Let us . . . leave for a while our own private judgement of what is pleasing to God and not pleasing, and turn to consider the picture which Scripture gives us of the true Christian life, and then attempt to measure our own life by it. He alone who gives us eternal happiness, has the power of determining the conditions for attaining it. Let us not take it for granted that we shall know them by our own common sense. Let us betake ourselves to Scripture to learn them.

. . . This is the very definition of a Christian,—one who looks for Christ; not who looks for gain, or distinction, or power, or pleasure, or comfort, but who looks "for the Saviour, the Lord Jesus Christ." This, according to Scripture, is the essential mark, this is the foundation of a Christian, from which every thing else follows; whether he is rich or poor, high or low, is a further matter, which may be considered apart; but he surely is a primitive Christian, and he only, who has no aim of this world, who has no wish to be other in this world than he is; whose thoughts and aims have relation to the unseen, the future world; who has lost his taste for this world, sweet and bitter being the same to him; who fulfils the same Apostle's exhortation in another Epistle, "Set your affection on things above, not on things on the earth, for ye are dead, and your life is hid with Christ in God." (Col 3: 2-4) . . .

In a word, there was no barrier, no cloud, no earthly object, interposed between the soul of the primitive Christian and its Saviour and Redeemer. Christ was in his heart, and therefore all that came from his heart, his thoughts, words, and actions, savoured of

Christ. The Lord was his light, and therefore he shone with the illumination. . . .

. . . [C]onsider the special prayer which the Lord Himself taught us, as a pattern of all prayer, and see how it corresponds to that one idea of a Christian. . . . We often hear it said, that the true way of serving God is to serve man, as if religion consisted merely in acting well our part in life, not in direct faith, obedience, and worship: how different is the spirit of this prayer! Evil round about him, enemies and persecutors in his path, temptation in prospect, help for the day, sin to be expiated, God's will in his heart, God's Name on his lips, God's kingdom in his hopes: this is the view it gives us of a Christian. What simplicity! What grandeur! and what definiteness! how one and the same, how consistent with all that we read of him elsewhere in Scripture!

. . . Times *are* changed, I grant; but without going on to the question of the obligation now of such a profession of the Gospel as I have been describing, do persuade yourselves, I entreat you, to contemplate the picture. Do not shut your eyes, do not revolt from it, do not fret under it, but look at it. Bear to look at the Christianity of the Bible; bear to contemplate the idea of a Christian, traced by inspiration, without gloss, or comment, or tradition of man. Bear to hear read to you a number of texts; texts which might be multiplied sevenfold; texts which can be confronted by no others; which are no partial selections, but a specimen of the whole of the New Testament. Before you go forward to the question, "How do they affect us, must we obey them or why need we not?" prevail on yourselves to realize the idea of a Scriptural Christian, and the fact that the first Christians really answered to it. Granting you have to apply and modify the pattern given you, before you can use it yourselves, which I am not denying, yet after all, your pattern it is; you have no other pattern of a Christian any where. No other view of Christianity is given you in Scripture. If Scripture is used, you must begin with accepting that pattern; how can you apply what you will not study? Study what a Bible Christian is; be silent over it; pray for grace to comprehend it, to accept it. . . .

. . . You know very well, most of us know it too well, that such precepts and examples do not directly apply to every one of us.

We are not severally bound to give up the world by so literal a surrender. The case of Ananias and Sapphira is enough to show us this. Their sin lay in professing to do what they need not have done; in making pretence of a voluntary renunciation which they did not execute. They kept back part of the price of the land which they made a show of giving up: and St. Peter urged it against them. "Whiles it remained, was it not thine own? and after it was sold, was it not in thine own power?" A most awful warning to every one, not to affect greater sanctity or self-denial than he attempts; but a proof withal, that those great surrenders which Scripture speaks of, are not incumbent on all Christians. They could not be voluntary if they were duties; they could not be meritorious if they were not voluntary. But though they are not duties to all, they may be duties to you; and though they are voluntary, you may have a call to them. It may be your duty to follow after merit. And whether it is you cannot learn, till first you have fairly surrendered your mind to the contemplation of that Christianity which Scripture delineates. After all, it may prove to be your duty to remains as others, and you may serve Him best and most acceptably in a secular life. But you cannot tell till you inquire. . . .

(SD 276, 278–79, 281, 288–92, "The Apostolical Christian")

16. Serving God from Our Youth

O may we ever bear in mind that we are not sent into this world to stand all the day idle, but to go forth to our work and to our labour until the evening! *Until* the evening, not *in* the evening only of life, but serving God from our youth, and not waiting till our years fail us. Until the *evening*, not in the day-time only, lest we begin to run well, but fall away before our course is ended. Let us "give glory to the Lord our God, before He cause darkness and before our feet stumble upon the dark mountains;" (Jer 13: 16) and, having turned to Him, let us see that our goodness be not "as the morning cloud, and as the early dew which passeth away." The *end* is the proof of the matter. When the sun shines, this earth pleases; but let us look towards that eventide and the cool of the day, when the Lord of the vineyard will walk amid the trees of His garden. . . .

May that day and that hour ever be in our thoughts! When we rise, when we lie down; when we speak, when we are silent; when we act, and when we rest: whether we eat or drink, or whatever we do, may we never forget that "for all these things God will bring us into judgement." (Eccles 11: 9) For "He cometh quickly, and His reward is with Him, to give every man according as His work shall be." (Rev 22: 12)

Let us turn from shadows of all kinds,—shadows of sense, or shadows of argument and disputation, or shadows addressed to our imagination and tastes. Let us attempt, through God's grace, to advance and sanctify the inward man. We cannot be wrong here. Whatever is right, whatever is wrong, in this perplexing world, we must be right in "doing justly, in loving mercy, in walking humbly with our God," in denying our wills, in ruling our tongues, in softening and sweetening our tempers, in mortifying our lusts; in learning patience, meekness, purity, forgiveness of injuries, and continuance in well-doing.

(SD 11–13, "The Work of the Christian")

17. God's Gift

It would be well if we were in the habit of looking at all we have as God's gift, undeservedly given, and day by day continued to us solely by His mercy. He gave; He may take away. He gave us all we have, life, health, strength, reason, enjoyment, the light of conscience; whatever we have good and holy within us; whatever faith we have; whatever of a renewed will; whatever love towards Him; whatever power over ourselves; whatever prospect of heaven. He gave us relatives, friends, education, training, knowledge, the Bible, the Church. All comes from Him. He gave; He may take away. Did He take away, we should be called on to follow Job's pattern, and be resigned: "The Lord gave, and the Lord hath taken away. Blessed be the Name of the Lord." . . . (Job 1: 21)

We are not our own, any more than what we possess is our

own. We did not make ourselves; we cannot be supreme over ourselves. We cannot be our own master. We are God's property by creation, by redemption, by regeneration. He has a triple claim upon us. Is it not our happiness thus to view the matter? Is it any happiness, or any comfort, to consider that we *are* our own? It may be thought so by the young and prosperous. These may think it a great thing to have everything, as they suppose, their own way— to depend on no one, to have to think of nothing out of sight, to be without the irksomeness of continual acknowledgment, continual prayer, continual reference of what they do to the will of another. But as time goes on, they, as all men, will find that independence was not made for man—that it is an unnatural state—may do for a while, but will not carry us on safely to the end. No, we are creatures; and, as being such, we have two duties, to be resigned and to be thankful.

Let us then view God's providences towards us more religiously than we have hitherto done. Let us try to gain a truer view of what we are, and where we are, in His kingdom. Let us humbly and reverently attempt to trace His guiding hand in the years which we have hitherto lived. Let us thankfully commemorate the many mercies He has vouchsafed to us in time past, the many sins He has not remembered, the many dangers He has averted, the many prayers He has answered, the many mistakes He has corrected, the many warnings, the many lessons, the much light, the abounding comfort which He has from time to time given. Let us dwell upon times and seasons, times of trouble, times of joy, times of trial, times of refreshment. How did He cherish us as children! How did He guide us in that dangerous time when the mind began to think for itself, and the heart to open to the world! How did He with His sweet discipline restrain our passions, mortify our hopes, calm our fears, enliven our heavinesses, sweeten our desolateness, and strengthen our infirmities! How did He gently guide us towards the strait gate! how did He allure us along His everlasting way, in spite of its strictness, in spite of its loneliness, in spite of the dim twilight in which it lay! . . . He has not made us for nought; He has brought us thus far, in order to bring us further, in order to bring us on to the end. He will never leave us nor forsake us. . . .

(PS 5:82–85, "Remembrance of Past Mercies")

18. The New Christian Character

Nothing short of suffering, except in rare cases, makes us what we should be; gentle instead of harsh, meek instead of violent, conceding instead of arrogant, lowly instead of proud, pure-hearted instead of sensual, sensitive of sin instead of carnal. This is the especial object which is set before us, to become holy as He who has called us is holy, and to discipline and chasten ourselves in order that we may become so; and we may be quite sure, that unless we chasten ourselves, God will chasten us. If we judge ourselves, through His mercy we shall not be judged of Him; if we do not afflict ourselves in light things, He will afflict us in heavy things; if we do not set about changing ourselves by gentle measures, He will change us by severe remedies. . . .

. . . He who has thrown himself out of this world, alone can overcome it; he who has cut himself loose of it, alone cannot be touched by it; he alone can be courageous, who does not fear it; he alone firm, who is not moved by it; he alone severe with it, who does not love it. Despair makes men bold, and so it is that he who has nothing to hope from the world, has nothing to fear from it. He who has really tasted of the true Cross, can taste no bitterer pain, no keener joy.

I have been trying to urge on you, my brethren, that the taking of Christ's yoke, and learning of Him, is something very distinct and special, and very unlike any other service and character. It is the result of a change from a state of nature, a change so great as to be called a death or even a crucifixion of our natural state. Never allow yourselves, my brethren, to fancy that the true Christian character can coalesce with this world's character, or is the world's character improved—merely a superior kind of worldly character. No, it is a new character; or, as St. Paul words it, "a new creation." . . . Where Christ is put on, St. Paul tells us, there is neither Jew nor Greek, bond nor free, male nor female, but all are one in Christ Jesus. (Gal 3: 28) What Lazarus is, that must Dives become; what Apostles were, that must each of us be. The high in this world think it suitable in them to show a certain pride and self-confidence; the wealthy claim deference on account of their wealth; kings and princes think themselves above instruction from any; men in the middle ranks consider it enough to be decent and respectable, and deem sanctity superfluous in them; the poor think to be saved by their poverty;—but to one and all Christ speaks, "Come unto Me," "Learn of Me." There is but one Cross and one character of mind formed by it. . . .

(PS 7:109–110, 112–114, "The Yoke of Christ")

19. Gradual Awakening

[W]e Christians, though born in our very infancy into the kingdom of God, and chosen above all other men to be heirs of heaven and witnesses to the world, and though knowing and believing this truth entirely, yet have very great difficulty and pass many years in learning our privilege. Not any one of course, fully understands it; doubtless;—but we have not even a fair, practical hold of it. . . .

Now this insensibility or want of apprehension rises in great measure, it is scarcely necessary to say, from our exceeding frailness and sinfulness. Our old nature is continually exerting itself against the new; "the flesh lusteth against the Spirit." (Eph 1: 18–20) Its desire is towards this world. This world is its food; its eyes apprehend this world. Because it is what it is, it allies itself to this world. The world and the flesh form a compact with each other; the one asks, and the other supplies. Therefore, in proportion as it seduces us into the world's company, of course, in an equal degree, it blunts our perception of that world which we do not see; it prevents our realizing it. . . .

We are born almost into the fulness of Christian blessings, long before we have reason. We could not apprehend them at all, and that without our own fault, when we were baptized; for we were infants. As, then, we acquire reason itself but gradually, so we acquire the knowledge of what we are but gradually also; and as it is no fault in us, but a blessing to us, that we were baptized so early, so, from the nature of the case, and not from any fault of ours, do we but slowly enter into the privileges of our baptism. So it is as regards all our knowledge of ourselves and of our position in the world; we but gradually gain it. . . . Thus a man differs from a boy; he has a general view of things; he sees their bearings on each other; he sees his own position, sees what is becoming, what is expected of him, what his duty is in the community, what his rights. He understands his place in the world, and, in a word, he is at home in it.

Alas, that while we thus grow in knowledge in matters of time and sense, yet we remain children in knowledge of our heavenly privileges! St. Paul says, that whereas Christ is risen, He "hath raised us up together, and made us sit together in heavenly places in Christ Jesus." (Eph 2: 6) This is what we have still to learn; to know our place, position, situation as "children of God, members of Christ, and inheritors of the kingdom of heaven." We are risen again, and we know it not. We begin our Catechism by confessing that we are risen, but it takes a long life to apprehend what we confess. We are like people waking from sleep, who cannot collect their thoughts at once, or understand where they are. By little and little the truth breaks upon us. Such are we in the present world; sons of light, gradually waking to a knowledge of themselves. For this let us meditate, let us pray, let us work,— gradually to attain to a real apprehension of what we are. Thus, as time goes on, we shall gain first one thing, then another. By little and little we shall give up shadows and find the substance. Waiting on God day by day, we shall make progress day by day, and approach to the true and clear view of what He has made us to be in Christ. . . .

This we shall find to be one great providential benefit arising from those duties which He exacts of us. Our duties to God and man are not only duties done to Him, but they are means of enlightening our eyes and making our faith apprehensive. Every act of obedience has a tendency to strengthen our convictions about heaven. Every sacrifice makes us more zealous; every self-denial makes us more devoted. This is a use, too, of the observance of sacred seasons; they wean us from this world, they impress upon us the reality of the world which we see not. We trust, if we thus proceed, we shall understand more and more where we are. We humbly trust that, as we cleanse ourselves from this world, our eyes will be enlightened to see the things which are only spiritually discerned. We hope that to us will be fulfilled in due measure the words of the beatitude, "Blessed are the pure in heart, for they shall see God." (Mt 5: 8)

(PS 6:96–100, "Difficulty of Realizing Sacred Privileges")

20. The Root of Charity

The great difficulty in our religious duties is their extent. This frightens and perplexes men,— naturally; those especially, who have neglected religion for a while, and on whom its obligations disclose themselves all at once. This, for example, is the great misery of leaving repentance till a man is in weakness or sickness; he does not know how to set about it. Now God's merciful Providence has in the natural course of things narrowed for us at first this large field of duty; He has given us a clue. We are to begin with loving our friends about us, and gradually to enlarge the circle of our affections, till it reaches all Christians, and then all men. Besides, it is obviously impossible to love all men in any strict and true sense. What is meant by loving all men, is, to feel well-disposed to all men, to be ready to assist them, and to act towards those who come in our way, as if we loved them. We cannot love those about whom we know nothing; except indeed we view them in Christ, as the objects of His Atonement, that is, rather in faith than in love. And love, besides, is a habit, and cannot be attained without actual *practice*, which on so large a scale is impossible. We see then how absurd it is, when writers (as is the manner of some who slight the Gospel) talk magnificently about loving the whole human race with a comprehensive affection, of being the friends of all mankind, and the like. Such vaunting professions, what do they come to? that such men have certain benevolent *feelings* towards the world,—feelings and nothing more;—nothing more than unstable feelings, the mere offspring of an indulged imagination, which exist only when their minds are wrought upon, and are sure to fail them in the hour of need. This is not to love men, it is but to talk about love.—The real love of man *must* depend on practice, and therefore, must begin by exercising itself on our friends around us, otherwise it will have not existence. By trying to love our relations and friends, by submitting to their wishes, though contrary to our own, by bearing with their infirmities, by overcoming their occasional waywardness by kindness, by dwelling on their excellences, and trying to copy them, thus it is that we form in our hearts that root of charity, which, though small at first, may, like the mustard seed, at last even overshadow the earth. . . .

(PS 2:54–55, "Love of Relations and Friends")

21. The One Happiness

I say, then, that the happiness of the soul consists in the exercise of the affection; not in sensual pleasures, not in activity, not in excitement, not in self-esteem, not in the consciousness of power, not in knowledge; in none of these things lies our happiness, but in our affections being elicited, employed, supplied. As hunger and thirst, as taste, sound, and smell, are the channels through which this bodily frame receives pleasure, so the affections are the instruments by which the soul has pleasure. When they are exercised duly, it is happy; when they are undeveloped, restrained, or thwarted, it is not happy. This is our real and true bliss, not to know, or to affect, or to pursue; but to love, to hope, to joy, to admire, to revere, to adore. Our real and true bliss lies in the possession of those objects on which our hearts may rest and be satisfied.

Now, if this be so, here is at once a reason for saying that the thought of God, and nothing short of it, is the happiness of man; for though there is much besides to serve as subject of knowledge, or motive for action, or means of excitement, yet the affections require a something more vast and more enduring than anything created. What is novel and sudden excites, but does not influence; what is pleasurable or useful raises no awe; self moves no reverence, and mere knowledge kindles no love. He alone is sufficient for the heart who made it. . . . We gain much for a time from fellowship with each other. It is a relief to us, as fresh air to the fainting, or meat and drink to the hungry, or a flood of tears to the heavy in mind. It is a soothing comfort to have those whom we may make our confidants; a comfort to have those to whom we may confess our faults; a comfort to have those to whom we may look for sympathy. Love of home and family in these and other ways is sufficient to make this life tolerable to the multitude of men, which otherwise it would not be; but still, after all, our affections exceed such exercise of them, and demand what is more stable. Do not all men die? are they not taken from us? are they not as uncertain as the grass of the field? We do not give our hearts to things irrational, because these have no permanence in them. We do not place our affections in sun, moon, and stars, or this rich and fair earth, because all things material come to nought, and vanish like day and night. Man, too, though he has an intelligence within him, yet in his best estate he is altogether vanity. If our happiness consists in our affections being employed and recompensed, "man that is born of a woman" cannot be our happiness. . . .

But there is another reason why God alone is the happiness of our souls, . . . the contemplation of Him, and nothing but it, is able fully to open and relieve the mind, to unlock, occupy, and fix our affections. We may indeed love things created with great intenseness, but such affection, when disjoined from the love of the Creator, is like a stream running in a narrow channel, impetuous, vehement, turbid. The heart runs out, as it were, only at one door; it is not an expanding of the whole man. Created natures cannot open us, or elicit the ten thousand mental senses which belong to us, and through which we really live. None but the presence of our Maker can enter us; for to none besides can the whole heart in all its thoughts and feelings be unlocked and subjected. . . . It is this feeling of simple and absolute confidence and communion, which soothes and satisfies those to whom it is vouchsafed. We know that even our nearest friends enter into us but partially, and hold intercourse with us only at times; whereas the consciousness of a perfect and enduring Presence, and it alone, keeps the heart open. Withdraw the Object on which it rests, and it will relapse again into its state of confinement and constraint; and in proportion as it is limited, either to certain seasons or to certain affections, the heart is straitened and distressed. If it be not over bold to say it, He who is infinite can alone be its measure. . . .

What a truly wretched state is that coldness and dryness of soul, in which so many live and die, high and low, learned and unlearned. Many a great man, many a peasant, many a busy man, lives and dies with closed heart, with affections undeveloped, unexercised. You see the poor man, passing day after day, Sunday after Sunday, year after year, without a thought in his mind, to appearance almost like a stone. You see the educated man, full of thought, full of intelligence, full of action, but still with a stone heart, as cold and dead as regards his affections, as if he were the poor ignorant countryman. You see others, with warm affections, perhaps, for their families, with benevolent feelings towards their fellow-men, yet stopping there; centering their hearts on what is sure to fail them, as being perishable. Life passes, riches fly away, popularity is fickle, the senses decay, the world changes, friends die. One alone is constant; One alone is true to us; One alone can be true; One alone can be all things to us; One alone can supply our needs; One alone can train us up to our full perfection; One alone can give a meaning to our complex and intricate nature; One alone can give us tune and harmony; One alone can form and possess us. . . .

(PS 5:315–19, 325–26, "The Thought of God, the Stay of the Soul")

22. Uniting High and Low

Let us adore the Sacred Presence within us with all fear, and "rejoice with trembling." Let us offer up our best gifts in sacrifice to Him who, instead of abhorring, has taken up His abode in these sinful hearts of ours. Prayer, praise, and thanksgiving, "good works and alms-deeds," a bold and true confession and a self-denying walk, are the ritual of worship by which we serve Him in these His Temples. How the distinct and particular works of faith avail to our final acceptance, we know not; neither do we know how they are efficacious in changing our wills and characters, which, through God's grace, they certainly do. All we know is, that as we persevere in them, the inward light grows brighter and brighter, and God manifests Himself in us in a way the world knows not of. In this, then, consists our whole duty, first in contemplating Almighty God, as in Heaven, so in our hearts and souls; and next, while we contemplate Him, in acting towards and for Him in the works of every day; in viewing by faith His glory without and within us, and in acknowledging it by our obedience. Thus we shall unite conceptions the most lofty concerning His majesty and bounty towards us, with the most lowly, minute, and unostentatious service to Him.

(PS 3:269–70, "The Gift of the Spirit")

23. Prayer without Ceasing

What does nature teach us about ourselves, even before opening the Bible?—that we are creatures of the Great God, the Maker of heaven and earth; and that, as His creatures, we are bound to serve Him and give Him our hearts; in a word, to be religious beings. And next, what is religion but a habit? and what is a habit but a state of mind which is always upon us, as a sort of ordinary dress or inseparable garment of the soul? A man cannot really be religious one hour, and not religious the next. We might as well say he could be in a state of good health one hour, and in bad health the next. A man who is religious, is religious morning, noon, and night; his religion is a certain character, a mould in which his thoughts, words, and actions are cast, all forming parts of one and the same whole. He sees God in all things; every course of action he directs towards those spiritual objects which God has revealed to him; every occurrence of the day, every event, every person met with, all news which he hears, he measures by the standard of God's will. And a person who does this may be said almost literally to pray without ceasing; for, knowing himself to be in God's presence, he is continually led to address Him reverently, whom he sets always before him, in the inward language of prayer and praise, of humble confession and joyful trust.

How is religious obedience described in Scripture? Surely as a certain kind of life. We know what life of the body is; it is a state of the body: the pulse beats; all things are in motion. The hidden principle of life, though we know not how or what it is, is seen in these outward signs of it. And so of the life of the soul. . . . Now how God quickens our souls we do not know; as little as how He quickens our bodies. Our spiritual "life" (as St. Paul says) "is *hid* with Christ in God." (Col 3: 3) But as our bodily life discovers itself by its activity, so is the presence of the Holy Spirit in us discovered by a spiritual activity; and this activity is the spirit of continual prayer. Prayer is to spiritual life what the beating of the pulse and the drawing of the breath are to the life of the body. It would be as absurd to suppose that life could last when the body was cold and motionless and senseless, as to call a soul alive which does not pray. The state or habit of spiritual life exerts itself, consists, in the continual activity of prayer. . . .

Most men indeed, I fear, neither pray at fixed times, nor do they cultivate an habitual communion with Almighty God. Indeed, it is too plain how most men pray. They pray now and then, when they feel particular need of God's assistance; when they are in trouble or in apprehension of danger; or when their feelings are unusually excited. They do not know what it is either to be habitually religious, or to devote a certain number of minutes at fixed times to the thought of God. Nay, the very best Christian, how lamentably deficient is he in the spirit of prayer! Let any man compare in his mind how many times he has prayed when in trouble, with how seldom he has returned thanks when his prayers have been granted; or the earnestness with which he prays against expected suffering, with the languor and unconcern of his thanksgivings afterwards, and he will soon see how little he has of the real habit of prayer, and how much his religion depends on accidental excitement, which is no test of a religious heart. Or supposing he has to repeat the same prayer for a month or two, the cause of using it continuing, let him compare the earnestness with which he first said it, and tried to enter into it, with the coldness with which he at length uses it. Why is this, except that his perception of the unseen world is not the true view which faith gives . . . but a mere dream, which endures for a night, and is succeeded by a hard worldly joy in the morning? Is God habitually in our thoughts? Do we think of Him, and of His Son our Saviour, through the day? When we eat and drink, do we thank Him, not as a mere matter of form, but in spirit? When we do things in themselves right, do we lift up our minds to Him, and desire to promote His glory? When we are in the exercise of our callings, do we still think of Him, acting ever conscientiously, desiring to know His will more exactly than we do at present and aiming at fulfilling it more completely and abundantly? Do we wait on His grace to enlighten, renew, strengthen us?

I do not ask whether we use many words about religion. There is no need to do this: nay, we should avoid a boastful display of our better feelings and practices, silently serving God without human praise, and hiding our conscientiousness except when it would dishonour God to do so. There are times, indeed, when, in the presence of a holy man, to confess is a benefit, and there are times when, in the presence of worldly men, to confess becomes a duty; but these seasons, whether of privilege or of duty, are comparatively rare. But we are always with ourselves and our God; and that silent inward confession in His presence may be sustained and continual, and will end in durable fruit.

(PS 7:205-06, 208-09, 211-13, "Mental Prayer")

24. Conscience

[W]hen He became Creator, He implanted this Law, which is Himself, in the intelligence of all His rational creatures. The Divine Law, then, is the rule of ethical truth, the standard of right and wrong, a sovereign, irreversible, absolute authority in the presence of men and Angels. "The eternal law," says St. Augustine, "is the Divine Reason or Will of God, commanding the observance, forbidding the disturbance, of the natural order of things." "The natural law," says St. Thomas "is an impression of the Divine Light in us, a participation of the eternal law in the rational creature.". . . This law, as apprehended in the minds of individual men is called "conscience;" and though it may suffer refraction in passing into the intellectual medium of each, it is not therefore so affected as to lose its character of being the Divine Law, but still has, as such, the prerogative of commanding obedience. . . .

This view of conscience, I know, is very different from that ordinarily taken of it, both by the science and literature, and by the public opinion, of this day. It is founded on the doctrine that conscience is the voice of God, whereas it is fashionable on all hands now to consider it in one way or another a creation of man.

Of course, there are great and broad exceptions to this statement. It is not true of many or most religious bodies of men; especially not of their teachers and ministers. . . . [T]hey mean what we mean, the voice of God in the nature and heart of man, as distinct from the voice of Revelation. They speak of a principle planted within us, before we have had any training, although training and experience are necessary for its strength, growth, and due formation. They consider it a constituent element of the mind, as our perception of other ideas may be, as our powers of reasoning, as our sense of order and the beautiful, and our other intellectual endowments. They consider it, as Catholics consider it, to be the internal witness of both the existence and the law of God. They think it holds of God, and not of man, as an Angel walking on the earth would be no citizen or dependent of the Civil Power. . . .

. . . The rule and measure of duty is not utility, nor expedience, nor the happiness of the greatest number, not State convenience, not fitness, order and the *pulchrum.* Conscience is not a long-sighted selfishness, nor a desire to be consistent with oneself; but it is a messenger from Him, who, both in nature and in grace, speaks to us behind a veil, and teaches and rules us by His representatives. Conscience is the aboriginal Vicar of Christ, a prophet in its informations, a monarch in its peremptoriness, a priest in its blessings and anathemas, and, even though the eternal priesthood throughout the Church could cease to be, in it the sacerdotal principle would remain and would have a sway.

(Diff. 2:246–49, "Conscience")

25. Vigilance against Sin

. . . [W]ith respect to this progress of sin from infirmity to transgression . . . we have no need to go to Scripture in proof of a truth which every day teaches us, that men begin with little sins and go on to great sins, that the course of sin is a continuous declivity, with nothing to startle those who walk along it, and that the worst transgressions seem trifles to the sinner, and that the lightest infirmities are grievous to the holy. . . . We are ever in a degree lame in this world, even in our best estate. All Christians are such; but when in consequence of their lameness they proceed to turn aside, or, as the text says, to "draw back," then they differ from those who are merely lame, as widely as those who halt along a road differ from those who fall out of it. Those who have turned aside, have to return, they have fallen into a different state: Those who are lame must be "healed" *in* the state of grace in which they are, and while they are in it; and that, *lest* they "turn out" of it. Thus lameness is at once distinct from backsliding, yet leads to it. . . .

On the whole, then, this may be considered a Christian's state, ever about to fall, yet by God's mercy never falling; ever dying, yet always alive; full of infirmities, yet free from transgressions: and, as time goes on, more and more free from infirmities also, as tending to that perfect righteousness which is the fulfilling of the Law;—on the other hand, should he fall, recoverable, but not without much pain, with fear and trembling.

. . . Come then continually to the Fount of cleansing for cleansing. St. John says that the Blood of Jesus Christ cleanseth from all sin. Use the means appointed,—confession, prayer, fasting, making amends, good resolves, and the ordinances of grace. Do not stop to ask the degree of your guilt,—whether you have actually drawn back from God or not. Let your ordinary repentance be as though you had. You cannot repent too much. Come to God day by day, entreating Him for all the sins of your whole life up to the very hour present. This is the way to keep your baptismal robe bright. Let it be washed as your garments of this world are, again and again; washed in the most holy, most precious, most awfully salutary of all streams, His blood, who is without blemish and without spot. It is thus that the Church of God, it is thus that each individual member of it, becomes all glorious within, and filled with grace.

(PS 5:204–208, "Transgressions and Infirmities")

26. True Christians and Professing Christians

An honest, unaffected *desire* of doing right is the test of God's true servant. On the other hand, a double mind, a pursuing other ends besides the truth, and in consequence an inconsistency in conduct, and a half-consciousness (to say the least) of inconsistency, and a feeling of the necessity of defending oneself to oneself, and to God, and to the world; in a word, hypocrisy; these are the signs of the merely professed Christian. . . .

. . . A true Christian, then, may almost be defined as one who has a ruling sense of God's presence within him. . . . A man is justified whose conscience is illuminated by God, so that he habitually realizes that all his thoughts, all the first springs of his moral life, all his motives and his wishes, are open to Almighty God. Not as if he was not aware that there is very much in him impure and corrupt, but he wishes that all that is in him should be bare to God. He believes that it is so, and he even joys to think that it is so, in spite of his fear and shame at its being so. He alone admits Christ into the shrine of his heart; whereas others wish in some way or other, to be by themselves, to have a home, a chamber, a tribunal, a throne, a self where God is not,—a home within them which is not a temple, a chamber which is not a confessional, a tribunal without a judge, a throne without a king;—that self may be king and judge; and that the Creator may rather be dealt with and approached as though a second party, instead of His being that true and better self, of which self itself should be but an instrument and minister.

. . . [The true Christian] enthrones the Son of God in his conscience, refers to Him as a sovereign authority, and uses no reasoning with Him. He does not reason, but he says, "Thou, God, seest me." He feels that God is too near him to allow of argument, self-defense, excuse, or objection. He appeals in matters of duty, not to his own reason, but to God Himself, whom with the eyes of faith he sees, and whom he makes the Judge; not to any fancied fitness, or any preconceived notion, or any abstract principle, or any tangible experience. . . .

And, now, on the other hand, let us contrast such a temper of mind, which loves to walk in the light, with that of the merely professing Christian, or, in Scripture language, of the *hypocrite*. Such are they who have two ends which they pursue, religion, *and* the world; and hence St. James calls them "double-minded." Hence, too, our Lord, speaking of the Pharisees who were hypocrites says, "Ye cannot serve God and mammon." (Lk 16: 13) A double-minded man, then, as having two ends in view, dare not come to God, lest he should be discovered. . . .

. . . [T]here being in the estimation of the double-minded man two parties, God and self, it follows (as I have said), that reasoning and argument is the mode in which he approaches his Saviour and Judge; and that for two reasons,—first, because he will not *give* himself up to God, but stands upon his rights and appeals to his notions of fitness; and next, because he has some secret misgiving after all that he is dishonest, or some consciousness that he may appear so to others; and therefore, he goes about to fortify his position, to explain his conduct, or to excuse himself.

Such is the conduct of insincere men in difficulty. Perhaps their difficulty may be a real one; but in this they differ from the sincere:—the latter seek God *in* their difficulty, feeling that He only who imposes it can remove it; but insincere men do not like to go to God; and to them the difficulty is only so much gain, for it gives them an apparent reason, a sort of excuse, for not going by God's rule, but for deciding in their own way. . . .

. . . This is most true, though it be not at all welcome doctrine to many. We cannot hide ourselves from Him; and our wisdom, as our duty, lies in embracing this truth, acquiescing in it, and acting upon it. Let us then beg Him to teach us the Mystery of His Presence in us, that, by acknowledging it, we may thereby possess it fruitfully. . . . In all circumstances, of joy or sorrow, hope or fear, let us aim at having Him in our inmost heart; let us have no secret apart from Him. Let us acknowledge Him as enthroned within us at the very springs of thought and affection. Let us submit ourselves to His guidance and sovereign direction; let us come to Him that He may forgive us, cleanse us, change us, guide us, and save us.

(PS 5:224–26, 229–30, 233, 235–36, "Sincerity and Hypocrisy")

27. Self-Surrender

We are ever sinning, we must ever be renewing our sorrow and our purpose of obedience, repeating our confessions and our prayers for pardon. . . . [W]e are *ever* but beginning; the most perfect Christian is to himself but a beginner, a penitent prodigal, who has squandered God's gifts, and comes to Him to be tried over again, not as a son, but as a hired servant. . . .

. . . The most noble repentance (if a fallen being can be noble in his fall), the most decorous conduct in a conscious sinner, is an *unconditional* surrender of himself to God—not a bargaining about terms, not a scheming (so to call it) to be received back again, but an instant *surrender* of himself in the first instance. Without knowing what will become of him, whether God will spare or not, merely with so much hope in his heart as not utterly to despair of pardon, still not looking merely to *pardon* as an *end*, but rather looking to the claims of the Benefactor whom he has offended, and smitten with shame, and the sense of his ingratitude, he must surrender himself to his lawful Sovereign. He is a runaway offender; he must come back, as a very first step, before anything can be determined about him, bad or good; he is a rebel, and must lay down his arms. Self-devised offerings might do in a less serious matter; as an atonement for sin, they imply a defective view of the evil and extent of sin in his own case. Such is that perfect way which nature shrinks from, but which our Lord enjoys in the parable—a surrender. The prodigal son waited not for his father to show signs of placability. He did not merely approach a space, and then stand as a coward, curiously inquiring, and dreading how his father felt towards him. He made up his mind at once to degradation at the best, perhaps to rejection. He arose and went straight on towards his father, with a collected mind; and though his relenting father saw him from a distance, and went out to meet him, still his purpose was that of an instant frank submission. Such must be Christian repentance: First we must put aside the idea of finding a remedy for our sin; then, though we feel the guilt of it, yet we must set out firmly towards God, not knowing for certain that we shall be forgiven. He, indeed, meets us on our way with the token of His favour, and so He bears up human faith, which else would sink under the apprehensions of meeting the Most High God; still, for our repentance to be Christian, there must be in it that generous temper of self-surrender, the acknowledgment that we are unworthy to be called any more His sons, the abstinence from all ambitious hopes of sitting on His right hand or His left, and the willingness to bear the heavy yoke of bond-servants, if He should put it upon us.

. . . The truest kind of repentance as little comes at first, as perfect conformity to any other part of God's Law. It is gained by long practice—it will come at length. The dying Christian will fulfil the part of the returning prodigal more exactly than he ever did in his former years. When first we turn to God in the actual history of our lives, our repentance is mixed with all kinds of imperfect views and feelings. Doubtless there is in it something of the true temper of simple submission; but the wish of appeasing God on the one hand, or a hard-hearted insensibility about our sins on the other, mere selfish dread of punishment, or the expectation of a sudden easy pardon, these, and such-like principles, influence us, whatever we may say or may think we feel. It is, indeed, easy enough to have good words put into our mouths, and our feelings roused, and to profess the union of utter self-abandonment and enlightened sense of sin; but to claim is not really to possess these excellent tempers. Really to gain these is a work of time. It is when the Christian has long fought the good fight of faith, and by experience knows how few and how imperfect are his best services; then it is that he is able to acquiesce, and most gladly acquiesces in the statement, that we are accepted by faith only in the merits of our Lord and Saviour. . . .

(PS 3:91, 96–98, "Christian Repentance")

28. The Duty of Intercession

By words and works we can but teach or influence a few; by our prayers we may benefit the whole world, and every individual of it, high and low, friend, stranger, and enemy. It is not fearful then to look back on our past lives even in this one respect? How can we tell but that our king, our country, our Church, our institutions, and our own respective circles, would be in far happier circumstances than they are, had we been in the practice of more earnest and serious prayer for them? How can we complain of difficulties, national or personal, how can we justly blame and denounce evil-minded and powerful men, if we have but lightly used the intercessions offered up in the Litany, the Psalms, and in the Holy Communion? How can we answer to ourselves for the souls who have, in our time, lived and died in sin; the souls that have been lost and are now waiting for judgement, the infidel, the blasphemer, the profligate, the covetous, the extortioner; or those again who have died with but doubtful signs of faith, the death-bed penitent, the worldly, the double-minded, the ambitious, the unruly, the trifling, the self-willed, seeing that, for what we know, we were ordained to influence or reverse their present destiny and have not done it?

(PS 3:364–65, "Intercession")

29. Intercession and Mary

To a candid pagan it must have been one of the most remarkable points of Christianity, on its first appearance, that the observance of prayer formed so vital a part of its organization; and that, though its members were scattered all over the world, and its rulers and subjects had so little opportunity of correlative action, yet they, one and all, found the solace of a spiritual intercourse and a real bond of union, in the practice of mutual intercession. Prayer indeed is the very essence of all religion; but in the heathen religions it was either public or personal; it was a state ordinance, or a selfish expedient for the attainment of certain tangible, temporal goods. Very different from this was its exercise among Christians, who were thereby knit together in one body, different, as they were, in races, ranks, and habits, distant from each other in country, and helpless amid hostile populations. Yet it proved sufficient for its purpose. Christians could not correspond; they could not combine; but they could pray one for another. Even their public prayers partook of this character of intercession; for to pray for the welfare of the whole Church was in fact a prayer for all the classes of men and all the individuals of which it was composed. It was in prayer that the Church was founded. For ten days all the Apostles "persevered with one mind in prayer and supplication, with women, and Mary the Mother of

Jesus, and with his brethren." Then again at Pentecost "they were all with one mind in one place;" and the converts then made are said to have "persevered in prayer." And when, after a while, St. Peter was seized and put in prison with a view to his being put to death, "prayer was made without ceasing" by the Church of God for him; and, when the Angel released him, he took refuge in a house "where many were gathered together in prayer.". . .

Intercession thus being a first principle of the Church's life, next it is certain again, that the vital force of that intercession, as an availing power, is, (according to the will of God), sanctity. . . .

I consider it impossible then, for those who believe the Church to be one vast body in heaven and on earth, in which every holy creature of God has his place, and of which prayer is the life, when once they recognize the sanctity and dignity of the Blessed Virgin, not to perceive immediately, that her office above is one of perpetual intercession for the faithful militant, and that our very relation to her must be that of clients to a patron, and that, in the eternal enmity which exists between the woman and the serpent, while the serpent's strength lies in being the Tempter, the weapon of the Second Eve and Mother of God is prayer.

(Diff. 2:68–69, 71, 73, "Belief of Catholics in Her Intercessory Power")

30. Worldly Ambition and Heavenly Ambition

The Gospel offers to us things supernatural. . . . But, alas! the multitude of men do not enter into the force of such an invitation, or feel its graciousness or desirableness. They are satisfied to remain where they find themselves by nature, to be what the world makes them, to bound their conceptions of things by sight and touch, and to conceive of the Gospel according to the thoughts, motives, and feelings which spring up spontaneously within them. They form their religion for themselves from what they are, and live and die in the ordinary and common-place round of hopes and fears, pleasures and pains. In the ordinary common-place round of *duties* indeed, they ought to be engaged, and are bound to find satisfaction. To be out of conceit with our lot in life, is no high feeling, it is discontent or ambition; but to be out of conceit with the ordinary way of *viewing* our lot, with the ordinary thoughts and feelings of mankind, is nothing but to be a Christian. This is the difference between worldly ambition and heavenly. It is a heavenly ambition which prompts us to soar above the vulgar and ordinary *motives* and *tastes* of the world, the while we abide *in* our calling; like our Saviour who, though the Son of God and partaking of His Father's fulness, yet all His youth long was obedient to His earthly parents, and learned a humble trade. But it is a sordid, narrow, miserable ambition to attempt to *leave* our earthly lot; to be wearied or ashamed of what we are, to hanker after greatness of station, or novelty of life. However, the multitude of men go neither in the one way nor the other; they neither have the high ambition nor the low ambition. It is well they have not the low, certainly; it is well they do not aim at being great men, or heroes; but they have no temptation to do so. What they are tempted to, is to settle down in a satisfied way in the world as they find it. . . . They tend to become part of the world, and be sucked in by it, and (as it were) changed into it; and so to lose all aspirations and thoughts, whether good or bad, after any thing higher than what they are. I do not know whether rich or poor are in greater temptation this way. . . .

. . . [I]s the superhuman life enjoined on us in the Gospel but a dream? is there no meaning in our own case, of the texts about the strait gate and the narrow way, and Mary's good part, and the rule of perfection, and the saying which "all cannot receive save they to whom it is given?" Holy men, certainly, do not throw themselves out of their stations. They are not gloomy, or morose, or overbearing, or restless; but still they are pursuing in their daily walk, and by their secret thoughts and actions, a conduct *above* the world. Whether rich or poor, high-born or low-born, married or single, they have never wedded themselves to the world; they have never surrendered themselves to be its captives; never looked out for station, fashion, comfort, credit, as the end of life. They have kept up the feeling which young people often have, who at first ridicule the artificial forms and usages of society, and find it difficult to conform themselves to its pomp and pretence. . . .

(PS 4:161–63, 166, "The Visible Church for the Sake of the Elect")

31. Fear and Love

In a Christian's course, *fear and love must go together*. And this is the lesson to be deduced from our Saviour's withdrawing from the world after His resurrection. He showed His love for men by dying for them, and rising again. He maintained His honour and great glory by retiring from them when His merciful purpose was attained, that they might seek Him if they would find Him. He ascended to His Father out of our sight. Sinners would be ill company for the exalted King of Saints. When we have been duly prepared to see Him, we shall be given to approach Him.

In heaven, love will absorb fear; but in this world, *fear and love must go together*. No one can love God aright without fearing Him; though many fear Him, and yet do not love Him. Self-confident men, who do not know their own hearts, or the reasons they have for being dissatisfied with themselves, do not fear God, and they think this bold freedom is to love Him. Deliberate sinners fear but cannot love Him. But devotion to Him consists in love and fear, as we may understand from our ordinary attachment to each other. No one really loves another, who does not feel a certain reverence towards him. When friends transgress this sobriety of affection, they may indeed continue associates for a time, but they have broken the bond of union. It is mutual respect which makes friendship lasting. So again, in the feelings of inferiors towards superiors. Fear must go before love. Till he who has authority shows he has it and can use it, his forbearance will not be valued duly; his kindness will look like weakness. We learn to contemn what we do not fear; and we cannot love what we contemn. So in religion also. We cannot understand Christ's mercies till we understand His power, His glory, His unspeakable holiness, and our demerits; that is, until we first fear Him. Not that fear comes first, and then love; for the most part they will proceed together. Fear is allayed by the love of Him, and our love sobered by our fear of Him. Thus He draws us on with encouraging voice amid the terrors of His threatenings. As in the young ruler's case, He loves us, yet speaks harshly to us that we may learn to cherish mixed feelings towards Him. He hides Himself from us, and yet calls us on, that we may hear His voice as Samuel did, and, believing, approach Him with trembling. This may seem strange to those who do not study the Scriptures, and to those who do not know what it is earnestly to seek after God. But in proportion as the state of mind is strange, so is there in it, therefore, untold and surpassing pleasure to those who partake it. The bitter and the sweet strangely tempered, thus leave upon the mind the lasting taste of Divine truth, and satisfy it; not so harsh as to be loathed; nor of that insipid sweetness which attends enthusiastic feelings, and is wearisome when it becomes familiar. Such is the feeling of conscience too, God's original gift; how painful! yet who would lose it? . . .

(PS 1:303-05, "Christian Reverence")

32. Devotion and Intellect

I wish the intellect to range with the utmost freedom, and religion to enjoy an equal freedom; but what I am stipulating for is, that they should be found in one and the same place, and exemplified in the same persons. I want to destroy that diversity of centres, which puts everything into confusion by creating a contrariety of influences. I wish the same spots and the same individuals to be at once oracles of philosophy and shrines of devotion. It will not satisfy me, what satisfies so many, to have two independent systems, intellectual and religious, going at once side by side, by a sort of division of labour, and only accidentally brought together. It will not satisfy me, if religion is here and science there, and young men converse with science all day, and lodge with religion in the evening. . . . Devotion is not a sort of finish given to the sciences; nor is science a sort of feather in the cap, if I may so express myself, an ornament and set-off to devotion. I want the intellectual layman to be religious, and the devout ecclesiastic to be intellectual.

This is no matter of terms, nor of subtle distinctions. Sanctity has its influence; intellect has its influence; the influence of sanctity is the greater in the long run; the influence of intellect is greater at the moment. . . .

(OS 13–14, "Intellect, the Instrument of Religious Training")

33. The Church and the Individual Soul

[The Church] contemplates, not the whole, but the parts; not a nation, but the men who form it; not society in the first place, but in the second place, and in the first place individuals; it looks beyond the outward act, on and into the thought, the motive, the intention, and the will; it looks beyond the world, and detects and moves against the devil, who is sitting in ambush behind it. It has, then, a foe in view; nay, it has a battlefield, to which the world is blind; its proper battlefield is the heart of the individual, and its true foe is Satan.

. . . I bear my own testimony to what has been brought home to me most closely and vividly as a matter of fact since I have been a Catholic; viz., that that mighty worldwide Church, like her Divine Author, regards, consults for, labours for the individual soul; she looks at the souls for whom Christ died, and who are made over to her; and her one object, for which everything is sacrificed—appearances, reputation, worldly triumph—is to acquit herself well of this most awful responsibility. Her one duty is to bring forward the elect to salvation and to make them as many as she can: to take offences out of their path, to warn them of sin, to rescue them from evil, to convert them, to teach them, to feed them, to protect them, and to perfect them. Oh, most tender loving Mother, ill-judged by the world, which thinks she is, like itself always minding the main chance; on the contrary, it is her keen view of things spiritual, and her love for the soul, which hampers her in her negotiations and her measures, on this hard cold earth, which is her place of sojourning. How easy would her course be, at least for a while, could she give up this or that point of faith, or connive at some innovation or irregularity in the administration of the Sacraments! . . .

No, my dear brethren, it is this supernatural sight and supernatural aim, which is the folly and the feebleness of the Church in the eyes of the world, and would be failure but for the providence of God. The Church overlooks everything in comparison of the immortal soul.

Good and evil to her are not lights and shades passing over the surface of society, but living powers, springing from the depths of the heart. Actions in her sight are not mere outward deeds and words, committed by hand or tongue, and manifested in effects over a range of influence wider or narrower, as the case may be; but they are the thoughts, the desires, the purposes of the solitary responsible spirit. She knows nothing of space or time, except as secondary to will; she knows no evil but sin, and sin is something personal, conscious, voluntary; she knows no good but grace, and grace again is something personal, private, special, lodged in the soul of the individual. She has one and one only aim—to purify the heart; she recollects who it is who has turned our thoughts from the external crime to the inward imagination; who said, that "unless our justice abounded more than that of Scribes and Pharisees, we should not enter in the kingdom of Heaven". . . .

The Church aims, not at making a show, but at doing a work. She regards this world, and all that is in it, as a mere shadow, as dust and ashes, compared with the value of one single soul. She holds that, unless she can, in her own way, do good to souls, it is no use her doing anything. . . .

(Diff. 1:236–40, "Social State of Catholic Countries No Prejudice to the Sanctity of the Church")

34. Advancement and Abasement

Under the dispensation of the Spirit all things were to become new and to be reversed. Strength, numbers, wealth, philosophy, eloquence, craft, experience of life, knowledge of human nature, these are the mean by which worldly men have ever gained the world. But in that kingdom which Christ has set up, all is contrariwise. "The weapons of our warfare are not carnal, but mighty through God to the pulling down of strongholds." What was before in honour, has been dishonoured; what before was in dishonour, has come to honour; what before was successful, fails; what before failed, succeeds. What before was great, has become little; what before was little, has become great. Weakness has conquered strength, for the hidden strength of God "is made perfect in weakness." Death has conquered life, for in that death is a more glorious resurrection. Spirit has conquered flesh; for that spirit is an inspiration from above. A new kingdom has been established, not merely different from all kingdoms before it, but contrary to them; a paradox in the eyes of man—the visible rule of the invisible Saviour.

Such is the kingdom of the sons of God; and while it endures, there is ever a supernatural work going on by which all that man thinks great is overcome, and what he despises prevails.

Yes, so it is; since Christ sent down gifts from on high, the Saints are ever taking possession of the kingdom, and with the weapons of Saints. The invisible powers of the heavens, truth, meekness, and righteousness, are ever coming in upon the earth, ever pouring in, gathering, thronging, warring, triumphing, under the guidance of Him who "is alive and was dead, and is alive for evermore." . . .

Now let us apply this great truth to ourselves. . . . The kingdom is within us, and among us, and around us. We are apt to speak of it as a matter of history; we speak of it as at a distance; but really we are a part of it, or ought to be; and, as we wish to be a living portion of it, which is our only hope of salvation, we must learn what its characters are in order to imitate them. It is the characteristic of Christ's Church, that the first should be last, and the last first; are we realizing in ourselves and taking part in this wonderful appointment of God? . . .

. . . Here is our rule. The way to mount up is to go down. Every step we take downward, makes us higher in the kingdom of heaven. Do you desire to be great? Make yourselves little. There is a mysterious connection between real advancement and self-abasement. If you minister to the humble and despised, if you feed the hungry, tend the sick, succour the distressed; if you bear with the forward, submit to insult, endure ingratitude, render good for evil, you are, as by a divine charm, getting power over the world and rising among the creatures. God has established this law. Thus He does His wonderful works. His instruments are poor and despised; the world hardly knows their names, or not at all. They are busied about what the world thinks petty actions, and no one minds them. They are apparently set on no great works; nothing is seen to come of what they do: They seem to fail. Nay, even as regards religious objects which they themselves profess to desire, there is no natural and visible connexion between their doings and sufferings and these desirable ends; but there is an unseen connexion in the kingdom of God. They rise by falling. Plainly so, for no condescension *can* be so great as that of our Lord *Himself.* Now the more they abase themselves the more *like* they are to Him; and the more like they are to Him, the greater must be their power with Him. . . .

Let us then, my brethren, understand our place, as the redeemed children of God. Some *must* be great in this world, but woe to those who make themselves great; woe to any who take one step out of their way with this object before them. Of course no one is safe from the intrusion of corrupt motives; but I speak of persons *allowing* themselves in such a motive, and acting mainly from such a motive. Let this be the settled view of all who would promote Christ's cause upon earth. If we are true to ourselves, nothing can really thwart us. Our warfare is not with carnal weapons, but with heavenly. The world does not understand what our real power is, and where it lies. And until we put ourselves into its hands of our own act, it can do nothing against us. Till we leave off patience, meekness, purity, resignation, and peace, it can do nothing against that Truth which is our birthright, that cause which is ours, as it has been the cause of all saints before us. But let all who would labour for God in a dark time beware of any thing which ruffles, excites, and in any way withdraws them from the love of God and Christ, and simple obedience to Him.

(PS 6:313, 316–17, 319–20, 325, "The Weapons of Saints")

35. Leaving the Goods of the Earth

These are thoughts wherewith to enter upon that solemn season of the year, when for a time we separate from each other, as far as may be, and from the other blessings which God has given us. Pass a few days and, like Abraham, we shall have been called to quit things visible and temporal for the contemplation and the hope of God's future presence. Come the fourth day from this and, like Moses, we shall have gone up into the Mount, to remain there forty days and forty nights in abstinence and prayer. We shall be called, as it were, out of sight; for though our worldly duties will remain and must be done, and our bodily presence is in the world as it was, yet for a season we must be, more or less, cut off from the intercourse, the fellowship, the enjoyment of each other, and be thrown upon the thought of ourselves and of our God. Earth must fade away from our eyes, and we must anticipate that great and solemn truth, which we shall not fully understand until we stand before God in judgement, that to us there are but two beings in the whole world, God and ourselves. The sympathy of others, the pleasant voice, the glad eye, the smiling countenance, the thrilling heart, which at present are our very life, all will be away from us, when Christ comes in judgement. Every one will have to think of himself. Every eye shall see *Him*; every heart will be full of *Him*. He will speak to every one; and every one will be rendering to Him his own account. By self-restraint, by abstinence, by prayer, by meditation, by recollection, by penance, we now anticipate in our measure that dreadful season. By thinking of it beforehand, we hope to mitigate its terrors when it comes. By humbling ourselves now, we hope to escape humiliation then. By owning our faults now, we hope to avert the disclosures of that day. By judging ourselves now, we hope to be spared that judgement which mercy tempers not. We prepare not to meet our God; we retire, as it were, to our sick room, and put our house in order. We "remember our Creator in the days of our youth" and strength, "while the evil days come not, nor the years draw nigh, in which is no pleasure;" ere "keepers of the house tremble, and the strong men bow themselves, and the doors are shut in the streets, and the daughters of music are brought low, and desire fails: or ever the silver cord be loosed, or the golden bowl be broken, or the pitcher be broken at the fountain, or the wheel broken at the cistern." (Eccles 12: 1, 3–4, 6) We leave the goods of earth before they leave us.

Let us not shrink from this necessary work; let us not suffer indolence or carnal habits to get the better of us. Let us not yield to disgust or impatience; let us not fear as we enter into the cloud.

Let us recollect that it is *His* cloud that overshadows us. It is no earthly sorrow or pain, such as worketh death; but it is a bright cloud of godly sorrow, "working repentance to salvation not to be repented of." (2 Cor 7: 10) It is the hand of God which is upon us; "let us humble ourselves therefor under the mighty hand of God, that He may exalt us in due time." (1 Pet 5: 6)

(SD 38–40, "Our Lord's Last Supper and His First")

36. Watching for Christ

[T]rue Christians, whoever they are, watch, and inconsistent Christians do not. Now what is watching? . . .

This . . . is to watch; to be detached from what is present, and to live in what is unseen; to live in the thought of Christ as He came once, and as He will come again; to desire His second coming, from our affectionate and grateful remembrance of His first. And this it is, in which we shall find that men in general are wanting. . . .

It is easy to exemplify what I mean, from the experience which we all have of love. Many men indeed are open revilers of religion, or at least openly disobey its laws; but let us consider those who are of a more sober and conscientious cast of mind. They have a number of good qualities, and are in a certain sense and up to a certain point religious; but they do not watch. Their notion of religion is briefly this: loving God indeed, but loving this world too; not only doing their *duty*, but finding their chief and highest *good*, in that state of life to which it has pleased God to call them, resting in it, taking it as their portion. They serve God, and they seek Him; but they look on the present world as if it were the eternal, not a mere temporary, scene of their duties and privileges, and never contemplate the prospect of being separated from it. It is not that they forget God, or do not live by principle, or forget that the goods of this world are His gift; but they love them for their own sake more than for the sake of the Giver, and reckon on their remaining, as if they had that permanence which their duties and religious privileges have. They do not understand that they are called to be strangers and pilgrims upon the earth, and that their worldly lot and worldly goods are a sort of accident of their existence, and that they really have no property, though human law guarantees property to them. Accordingly, they set their heart upon their goods, be they great or little, not without a sense of religion the while, but still idolatrously. *This* is their fault,—an identifying God with this world, and therefore an idolatry towards this world; and so they are rid of the trouble of looking out for their God, for they think they have found Him in the goods of this world. While, then, they are really praiseworthy in many parts of their conduct, benevolent, charitable, kind, neighbourly, and useful in their generation, nay, constant perhaps in the ordinary religious duties which custom has established, and while they display much right and amiable feeling, and much correctness in opinion, and are even in the way to improve in character and conduct as time goes on, correct much that is amiss, gain greater command over themselves, mature in judgement, and are much looked up to in consequence; yet still it is plain that they love this world, would be loath to leave it, and wish to have more of its good things. They like wealth, and distinction, and credit, and influence. They may improve in conduct, but not in aims; they advance, but they do not mount; they are moving on a low level, and were they to move on for centuries, would never rise above the atmosphere of this world. "I will stand upon my watch, and set me upon the tower, and will watch to see what He will say unto me, and what I shall answer when I am reproved." (Hab 2: 1) This is the temper of mind which they have not; and when we reflect how rarely it is found among professing Christians, we shall see why our Lord is so urgent in enforcing it;—as if He said, "I am not warning you, My followers, against open apostasy; that will not be; but I foresee that very few will keep awake and watch while I am away. Blessed are the servants who do so; few will open to me *immediately*, when I knock. They will have something to do first; they will have to get ready. They will have to recover from the surprise and confusion which overtake them on the first news of My coming, and will need time to collect themselves, and summon about them their better thoughts and affections. They feel themselves very well off as they are; and wish to serve God as they are. They are satisfied to remain on earth; they do not wish to move; they do not wish to change."

Without denying, then, to these persons the praise of many religious habits and practices, I would say that they want the tender and sensitive heart which hangs on the thought of Christ, and lives in His love. The breath of the world has a peculiar power in what may be called rusting the soul. The mirror within them, instead of reflecting back the Son of God their Saviour, has become dim and discoloured; and hence, though (to use a common expression) they have a good deal of good in them, it is only in them, it is not through them, around them, and upon them. An evil crust is *on* them: they think with the world; they are full of the world's notions and modes of speaking; they appeal to the world and have a sort of reverence for what the world will say. There is a want of naturalness, simplicity, and childlike teachableness in them. It is difficult to touch them, or (what may be called) get at them, and to persuade them to a straightforward course in religion. They start off when you least expect it; they have reservations, make distinctions, take exceptions, indulge in refinement, in questions where there are really but two sides, a right and a wrong. Their religious feelings do not flow forth easily, at times when they ought to flow; either they are diffident, and can say nothing, or else they are affected and strained in their mode of conversing. And as a rust preys upon metal and eats into it, so does this worldly spirit penetrate more and more deeply into the soul which once admits it. And this is one great end; as it would appear, of afflictions, viz., to rub away and clear off these outward defilements, and to keep the soul in a measure of its baptismal purity and brightness.

This is our state, or something like this, and the Day will declare it; the Day is at hand, and the Day will search our hearts, and bring it home even to ourselves, that we have been cheating ourselves with words, and have not served Christ, as the Redeemer of the soul claims, but with a meagre, partial, worldly service, and without really contemplating Him who is above and apart from this world.

. . . O, my brethren, pray Him to give you the heart to seek Him in sincerity. Pray Him to make you in earnest. You have one work only, to bear your cross after Him. . . . Pray Him to give you what Scripture calls "an honest and good heart," or "a perfect heart," and, without waiting begin at once to obey Him with the best heart you have. Any obedience is better than none,—any profession which is disjoined from obedience, is a mere pretence and deceit. Any religion which does not bring you nearer to God is of the world. You have to seek His face; obedience is the only way of seeking Him. All your duties are obediences. If you are to believe the truths He has revealed, to regulate yourselves by His precepts, to be frequent in His ordinances, to adhere to His Church and people, why is it, except because *He* has bid you? and to do what He bids is to obey Him, and to obey Him is to approach Him. Every act of obedience is an approach, an approach to Him who is not far off though He seems so, but close behind this visible screen of things which hides Him from us. He is behind this material framework; earth and sky are but a veil going between Him and us; the day will come when He will rend that veil, and show Himself to us. And then, according as we have waited for Him, will He recompense us. . . .

(PS 4:322, 325–28, 331–32, "Watching")

37. Watching and Waiting

[T]here is just one Name in the whole world that lives; it is the Name of One who passed His years in obscurity, and who died a malefactor's death. Eighteen hundred years have gone since that time, but still It has Its hold upon the human mind. It has possessed the world, and It maintains possession. Amid the most various nations under the most diversified circumstances, in the most cultivated, in the rudest races and intellects, in all classes of society, the Owner of that great Name reigns. High and low, rich and poor acknowledge Him. Millions of souls are conversing with Him, are venturing at His word, are looking for His presence. Palaces, sumptuous, innumerable, are raised to His honour; His image in its deepest humiliation, is triumphantly displayed in the proud city, in the open country; at the corners of streets, on the tops of mountains. It sanctifies the ancestral hall, the closet, and the bedchamber; it is the subject for the exercise of the highest genius in the imitative arts. It is worn next the heart in life; it is held before the failing eyes in death. Here, then, is One who is not a mere name; He is no empty fiction; He is a substance; He is dead and gone, but still He lives—as the living, energetic thought of successive generations, and as the awful motive power of a thousand great events. He has done without effort what others with lifelong, heroic struggles have not done. Can He be less than Divine? Who is He but the Creator Himself, who is sovereign over His own works; towards whom our eyes and hearts turn instinctively, because He is our Father and our God?

. . . If there be any who are not waiting on their Lord and Saviour, not keeping watch for Him, not longing for Him, not holding converse with Him, it is they who, like ourselves, are in the possession or in the search of temporal goods. Those saintly souls, whose merits and satisfactions almost make them sure of heaven, they, by the very nature of their state, are feeding on Christ. Those holy communities of men and women, whose life is a mortification, they, by their very profession of perfection, are waiting and watching for Him. The poor, those multitudes who pass their days in constrained suffering, they, by the stern persuasion of that suffering, are looking out for Him. But we, my Brethren, who are in easy circumstances, or in a whirl of business, or in a labyrinth of cares, or in a war of passions, or in the race of wealth, or honour, or station, or in the pursuits of science or of literature, alas! we are the very men who are likely to have no regard, no hunger or thirst, no relish for the true bread of heaven and the living water. . . . God in His mercy rouse our sluggish spirits, and inflame our earthly hearts, that we may cease to be an exception in His great family, which is ever adoring, praising, and loving Him.

(OS 44–46, "Waiting for Christ")

38. Serving Our Lord in the World

[I]t should be recollected that the employments of this world, though not themselves heavenly, are, after all, the way to heaven—though not the fruit, are the seed of immortality—and are valuable, though not in themselves, yet for that to which they lead: but it is difficult to realize this. It is difficult to realize both truths at once, and to connect both truths together; steadily to contemplate the life to come, yet to act in this. . . .

Now I am far from denying that a man's worldly occupation *may* be his cross. Again, I am far from denying that under circumstances it may be right even to retire from the world. But I am speaking of cases when it is a person's duty to remain in his worldly calling, and when he does remain in it, but when he cherishes dissatisfaction with it: whereas what he ought to feel is this,—that *while* in it he is to glorify God, not *out* of it, but *in* it, and *by means* of it, according to the Apostle's direction, "not slothful in business, fervent in spirit, serving the Lord." The Lord Jesus Christ our Saviour is best served, and with the most fervent spirit, when men are not slothful in business, but do their duty in that state of life in which it has pleased God to call them.

Now what leads such a person into this mistake is, that he sees that most men who engage cheerfully and diligently in worldly business, do so from a worldly spirit, from a low carnal love of the world; and so he thinks it is *his* duty, on the contrary, *not* to take a cheerful part in the world's business at all. And it cannot be denied that the greater part of the world is *absorbed* in the world; so much so that I am almost afraid to speak of the duty of being active in our worldly business, lest I should seem to give countenance to that miserable devotion to the things of time and sense, that love of bustle and management, that desire of gain, and that aiming at influence and importance, which abound on all sides. . . . [T]his most fearfully earthly and groveling spirit is likely, alas! to extend itself more and more among our countrymen,—an intense, sleepless, restless, never-wearied, never-satisfied, pursuit of Mammon in one shape or other, to the exclusion of all deep, all holy, all calm, all reverent thoughts. *This* is the spirit in which, more or less (according to their different tempers), men do commonly engage in concerns of this world; and I repeat it, better, far better, were it to retire from the world altogether than thus to engage in it—better with Elijah to fly to the desert, than to serve Baal and Ashtoreth in Jerusalem.

But surely it is possible to "serve the Lord," yet not to be "slothful in business;" not over devoted to it, but not to retire from it. We may do *all things* whatever we are about to God's glory; we may do all things heartily, as to the Lord, and not to man, being both active yet meditative. . . .

Thankfulness to Almighty God, nay, and the inward life of the Spirit itself, will be . . . principles causing the Christian to labour diligently in his calling. He will see God in all things. He will recollect our Saviour's life. Christ was brought up to a humble trade. When he labours in his own, he will think of his Lord and Master in His. He will recollect that Christ went down to Nazareth and was subject to His parents, that He walked long journeys, that He bore the sun's heat and the storm, and had not where to lay His head. Again, he knows that the Apostles had various employments of this world before their calling; St. Andrew and St. Peter fishers, St. Matthew a tax-gatherer, and St. Paul, even after his calling, still a tentmaker. Accordingly, in whatever comes upon him, he will endeavour to discern and gaze (as it were) on the countenance of his Saviour. He will feel that the true contemplation of that Saviour lies *in* his worldly business; that as Christ is seen in the poor, and in the persecuted, and in children, so is He seen in the employments which He puts upon His chosen, whatever they be; that in attending to his own calling he will be meeting Christ; that if he neglect it, he will not on that account enjoy His presence at all the more, but that while performing it, he will see Christ revealed to his soul amid the ordinary actions of the day, as by a sort of sacrament. Thus he will take his worldly business as a gift from Him, and will love it as such.

It is very easy to speak and teach this, difficult to do it; very difficult to steer between the two evils,—to use this world as not abusing it, to be active and diligent in this world's affairs, yet not for this world's sake, but for God's sake. . . .

(PS 8:154–55, 158–61, 164–65, 170, "Doing Glory
to God in Pursuits of the World")

39. Living by a Higher Law

[T]he Christian's character is formed by a rule higher than that of calculation and reason, consisting in a Divine principle or life, which transcends the anticipations and criticisms of ordinary men. Judging by mere worldly reasons, the Christian ought to be self-conceited, for he is gifted; he ought to understand evil, because he sees and speaks of it; he ought to feel resentment, because he is conscious of being injured; he ought to act from self-interest, because he knows that what is right is also expedient; he ought to be conscious and fond of the exercises of private judgement, because he engages in them; he ought to be doubting and hesitating in his faith, because his evidence for it might be greater than it is; he ought to have no expectation of Christ's coming, because Christ has delayed so long; but not so: his mind and heart are formed on a different mould. In these and ten thousand other ways he is open to the misapprehensions of the world, which neither has his feelings nor can enter into them. Nor can he explain and defend them on considerations which all men, good and bad, can understand. He goes by a law which others know not; not his own wisdom or judgement, but by Christ's wisdom and the judgement of the Spirit, which is imparted to him,—by that inward incommunicable perception of truth and duty, which is the rule of his reason, affections, wishes, tastes, and all that is in him, and which is the result of persevering obedience. This it is which gives so unearthly a character to his whole life and conversation, which is "hid with Christ in God;" he has ascended with Christ on high, and there "in heart and mind continually dwells;" and he is obliged, in consequence, to put a veil upon his face, and is mysterious in the world's judgement. . . .

. . . It must not be supposed, then, that this implies a neglect of our duties in this world. As it is possible to watch for Christ in spite of earthly reasonings to the contrary, so is it possible to engage in earthly duties, in spite of our watching. Christ has told us, that when He comes two men shall be in the field, two women at the mill, "the one shall be taken, and the other left." You see that good and bad are engaged in the same way; nor need it hinder any one from having his heart firmly fixed on God, that he is engaged in worldly business with those whose hearts are upon the world. Nay, we may form large plans, we may busy ourselves in new undertakings, we may begin great works which we cannot do more than begin; we may make provision for the future and anticipate in our acts the certainty of centuries to come, yet be looking out for Christ. Thus indeed we are bound to proceed and to leave "times and seasons in His Father's power." Whenever He comes, He will cut things short; and, for what we know, our efforts and beginnings, though they be nothing more, are just as necessary in the course of His providence, as could be the most successful accomplishment. Surely, He will end the world abruptly, whenever He comes. . . . And as He began without beginning, so will He end without an ending; or rather, all that we do—whatever we are doing—whether we have time for more or time for less—yet our work, finished or unfinished, will be acceptable, if done for Him. There is no inconsistency, then, in watching yet working, for we may work without setting our hearts on our work. Our sin will be if we idolize the work of our hands; if we love it so well as not to bear to part with it. The test of our faith lies in our being able to fail without disappointment.

(PS 6:266–69, "Subjection of the Reason and Feelings
to the Revealed Word")

40. Private Judgement and Divine Aid

[We] suspect that the doctrine of private judgement, in its simplicity, purity, and integrity, private judgement, all private judgement, and nothing but private judgement—is held by very few persons indeed; and that the great mass of the population are either stark unbelievers in it or deplorably dark about it; and that even the minority who are in a manner faithful to it, have glossed and corrupted the true sense of it by a miserably faulty reading, and hold, not the right of private judgement, but the private right of judgement; in other words, their own private right, and no one's else. To us it seems as clear as day, that they consider that they themselves, indeed, individually can and do act on reason, and on nothing but reason; that they have the gift of advancing, without bias or unsteadiness, throughout their search, from premise to conclusion, from text to doctrine; that they have sought aright, and no one else, who does not agree with them;

that they alone have found out the art of putting the salt upon the bird's tail and have rescued themselves from being the slaves of circumstance and the creatures of impulse. It is undeniable, then, if the popular feeling is to be our guide, that, high and mighty as the principle of private judgement is in religious inquiries, as we most fully grant it is, still it bears some similarity to Saul's armour which David rejected, or to edged tools which have a bad trick of chopping at our fingers, when we are but simply and innocently meaning them to make a dash forward at truth.

Any tolerably serious man will feel this in his own case more vividly than in that of any one else. Who can know ever so little of himself without suspecting all kinds of imperfect and wrong motives in everything he attempts? And then there is the bias of education and of habit; and, added to the difficulties thence resulting, those which arise from weakness of the reasoning faculty, ignorance or imperfect knowledge of the original languages of Scripture, and again, of history and antiquity. These things being considered, we lay it down as a truth, about which, we think, few ought to doubt, that Divine aid alone can carry any one safely and successfully through an inquiry after religious truth. . . . It is useless, surely, attempting to . . . judge, unless a Divine command enjoin the work upon us, and a Divine promise sustain us through it. Supposing, indeed, such a command and promise be given, then, of course, there is no difficulty in the matter. Whatever be our personal infirmities, He whom we serve can overrule or supersede them. An act of duty must always be right; and will be accepted, whatever be its success, because done in obedience to His will. And He can bless the most unpromising circumstances; He can even lead us forward by means of our mistakes; He can turn our mistakes into a revelation; He can convert us, if He will, through the very obstinacy, or self-will, or superstition, which mixes itself up with our better feelings, and defiles, yet is sanctified by our sincerity. And much more can he shed upon our path supernatural light, if He so will, and give us an insight into the meaning of Scripture, and a hold of the sense of Antiquity, to which our own unaided powers never could have attained.

All this is certain; He continually leads us forward in the mist of darkness; and we live, not by bread only, but by His word converting the hard rock or salt sea into nourishment.

(Ess. 2:340–43, "Private Judgement")

41. His Gifts

Gloom is no Christian temper; that repentance is not real, which has not love in it; that self-chastisement is not acceptable, which is not sweetened by faith and cheerfulness. We must live in sunshine, even when we sorrow; we must live in God's presence, we must not shut ourselves up in our own hearts, even when we are reckoning up our past sins.

He has promised that this shall be His rule,—that thus shall it be fulfilled to us as His ordinary providence, viz.—that life shall not be a burden to us, but a blessing, and shall contain more to comfort than to afflict. And giving us as much as this, He bids us be satisfied with it; He bids us confess that we "have all" when we have so much: that we "abound" when we have enough; He promises us food, raiment, and lodging; and He bids us, "having food and raiment, therewith to be content." (1 Tim 6: 8) He bids us be content with those gifts, and withal unsolicitous about them; tranquil, secure, and confident, because He has promised them; He bids us be sure that we shall have so much, and not be disappointed that it is no more. Such is His merciful consideration of us; He does not separate us from this world, though He calls us out of it; He does not reject our old nature when He gives us a new one; He does but redeem it from the curse, and purify it from the infection which came through Adam, and is none of His. He especially blesses the creation to our use. . . . He does not bid us renounce the creation, but associates us with the most beautiful portions of it. He likens us to the flowers with which He has ornamented the earth, and to the birds that live solitary under heaven, and makes them the type of a Christian. He denies us Solomon's regal magnificence to unite us to the lilies of the field and the fowls of the air. . . .

It is often said, and truly, that the Christian is born to trouble,—that sorrow is the rule with him, and pleasure the exception. But when this is said, it is with reference to seasons, circumstances, events, such things as are adventitious and additional to the gift of life itself. The Christian's *lot* is one of sorrow, but, as the regenerate *life* with him is happiness, so is the gift of natural life also. We live, therefore we are happy; *upon* this life of ours come joys and sorrows; and in proportion as we are favourites of God, it is sorrow that comes, not joy. Still after all considered in ourselves, that we live; that God breathes in us; that we exist in Him; that we think and act; that we have the means of life; that we have food, and sleep, and raiment, and lodging, and that we are not lonely, but in God's Church, and are sure of brethren by the very token of our having a Father which is in heaven; so far, rejoicing is the very condition of our being, and all pain is little more than external, not reaching to our inmost heart. So far all men almost are on a level, seasons of sickness excepted. Even delicate health and feebleness of life does not preclude these pleasures. And as to seasons of sickness, or even long and habitual pain or disease, the good Lord can compensate for them in His own way by extraordinary supplies of grace. . . .

. . . [L]et us acknowledge the blessing, whether of the holy marriage bond, or of family affection, or of the love of friends, which He so bounteously bestows. He gives, He takes away; blessed be His Name. But He takes away to give again, and He withdraws one blessing, to restore fourfold. . . . We too, through God's mercy, whether we be young or old, whether we have many friends or few, if we be Christ's shall all along our pilgrimage find those in whom we may live, who will love us and whom we may love, who will aid us and help us forward, and comfort us, and close our eyes. For His love is a secret gift, which, unseen by the world, binds together those in whom it lives, and makes them live and sympathise in one another.

. . . [G]reat thanks to God, who has made use of the world, and has overruled its course of opinion to our benefit. We have large and noble churches to worship in; we may go freely to worship when we will; we may enjoy the advice of those who know better than ourselves; we may speak our mind one to another; we may move about freely; we may hold intercourse with whom we will; we may write what we will, explaining, defending, recommending, spreading the truth, without suffering or inconvenience. . . .

Lastly, and very briefly, my brethren, let us remind ourselves of our own privileges here in this place. How great is our privilege, my brethren!—every one of us enjoys the great privilege of daily Worship. . . . This great privilege God has given to me and to you,—let us enjoy it while we have it. Not any one of us knows how long it may be his own. Perhaps there is no one among us all who can reckon upon it for a continuance. Perhaps, or rather probably, it is a bright spot in our lives. Perhaps we shall look upon these days or years, time hence; and then reflect, when all is over, how pleasant they were; how pleasant to come, day after day, quietly and calmly, to kneel before our Maker,—week after week, to meet our Lord and Saviour. How soothing will then be the remembrance of His past gifts! we shall remember how we got up early in the morning, and how all things, light or darkness, sun or air, cold or freshness, breathed of Him,—of Him, the Lord of glory, who stood over us, and came down upon us, and gave Himself to us, and poured forth milk and honey for our sustenance, though we saw Him not. Surely we have all, and abound: we are full.

(PS 5:271, 274–75, 277–78, 280–83, "Present Blessings")

42. The Defect of "Cheerful" Religion

[T]he age, whatever be its peculiar excellences, has this serious defect, it loves an exclusively cheerful religion. It determined to make religion bright and sunny and joyous, whatever be the form of it which it adopts. And it will handle the Catholic doctrine in this spirit; it will skim over it; it will draw it out in mere buckets-full; it will substitute its human cistern for the well of truth; it will be afraid of the deep well, the abyss of God's judgements and God's mercies.

. . . Surely we are pretending allegiance to the Church to no purpose, or rather to our own serious injury, if we select her doctrines and precepts at our pleasure; choose this, reject that; take what is beautiful and attractive, shrink from what is stern and painful. . . .

Christianity, considered as a moral system, is made up of two elements, beauty and severity; whenever either is indulged to the loss or disparagement of the other, evil ensues. . . .

. . . Thus let us proceed in the use of all our privileges, all will be benefits. Let us not keep festivals without keeping vigils; let us not keep Eastertide without observing Lent; let us not approach the Sunday feast without keeping the Friday abstinence; let us not adorn churches without studying personal simplicity and austereness; let us not cultivate the accomplishments of taste and literature without the corrective of personal discomfort; let us not attempt to advance the power of the Church, to enthrone her rulers, to rear her palaces, and to ennoble her name, without recollecting that she must be mortified within while she is in honour in the world. . . .

. . . [L]et us beware, on the other hand, of dishonouring and rudely rejecting God's gifts, out of gloominess or sternness; let us beware of fearing without feasting. "Every creature of God is good, and nothing to be refused." Let us beware, though it must be a sad perversion of mind which admits of it,—let us beware of afflicting ourselves for sin, without first coming to the Gospel for strength to do so. And let us not so plunge ourselves in the sense of our offences, as not withal to take delight in the contemplation of our privileges. Let us rejoice while we mourn. Let us look up to our Lord and Saviour the more we shrink from the sight of ourselves; let us have the more faith and love the more we exercise repentance. Let us, in our penitence, not substitute the Law *for* the Gospel, but add the Law *to* the Gospel. . . .

. . . [A]s they must not defraud themselves of Christian privileges, neither need they give up God's temporal blessings. All the beauty of nature, the kind influences of the seasons, the gifts of sun and moon, and the fruits of the earth, the advantages of civilized life, and the presence of friends and intimates; all these good things are but one extended and wonderful type of God's benefits in the Gospel. Those who aim at perfection will not reject the gift, but add a corrective; they will add the bitter herbs to the fatted calf and music and dancing; they will not refuse the flowers of earth, but they will toil in plucking up the weeds. Or if they refrain from one temporal blessing, it will be to reserve another; for this is one great mercy of God, that while He allows us a discretionary use of His temporal gifts, He allows a discretionary abstinence also. . . .

(SD 117, 120, 122–24, "Indulgence in Religious Privileges")

43. Abstinence and Christian Love

Now at first sight it may not be clear why this moderation, and at least occasional abstinence, in the use of God's gifts, should be so great a duty, as our Lord, for instance, seems to imply, when He places fasting in so prominent a place in the Sermon on the Mount, with almsgiving and prayer. But thus much we are able to see, that the great duty of the gospel is love to God and man; and that this love is quenched and extinguished by self-indulgence, and cherished by self-denial. They who enjoy this life freely, make it or self their idol; they are gross-hearted, and have no eyes to see God withal. Hence it is said, "Blessed are the pure in heart, for they shall see God." (Mt 5: 8) And again, it was the rich man who fared sumptuously every day, who neglected Lazarus; for sensual living hardens the heart, while abstinence softens and refines it. Now, observe, I do not mean that abstinence produces this effect as a matter of course in any given person,—else all the poor ought to be patterns of Christian love,—but that where men are religiously-minded, there those out of the number will make greater attainments in love and devotional feeling, who do exercise themselves in self-denial of the body. I should really be disposed to say,—You must make your choice, you must in some way or another deny the flesh, or you cannot possess Christian love. Love is no common grace in its higher degrees. It is true, indeed, that, as being the necessary token of every true Christian, it must be possessed in some degree even by the weakest and humblest of Christ's servants—but in any of its higher and maturer stages, it is rare and difficult. It is easy to be amiable or upright; it is easy to live in regular habits;—it is easy to live conscientiously, in the common sense of the word. I say, all this is comparatively easy; but one thing is needful, and one thing is often lacking,—love. We may act rightly, yet without doing our right actions from the love of God. Other motives, short of love, are good in themselves; these we may have, and not have love. Now I do not think that this defect arises from any one cause, or can be removed by any one remedy; and yet still, it does seem as if abstinence and fasting availed much towards its removal; so much so, that, granting love is necessary, then these are necessary; assuming love to be the characteristic of a

Christian, so is abstinence. You may think to dispense with fasting; true; and you may neglect also to cultivate love.

(PS 6:29–30, "Apostolic Abstinence a Pattern for Christians")

44. Fasting and Feasting

None rejoice in Easter-tide less than those who have not grieved in Lent. This is what is seen in the world at large. To them, one season is the same as another, and they take no account of any. Feast-day and fast-day, holy tide and other tide, are one and the same to them. Hence they do not realize the next world at all. To them the Gospels are but like another history; a course of events which took place eighteen hundred years since. They do not make our Saviour's life and death present to them: they do not transport themselves back to the time of His sojourn on earth. They do not act over again, and celebrate His history, in their own observance; and the consequence is, that they feel no interest in it. They have neither faith nor love towards it; it has no hold on them. They do not form their estimate of things upon it; they do not hold it as a sort of practical principle in their heart. This is the case not only with the world at large, but too often with men who have the Name of Christ in their mouths. They think they believe in Him, yet when trial comes, or in the daily conduct of life, they are unable to act upon the principles which they profess: and why? because they . . . have considered it a simpler and more spiritual religion, not to act religiously except when called to it by extraordinary trial or temptation; because they have thought that, since it is the Christian's duty to rejoice evermore, they would rejoice better if they never sorrowed and never travailed with righteousness. On the contrary, let us be sure that, as previous humiliation sobers our joy, it alone secures it to us. Our Saviour says, "Blessed are they that mourn, for they shall be comforted;" and what is true hereafter, is true here. . . .

. . . In the world feasting comes first and fasting afterwards; men first glut themselves, and then loathe their excesses; they take their fill of good, and then suffer; they are rich that they may be poor; they laugh that they may weep; they rise that they may fall. But in the Church of God it is reversed; the poor *shall* be rich, the lowly shall be exalted, those that sow in tears shall reap in joy, those that mourn shall be comforted, those that suffer with Christ shall reign with Him. . . . And what is true of the general course of our redemption is, I say, fulfilled also in the yearly and other commemorations of it. Our Festivals are preceded by humiliation, that we may keep them duly; not boisterously or fanatically, but in a refined, subdued, chastised spirit, which is the true rejoicing in the Lord.

(PS 4:338–39, "Keeping Fast and Festival")

45. The Christian Temper

[W]hen we lie on the bed of death, what will it avail us to have been rich, or great, or fortunate, or honoured, or influential? All things will then be vanity. Well, what this world will be understood by all to be then, such is it felt to be by the Christian now. He looks at things as he then will look at them, with an uninterested and dispassionate eye, and is neither pained much nor pleased much at the accidents of life, because they are accidents.

. . . The truth is, as soon and in proportion as a person believes that Christ is coming, and recognises his own position as a stranger on earth, who has but hired a lodging in it for a season, he will feel indifferent to the course of human affairs. He will be able to look on, instead of taking a part in them. They will be nothing to him. He will be able to criticize them, and pass judgement without partiality. . . . Those who have strong interest one way or the other, cannot be dispassionate observers and candid judges. They are partisans; they defend one set of people, and attack another. They are prejudiced against those who differ from them, or who thwart them. They cannot make allowances, or show sympathy for them. But the Christian has no keen expectations, no acute mortifications. He is fair, equitable, considerate towards all men, because he has no temptation to be otherwise. He has no violence, no animosity, no bigotry, no party feeling. He knows that his Lord and Saviour must triumph; he knows that He will one day come from heaven, no one can say how soon. Knowing then the end to which all things tend, he cares less for the road which is to lead to it. When we read a book of fiction, we are much excited with the course of the narrative, till we know how things will turn out; but when we do, the interest ceases. So is it with the Christian. He knows Christ's battle will last till the end; that Christ's cause will triumph in the end; that His Church will last till He comes. He knows what is truth and what is error, where is safety and where is danger; and all this clear knowledge enables them to make concessions, to own difficulties, to do justice to the erring, to acknowledge their good points, to be content with such countenance, greater or less, as he himself receives from others. He does not fear; fear it is that makes men bigots, tyrants, and zealots; but for the Christian, it is his privilege, as he is beyond hopes and fears, suspense and jealousy, so also to be patient, cool, discriminating, and impartial—so much so, that this very fairness marks his character in the eyes of the world, is "known unto all men."

. . . [P]eace is part of this same temper also.

. . . [T]he Christian has a deep, silent, hidden peace, which the world sees not—like some well in a retired and shady place, difficult of access. He is the greater part of his time by himself and when he is in solitude, that is his real state. What he is when left to himself and to his God, that is his true life. He can bear himself; he can (as it were) joy in himself; for it the grace of God within him, it is the presence of the Eternal Comforter, in which he joys. He can bear, he finds it pleasant, to be with himself at all times— "never less alone than when alone." He can lay his head on his pillow at night, and own in God's sight, with overflowing heart, that he wants nothing—that he "is full and abounds,"—that God has been all things to him, and that nothing is not his which God could give him. More thankfulness, more holiness, more of heaven he needs indeed, but the thought that he can have more is not a thought of trouble, but of joy. It does not interfere with his peace to know that he may grow nearer God. Such is the Christian's peace, when, with a single heart and the Cross in his eye, he addresses and commends himself to Him with whom the night is as clear as the day. St. Paul says that "the peace of God shall *keep* our hearts and minds." By "keep" is meant "guard," or "garrison," our hearts; so as to keep out enemies. And he says, our "hearts and minds" in contrast to what the world sees of us. Many hard things may be said of the Christian, and done against him, but he has a secret preservative or charm, and minds them not.

. . . The Christian is cheerful, easy, kind, gentle, courteous, candid, unassuming; has no pretence, no affectation, no ambition, no singularity; because he has neither hope nor fear about this world. He is serious, sober, discreet, grave, moderate, mild, with so little that is unusual or striking in his bearing, that he may easily be taken at first sight for an ordinary man. There are persons who think religion consists in ecstasies, or in set speeches—he is not of those. And it must be confessed, on the other hand, that there is a commonplace state of mind which does show itself calm, composed, and candid, yet is very far from the true Christian temper. In this day especially it is very easy for men to be benevolent, liberal, and dispassionate. It costs nothing to be dispassionate when you feel nothing, to be cheerful when you have nothing to fear, to be generous or liberal when what you give is not your own, and to be benevolent and considerate when you have no principles and no opinions. Men nowadays are moderate and equitable, not because the Lord is at hand, but because they do not feel that He is coming. Quietness is a grace, not in itself, only when it is grafted on the stem of faith, zeal, self-abasement, and diligence.

May it be our blessedness, as years go on, to add one grace to another, and advance upward, step by step, neither neglecting the lower after attaining the higher, nor aiming at the higher before attaining the lower. The first grace is faith, the last is love; first comes zeal, afterwards comes loving-kindness; first comes humiliation, then comes peace; first comes diligence, then comes resignation. May we learn to mature all graces in us;—fearing and trembling, watching and repenting, because Christ is coming; joyful, thankful, and careless of the future, because He is come.

(PS 5:63–65, 68–71, "Equanimity")

46. Perfecting Natural Virtue

The difference, then, between the extraordinary Christian "spirit," and human faith and virtue, viewed apart from Christianity, is simply this: that, while the two are the same in nature, the former is immeasurably higher than the other, more deeply rooted in the mind it inhabits, more consistent, more vigorous, of more intense purity, of more sovereign authority, with greater promise of victory—the choicest elements of our moral nature being collected, fostered and matured into a determinate character by the gracious influences of the Holy Ghost. . . .

And let us view [men who manifest such spirit], whom we rightly call Saints, in the combination of graces which form their character, and we shall gain a fresh insight into the nature of that sublime morality which the Spirit enforces. St. Paul exhibits the union of zeal and gentleness; St. John, of overflowing love with uncompromising strictness of principle. Firmness and meekness is another combination of virtues, which is exemplified in Moses, even under the first Covenant. To these we may add such as self-respect and humility, the love and fear of God, and the use of the world without the abuse of it. This necessity of being "sanctified wholly," in the Apostle's language, is often forgotten. It is indeed comparatively easy to profess one side only of moral excellence, as if faith were to be all in all, or zeal, or amiableness; whereas in truth, religious obedience is a very intricate problem, and the more so the farther we proceed in it. The moral growth within us must be symmetrical, in order to be beautiful or lasting; hence mature sanctity is seldom recognized by others, where it really exists, never by the world at large. Ordinary spectators carry off one or other impression of a good man, according to the accidental circumstances under which they see him. Much more are the attributes and manifestations of the Divine Mind beyond our understanding, and, appearing inconsistent, are rightly called mysterious.

Such, then, is the present benefit which Christianity offers us; not only a renewal of our moral nature after Adam's original likeness, but a blending of all its powers and affections into the one perfect man, "after the measure of the stature of the fulness of Christ." . . .

The day, we know, will come, when every Christian will be judged, not by what God has done for him, but by what he has done for himself: when, of all the varied blessings of Redemption, in which he was clad here, nothing will remain to him, but what he has incorporated in his own moral nature, and made part of himself. And, since we cannot know that measure of holiness will be then accepted in our own case, it is but left to us to cast ourselves individually on God's mercy in faith, and to look steadily, yet humbly, at the Atonement for sin which He has appointed; so that when He comes to judge the world He may remember us in His kingdom.

(US 43, 47–48, 53, "Evangelical Sanctity
the Completion of Natural Virtue")

47. Obedience

[D]eeds of obedience are an intelligible evidence, nay, the sole evidence possible, and, on the whole, a satisfactory evidence of the reality of our faith. I do not say that this or that good work tells anything; but a course of obedience says much. Various deeds, done in different departments of duty, support and attest each other. Did a man act merely a bold and firm part, he would have cause to say to himself, "Perhaps all this is mere pride and obstinacy." Were he merely yielding and forgiving—he might be indulging a natural indolence of mind. Were he merely industrious, this might consist with ill-temper, or selfishness. Did he merely fulfil the duties of his temporal calling, he would have no proof that he had given his heart to God at all. Were he merely regular at Church and Holy Communion—many a man is such who has a lax conscience, who is not scrupulously fair-dealing, or is censorious, or niggardly. Is he what is called a domestic character, amiable, affectionate, fond of his family? Let him beware lest he put wife and children in the place of God who gave them. Is he only temperate, sober, chaste, correct in his language? It may arise from mere dulness and insensibility, or may consist with spiritual pride. Is he cheerful and obliging? It may arise from youthful spirits and ignorance of the world. Does he choose his friends by a strictly orthodox rule? He may be harsh and uncharitable; or is he zealous and serviceable in defending the Truth? Still he may be unable to condescend to men of low estate, to rejoice with those who rejoice, and to weep with those who weep. No one is without some good quality or other: Balaam had a scruple about misrepresenting God's message, Saul was brave, Joab was loyal, the

Bethel Prophet reverenced God's servants, the witch of Endor was hospitable; and therefore, of course, no one good deed or disposition is the criterion of a spiritual mind. Still, on the other hand, there is no one of its characteristics which has not its appropriate outward evidence; and in proportion as these external acts are multiplied and varied, so does the evidence of it become stronger and more consoling. General conscientiousness is the only assurance we can have of possessing it; and at this we must aim, determining to obey God consistently, with a jealous carefulness about all things, little and great. This is, in Scripture language, to "serve God with a perfect heart." . . .

(PS 2:157–59, "Saving Knowledge")

48. Watching and Praying and Meditating

[I]t is true that the Father and the Son are invisible, that They have an ineffable union with each other, and are not in any dependence upon the mortal concerns of this world; and so we, in our finite measure, must live after Their Divine pattern, holding communion with Them, as if we were at the top of the Mount, while we perform our duties towards that sinful and irreligious world which lies at the foot of it. . . .

It is then the duty and the privilege of all disciples of our glorified Saviour, to be exalted and transfigured with Him; to live in heaven in their thoughts, motives, aims, desires, likings, prayers, praises, intercessions, even while they are in the flesh; to look like other men, to be busy like other men, to be passed over in the crowd of men, or even to be scorned or oppressed, as other men may be, but the while to have a secret channel of communication with the Most High, a gift the world knows not of; to have their life *hid* with Christ in God. . . .

. . . Wonderful things had taken place, while the world seemed to go on as usual. Pontius Pilate thought himself like other governors. The Jewish rulers went on with the aims and the prejudices which had heretofore governed them. Herod went on in his career of sin, and having seen and put to death one prophet, hoped to see miracles from a second. They all viewed all things as of this world; they said, "tomorrow shall be as to-day, and much more abundant." They heard the news and saw the sights and provided for the needs of the moment, and forgot the thought of God. Thus men went on at the foot of the mount, and they cared not for what was on the summit. They did not understand that another and marvelous system, contrary to this world, was proceeding forward under the veil of this world. So it was then: so it is now. The world witnesses not the secret communion of the Saints of God, their prayers, praises, and intercessions. But *they* have the present privileges of saints, notwithstanding,—a knowledge, and a joy, and a strength, which they cannot compass or describe, and would not if they could. . . .

. . . If you have hitherto thought too little of these things, if you have thought religion lies *merely* in what it certainly does consist in also, in filling your worldly station well, in being amiable, and well-behaved, and considerate, and orderly,—but if you have thought it was nothing more than this, if you have neglected to stir up the great gift of God which is lodged deep within you . . . if you have been scanty in your devotions, in intercession, prayer, and praise, and if, in consequence, you have little or nothing of the sweetness, the winning grace, the innocence, the freshness, the tenderness, the cheerfulness, the composure of the elect of God, if you are at present really deficient in praying, and other divine exercises, make a new beginning henceforth. . . . Mount up from the grave of the old Adam; from groveling cares, and jealousies, and fretfulness, and worldly aims; from the thraldom of habit, from the tumult of passion, from the fascinations of the flesh, from a cold, worldly, calculating spirit, from frivolity, from selfishness, from effeminacy, from self-conceit and high-mindedness. Henceforth set about doing what it is so difficult to do, but what should not, must not be left undone; watch, and pray, and meditate, that is, according to the leisure which God has given you. Give freely of your time to your Lord and Saviour, if you have it. If you have little, show your sense of the privilege by giving that little. But any how, show that your heart and your desires, show that your life is with your God. Set aside every day times for seeking Him. Humble yourself that you have been hitherto so languid and uncertain. Live more strictly to Him; take His yoke upon your shoulder; live by rule. I am not calling on you to go out of the world, or to abandon your duties in the world, but to redeem the time; not to give hours to mere amusement or society, while you give minutes to Christ; not to pray to Him only when you are tired, and fit for nothing but the world and the Church; but in good measure to realize honestly the words of the text, to "set your affection on things above;" and to prove that you are His, in that your heart is risen with Him, and your life hid in Him.

(PS 6:210–11, 214, 216–17, 219–20, "Rising with Christ")

49. Self-Examination

[O]ur obedience may be in some sort religious, and yet hardly deserve the title of Christian. This may be at first sight a startling assertion. It may seem to some of us as if there were no difference between being religious and being Christian; and that to insist on a difference is to perplex people. But listen to me. Do you not think it possible for men to do their duty, i.e. be religious, in a heathen country? Doubtless it is. St. Peter says, that in every nation he that feareth God and worketh righteousness is accepted with Him. Now are such persons, therefore, Christians? Certainly *not*. It would seem, then, it is possible to fear God and work righteousness, yet without being Christians; for (if we would know the truth of it) to be a Christian is to do this, and to do *much more* than this. Here, then, is a fresh subject for self-examination. Is it not the way of men to dwell with satisfaction on their good deeds, particularly when, for some reason or other, their conscience smites them? Or when they are led to the consideration of death, then they begin to turn in their minds how they shall acquit themselves before the judgement-seat. And then it is they feel a relief in being able to detect, in their past lives, any deeds which may be regarded in any sense religious. You may hear some persons comforting themselves that they never harmed any one; and that they have not given in to an openly profligate and riotous life. Others are able to say more; they can speak of their honesty, their industry, or their general conscientiousness. We will say they have taken good care of their families; they have never defrauded or deceived any one;

and they have a good name in the world; nay, they have in one sense lived in the fear of God. I will grant them this and more; yet possibly they are not altogether Christians in their obedience. I will grant that these virtuous and religious deeds are really fruits of faith, not external merely, done without thought, but proceeding from the heart. I will grant they are really praiseworthy, and, when a man from want of opportunity knows no more, really acceptable to God; yet they determine nothing about his having received the Gospel of Christ in power. Why? For the simple reason that they are *not enough*. A Christian's faith and obedience is *built* on all this, but is only built on it. It is not the same as it. To be Christians, surely it is not enough to be that which we are enjoined to be, and must be, even without Christ; not enough to be no better than good heathens; not enough to be, in some slight measure, just, honest, temperate, and religious. We must indeed be just, honest, temperate, and religious, before we can rise to Christian Graces, and to *be* practised in justice and the like virtues is the way, the ordinary way, in which we receive the fulness of the kingdom of God. . . . I am not wishing to frighten these imperfect Christians, but to lead them on; to open their minds to the greatness of the work before them, to dissipate the meagre and carnal views in which the Gospel has come to them, to warn them that they must never be contented with themselves, or stand still and relax their efforts but must go on *unto perfection*; that till they are much more than they are at present, they have received the kingdom of God in word, not in power; that they are not spiritual men, and can have no comfortable sense of Christ's presence in their souls, for to whom much is given, of him is much required.

. . . Now it is plain that this is a very different mode of obedience from any which natural reason and conscience tell us of; different, *not in its nature*, but *in its excellence and peculiarity*. It is much more than honesty, justice, and temperance; and *this* is to be a Christian. Observe in what respect it is different from that lower degree of religion which we may possess without entering into the mind of the Gospel. First of all in its faith; which is placed, not simply in God, but in God as manifested in Christ, according to His own words, "Ye believe in God, believe also in Me." (Jn 14: 1) Next, we must adore Christ as our Lord and Master, and love Him as our most gracious Redeemer. We must have a deep sense of our guilt, and of the difficulty of securing heaven; we must live as in His presence, daily pleading His cross and passion, thinking of His holy commandments, imitating His sinless pattern, and depending on the gracious aids of His Spirit; that we may really and truly be servants of Father, Son, and Holy Ghost, in whose name we were baptized. Further, we must, for His sake, aim at a noble and unusual strictness of life, perfecting holiness in His fear, destroying our sins, mastering our whole soul, and bringing it into captivity to His law, denying ourselves lawful things, in order to do Him service, exercising a profound humility, and an unbounded, never-failing love, giving away much of our substance in religious and charitable works, and discountenancing and shunning irreligious men. This is to be a Christian; a gift easily described, and in a few words, but attainable only with fear and much trembling; promised, indeed, and in a measure accorded at once to every one who asks for it, but not secured till after many years, and never in this life fully realized. . . .

With others we have no concern; we do not know what their opportunities are. There may be thousands in this populous land who never had the means of hearing Christ's voice fully, and in whom virtues short of evangelical will hereafter be accepted as the fruit of faith. Nor can we know the *hearts* of *any* men, or tell what is the degree in which they have improved their talents. It is enough to keep to ourselves. We dwell in the full light of the Gospel, and the full grace of the Sacraments. We ought to have the holiness of Apostles. There is no reason except our own wilful corruption, that we are not by this time walking in the steps of St. Paul or St. John, and following them as they followed Christ. What a thought is this! Do not cast it from you, my brethren, but take it to your homes, and may God give you grace to profit by it!

(PS 1:76–82, "The Spiritual Mind")

50. The Spirit of Love

Faith and hope are graces of an imperfect state, and they cease with that state; but love is greater, because it is perfection. Faith and hope are graces, as far as we belong to this world, which is for a time; but love is a grace, because we are creatures of God whether here or elsewhere, and partakers in a redemption which is to last for ever. Faith will not be when there is sight, nor hope when there is enjoyment; but love will (as we believe) increase more and more to all eternity. Faith and hope are means by which we express our love: we believe God's word, because we love it; we hope after heaven because we love it. We should not have any hope or concern about it, unless we loved it; we should not trust or confide in the God of heaven, unless we loved Him. Faith, then, and hope are but instruments or expressions of love; but as to love itself, we do not love because we believe, for the devils believe, yet do not love; nor do we love because we hope, for hypocrites hope, who do not love. But we love for no cause beyond itself: we love, because it is our nature to love; and it is our nature, because God the Holy Ghost has made it our nature. Love is the immediate fruit and the evidence of regeneration. . . .

Faith is the first element of *religion*, and love, of *holiness*; and as holiness and religion are distinct, yet united, so are love and faith. Holiness can exist without religion; religion cannot exist without holiness. Baptized infants, before they come to years of understanding, are holy; they are not religious. Holiness is love of the Divine Law. When God regenerates an infant, He imparts to it the gift of His Holy Spirit; and what is the Spirit thus imparted but the Law written on its heart? . . . God comes to us as a Law, before He comes as a Lawgiver; that is, He sets up His throne within us, and enables us to obey Him, before we have learned to reflect on our own sensations, and to know the voice of God. Such, as if in a type, was Samuel's case; he knew not who it was who called him, till Eli the priest told him. Eli stands for religion, Samuel for holiness; Eli for faith, Samuel for love. . . .

Too true is it, that the mass of men live neither with faith nor love; they live to themselves, they love themselves selfishly, and do not desire any thing beyond the visible framework of things. This world is their all in all. But I speak of religious persons; and these, I think, will confess that distaste for the world is quite a distinct thing from the spirit of love. As years go on, the disappointments, troubles, and cares of life, wean a religious mind from attachment to this world. A man sees it is but vanity. He neither receives, nor looks for enjoyment from it. He does not look to the future with hope; he has no prospects; he cares not for the world's smile or frown; for what it can do, what it can withhold. . . . And thus in the course of time, with a very scanty measure of true divine love, he is enabled, whatever his sphere is, to act above the world, in his degree; to do his plain straightforward duty, because reason tells him he should do it, and because he has no great temptation seducing him from it. Observe, *why* he keeps God's commandments; from *reason*, because he knows he ought, and because he has no strong motives keeping him from doing so. Alas! Not from *love* towards those commandments. He has only just so much of the spirit of love as suffices to hinder his resignation from being despondent, and his faith from being dead. . . .

This then is that middle state in which some of us may be standing in our progress from earth to heaven, and which the text warns us against. It tells us that faith at most only makes a hero, but that love makes a saint; that faith can but put us above the world, but that love brings us under God's throne; that faith can but make us sober, but love makes us happy. It warns us that it is possible for a man to have the clearest, calmest, exactest view of the realities of heaven; that he may most firmly realize and act upon the truths of the gospel; that he may understand that all about him is but a veil, not a substance; that he may have that full confidence in God's word as to be able to do miracles; that he may have such simple absolute faith as to give up his property, give up all his goods to feed the poor; that he may so scorn the world, that he may with so royal a heart trample on it, as even to give his body to be burned by a glorious martyrdom; and yet I do not say, be without love; God forbid! I do not suppose the Apostle means there ever *was* actually such a case, but that it is abstractedly possible; that no one of the proper acts of faith, in itself, and necessarily, implies love; that it is distinct from love. He says this, that, though a person *be* all that has been said, yet unless he be also something besides, unless he have love, it profiteth him nothing. O fearful lesson, to all those who are tempted to pride themselves in their labours, or sufferings, or sacrifices, or works! We are Christ's, not by faith merely, nor by works merely, but by love;

not by hating the world, nor by hating sin, nor by venturing for the world to come, nor by calmness, nor by magnanimity,— though we must do and be all this; and if we *have* love in perfection we *shall*, but it is love makes faith, not faith love. We are saved, not by any of these things, but by that heavenly flame within us, which, while it consumes what is seen, aspires to what is unseen. Love is the gentle, tranquil, satisfied acquiescence and adherence of the soul in the contemplation of God; not only a preference of God before all things, but a delight in Him because He is God, and because His commandments are good; not any violent emotion or transport, but as St. Paul describes it, long-suffering, kind, modest, unassuming, innocent, simple, orderly, disinterested, meek, pure-hearted, sweet-tempered, patient, enduring. Faith without charity is dry, harsh, and sapless; it has nothing sweet, engaging, winning, soothing; but it was Charity which brought Christ down. Charity is but another name for the Comforter. It is eternal Charity which is the bond of all things in heaven and earth; it is charity wherein the Father and the Son are one in the unity of the spirit; by which the angels in heaven are one, by which all Saints are one with God, by which the Church is one upon earth.

(PS 4:309–10, 312–13, 315–18, "Faith and Love")

Temptations

51. The Lack of Will

Let us ask ourselves, why is it that we so often wish to do right and cannot? Why is it that we are so frail, feeble, languid, wayward, dim-sighted, fluctuating, perverse? Why is it that we cannot "do the things that we would?" Why is it that, day after day, we remain irresolute, that we serve God so poorly, that we govern ourselves so weakly and so variably, that we cannot command our thoughts, that we are so slothful, so cowardly, so discontented, so sensual, so ignorant? Why is it that we, who trust that we are not by wilful sin thrown out of grace (for of such I am all along speaking), why is it that we, who are ruled by no evil masters and bent upon no earthly ends, who are not covetous, or profligate livers, or worldly-minded, or ambitious, or envious, or proud, or unforgiving, or desirous of name—why is it that we, in the very kingdom of grace, surrounded by Angels, and preceded by Saints, nevertheless can do so little, and instead of mounting with wings like eagles, grovel in the dust, and do but sin, and confess sin, alternately? Is it that the *power* of God is not within us? Is it literally that we are *not able* to perform God's commandments? God forbid! We are able. We have that given us which makes us able. We are not in a state of nature. We have had the gift of grace implanted in us. We have a power within us to do what we are commanded to do. What is it we lack? The power? No; the will. What we lack is the real, simple, earnest, sincere inclination and aim to use what God has given us, and what we have in us. I say, our experience tells us this. It is no matter of mere doctrine, much less a matter of words, but of things; a very practical plain matter. . . .

There is a famous instance of a holy man of old time, who, before his conversion, felt indeed the excellence of purity, but could not get himself to say more in prayer than "Give me chastity, but not yet." I will not be inconsiderate enough to make light of the power of temptation of any kind, nor will I presume to say that Almighty God will certainly shield a man from temptation for his wishing it; but whenever men complain, as they often do, of the arduousness of a high virtue, at least it were well that they should first ask themselves the question, whether they desire to have it. . . . O ye men of the world, when ye talk, as ye do, so much of the impossibility of this or that supernatural grace, when you disbelieve in the existence of severe self-rule, when you scoff at holy resolutions, and affix a slur on those who make them, are you sure that the impossibility which you insist upon does not lie, not in nature, but in the will? Let us but will, and our nature is changed, "according to the power that worketh in us." Say not, in excuse for others or for yourselves, that you cannot be other than Adam made you; you have never brought yourselves to will it,— you cannot bear to will it. You cannot bear to be other than you are. Life would seem a blank to you, were you other; yet what you are from not desiring a gift, this you made an excuse for not possessing it.

(PS 5:347–50, "The Power of the Will")

52. Neglecting the One Thing Needful

Now let every one consider what his weak point is; in that is his trial. His trial is not in those things which are easy to him, but in that one thing, in those several things, whatever they are, in which to do his duty is against his nature. Never think yourself safe because you do your duty in ninety-nine points; it is the hundredth which is to be the ground of your self-denial, which must evidence, or rather instance and realize your faith. It is in reference to this you must watch and pray; pray continually for God's grace to help you, and watch with fear and trembling lest you fall. . . . Be quite sure that your judgement of persons, and of events, and of actions, and of doctrines, and your spirit towards God and man, your faith in the high truths of the Gospel, and your knowledge of your duty, all depend in a strange way on this strict endeavour to observe the whole law, on this self-denial in those little things in which obedience *is* a self-denial. Be not content with a warmth of faith carrying you over many obstacles even in your obedience, forcing you past the fear of men, and the usages of society, and the persuasions of interest; exult not in your experience of God's past mercies, and your assurance of what He has already done for your soul, if you are conscious you have neglected the one thing needful, the "one thing" which "thou lackest,"—daily self-denial.

. . . [O]ur Lord bids you take up your cross daily, and because it proves your earnestness, and because by doing so you strengthen your general power of self-mastery, and come to have such an habitual command of yourself, as will be a defense ready prepared when the season of temptation comes. Rise up then in the morning with the purpose that (please God) the day shalt not pass without its self-denial, with a self-denial in innocent plea-sures and tastes, if one occurs to mortify sin. Let your very rising from your bed be a self-denial; let your meals be self-denials. Determine to yield to others in things indifferent, to go out of your way in small matters, to inconvenience yourself (so that no direct duty suffers by it), rather than you should not meet with your daily discipline. . . . Make some sacrifice, do some distasteful thing, which you are not actually obliged to do,—so that it be lawful,—to bring home to your mind that in fact you do love your Saviour: That you do hate sin, that you do hate your sinful nature, that you have put aside the present world. Thus you will have an evidence (to a certain point) that you are not using mere words. It is easy to make professions, easy to say fine things in speech or in writing, easy to astonish men with truths which they do not know, and sentiments which rise above human nature. . . . Let not your words run on; force every one of them into action as it goes, and thus, cleansing yourself from all pollution of the flesh and spirit, perfect holiness in the fear of God. In dreams we sometimes move our arms to see if we are awake or not, and so we are awakened. This is the way to keep your heart awake also. Try yourself daily in little deeds, to prove that your faith is more than a deceit.

(PS 1:68–71, "Self-Denial the Test of Religious Earnestness")

53. Enduring the World's Ridicule

You must love the praise of God more than the praise of men. It is the very trial suited to you, appointed for you, to establish you in the faith. You are not tempted with gain or ambition, but with ridicule. And be sure, that unless you withstand it, you cannot endure hardships as good soldiers of Jesus Christ, you will not endure other temptations which are to follow. How can you advance a step in your after and more extended course till the first difficulty is overcome? You need faith, and "a double-minded man," says St. James, "is unstable in all his ways." Moreover, be not too sure that all who show an inclination to ridicule you, feel exactly as they say. They speak with the loudest speaker; speak you boldly, and they will speak with you. They have very little of definite opinion themselves, or probably they even feel with you, though they speak against you. Very likely they have uneasy, unsatisfied consciences, though they seem to sin so boldly; and are as afraid of the world as you can be, nay more so; they join in ridiculing you, lest others should ridicule them; or they do so in a sort of self-defence against the reproaches of their own consciences. Numbers in this bad world talk loudly against religion in order to encourage each other in sin, because they need encouragement. They are cowards, and rely on each other for support against their fears. They know they ought to be other than they are, but are glad to avail themselves of any thing that looks like argument, to overcome their consciences withal. . . . Those who serve God faithfully have a friend of their own, in each man's bosom, witnessing for them; even in those who treat them ill. . . .

Let us, then, rouse ourselves, and turn from man to God; what have we to do with the world, who from our infancy have been put on our journey heavenward? Take up your cross and follow Christ. He went through shame far greater than can be yours. Do you think He felt nothing when He was lifted up on the Cross to public gaze, amid the contempt and barbarous triumphings of His enemies, the Pharisees, Pilate and his Roman guard, Herod and his men of war, and the vast multitude collected from all parts of the world? . . . It is a high privilege to be allowed to be conformed to Christ; St. Paul thought it so, so have all good men. The whole church of God, from the days of Christ to the present, has been ever held in shame and contempt by men of this world. Proud men have reasoned against its Divine origin: crafty men have attempted to degrade it to political purposes: still it has lasted for many centuries; it will last still, through the promised help of God the Holy Ghost; and that same promise which is made to it first as a body, is assuredly made also to every one of us who seeks grace from God through it. The grace of our Lord and Saviour is pledged to every one of us without measure, to give us all necessary strength and holiness when we pray for it; and Almighty God tells us Himself, "Fear ye not the reproach of men, neither be ye afraid of their revilings. For the moth shall eat them up like a garment, and the worm shall eat them like wool; but My righteousness shall be for ever, and My salvation from generation to generation."

(PS 7:46–48, 56–57, "The Praise of Men")

54. Self-Deceit and Self-Knowledge

Now . . . unless we have some just idea of our hearts and of sin, we can have no right idea of a Moral Governor, a Saviour or a Sanctifier, that is, in professing to believe in Them, we shall be using words without attaching distinct meaning to them. Thus self-knowledge is at the root of all real religious knowledge; and it is in vain—worse than vain,—it is a deceit and a mischief, to think to understand the Christian doctrines as a matter of course, merely by being taught by books, or by attending sermons, or by any outward means, however excellent, taken by themselves. For it is in proportion as we search our hearts and understand our own nature, that we understand what is meant by an Infinite Governor and Judge; in proportion as we comprehend the nature of disobedience and our actual sinfulness, that we feel what is the blessing of the removal of sin, redemption, pardon, sanctification, which otherwise are mere words. God speaks to us primarily in our hearts. Self-knowledge is the key to the precepts and doctrines of Scripture. The very utmost any outward notices of religion can do, is to startle us and make us turn inward and search our hearts;

and then, when we have experienced what it is to read ourselves, we shall profit by the doctrine of the Church and the Bible.

. . . Should all the world speak well of us, and good men hail us as brothers, after all there is a Judge who trieth the hearts and the reins. He knows our real state; have we earnestly besought Him to teach us the knowledge of our own hearts? If we have not, that very omission is a presumption against us. Though our praise were throughout the Church, we may be sure He sees sins without number in us, sins deep and heinous, of which we have no idea. If man sees so much evil in human nature, what must God see? "If our heart condemn us, God is greater than our heart, and knoweth all things." Not *acts* alone of sin does He set down against us daily, of which we know nothing, but the thoughts of the heart too. The stirrings of pride, vanity, covetousness, impurity, discontent, resentment, these succeed each other through the day in momentary emotions, and are known to Him. We know them not, but how much does it concern us to know them! . . .

. . . [S]elf-knowledge does not come as a matter of course; it implies an effort and a work. As well may we suppose, that the knowledge of the languages comes by nature, as that acquaintance with our own heart is natural. Now the very effort of steadily reflecting is itself painful to many men; not to speak of the difficulty of reflecting correctly. To ask ourselves *why* we do this or that, to take account of the principles which govern us, and see whether we act for conscience' sake or from some lower inducement, is painful. We are busy in the World, and what leisure time we have we readily devote to a less severe and wearisome employment.

. . . Health of body and mind is a great blessing, if we can bear it; but unless chastened by watchings and fastings (2 Cor 11: 27), it will commonly seduce a man into the notion that he is much better than he really is. . . . When a man's spirits are high, he is pleased with every thing; and with himself especially. He can act with vigour and promptness, and he mistakes this mere constitutional energy for strength of faith. He is cheerful and contented; and he mistakes this for Christian peace. And, if happy in his family, he mistakes mere natural affection for Christian benevolence, and the confirmed temper of Christian love. In short, he is in a dream, from which nothing could have saved him except deep humility, and nothing will ordinarily rescue him except sharp affliction.

Other accidental circumstances are frequently causes of a similar self-deceit. While we remain in retirement from the world, we do not know ourselves; or after any great mercy or trial, which has affected us much, and given a temporary strong impulse to our obedience; or when we are in keen pursuit of some good object, which excites the mind, and for a time deadens it to temptation. Under such circumstances we are ready to think far too well of ourselves. The world is away; or, at least, we are insensible to its seductions; and we mistake our merely temporary tranquillity, or our overwrought fervour of mind, on the one hand for Christian peace, on the other for Christian zeal. . . .

. . . Can we content ourselves with such an unreal faith in Christ, as in no sufficient measure includes self-abasement, or thankfulness, or the desire or effort to be holy? for how can we feel our need of His help, or our dependence on Him, or our debt to Him, or the nature of His gift to us, unless we know ourselves? How can we in any sense be said to have that "mind of Christ," to which the Apostle exhorts us, if we cannot follow Him to the height above, or the depth beneath; if we do not in some measure discern the cause and meaning of His sorrows, but regard the world, and man, and the system of Providence, in a light different from that which His words and acts supply? If you receive revealed truth merely through the eyes and ears, you believe words, not things; you deceive yourselves. You may conceive yourselves sound in faith, but you know nothing in any true way. Obedience to God's commandments, which implies knowledge of sin and of holiness, and the desire and endeavour to please Him, this is the only practical interpreter of Scripture doctrine. Without self-knowledge you have no root in yourselves personally; you may endure for a time, but under affliction or persecution your faith will not last. This is why many in this age (and in every age) become infidels, heretics, schismatics, disloyal despisers of the Church. They cast off the form of truth, because it never has been to them more than a form. They endure not, because they never have tasted that the Lord is gracious; and they never have had experience of His power and love, because they have never known their own weakness and need.

(PS 1:42–45, 49–51, 54, "Secret Faults")

55. Individual Professions of Faith

If indeed a man stands forth *on his own ground*, declaring himself as an individual a witness for Christ, then indeed he *is* grieving and disturbing the calm spirit given us by God. But God's merciful providence has saved us this temptation, and forbidden us to admit it. He bids us unite together in one, and to shelter our personal profession under the authority of the general body. Thus, while we show ourselves as lights to the world far more effectively than if we glimmered separately in the lone wilderness without communication with others, at the same time we do so with far greater secrecy and humility. Therefore it is, that the Church does so many things for us, appoints fasts and feasts, times of public prayer, the order of the sacraments, the services of devotion at marriages and deaths, and all accompanied by a fixed form of sound words; in order (I say) to remove from us individually the burden of a high profession, of implying great things of ourselves by inventing for ourselves solemn prayers and praises, a task far above the generality of Christians, to say the least, a task which humble men will shrink from, lest they prove hypocrites, and which will hurt those who *do* undertake it, by making them rude-spirited and profane. I am desirous of speaking on this subject as a matter of *practice*; for I am sure, that if we wish really and in fact to spread the knowledge of the Truth, we shall do so far more powerfully as *well* as purely, by keeping together, than by witnessing one by one. Men are to be seen adopting all kinds of strange ways of giving glory (as they think) to God. If they would but follow the church; come together in prayer on Sundays and Saints' days, nay, every day; honour the rubric by keeping to it obediently, . . . I say that on the whole they would practically do vastly more good than by trying new religious plans, founding new religious societies, or striking out new religious views. . . .

. . . Now in the next place, consider how great a profession, and yet a profession how unconscious and modest, arises from the mere ordinary manner in which any strict Christian lives. Let this thought be a satisfaction to uneasy minds which fear lest they are not confessing Christ, yet dread to display. Your *life* displays Christ without your intending it. You cannot help it. Your *words and deeds* will show on the long run (as it is said), where your treasure is, and your heart. . . . We sometimes find men who aim at doing their duty in the common course of life, *surprised* to hear that they are ridiculed, and called hard names by careless or worldly persons. This is as it should be; it is as it should, that they are *surprised* at it. If a private Christian sets out with *expecting* to make a disturbance in the world, the fear is, lest he be not so humble-minded as he should be. But those who go on quietly in the way of obedience, and yet are detected by the keen eye of the jealous, self-condemning, yet proud world, and who on discovering their situation, first shrink from it and are distressed, then look to see if they have done aught wrongly, and after all are sorry for it, and but slowly and very timidly (if at all) learn to rejoice in it, these are Christ's flock. These are they who follow Him who was meek and lowly of heart. . . .

. . . The question is often raised, whether a man can do his duty simply and quietly, without being thought ostentatious by the world. It is no great matter to himself whether he is thought so or not, if he has not provoked the opinion. As a general rule, I would say the Church itself is always hated and calumniated by the world, as being in duty bound to make a bold profession. But whether individual members of the Church are so treated, depends on various circumstances in the case of each. There *are* persons, who, though very strict and conscientious Christians, are yet praised by the world. These are such, as having great meekness and humility, are not so prominent in station or so practically connected with the world as to offend it. Men admire religion, while they can gaze on it as a picture. They think it lovely in books: and as long as they can look upon Christians at a distance, they speak well of them. . . . Christians in active life thwarting (as they do) the pride and selfishness of the world, are disliked by the world, and have "all manner of evil said against them falsely for Christ's sake." (Mt 5: 11) Still, even under these circumstances, though they must not shrink from the attack on a personal account, it is still their duty to shelter themselves, as far as they can, under the name and authority of the Holy Church; to keep to its ordinances and rules; and, if they are called to suffer for the Church, rather to be drawn forward to the suffering in the common course of duty, than boldly to take upon them the task of defending it. There is no cowardice in this. Some men are placed in posts of danger, and to these danger comes in the way of duty; but others must not intrude into their honourable office. Thus in the first age of the Gospel, our Lord told His followers to flee from city to city, when persecuted; and even the heads of the Church, in the early persecutions, instead of exposing themselves to the fury of the heathen, did their utmost to avoid it. We are a suffering people from the first; but while, on the one hand, we do not defend ourselves illegally, we do not court suffering on the other. We must witness and glorify God, as lights on a hill, through evil report and good report; but the evil and the good report is not so much of our own making as the natural consequence of our Christian profession.

(PS 1:153–55, 162–63, "Profession without Ostentation")

56. The Paradox of Christian Knowledge

Do we think to become better men by knowing more? Little knowledge is required for religious obedience. The poor and rich, the learned and unlearned, are here on a level. We have all of us the means of doing our duty; we have not the *will*, and this no knowledge can give. We have need to subdue our own minds, and this no other person *can* do for us. The case is different in matters of learning and science. The others can and do labour for us; *we* can make use of *their* labours; we begin where they ended; these things progress, and each successive age knows more than the preceding. But in religion each must begin, go on, and end, for himself. The religious history of each individual is as solitary and complete as the history of the world. Each man will, of course, gain more knowledge as he studies Scripture more, and prays and meditates more; but he cannot make another man wise or holy by his own advance in wisdom or holiness. . . . The character will always require forming, evil will ever need rooting out of each heart; the grace to go before and to aid us in our moral discipline must ever come fresh and immediate from the Holy Spirit. So the world ever remains in its infancy, as regards the cultivation of moral truth. . . .

Practical religious knowledge, then, is a personal gift, and, further, a gift from God; and, therefore, as experience has hitherto shown, more likely to be obscured than advanced by the lapse of time. But further, we know of the existence of an evil principle in the world, corrupting and resisting the truth in its measure, according to the truth's clearness and purity. Whether it be from the sinfulness of our nature, or from the malignity of Satan, striving with peculiar enmity against Divine truth, certain it is that the best gifts of God have been the most woefully corrupted. It was prophesied from the beginning, that the serpent should bruise the heel of Him who was ultimately to triumph over him; and so it has ever been. Our Saviour, who was the Truth itself, was the most spitefully treated of all by the world. It has been the case with His followers too. . . .

. . . While we think it possible to make some great and important improvements in the subject of religion, we shall be unsettled, restless, impatient; we shall be drawn from the consideration of improving ourselves, and from using the day while it is given us, by the visions of a deceitful hope, which promises to make rich but tendeth to penury. On the other hand, if we feel that the way is altogether closed against discoveries in religion, as being neither practicable nor desirable, it is likely we shall be drawn more entirely and seriously to our own personal advancement in holiness; our eyes, being withdrawn from external prospects, will look more at home. We shall think less of circumstances, and more of our duties under them, whatever they are. In proportion as we cease to be theorists we shall become practical men; we shall have less of self-confidence and arrogance, more of inward humility and diffidence; we shall be less likely to despise others, and think of our own intellectual powers with less complacency.

It is one great peculiarity of the Christian character to be dependent. Men of the world, indeed, in proportion as they are active and enterprising, boast of their independence, and are proud of having obligations to no one. But it is the Christian's excellence to be diligent and watchful, to work and persevere, and yet to be in spirit *dependent*; to be willing to serve, and to rejoice in the permission to do so; to be content to view himself in a subordinate place; to love to sit in the dust. Though in the Church a son of God, he takes pleasure in considering himself Christ's "servant" and "slave," he feels glad whenever he can put himself to shame. So it is the natural bent of his mind freely and affectionately to visit and trace the footsteps of the saints, to sound the praises of the great men of old who have wrought wonders in the Church and whose words still live. . . .

. . . We have been granted Apostles, Prophets, Evangelists, pastors, and teachers. . . . For us Christ has died; on us the Spirit has descended. In these respects we are honoured and privileged, oh how far above all ages before He came! Yet our honours are our shame, when we contrast the glory given us with our love of the world, our fear of men, our lightness of mind, our sensuality, our gloomy tempers. What need have we to look with wonder and reverence at those saints of the Old Covenant, who with less advantages yet so far surpassed us; and still more at those of the Christian Church, who both had higher gifts of grace and profited by them! What need have we to humble ourselves; to pray God not to leave us, though we have left Him; to pray Him to give us back what we have lost, to receive a repentant people, to renew in us a right heart and give us a religious will, and to enable us to follow Him perseveringly in His narrow and humbling way.

(PS 7:247–49, 251–52, 256, "Stedfastness in the Old Paths")

57. A Smooth and Easy Life

I suppose most men, or at least a great number of men, have to lament over their hardness of heart, which, when analysed, will be found to be nothing else but the absence of love. I mean that hardness which, for instance, makes us unable to repent as we wish. No repentance is truly such without love; it is love which gives it its efficacy in God's sight. Without love there may be remorse, regret, self-reproach, self-condemnation, but there is not saving penitence. There may be conviction of the reason, but not conversion of the heart. Now, I say a great many men lament in themselves this want of love in repenting; they are hard-hearted; they are deeply conscious of their sins; they abhor them; and yet they can take a lively interest in what goes on around them. . . . [T]hey cannot abstain from any indulgence ever so trivial, which would be (as their reason tells them) a natural way of showing sorrow. They eat and drink with as good a heart, as if they had no distress upon their minds; they find no difficulty in entering into any of the recreations or secular employments which come in their way. They sleep as soundly; and, in spite of their grief, perhaps find it most difficult to persuade themselves to rise early to pray for pardon. These are signs of want of love.

Or, again, without reference to the case of penitence, they have a general indisposition towards prayer and other exercises of devotion. They find it most difficult to get themselves to pray; most difficult, too, to rouse their minds to attend to their prayers. At very best they do but feel satisfaction in devotion *while* they are engaged in it. Then perhaps they find a real pleasure in it, and wonder they can ever find it irksome; yet if any chance throws them out of their habitual exercises, they find it most difficult to return to them. They do not like them well enough to seek them *from* liking them. They are kept in them by habit, by regularity in observing them; not by love. When the regular course is broken, there is no inward principle to act at once in repairing the mischief. In wounds of the body, nature works towards a recovery, and, left to itself, would recover; but we have no spiritual principle strong and healthy enough to set religious matters right in us when they have got disordered, and to supply for us the absence of rule and custom. Here, again, is obedience, more or less mechanical, or without love.

Again—a like absence of love is shown in our proneness to be taken up and engrossed with trifles. Why is it that we are so open to the power of excitement? Why is it that we are looking out for novelties? Why is it that we complain of want of variety in a religious life? Why that we cannot bear to go on in an ordinary round of duties year after year? Why is it that lowly duties, such as condescending to men of low estate, are distasteful and irksome? Why is it that we need powerful preaching, or interesting and touching books, in order to keep our thoughts and feelings on God? Why is it that our faith is so dispirited and weakened by hearing casual objections urged against the doctrine of Christ? Why is it that we are so impatient that objections should be answered? Why are we so afraid of worldly events, or the opinion of men? Why do we so dread their censure or ridicule? Clearly because we are deficient in love. He who loves, cares little for any thing else. The world may go as it will; he sees and hears it not, for his thoughts are drawn another way; he is solicitous mainly to walk with God, and to be found with God; and is in perfect peace because he is stayed in Him.

. . . I must say plainly this, that, fanciful though it may appear at first sight to say so, the comforts of life are the main cause of [our want of love to God]; and, much as we may lament and struggle against it, till we learn to dispense with them in good measure, we shall not overcome it. Till we, in a certain sense, detach ourselves from our bodies, our minds will not be in a state to receive divine impressions, and to exert heavenly aspirations. A smooth and easy life, and uninterrupted enjoyment of the goods of Providence, full meals, soft raiment, well-furnished homes, the pleasures of sense, the feeling of security, the consciousness of wealth—these, and the like, if we are not careful, choke up all the avenues of the soul, through which the light and breath of heaven might come to us. A hard life is, alas! No certain method of becoming spiritually minded, but it is one out of the means by which almighty God makes us so. We must, at least at seasons, defraud ourselves of nature, if we would not be defrauded of grace. If we attempt to force our minds into a loving and devotional temper, without this preparation, it is too plain what will follow—the grossness and coarseness, the affectation, the effeminacy, the unreality, the presumption, the hollowness, in a word, what Scripture calls the Hypocrisy, which we see around us; that state of mind in which the reason, seeing what we should be, and the conscience enjoining it, and the heart being unequal to it, some or other pretence is set up, by way of compromise. . . .

. . . [L]et me bid you cherish . . . a constant sense of the love of your Lord and Saviour in dying on the cross for you. . . . Think of the Cross when you rise and when you lie down, when you go out and when you come in, when you eat and when you walk and when you converse, when you buy and when you sell, when you labour and when you rest, consecrating and sealing all your doings with this one mental action, the thought of the Crucified. Do not talk of it to others; be silent, like the penitent woman, who showed her love in deep subdued acts. She "stood at His feet behind Him weeping, and began to wash His feet with tears, and did wipe them with the hairs of her head, and kissed His feet, and anointed them with the Ointment." And Christ said of her, "Her sins, which are many, are forgiven her, for she loved much; but to whom little is forgiven, the same loveth little." (Lk 7: 38, 47)

(PS 5:334–39, "Love, the One Thing Needful")

58. Self-Satisfaction

Satisfaction with our own doings, as I have said, arises from fixing the mind on some *one part* of our duty, instead of attempting the whole of it. In proportion as we narrow the field of our duties, we become able to compass them. Men who pursue only this duty or only that duty, are in danger of self-righteousness. Zealots, bigots, devotees, men of the world, sectarians, are for this reason self-righteous. For the same reason, persons beginning a religious course are self-righteous, though they often think themselves just the reverse. They consider, perhaps, all religion to be in confessing themselves sinners, and having warm feelings concerning their redemption and justification—in having what they consider faith; and, as all this is fulfilled in them, they come to think they have attained and are sure of heaven; and all because they have so very contracted a notion of the range of God's commandments, of the rounds of that ladder which reaches from earth to heaven. And in the same way, I admit that religious persons who for one reason or another are led to begin a greater strictness than hitherto in their devotional observances, in attending prayers or the Lord's Supper, or in fasting, or in almsgiving, are, on beginning, in some danger of becoming self-satisfied for the same reason; that is, by fixing their minds on one certain portion of their duty and becoming excited about *it*; and this the more, inasmuch as the observances in question are something definite and precise, and on the other hand are evidently neglected by others.

But the remedy of the evil is obvious, and one which, since it will surely be applied by every religious person because he *is* religious, will, under God's grace, effect in no long time a cure. Try to do your *whole* duty, and you will soon cease to be well-pleased with your religious state. If you are in earnest, you will try to add to your faith virtue; and the more you effect, the less will you seem to yourself to do. On the other hand, attend prayer and the Holy Eucharist without corresponding strictness in other matters; and it is plain what will follow, from the nature of the human mind, without going to more solemn considerations. The more you neglect your daily, domestic, relative, temporal, duties, the more you will prize yourself on your (I cannot call them religious, your) formal, ceremonial observances. Thus it is plain that self-satisfaction is the feeling either of a beginner, or of a very defective and negligent Christian.

(PS 4:73–74, "Reliance on Religious Observances")

59. Unmeaning Benevolence

I ask . . . does not our kindness too often degenerate into weakness, and thus become not Christian Charity, but lack of Charity, as regards the objects of it? Are we sufficiently careful to do what is right and just, rather than what is pleasant? Do we clearly understand our professed principles, and do we keep to them under temptation? . . .

. . . [T]he very problem which Christian duty requires us to accomplish, is the reconciling in our conduct opposite virtues. It is not difficult (comparatively speaking) to cultivate single virtues. A man takes some one partial view of his duty whether severe or kindly, whether of action or of meditation: he enters into it with all his might, he opens his heart to its influence, and allows himself to be sent forward on its current. This is not difficult: there is no anxious vigilance or self-denial in it. On the contrary, there is a pleasure often in thus sweeping along in one way; and especially in matters of giving and conceding. Liberality is always popular, whatever be the subject of it, and excites a glow of pleasure and self-approbation in the giver, even though it involves no sacrifice, nay, is exercised upon the property of others. Thus in the sacred province of religion, men are led on,—without any bad principle, without that utter dislike or ignorance of the Truth, or that self-conceit, which are chief instruments of Satan at this day, nor again from mere cowardice or worldliness, but from thoughtlessness, a sanguine temper, the excitement of the moment, the love of making others happy, susceptibility of flattery, and the habit of looking only one way,—led on to give up Gospel Truths, to consent to open the Church to the various denominations of error which abound among us, or to alter our Services so as to please the scoffer, the lukewarm, or the vicious. To be kind is their one principle of action; and, when they find offence taken at the Church's creed, they begin to think how they may modify or curtail it, under the same sort of feeling as would lead them to be generous in a money transaction, or to accommodate another at the price of personal inconvenience. Not understanding that their religious privileges are a trust to be handed on to posterity, a sacred property entailed upon the Christian family, and their own in enjoyment rather than in possession, they act the spendthrift, and are lavish of the goods of others. . . .

. . . Who can deny that the apocalypse from beginning to end is a very fearful book; I may say, the most fearful book in Scripture, full of accounts of the wrath of God? Yet, it is written by the apostle of love. It is possible, then, for a man to be at once kind as Barnabas, yet zealous as Paul. Strictness and tenderness had no "sharp contention" in the breast of the Beloved Disciple; they found their perfect union, yet distinct exercise, in the grace of Charity, which is the fulfilling of the whole Law.

I wish I saw any prospect of this element of zeal and holy sternness springing up among us, to temper and give character to the languid, unmeaning benevolence which we misname Christian love. I have no hope of my country till I see it. Many schools of religion and Ethics are to be found among us, and they all profess to magnify, in one shape or other, what they consider the principle of love; but what they lack is a firm maintenance of that characteristic of the divine Nature which, in accommodation to our infirmity, is named by St. John and his brethren the wrath of God. . . .

(PS 2:280, 282–83, 286–87, "Tolerance of Religious Error")

60. Unreal Words

Persons are aware from the mere force of the doctrines of which the Gospel consists, that they ought to be variously affected, and deeply and intensely too, in consequence of them. The doctrines of original and actual sin, of Christ's Divinity and atonement, and of Holy Baptism, are so vast, that no one can realize them without very complicated and profound feelings. Natural reason tells a man this, and that if he simply and genuinely believes the doctrines, he must have these feelings; and he professes to believe the doctrines absolutely, and therefore he professes the correspondent feelings. But in truth he perhaps does *not* really believe them absolutely, because such absolute belief is the work of long time, and therefore his profession of feeling outruns the real inward existence of feeling, or he becomes unreal. Let us never lose sight of two truths,—that we ought to have our hearts penetrated with the love of Christ and full of self-renunciation; but that if they be not, professing that they are does not make them so. . . .

. . . It takes a long time really to feel and understand things as they are; we learn to do so only gradually. Profession beyond our feelings is only a fault when we might help it;—when either we speak when we need not speak, or do not feel when we might have felt. Hard insensible hearts, ready and thoughtless talkers, these are they whose unreality, as I have termed it, is a sin; it is the sin of every one of us, in proportion as our hearts are cold, or our tongues excessive. . . .

It is not an easy thing to learn that new language which Christ has brought us. He has interpreted all things for us in a new way; He has brought us a religion which sheds a new light on all that happens. Try to learn this language. Do not get it by rote, or speak it as a thing of course. Try to understand what you say. Time is short, eternity is long; God is great, man is weak; he stands between heaven and hell; Christ is his Saviour; Christ has suffered for him. The Holy Ghost sanctifies him; repentance purifies him, faith justifies, works save. These are solemn truths, which need not be actually spoken, except in the way of creed or of teaching; but which must be laid up in the heart. That a thing is true, is no reason that it should be said, but that it should be done;

that it should be acted upon; that it should be made our own inwardly.

Let us avoid talking, of whatever kind; whether mere empty talking, or censorious talking, or idle profession, or descanting upon Gospel doctrines, or the affectation of philosophy, or the pretence of eloquence. Let us guard against frivolity, love of display, love of being talked about, love of singularity, love of seeming original. Let us aim at meaning what we say, and saying what we mean; let us aim at knowing when we understand a truth, and when we do not. When we do not, let us take it on faith, and let us profess to do so. Let us receive the truth in reverence, and pray God to give us a good will, and divine light, and spiritual strength, that it may bear fruit within us.

(PS 5:38–39, 43–45, "Unreal Words")

61. Looking at Sin as He Would Look at It

[N]o one among us, but, if he shut his eyes to the external world, and opened them to the world within him, contemplated his real state and prospects, and called to mind his past life, would be brought to repentance and amendment. Endeavour then, my brethren, to realize that you have souls, and pray God to enable you to do so. Endeavour to disengage your thoughts and opinions from the things that are seen; look at things as God looks at them, and judge of them as He Judges. Pass a very few years and you will actually experience what as yet you are called on to believe. There will be no need of the effort of mind to which I invite you, when you have passed into the unseen state. There will be no need of shutting your eyes to this world, when this world has vanished from you, and you have nothing before you but the throne of God, and the slow but continual movements about it in preparation of the judgement. In that interval, when you are in that vast receptacle of disembodied souls, what will be your thoughts about the world which you have left! How poor will then seem to you its highest aims, how faint its keenest pleasures, compared with the eternal aims, the infinite pleasures, of which you will at length feel your souls to be capable! O, my brethren, let this thought be upon you day by day, especially when you are tempted to sin. Avoid sin as a serpent; it looks and promises well; it bites afterwards. It is dreadful in memory, dreadful even on earth; but in that awful period, when the fever of life is over, and you are waiting in silence for the judgement, with nothing to distract your thoughts, who can say how dreadful may be the memory of sins done in the body? Then the very apprehension of their punishment, when Christ shall suddenly visit, will doubtless outweigh a thousand-fold the gratification, such as it was, which you felt in committing them. . . .

(PS 4:91–92, "The Individuality of the Soul")

THE WORLD

62. Worldly Unbelief

May we not be sure that men nowadays, had they been alive when He came, would have disbelieved and derided the holy and mysterious doctrines which He brought? Alas! is there any doubt at all, that they would have fulfilled St. John's words,—"the darkness comprehended it not?" Their hearts are set on schemes of this world: there would have been no *sympathy* between them and the calm and heavenly mind of the Lord Jesus Christ. They would have said that His Gospel was strange, extravagant, incredible. The only reason they do not say so now is, that they are used to it, and do not really dwell on what they profess to believe. What! (it would have been said,) the Son of God taking human flesh, impossible! The Son of God, separate from God yet one with Him! "How can these things be?" God Himself suffering on the Cross, the Almighty Everlasting God in the form of a servant, with human flesh and blood, wounded, insulted, dying? And all this as an Expiation for human sin? Why (they would ask) was an Expiation necessary? Why could not the All-merciful Father pardon without one? Why is human sin to be accounted so great an evil? We see no necessity for so marvelous a remedy; we refuse to admit a course of doctrine so utterly unlike any thing which the face of this world tells us of. These are events without parallels; they belong to a new and distinct order of things; and, while our heart has no sympathy with them, our reason utterly rejects them. And as for Christ's miracles, if they had not seen them, they would not have believed the report; if they had, they would have been ready enough to refer them to juggling craft—if not, as the Jews did, to Beelzebub.

Such will the holy truths of the Gospel ever appear to those who live to this world, whether they love its pleasures, its comforts, its prizes, or its struggles; their eyes are waxen gross, they cannot see Christ spiritually. When they see Him, there is no beauty in Him that they should desire Him. Thus they become unbelieving. In our Lord's words, "No servant can serve two masters: for either he will hate the one and love the other, or else he will hold to the one and despise the other. *Ye cannot serve God and mammon.*" (Lk 16: 13–15) . . . God grant that we may not attempt to deceive our consciences, and to reconcile together, by some artifice or other, the service of this world and of God! God grant that we may not pervert and dilute His holy Word, put upon it the false interpretations of men, reason ourselves out of its strictness, and reduce religion to an ordinary commonplace matter—instead of thinking it what it *is*, a mysterious and supernatural subject, as distinct from any thing that lies on the surface of this world, as day is from night and heaven from earth!

(PS 6:80–82, "The Incarnate Son, a Sufferer and Sacrifice")

63. Consolation in the Midst of the World

What is man, what are we, what am I, that the Son of God should be so mindful of me? What am I, that He should have raised me from almost a devil's nature to that of an Angel's? That He should have changed my soul's original constitution, new-made me, who from my youth up have been a transgressor, and should Himself dwell personally in this very heart of mine, making me His temple? What am I, that God the Holy Ghost should enter into me, and draw up my thoughts heavenward "with plaints unutterable?"

These are the meditations which come upon the Christian to console him, while he is with Christ upon the holy mount. And, when he descends to his daily duties, they are still his inward strength, though he is not allowed to tell the vision to those around him. They make his countenance to shine, make him cheerful, collected, serene, and firm in the midst of all temptation, persecution, or bereavement. And with such thoughts before us, how base and miserable does the world appear in all its pursuits and doctrines! How truly miserable does it seem to seek good from the creature; to covet station, wealth, or credit; to choose for ourselves, in fancy, this or that mode of life; to affect the manners and fashions of the great; to spend our time in follies; to be discontented, quarrelsome, jealous or envious, censorious or resentful; fond of unprofitable talk, and eager for the news of the day; busy about public matters which concern us not; hot in the cause of this or that interest or party; or set upon gain; or devoted to the increase of barren knowledge! And at the end of our days, when flesh and heart fail, what will be our consolation, though we have made ourselves rich, or have served an office, or been the first man among our equals, or have depressed a rival, or managed things our own way, or have settled splendidly, or have been intimate with the great, or have fared sumptuously, or have gained a name! Say, even if we obtain that which lasts longest, a place in history, yet, after all, what ashes shall we have eaten for bread! And, in that awful hour, when death is in sight, will He, whose eye is now so loving towards us, and whose hand falls on us so gently, will He acknowledge us any more? Or, if He still speaks, will His voice have any power to stir us? Rather will it not repel us, as it did Judas, by the very tenderness with which it would invite us to Him?

Let us then endeavour, by His grace, rightly to understand where we stand, and what He is towards us; most tender and pitiful, yet, for all His pity, not passing by the breadth of a single hair the eternal lines of truth, holiness, and justice. . . .

(PS 3:126–27, "A Particular Providence as Revealed in the Gospel")

64. The Dangers of Worldly Advantages

Much intercourse with the world, which eminence and station render a duty, has a tendency to draw off the mind from God, and deaden it to the force of religious motives and considerations. There is a want of sympathy between much business and calm devotion, great splendour and a simple faith, which will be to no one more painful than to the Christian, to whom God has assigned some post of especial responsibility or distinction. To maintain a religious spirit in the midst of engagements and excitements of this world is possible only to a saint. . . .

Again, these worldly advantages, as they are called, will seduce us into an excessive love of them. We are too well inclined by nature to live by sight, rather than by faith; and besides the immediate enjoyment, there is something so agreeable to our natural tastes in the honours and emoluments of the world, that it requires an especially strong mind, and a large measure of grace, not to be gradually corrupted by them. We are led to set our hearts upon them, and in the same degree to withdraw them from God. We become unwilling to leave this visible state of things, and to be reduced to a level with those multitudes who are at present inferior to ourselves. Prosperity is sufficient to seduce, although not to satisfy. Hence death and judgement are unwelcome subjects of reflection to the rich and powerful; for death takes from them those comforts which habit has made necessary to them, and throws them adrift on a new order of things, of which they know nothing, save that in it there is no respect of persons. . . .

And moreover, these temporal advantages, as they are considered, have a strong tendency to render us self-confident. When a man has been advanced in the world by means of his own industry and skill, when he began poor and ends rich, how apt will he be to pride himself, and confide, in his own contrivances and his own resources! Or when a man feels himself possessed of good abilities; of quickness in entering into a subject, or of powers of argument to discourse readily upon it, or of acuteness to detect fallacies in dispute with little effort, or of a delicate and cultivated taste, so as to separate with precisions the correct and beautiful in thought and feeling from the faulty and irregular, how will such an one be tempted to self-complacency and self-approbation! How apt will he be to rely upon himself, to rest contented with himself; to be harsh and impetuous; or supercilious; or to be fastidious, indolent, unpractical; and to despise the pure, self-denying, humble temper of religion, as something irrational, dull, enthusiastic, or needlessly rigorous! . . .

From what I have said concerning the danger of possessing the things which the world admires, we may draw the following rule: use them, as far as given, with gratitude for what is really good in them, and with a desire to promote God's glory by means of them; but do not go out of the way to seek them. They will not on the whole make you happier, and they may make you less religious.

. . . The time is short; year follows year, and the world is passing away. It is of small consequence to those who are beloved of God, and walk in the Spirit of truth, whether they pay or receive honour, which is but transitory and profitless. To the true Christian the world assumes another and more interesting appearance; it is no longer a stage for the great and noble, for the ambitious to fret in, and the wealthy to revel in; but it is a scene of probation. Every soul is a candidate for immortality. And the more we realize this view of things, the more will the accidental distinctions of nature or fortune die away from our view, and we shall be led habitually to pray, that upon every Christian may descend, in rich abundance, not merely worldly goods, but that heavenly grace which alone can turn this world to good account for us, and make it the path of peace and of life everlasting.

(PS 7:62–65, 72–73, "Temporal Advantages")

65. The Religion of the Natural Man

The natural conscience of man, if cultivated from within, if enlightened by those external aids which in varying degrees are given him in every place and time, would teach him much of his duty to God and man, and would lead him on, by the guidance both of Providence and grace, into the fulness of religious knowledge; but, generally speaking, he is contented that it should tell him very little, and he makes no efforts to gain any juster views than he has at first, of his relations to the world around him and to his Creator. . . .

So it was with the Pharisee. . . . He looked upon himself with great complacency, for the very reason that the standard was so low, and the range so narrow, which he assigned to his duties towards God and man. He used, or misused, the traditions in which he had been brought up, to the purpose of persuading himself that perfection lay in merely answering the demands of society. He professed, indeed, to pay thanks to God, but he hardly apprehended the existence of any direct duties on his part towards his Maker. He thought he did all that God required, if he satisfied public opinion. To be religious, in the Pharisee's sense, was to keep the peace towards others, to take his share in the burdens of the poor, to abstain from gross vice, and to set a good example. His alms and fastings were not done in penance, but because the world asked for them; penance would have implied the consciousness of sin; whereas it was only Publicans, and such as they, who had anything to be forgiven. And these indeed were the outcasts of society, and despicable; but no account lay against men of well-regulated minds such as his: men who were well-behaved, decorous, consistent, and respectable. He thanked God he was a Pharisee, and not a penitent. . . .

And such, I say, is the religion of the natural man in every age and place; often very beautiful on the surface, but worthless in God's sight; good, as far as it goes, but worthless and hopeless, because it does not go further, because it is based on self-sufficiency, and results in self-satisfaction. I grant, it may be beautiful to look at, as in the instance of the young ruler whom our Lord looked at and loved, yet sent away sad; it may have all the delicacy, the amiableness, the tenderness, the religious sentiment, the kindness, which is actually seen in many a father of a family, many a mother, many a daughter, in the length and breadth of these kingdoms, in a refined and polished age like this; but still it is rejected by the heart-searching God, because all such persons walk by their own light, not by the True Light of men, because self is their supreme teacher, and because they pace round and round in the small circle of their own thoughts and of their own judgements, careless to know what God says to them, and fearless of being condemned by Him, if only they stand approved in their own sight. . . .

(OS 20–22, 25–26, "The Religion of the Pharisee, the Religion of Mankind")

66. Putting Away Childish Things

When our Lord was going to leave the world and return to His Father, He called His disciples *orphans*; children, as it were, whom He had been rearing, who were still unable to direct themselves, and who were soon to lose their Protector; but He said, "I will not leave you comfortless orphans, I will come to you;" (Jn 14: 18) meaning to say, He would come again to them in the power of His Holy Spirit, who should be their present all-sufficient Guide, though He Himself was away. And we know, from the sacred history, that when the Holy Spirit came, they ceased to be the defenseless children they had been before. He breathed into them a divine life, and gifted them with spiritual manhood, or *perfection*, as it is called in Scripture. From that time forth, they put away childish things; they spake, they understood, they thought, as those who had been taught to govern themselves; and who, having "an unction from the Holy One, knew all things."

That such a change was wrought in the Apostles, according to Christ's promise, is evident from comparing their conduct *before* the day of Pentecost, when the Holy Spirit descended on them, and *after*. I need not enlarge on their wonderful firmness and zeal in their Master's cause afterwards. On the other hand, it is plain from the Gospels, that before the Holy Ghost came down, that is, while Christ was still with them, they were as helpless and ignorant as children; had no clear notion what they ought to seek after, and how; and were carried astray by their accidental feelings and their long-cherished prejudices. . . .

Children have evil tempers and idle ways which we do not deign to speak seriously of. Not that we, in any degree, approve them or endure them on their own account; nay, we punish some of them; but we bear them *in* children, and look for their disappearing as the mind becomes more mature. And so in religious matters there are many habits and views, which we bear with in the unformed Christian, but which we account disgraceful and contemptible should they survive that time when a man's character may be supposed to be settled. Love of display is one of these; whether we are vain of our abilities, or our acquirements, or our wealth, or our personal appearance; whether we discover our weakness in talking much, or in love of managing, or again in love of dress. Vanity, indeed, and conceit are always disagreeable, for the reason that they interfere with the comfort of other persons, and vex them; but I am here observing, that they are *in themselves* odious, when discerned in those who enjoy the full privileges of the Church, and are by profession men in Christ Jesus, odious from their inconsistency with Christian faith and earnestness.

And so with respect to the love of worldly comforts and luxuries (which, unhappily, often grows upon us rather than disappears, as we get old), whether or not it be natural in youth, at least, it is (if I may so say) *shocking* in those who profess to be "perfect," if we would estimate things aright; and this from its great incongruity with the spirit of the Gospel. Is it not something beyond measure strange and monstrous (if we could train our hearts to possess a right judgement in all things), to profess that our treasure is not here, but in heaven with Him who is ascended thither, and to own that we have a cross to bear after Him, who first suffered before He triumphed; and yet to set ourselves *deliberately* to study our own comfort as some great and sufficient end, to go much out of our way to promote it, to sacrifice any thing considerable to guard it, and to be downcast at the prospect of the loss of it? . . .

. . . [T]ime goes slowly, yet surely, from birth to the age of manhood, and in like manner, our minds, though slowly formed to love Christ, must still be forming. It is when men are mature in years, and yet are "children in understanding," then they are intolerable, because they have exceeded their season, and are out of place. Then it is that ambitious thoughts, trifling pursuits and amusements, passionate wishes and keen hopes, and the love of display, are directly sinful, because they are by that time deliberate sins. While they were children, "they spake as children, understood, thought as children," but when they became men, "it was high time to awake out of sleep;" and "put away childish things." And if they have continued children instead of "having their senses exercised to discriminate between the excellent and the base," alas! what deep repentance must be theirs, before they can know what true peace is!—what self-reproach and sharp self-discipline, before their eyes can be opened to see effectually those truths which are "spiritually discerned!" . . .

What is it your Saviour requires of you, more than will also be exacted from you by that hard and evil master, who desires your ruin? Christ bids you give up the world; but will not, at any rate, the world soon give up you? Can you keep it, by being its slave? Will not he, whose creature of temptation it is, the prince of the world, take it from you, whatever he at present promises? What does your Lord require of you, but to look at all things as they really are, to account them merely as His instruments, and to believe that good is good because He wills it, that He can bless as easily by hard stone as by bread, in the desert as in the fruitful field, if we have faith in Him who gives us the true bread from heaven? . . . Be not afraid,—it is but a pang now and then, and a struggle; a covenant with your eyes, and a fasting in the wilderness, some calm habitual watchfulness, and the hearty effort to obey, and all will be well. Be not afraid. He is most gracious, and will bring you on by little and little. He does not show you whither He is leading you; you might be frightened did you see the whole prospect at once. Sufficient for the day is its own evil. Follow His plan; look not on anxiously; look down at your present footing "lest it be turned out of the way," but speculate not about the future. I can well believe that you have hopes now, which you cannot give up, and even which support you in your present course. Be it so; whether they will be fulfilled, or not, is in His hand. He may be pleased to grant the desires of your heart; if so, thank Him for His mercy; only be sure, that all will be for your highest good. . . .

(PS 1:336–37, 340–42, 346–49, "Christian Manhood")

67. The Pursuit of Gain

The danger of *possessing* riches is the carnal security to which they lead; that of "*desiring*" and *pursuing* them, is, that an object of this world is thus set before us as the aim and end of life. It seems to be the will of Christ that His followers should have no aim or end, pursuit or business, merely of this world. . . . It is His will that all we do should be done, not unto men, or to the world, or to self, but to His glory; and the more we are enabled to do this simply, the more favoured we are. Whenever we act with reference to an object of this world even though it be ever so pure, we are exposed to the temptation—not irresistible, God forbid!—still to the temptation of setting our hearts upon obtaining it. And therefore, we call all such objects *excitements*, as stimulating us incongruously, casting us out of the serenity and stability of heavenly faith, attracting us aside by their proximity from our harmonious round of duties, and making our thoughts converge to something short of that which is infinitely high and eternal. Such excitements are of perpetual occurrence, and the mere undergoing them, so far from involving guilt in the act itself or its results, is the great business of life and the discipline of our hearts. . . .

. . . [I]t is a part of Christian caution to see that our engagements do not become pursuits. Engagements are our portion, but pursuits are for the most part of our own choosing. We may be engaged in worldly business, without pursuing worldly objects; "not slothful in business," yet "serving the Lord." In this then consists the danger of the pursuit of gain, as by trade and the like. It is the most common and widely extended of all excitements. It is one in which every one almost may indulge, nay and will be praised by the world for indulging. And it lasts through life; in that differing from the amusements and pleasures of the world, which are short-lived, and succeed one after another. Dissipation of mind, which these amusements create, is itself indeed miserable enough: but far worse than this dissipation is the concentration of mind upon some worldly object, which admits of being constantly pursued, and such is the pursuit of gain. Nor is it a slight aggravation of the evil, that anxiety is almost sure to attend it. A life of money-getting is a life of care; from the first there is a fearful anticipation of loss in various ways to depress and unsettle the mind; nay to haunt it, till a man finds he can think about nothing else, and is unable to give his mind to religion, from the constant whirl of business in which he is involved. It is well this should be understood. You may hear men talk as if the pursuit of wealth was the business of life. They will argue, that by the law of nature a man is bound to gain a livelihood for his family, and that he finds a reward in doing so, an innocent and honourable satisfaction, as he adds one sum to another, and counts up his gains. . . .

. . . Money is a sort of creation, and gives the acquirer, even more than the possessor, an imagination of his own power; and tends to make him idolize self. Again, what we have hardly won, we are unwilling to part with; so that a man who has himself made his wealth will commonly be penurious, or at least will not part with it except in exchange for what will reflect credit upon himself, or increase his importance. Even when his conduct is most disinterested and amiable (as in spending for the comfort of those who depend upon him), still this indulgence of self, of pride and worldliness, insinuates itself. Very unlikely therefore is it that he should be liberal towards God; for religious offerings are an expenditure without sensible return, and that upon objects for which the very pursuit of wealth has indisposed his mind. Moreover, if it may be added, there is a considerable tendency in occupations connected with gain to make a man unfair in his dealings, that is, in a subtle way. There are so many conventional deceits and prevarications in the details of the world's business, so much intricacy in the management of accounts, so many perplexed questions about justice and equity, so many plausible subterfuges and fictions of law, so much confusion between the distinct yet approximating outlines of honesty and civil enactment, that it requires a very straightforward mind to keep firm hold of strict conscientiousness, honour, and truth, and to look at matters in which he is engaged, as he would have looked on them, supposing he now came upon them all at once as a stranger.

. . . Only let us consider the fact, that we are money-making people, with our Saviour's declarations before us against wealth, and trust in wealth: and we shall have abundant matter for serious thought.

(PS 2:349–50, 352–53, 355–57, "The Danger of Riches")

68. The Religion of the Day

In every age of Christianity, since it was first preached, there has been what may be called a *religion of the world*, which so far imitates the one true religion, as to deceive the unstable and unwary. The world does not oppose religion *as such*. I may say, it never has opposed it. In particular, it has, in all ages, acknowledged in one sense or other the Gospel of Christ, fastened on one or other of its characteristics, and professed to embody this in its practice; while by neglecting the other parts of the holy doctrine, it has, in fact, distorted and corrupted even that portion of it which it has exclusively put forward, and so has contrived to explain away the whole;—for he who cultivates only one precept of the gospel to the exclusion of the rest, in reality attends to no part at all. Our duties *balance* each other; and though we are too sinful to perform them all perfectly, yet we may in some measure be performing them all, and preserving the balance on the whole; whereas, to give ourselves only to this or that commandment, is to incline our minds in a wrong direction, and at length to pull them down to the earth, which is the aim of our adversary, the Devil.

What is the world's religion now? It has taken the brighter side of the Gospel,—its tidings of comfort, its precepts of love; all darker, deeper views of man's condition and prospects being comparatively forgotten. This is the religion *natural* to a civilized age, and well has Satan dressed and completed it into an idol of the Truth. . . . Conscience is no longer recognized as an independent arbiter of actions, its authority is explained away; partly it is superseded in the minds of men by the so-called moral sense, which is regarded merely as the love of the beautiful; partly by the rule of expediency, which is forthwith substituted for it in the details of conduct. Now conscience is a stern, gloomy principle; it tells us of guilt and of prospective punishment. Accordingly, when its terrors disappear, then disappear also, in the creed of the day, those fearful images of divine wrath with which the Scriptures abound. They are explained away. Every thing is bright and cheerful. Religion is pleasant and easy; benevolence is the chief virtue; intolerance, bigotry, excess of zeal, are the first of sins. Austerity is an absurdity; even firmness is looked on with an unfriendly, suspicious eye. . . .

. . . Here is an existing teaching, only partially evangelical, built upon worldly principle, yet pretending to be the Gospel, dropping one whole side of the Gospel, its austere character, and considering it enough to be benevolent, courteous, candid and correct in conduct—delicate, though it includes no true fear of God, no fervent zeal for His honour, no deep hatred of sin, no horror at the sight of sinners, no indignation and compassion at the blasphemies of heretics, no jealous adherence to doctrinal truth, no especial sensitiveness about the particular means of gaining ends, provided the ends be good, no loyalty to the Holy apostolic Church, of which the Creed speaks, no sense of the authority of religion as external to the mind: in a word, no seriousness, and therefore is neither hot nor cold, but (in Scripture language) *luke-warm*. Thus the present age is the very contrary to what are commonly called the dark ages; and together with the faults of those ages we have lost their virtues. I say their virtues; for even the errors then prevalent, a persecuting spirit, for instance, fear of religious inquiry, bigotry, these were, after all, but perversions and excesses of *real virtues*, such as zeal and reverence; and we, instead of limiting and purifying them, have taken them away root and branch. Why? Because we have not acted from a love of the Truth, but from the influence of the Age. . . .

. . . [T]he religion of the day, is especially adapted to please men of sceptical minds . . . who have never been careful to obey their conscience, who cultivate the intellect without disciplining the heart, and who allow themselves to speculate freely about what religion *ought to be*, without going to Scripture to discover what it really is. Some persons of this character almost consider religion itself to be an obstacle in the advance of our social and political well-being. But they know human nature requires it; therefore they select the most *rational* form of religion (so they call it) which they can find. Others are far more seriously disposed, but are corrupted by bad example or other cause. But they all discard (what they call) gloomy views of religion; they all trust themselves more then God's word, and thus may be classed together; and are ready to embrace the pleasant consoling religion natural to a polished age. . . .

. . . It cannot be denied that, pleasant as religious observances are declared in Scripture to be to the holy, yet to men in general they are said to be difficult and distasteful; to all men *naturally* impossible, and by few fulfilled even with the assistances of grace, on account of their wilful corruption. Religion is pronounced to be against nature, to be against our original will, to require God's aid to make us love and obey it, and to be commonly refused and opposed in spite of that aid. We are expressly told, that "strait is the gate and narrow the way that leads to life, and few there be that find it." . . . This is the dark side of religion; and the men I have been describing cannot bear to think of it. They shrink from it as too terrible. They easily get themselves to believe that those strong declarations of Scripture do not belong to the present day, or that they are figurative. They have no language within their heart responding to them. Conscience has been silenced. The only information they have received concerning God has been from Natural Theology, and that speaks only of benevolence and harmony; so they will not credit the plain word of Scripture. . . .

Here I will not shrink from uttering my firm conviction, that it would be a gain to this country, were it vastly more superstitious, more bigoted, more gloomy, more fierce in its religion, than at present it shows itself to be. Not, of course, that I think the tempers of mind herein implied desirable, which would be an evident absurdity; but I think them infinitely more desirable and more promising than a heathen obduracy, and a cold, self-sufficient, self-wise tranquillity. . . .

(PS 1:309–14, 316, 318–20, "The Religion of the Day")

69. Artificiality and Simplicity

All exercises of mind which lead us to reflect upon and ascertain our state; to know what worship is, and why we worship; what service is, and why we serve; what our feelings imply, and what our words mean, tend to divert our minds from the one thing needful, unless we are practised and expert in using them. All proofs of religion, evidences, proofs of particular doctrines, scripture proofs, and the like—these certainly furnish scope for the exercise of great and admirable powers of mind, and it would be fanatical to disparage or disown them; but it requires a mind rooted and grounded in love not to be dissipated by them. As for truly religious minds, they, when so engaged, instead of mere disputing, are sure to turn inquiry into meditation, exhortation into worship, and argument into teaching.

Reflections such as these, followed up, show us how different is our state from that for which God made us. He meant us to be simple, and we are unreal; He meant us to think no evil, and a thousand associations, bad, trifling, or unworthy, attend our every thought. He meant us to be drawn on to the glories without us, and we are drawn back and (as it were) fascinated by the miseries within us. And hence it is that the whole structure of society is so artificial; no one trusts another, if he can help it; safeguards, checks, and securities are ever sought after. No one means exactly what he says, for our words have lost their natural meaning, and even an Angel could not use them naturally, for every mind being different from every other, they have no distinct meaning. What, indeed, is the very function of society, as it is at present, but a rude attempt to cover the degradation of the fall, and to make men feel respect for themselves, and enjoy it in the eyes of others, without returning to God. This is what we should especially guard against, because there is so much of it in the world. I mean, not an abandonment of evil, not a sweeping away and cleansing out of the corruption which sin has bred within us, but a smoothing it over, an outside delicacy and polish, an ornamenting the surface of things while "within are dead men's bones and all uncleanness," making the garments, which at first were given for decency, a means of pride and vanity. Men give good names to what is evil, they sanctify bad principles and feelings; and, knowing that there is vice and error, selfishness, pride, and ambition, in the world, they attempt, not to root out these evils, not to withstand these errors that they think a dream, the dream of theorists who do not know the world, but to cherish and form alliance with them, to use them, to make a science of selfishness, to flatter and indulge error, and to bribe vice with the promise of bearing with it, so that it does but keep in the shade.

... But Christ has purchased for us what we lost in Adam, our garment of innocence. He has bid us and enabled us to become as little children; He has purchased for us the grace of *simplicity* which, though one of the highest, is very little thought about, is very little sought after. We have, indeed, a general idea what love is, and hope, and faith, and truth, and purity, though a poor idea; but we are almost blind to what is one of the first elements of Christian perfection, that simple-mindedness which springs from the heart's being *whole* with God, entire, undivided. And those who think they have an idea of it, commonly rise no higher than to mistake for it a mere weakness and softness of mind, which is but its counterfeit. To be simple is to be like the apostles and first Christians. Our Saviour says, "Be ye harmless," or simple, "as doves." And St. Paul, "I would have you wise unto that which is good, and *simple concerning evil.*" (Rom 16: 19) . . . Let us pray God to give us this great and precious gift; that we may blot out from our memory all that offends Him; unlearn all that knowledge which sin has taught us; rid ourselves of selfish motives, self-conceit, and vanity, littlenesses, envying, grudgings, meannesses; turn from all cowardly, low, miserable ways; and escape from servile fears, the fear of man, vague anxieties of conscience, and superstitions. So that we may have the boldness and frankness of those who are as if they had no sin, from having been cleansed from it; the uncontaminated hearts, open countenances, and untroubled eyes of those who neither suspect, nor conceal, nor shun, nor are jealous; in a word, so that we may have confidence in Him, that we may stay on Him, and rest in the thoughts of Him, instead of plunging amid the thickets of this world. . . .

(PS 8:265, "Ignorance of Evil")

70. The Inventions of Reason

Take the world as it is, with its intelligence, its bustle, its feverish efforts, its works, its results, the ceaseless ebb and flow of the great tide of mind: view society, I mean, not in its adventitious evil, but in its essential characters, and what is all its intellectual energy but a fruit of the tree of the knowledge of good and evil, and though not sinful, yet, in fact, the consequence of sin? Consider its professions, trades, pursuits, or, in the words of the text, "inventions;" trace them down to their simplest forms and first causes, and what is their parent, but the loss of original uprightness? What place have its splendours, triumphs, speculations, or theories in that pure and happy region which was our cradle, or in that heaven which is to be our rest? Dexterity, promptness, presence of mind, sagacity, shrewdness, powers of persuasion, talent for business, what are these but developments of intellect which our fallen state has occasioned, and probably far from the highest which our mind is capable of? And are not these and others at best only of use in remedying the effects of the fall, and, so far, indeed, demanding of us deep thankfulness towards the Giver, but not having a legitimate employment except in a world of sickness and infirmity?

Now, in thus speaking, let it be observed, I am not using light words of what is a great gift of God, and one distinguishing mark of man over the brutes, our reason; I have but spoken of the *particular exercises and developments*, in which it has its life in the world, as we see them; and these, though in themselves excellent, and often admirable, yet would not have been but for sin, and now that they are, subserve the purposes of sin. Reason, I say, is God's gift; but so are the passions; Adam had the gift of reason, and so had he passions; but he did not *walk* by reason, nor was he led by his passions; he, or at least Eve, was tempted to follow passion and reason, instead of her Maker, and she fell. Since that time passion and reason have abandoned their due place in man's nature, which is one of subordination, and conspired together against the Divine light within him, which is his proper guide. Reason has been as guilty as passion here. God made man upright, and grace was his strength; but he has found out many inventions, and his strength is reason.

To conclude: Let us learn from what has been said, whatever gifts of mind we have, henceforth to keep them under, and to subject them to innocence, simplicity, and truth. Let our characters be formed upon faith, love, contemplativeness, modesty, meekness, humility. . . . Let us labour to approve ourselves to Christ. If we be in a crowd, still be we as hermits in the wilderness; if we be rich as if poor, if married as single, if gifted in mind, still as little children. Let the tumult of error teach us the simplicity of truth; the miseries of guilt the peace of innocence; and "the many inventions" of the reason the stability of faith. Let us, with St. Paul, be "all things to all men," while we "live unto God;" "wise as serpents and harmless as doves". . . .

(PS 5:113–15, "The State of Innocence")

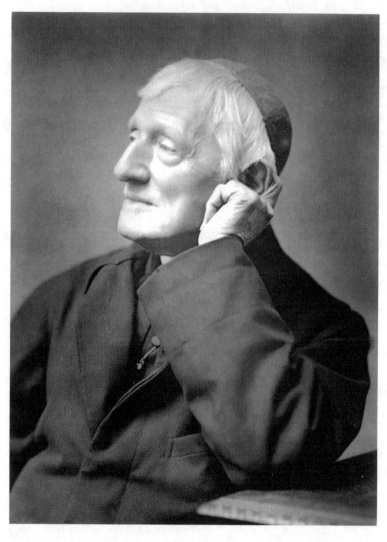

Cardinal John Henry Newman, photographed by Barrand, 1888.

DOUBTS

71. The Hidden God

This established order of things, in which we find ourselves, if it has a Creator, must surely speak of His will in its broad outlines and its main issues. This principle being laid down as certain, when we come to apply it to things as they are, our first feeling is one of surprise and (I may say) of dismay, that His control of this living world is so indirect, and His action so obscure. This is the first lesson that we gain from the course of human affairs. What strikes the mind so forcibly and so painfully is, His absence (if I may so speak) from His own world. It is a silence that speaks. It is as if others had got possession of His work. Why does not He, our Maker and Ruler, give us some immediate knowledge of Himself? Why does He not write His Moral Nature in large letters upon the face of history, and bring the blind, tumultuous rush of its events into a celestial, hierarchical order? Why does He not grant us in the structure of society at least so much of a revelation of Himself as the religions of the heathen attempt to supply? Why from the beginning of time has no one uniform steady light guided all families of the earth, and all individual men, how to please Him? Why is it possible without absurdity to deny His will, His attributes, His existence? Why does He not walk with us one by one, as He is said to have walked with His chosen men of old time? We both see and know each other; why, if we cannot have the sight of Him, have we not at least the knowledge? On the contrary, He is specially "a Hidden God;" and with our best efforts we can only glean from the surface of the world some faint and fragmentary views of Him. I see only a choice of alternatives in explanation of so critical a fact: either there is no Creator, or He has disowned His creatures. Are then the dim shadows of His Presence in the affairs of men but a fancy of our own, or, on the other hand, has He hid His face and the light of His countenance, because we have in some special way dishonoured His? My true informant, my burdened conscience, gives me at once the true answer to each of these antagonist questions. It pronounces without any misgiving that God exists, and it pronounces quite as surely that I am alienated from Him; that "His hand is not shortened, but that our iniquities have divided between us and our God." Thus it solves the world's mystery, and sees in that mystery only a confirmation of its own original teaching.

(GA 396–98, "Natural Religion")

72. Christianity in the World

Unless it be maintained that the Church has never done her duty towards the nations where she has sojourned, it must be granted that success in the hearts of the many is not promised her. Christianity has raised the tone of morals, has restrained the passions, and enforced external decency and good conduct in the world at large; it has advanced certain persons in virtuous or religious habits, who otherwise might have been imbued with the mere rudiments of truth and holiness; it has given a firmness and consistency to religious profession in numbers, and perhaps has extended the range of really religious practice. Still on the whole the great multitude of men have to all appearance remained, in a spiritual point of view, no better than before. The state of great cities now is not so very different from what it was of old; or at least not so different as to make it appear that the main work of Christianity has lain with the face of society, or what is called the world. Again, the highest class in the community and the lowest, are not so different from what they would be respectively without the knowledge of the Gospel, as to allow it to be said that Christianity has succeeded with the world, as the world, in its several ranks and classes. And so of its pursuits and professions; they are in character what they were, softened or restrained in their worst consequences, but still with the same substantial fruits. Trade is still avaricious, not in tendency only but in fact, though it has heard the Gospel; physical science is still sceptical as it was when heathen. Lawyers, soldiers, farmers, politicians, courtiers, nay, shame to say, the priesthood, still savour of the old Adam. Christian states move forward upon the same laws as before, and rise and fall as time goes on, upon the same internal principles. Human nature remains what it was, though it has been baptized; the proverbs, the satires, the pictures, of which it was the subject in heathen times, have their point still. In a word, taking religion to mean as it well may, the being bound by God's law, the acting under God's will instead of our own, how few are there in a country called Christian who even profess religion in this sense! How few there are who live by any other rule than that of their own ease, habit, inclination, as the case may be, on the one hand, and of external circumstances on the other! With how few is the will of God an habitual object of thought, or search, or love, or obedience! All this is so notorious that unbelievers taunt us with it. They see, and scoff at seeing, that Christians, whether the many or the educated or the old, nay, or the sacred ministry, are open to the motives, and unequal to the temptations, which prevail with human nature generally.

The knowledge of the Gospel then has not materially changed more than the surface of things; it has made clean the outside; but as far as we have the means of judging, it has not acted on a large scale upon the mind within, upon that "heart" out of which proceed the evil things "which defile a man." Nor did it ever promise it would do so. Our Saviour's words, spoken of the apostles in the first instance, relate to the Church at large,—"I pray not for the world, but for them which Thou has given Me, for they are Thine." In like manner St. Paul says that Christ came, not to convert the world, but "to purify unto Himself a *peculiar people*, zealous of good works;" not to sanctify this evil world, but to "deliver us *out of* this present evil world according to the will of God and our Father;" not to turn the whole earth into a heaven, but to bring down a heaven upon earth. This has been the real triumph of the Gospel, to raise those beyond themselves and beyond human nature, in whatever rank and condition of life, whose wills mysteriously cooperate with God's grace, who, while God visits them, really fear and really obey God, whatever be the unknown reason why one man obeys Him and another not. It has made men saints, and brought into existence specimens of faith and holiness, which without it are unknown and impossible. . . .

(PS 4:154–56, "The Visible Church for the Sake of the Elect")

73. Enlarging the Mind

[W]hat is called seeing the world, entering into active life, going into society, travelling, gaining acquaintance with the various classes of the community, coming into contact with the principles and modes of thought of various parties, interests, and races, their views, aims, habits and manners, their religious creeds and forms of worship—gaining experience how various yet how alike men are, how low-minded, how bad, how opposed, yet how confident in their opinions; all this exerts a perceptible influence upon the mind, which it is impossible to mistake, be it good or be it bad, and is popularly called its enlargement.

And then again, the first time the mind comes across the arguments and speculations of unbelievers, and feels what a novel light they cast upon what he has hitherto accounted sacred; and still more, if it gives in to them and embraces them, and throws off as so much prejudice what it has hitherto held, and, as if waking from a dream, begins to realize to its imagination that there is now no such thing as law and the transgression of law, that sin is a phantom, and punishment a bugbear, that it is free to sin, free to enjoy the world and the flesh; and still further, when it does enjoy them, and reflects that it may think and hold just what it will, that "the world is all before it where to choose," and what system to build up as its own private persuasion; when this torrent of wilful thoughts rushes over and inundates it, who will deny that the fruit of the tree of knowledge, or what the mind takes for knowledge, has made it one of the gods, with a sense of expansion and elevation—an intoxication in reality, still, so far as the subjective state of the mind goes, an illumination? Hence the fanaticism of individuals or nations, who suddenly cast off their Maker. Their eyes are opened; and, like the judgement-stricken king in the Tragedy, they see two suns, and a magic universe, out of which they look back upon their former state of faith and innocence with a sort of contempt and indignation, as if they were then but fools, and the dupes of imposture.

On the other hand, religion has its own enlargement, and an enlargement, not of tumult, but of peace. It is often remarked of uneducated persons, who have hitherto thought little of the unseen world, that, on their turning to God, looking into themselves, regulating their hearts, reforming their conduct, and meditating on death and judgement, heaven and hell, they seem to become, in point of intellect, different beings from what they were. Before, they took things as they came, and thought no more of one thing than another. But now every event happens to them; they are mindful of times and seasons, and compare the present with the past; and the world, no longer dull, monotonous, unprofitable, and hopeless, is a various and complicated drama, with parts and an object, and an awful moral.

(Idea 132–33, "Knowledge Viewed in Relation to Learning")

74. Doubt and Devotion

[M]any a man seems to have no grasp at all of doctrinal truth. He cannot get himself to think it of importance what a man believes, and what not. He tries to do so; for a time he does; he does for a time think that a certain faith is necessary for salvation, that certain doctrines are to be put forth and maintained in charity to the souls of men. Yet though he thinks so one day, he changes the next; he holds the truth, and then lets it go again. He is filled with doubts; suddenly the question crosses him, "Is it possible that such and such a doctrine *is* necessary?" and he relapses into an uncomfortable sceptical state, out of which there is no outlet. Reasonings do not convince him; he *cannot* be convinced; he has no grasp of truth. Why? Because the next world is not a reality to him; it only exists in his mind in the form of certain conclusions from certain reasonings. It is but an inference; and never can be more, never can be present to his mind, until he acts, instead of arguing. Let him but act as if the next world were before him; let him but give himself to such devotional exercises as we ought to observe in the presence of an Almighty, All-holy, and All-merciful God, and it will be a rare case indeed if his difficulties do not vanish. . . .

. . . [T]here *are* cases where this wavering of mind *does* arise from scantiness of prayer; and if so, it is worth a man's considering, who is thus unsteady, timid, and dimsighted, whether this scantiness be not perchance the true reason of such infirmities in his own case, and whether a "continuing instant in prayer,"—by which I mean, not merely prayer morning and evening, but something suitable to his disease, something extraordinary, as medicine is extraordinary, a "redeeming of time" from society and recreation in order to pray more—whether such a change in his habits would not remove them?

For what is the very promise of the New Covenant but stability? what is it, but a clear insight into the truth, such as will enable us to know how to walk, how to profess, how to meet the circumstances of life, how to withstand gainsayers? Are we built upon a rock or upon the sand? are we after all tossed about on the sea of opinion, when Christ has stretched out His hand to us, to help and encourage us? . . . Can we possibly have apprehensions about what man will do to us or say of us, can we flatter the great ones of earth, or timidly yield to the many, or be dazzled by talent, or drawn aside by interest, who are in the habit of divine conversations?

(PS 4:231, 233–34, "Moral Effects of Communion with God")

75. Trials of Faith

When Christians have but a little, they are thankful; they gladly pick up the crumbs from under the table. Give them much, they soon forget it is much; and when they find it is not all, and that for other men, too, even for penitents, God has some good in store, straightway they are offended. Without denying in words their own natural unworthiness, and still having real convictions of it to a certain point, nevertheless, somehow, they have a certain secret over-regard for themselves; at least they *act* as if they thought that the Christian privileges belonged to them over others, by a sort of fitness. And they like respect to be shown them by the world, and are jealous of anything which is likely to interfere with the continuance of their credit and authority. Perhaps, too, they have pledged themselves to certain received opinions, and this is an additional reason for their being suspicious of what to them is a novelty. Hence such persons are least fitted to deal with difficult times. God works wondrously in the world; and at certain eras His providence puts on a new aspect. Religion seems to be failing, when it is merely changing its form. God seems for an instant to desert His own appointed instruments, and to be putting honour upon such as have been framed in express disobedience to His commands. For instance, sometimes He brings about good by means of wicked men, or seems to bless the efforts of those who have separated from His Holy Church more than those of His true labourers. Here is the trial of the Christian's faith, who, if the fact is so, must not resist it, lest haply he be found fighting against God, nor must he quarrel with it after the manner of the elder brother. But he must take everything as God's gift, hold fast his *principles*, not give *them* up because appearances are for the moment against them, but believe all things will come round at length. On the other hand, he must not cease to beg of God, and try to gain, the spirit of a sound mind, the power to separate truth from falsehood, and to try the spirits, the disposition to submit to God's teaching, and the wisdom to act as the varied course of affairs requires; in a word, a portion of that spirit which rested on the great Apostle, St. Paul.

(PS 3:110–11, "Contracted Views in Religion")

76. Difficulties and Obscurities

When the many own Christ with their lips, what shall try and discipline His true servant, and detect the self-deceiver? Difficulties in revelation mainly contribute to this end. They are stumbling-blocks to proud and unhumbled minds, and were intended to be such. Faith is unassuming, modest, thankful, obedient. It receives with reverence and love whatever God gives, when convinced it is His gift. But when men do not feel rightly their need of His redeeming mercy, their lost condition and their inward sinfulness, when, in fact, they do not seek Christ in good earnest, in order to gain something, and do something, but as a matter of curiosity, or speculation, or form, *of course* these difficulties will become great objections in the way of their receiving His word simply. And I say these difficulties were intended to be such by Him who "scattereth the proud in the imagination of their hearts." . . . [O]ur Lord's conduct through His ministry is a continued example of this. He spoke in parables, that they might see and hear, yet not understand,—a righteous detection of insincerity; whereas the same difficulties and obscurities, which offended irreligious men, would but lead the humble and meek to seek for more light, for information as far as it was to be obtained, and for resignation and contentedness, where it was not given. When Jesus said, ". . . Except ye eat the flesh of the Son of Man, and drink His blood, ye have no life in you . . . Many of His disciples . . . said, This is a hard saying: who can hear it? . . . and from that time many . . . went back, and walked no more with Him. . . . Then said Jesus unto the twelve, Will ye also go away? Then Simon Peter answered Him, Lord, to whom shall we go? Thou hast the words of eternal life." Here is the trial of faith, *a difficulty*. Those "that believe not" fall away; the true disciples remain firm, for they feel their *eternal interests* at stake, and ask the very plain and practical, as well as affectionate question, "*To whom* shall we go," if we leave Christ? (Jn 6: 53–68)

Therefore, if we feel the necessity of coming to Christ, yet the difficulty, let us recollect that the gift of coming is in God's hands, and that we must pray Him to give it to us. Christ does not merely tell us, that we cannot come of ourselves (though this He does tell us), but He tells us also with whom the power of coming is lodged, with His Father,—that we may seek it of Him. It is true, religion has an austere appearance to those who never have tried it; its doctrines full of mystery, its precepts of harshness; so that it is uninviting, offending different men in different ways, but in some way offending all. When then we feel within us the risings of this opposition to Christ, proud aversion to His Gospel, or a low-minded longing after this world, let us pray God to draw us; and though we cannot move a step without Him, at least let us try to move. He looks into our hearts and sees our strivings even before we strive, and He blesses and strengthens even our feebleness. Let us get rid of curious and presumptuous thoughts by going about our business, whatever it is; and let us mock and baffle the doubts which Satan whispers to us by *acting* against them. No matter whether we believe doubtingly or not, or know clearly or not, so that *we act* upon our belief. The rest will follow in time; part in this world, part in the next. Doubts may pain, but they cannot harm, unless we give way to them; and that we *ought not* to give way, our conscience tells us, so that our course is plain. And the more we are in earnest to "work out our salvation," the less shall we care to know how those things really are, which perplex us. At length, when our hearts are in our work, we shall be indisposed to take the trouble of listening to curious truths (if they are but curious), though we might have them explained to us. For what says the Holy Scripture? That of speculations "there is no end," and they are "a weariness of the flesh;" but that we must "fear God and keep His commandments; for this is the whole duty of man." (Eccles 12: 12–13)

(PS 1:211, "The Christian Mysteries")

77. Deferred Rewards

Alas! Is it not discouragement enough to walk in a path of self-denial, to combat our natural lusts and high imaginations, to have the war of the flesh, that the war with the world must be added to it? Is it not enough to be pilgrims and soldiers all our days, but we must hear the mutual greetings, and exulting voices of those who choose the way of death, and must walk not only in pain but in solitude? Where is the blessing upon the righteous, where the joy of faith, the comfort of love, the triumph of self-mastery, in such dreariness and desolateness? Who are to sympathize with us in our joys and sorrows, who are to spur us on by the example of their own success? St. Paul answers us—the cloud of witnesses of former days. . . .

In truth, do what he will, Satan cannot quench or darken the light of the Church. He may incrust it with his own evil creations, but even opaque bodies transmit rays, and Truth shines with its own heavenly lustre, though "under a bushel." The Holy Spirit has vouchsafed to take up His abode in the Church, and the Church will ever bear, on its front, the visible signs of its hidden privilege. Viewed at a little distance, its whole surface will be illuminated, though the light really streams from apertures which might be numbered. The scattered witnesses thus become, in the language of the text, "a cloud," like the Milky Way in the heavens.

We have, in Scripture, the records of those who lived and died by faith in the old time, and nothing can deprive us of them. The strength of Satan lies in his being seen to have the many on his side; but, when we read the Bible, this argument loses its hold over us. There we find that we are not solitary; that others, before us, have been in our very condition, have had our feelings, undergone our trials, and laboured for the prize which we are seeking. Nothing more elevates the mind than the consciousness of being one of a great and victorious company. . . . He finds, in the history of the past, a peculiar kind of consolation, counteracting the influence of the world that is seen. . . .

. . . I will own that a man cannot profit by these considerations all at once. A man, who has never thought of the history of the Saints, will gain little benefit from it on first taking up the subject when he comes into trouble. He will turn from it disappointed. He may say, "My pain or my trial is not the less because another had it a thousand years since." But the consolation in question comes not in the way of argument but by habit. A tedious journey seems shorter when gone in company, yet, be the travellers many or few, each goes over the same ground.

Such is the Christian's feeling towards all Saints, but it is especially excited by the Church of Christ and by all that belong to it. For what is that Church but a pledge and proof of God's never-dying love and power from age to age? He set it up in mercy to mankind, and its presence among us is a proof that in spite of our sins He has not yet forsaken us;—"Hitherto hath the Lord helped us." He set it up on the foundation of His Twelve Apostles, and promised that the gates of hell should not prevail against it; and its presence among us is a proof of His power. . . . He said, He would be with His Church: He has continued it alive to this day. He has continued the line of His Apostles onwards through every age and all troubles and perils of the world. Here then, surely, is somewhat of encouragement for us amid our loneliness and weakness. . . .

. . . A prayer we read daily is called the prayer of St. Chrysostom; a creed is called the Creed of St. Athanasius; another creed is called the Nicene Creed; . . . in the Homilies of many other such besides. What do these names mean? Sad it is, you have no heart to inquire after or celebrate those who are fellow-citizens with you, and your great benefactors! Men of this world spread each other's fame—they vaunt loudly; you see in every street the names and the statues of the children of men, you hear of their exploits in speeches and histories; yet you care not to know concerning those to whom you are indebted for the light of Gospel truth. Truly they were in their day men of God; they were rulers and teachers in the Church; they had received by succession of hands the power first given to the apostles and their writings remain to this day. Now a person who cultivates this thought, finds therein, through God's mercy, great encouragement. Say he is alone, his faith counted a dream, and his efforts to do good a folly, what then? He knows there have been times when his opinions were those of the revered and influential, and the opinions now in repute only not reprobated because they were not heard of. He knows that present opinions are the accident of the day, and that they will fall as they have risen. They will surely fall even though at a distant date! He labours for that time; he labours for five hundred years to come. He can bear in faith to wait five hundred years, to wait for an era long, long after he has mouldered into dust. The Apostles lived eighteen hundred years since; and as far as the Christian looks back, so far can he afford to look forward. There is one Lord, one faith, one baptism, one God and Father of all, from first to last.

. . . When we read the Bible and religious books in private, there is great comfort; but our minds are commonly more roused and encouraged in Church, when we see those great truths displayed and represented which Scripture speaks of. There we see "Jesus Christ, evidently set forth, crucified among us." The ordinances which we behold, force the unseen truth upon our senses. The very disposition of the building, the subdued light, the aisles, the Altar, with its pious adornments, are figures of things unseen, and stimulate our fainting faith. We seem to see the heavenly courts, with Angels chanting, and Apostles and Prophets listening, as we read their writings in due course. . . . I say it with confidence, he who observes it, will grow in time a different man from what he was, God working in him. His heart will be more heavenly and aspiring; the world will lie under his feet; he will be proof against its opinions, threats, blandishments, ridicule. His very mode of viewing things, his very voice, his manner, gait, and countenance, will speak of Heaven to those who know him well, though the many see nothing in him.

The many understand him not, and even in St. Paul or St. John would see but ordinary men. Yet at times such a one will speak effectually even to the many. In seasons of unusual distress or alarm, when men's minds faint for fear, then he will have a natural power over the world, and will seem to speak, not as an individual, but as if in him was concentrated all the virtue and the grace of those many Saints who have been his lifelong companions. He has lived with those who are dead, and he will seem to the world as one coming from the dead, speaking in the name of the dead, using the language of souls dead to things that are seen, revealing the mysteries of the heavenly world, and awing and controlling those who are wedded to this. . . . One living Saint, though there be but one, is a pledge of the whole Church Invisible. Let this thought console us as it ought to do; let it have its full influence in us, and possess us.

(PS 3:237–38, 243–44, 246–53, "The Visible Church
an Encouragement to Faith")

78. The Sternness of Scripture

"Vanity of vanities, all is vanity;" "man is born to trouble:" these are its customary lessons. The text is but a specimen of the descriptions repeated again and again throughout Scripture of human infirmity and misery.

So much is this the case, that thoughtless persons are averse to the Scripture narrative for this very reason. I do not mean bad men, who speak hard, presumptuous words against the Bible, and in consequence expose themselves to the wrath of God; but I speak of *thoughtless* persons; and of these there are many, who consider the Bible a gloomy book, and on that account seldom look into it, saying that it makes them melancholy. Accordingly, there have been attempts made on the other hand to hide this austere character of Scripture, and make it a bright interesting picture of human life. Its stories have before now been profanely embellished in human language, to suit the taste of weak and cowardly minds. All this shows, that in the common opinion of mankind, the Bible does not take a pleasant sunshine view of the world.

. . . God does nothing without some wise and good reason, which it becomes us devoutly to accept and use. He has not given us this dark view of the world without a cause. In truth, this view is the ultimate *true* view of human life. But this is not all; it is a view which it concerns us much to know. It concerns us (I say) much to be told that this world is, after all, in spite of first appearances and partial exceptions, a dark world; else we shall be obliged to learn it (and, sooner or later, we must learn it) by sad *experience*, whereas, if we are forewarned, we shall unlearn false notions of its excellence, and be saved the disappointment which follows them. And therefore it is that Scripture omits even what might be said in praise of this world's pleasures—not denying their value, such as it is, or forbidding us to use them religiously, but knowing that we are sure to find them out for ourselves without being told of them, and that our danger is on the side, not of undervaluing, but of overvaluing them; whereas, by being told of the worldly vanity, *at first*, we shall learn (what else we should only attain *at last*), not indeed to be gloomy and discontented, but to bear a sober and calm heart under a smiling cheerful countenance. This is one chief reason of the solemn character of the Scripture history; and if we keep it in view, so far from being offended and frightened away by its notes of sorrow, because they grate on the ear at first, we shall stedfastly listen to them, and get them by heart, as a gracious gift from God sent to us, as a remedy for all dangerous overflowing joy in present blessings, in order to save us far greater pain (if we use the lesson well), the pain of actual disappointment, such as the overthrow of vainly cherished hopes of lasting good upon earth, will certainly occasion. . . .

. . . The great rule of our conduct is to take things as they come. He who goes out of his way as shrinking from the varieties of human life which meet him has weak faith, or a strangely perverted conscience; he wants elevation of mind. The true Christian rejoices in those earthly things which give joy, but in such a way as not to care for them when they go. For no blessing does he care much, except those which are immortal, knowing that he shall receive all such again in the world to come. But the least and the most fleeting he is too religious to contemn, considering them God's gift; and the least and most fleeting, thus received, yield a purer and deeper, though a less tumultuous joy. And if he at time refrains, it is lest he should encroach upon God's bounty, or lest by a constant use of it he should forget how to do without it.

. . . Only look upon the world in this light; its sights of sorrows are to calm you, and its pleasant sights to try you. There is a bravery in thus going straightforward, shrinking from no duty little or great, passing from high to low, from pleasure to pain, and making your principles strong without their becoming formal. Learn to be as the Angel, who could descend among the miseries of Bethesda, without losing his heavenly purity or his perfect happiness. Gain healing from troubled waters. Make up your mind to the prospect of sustaining a certain measure of pain and trouble in your passage through life; by the blessing of God this will prepare you for it, it will make you thoughtful and resigned without interfering with your cheerfulness.

(PS 1:327–29, 333–34, "Scripture a Record of Human Sorrow")

79. The Mystery of Religion

Christians especially incur the charge of craft at the hands of the world, because they pretend to so little, yet effect so much. . . .

First: sobriety, self-restraint, control of word and feeling, which religious men exercise, have about them an appearance of being artificial, because they are not natural; and of being artful, because artificial. . . . [T]hose who would be holy and blameless, the sons of God, find so much in the world to unsettle and defile them, that they are necessarily forced upon a strict self-restraint, lest they should receive injury from such intercourse with it as is unavoidable; and this self-restraint is the first thing which makes holy persons seem wanting in openness and manliness.

Next let it be considered that the world, the gross, carnal, unbelieving world, is blind to the peculiar feelings, objects, hopes, fears, affections of religious people. It cannot understand them. Religious men are a mystery to it; and, being a mystery, they will be called by the world, in mere self-defence, mysterious, dark, subtle, designing; and that the more, because, as living to God, they are at no pains to justify themselves to the world, or to open their hearts, or account to it for their conduct. . . . It cannot believe that men will deliberately sacrifice this life to the next; and when they profess to do so, it thinks that of necessity there must be something behind which they do not divulge. And, again, all the reasons which religious men allege, seem to the world unreal, and all the feelings fantastical and strained; and this strengthens it in its idea that it has not fathomed them, and that there is some secret to be found out. And indeed it has not fathomed them, and there is a secret; but it is the power of Divine grace, their state of heart, which is the secret; not their motives or their ends, which the world is told to the full. . . .

To this must be added, that the truth has in itself the gift of spreading, without instruments; it makes its way in the world, under God's blessing, by its own persuasiveness and excellence; . . . The Word, when once uttered, runs its course. He who speaks it has done his work in uttering it, and cannot recall it if he would. It runs its course; it prospers in the thing whereunto God sends it. It seizes many souls at once, and subdues them to the obedience of faith. Now when bystanders see these effects and see no cause, for they will not believe that the Word itself is the cause, which is to them a dead-letter—when it sees many minds moved in one way in many places, it imputes to secret management that uniformity which is nothing but the echo of the One Living and True Word.

And of course all this happens to the surprise of Christians as well as of the world; they can but marvel and praise God, but cannot account for it more than the world. . . . Moreover, meekness, gentleness, patience, and love, have in themselves a strong power to melt the heart of those who witness them. Cheerful suffering, too, leads spectators to sympathy, till, perhaps, a reaction takes place in the minds of men, and they are converted by the sight, and glorify their Father which is in heaven. But it is easy to insinuate, when men are malevolent, that those who triumph through meekness have affected the meekness to secure the triumph.

. . . Those who surrender themselves to Christ in implicit faith are graciously taken into His service; and, "as men under authority," they do great things without knowing it, by the Wisdom of their Divine Master. They act on conscience, perhaps in despondency, and without foresight; but what is obedience in them, has a purpose with God, and they are successful, when they do but mean to be dutiful. But what duplicity does the world think it, to speak of conscience, or honour, or propriety, or delicacy, or to give other tokens of personal motives, when the event seems to show that a calculation of results has been the actuating principle at bottom! It is God who designs, but His servants seem designing. . . .

But for us, let us glory in what they disown; let us beg of our Divine Lord to take to Him His great power, and manifest Himself more and more, and reign both in our hearts and in the world. Let us beg of Him to stand by us in trouble, and guide us on our dangerous way. May He, as of old, choose "the foolish things of the world to confound the wise, and the weak things of the world to confound the things which are might"! May He support us all the day long, till the shades lengthen, and the evening comes, and the busy world is hushed, and the fever of life is over, and our work is done! . . .

(SD 299–301, 303-05, 307, "Wisdom and Innocence")

80. Recognizing the Holy Spirit

And what the power of the Spirit has been in the world at large, that it is also in every human heart to which it comes . . . [T]he characteristics of the Spirit's influence are, that it is the same everywhere, that it is silent, that it is gradual, that it is thorough; not violent, or abrupt, or fitful, or partial, or detached; and if, on the other hand, the stirrings of heart which we experience, the impulses and the changes, are of this imperfect character, we have cause to suspect that in no sense do they come from the One True Sanctifier, the Holy Ghost, the Comforter.

For instance: any spirit which professes to come to us alone, and not to others, which makes no claim of having moved the body of the Church at all times and places, is not of God, but a private spirit of error. . . .

Again: vehemence, tumult, confusion, are no attributes of that benignant flood with which God has replenished the earth. That flood of grace is sedate, majestic, gentle in its operation. If at any time it seems to be violent, that violence is occasioned by some accident or imperfection of the earthen vessels into which it vouchsafes to pour itself; and is no token of the coming of Divine Power. Sudden changes of feeling, restlessness, terror, vehement emotions, impetuous resolves, ecstasies and transports, are no signs of it; and often they proceed from false spirits, who are but imitating heavenly influences as best they may and seducing souls to their ruin.

And again: the Divine Baptism, wherewith God visits us, penetrates through our whole soul and body. It leaves no part of us uncleansed, unsanctified. It claims the whole man for God. Any spirit which is content with what is short of this, which does not lead us to utter self-surrender and devotion; which reserves something for ourselves; which indulges our self-will; which flatters this or that natural inclination or affection; which does not tend to consistency of religious character—is not from God. The heavenly influence which He has given us is as intimately present, and as penetrating—as catholic—in an individual heart as it is in the world at large. It is every where, in every faculty, every affection, every design, every work. . . .

Thus the heart of every Christian ought to represent in miniature the Catholic Church, since one Spirit makes both the whole Church and every member of it to be His Temple. As He makes the Church one, which, left to itself, would separate into many parts; so He makes the soul one, in spite of its various affections and faculties, and its contradictory aims. As He gives peace to the multitude of nations, who are naturally in discord one with another, so does He give an orderly government to the soul, and set reason and conscience as sovereigns over the inferior parts of our nature. As He leavens each rank and pursuit of the community with the principles of the doctrine of Christ, so does that same Divine Leaven spread through every thought of the mind, every member of the body, till the whole is sanctified. And let us be quite sure that these two operations of our Divine Comforter depend upon each other, and that while Christians do not seek after inward unity and peace in their own breasts, the Church itself will never be at unity and peace in the world around them. . . .

. . . Till we look at home, no good shall we be able to perform for the Church at large; we shall but do mischief, when we intend good, and to us will apply that proverb—"Physician, heal thyself." . . . And let us not doubt that if we do thus proceed, we shall advance the cause of Christ in the world, whether we see it or not, whether we will it or not, whether the world wills it or not. Let us but raise the level of religion in our hearts, and it will rise in the world. He who attempts to set up God's kingdom in his heart, furthers it in the world. He whose prayers come up for a memorial before God, opens the "windows of Heaven, and the foundations of the great deep," and the waters rise. . . .

(SD 130–34, "Connexion between Personal and Public Improvement")

MYSTERIES

81. Divine Ordinance

I fear, indeed, that most men, though they profess and have a regard for religion, yet have very low and contracted notions of the dignity of their station as *Christians*. To be a Christian is one of the most wondrous and awful gifts in the world. It is, in one sense, to be higher than Angel or Archangel. If we have any portion of an enlightened faith, we shall understand that our state, as members of Christ's Church, is full of mystery. What so mysterious as to be born, as we are, under God's wrath? What so mysterious as to be redeemed by the death of the Son of God made flesh? What so mysterious as to receive the virtue of that death one by one through Sacraments? What so mysterious as to be able to teach and train each other in good or evil? When a man at all enters into such thoughts, how is his view changed about the birth of children! In what a different light do his duties, as a parent, break upon him! The notion entertained by most men seems to be, that it is a pleasant thing to have a home—this is what would be called an innocent and praiseworthy reason for marrying—that a wife and family are comforts. And the highest view a number of persons take is that it is decent and respectable to be a married man; that it gives a man a station in society, and settles him. All this is true. Doubtless wife and children *are* blessings from God: and it *is* praiseworthy and right to be domestic, and to live in orderly and honourable habits. But a man who limits his view to these thoughts, who does not look at marriage and at the birth of children as something of a much higher and more heavenly nature than anything we see, who does not discern in Holy Matrimony a divine ordinance, shadowing out the union between Christ and the Church, and does not associate the birth of children with the Ordinance of their new birth, such a one, I can only say, has very carnal views. It is well to go on labouring, year after year, for the bread that perisheth; and if we are well off in the world, to take interest and pleasure in our families rather than to seek amusements out of doors; it is very well, but it is not religion; and let us endeavour to make our feelings towards them more, and more religious. Let us beware of aiming at nothing higher than their being educated well before this world, their forming respectable connections, succeeding in their callings, and settling well. Let us never think we have absolved ourselves from the responsibility of being their parents till we have brought them to Christ, as in Baptism, so by religious training. Let us bear in mind ever to pray for their eternal salvation; let us "watch for their souls as those who must give account." Let us remember that salvation does not come as a matter of course; that Baptism, though administered to them once and long since, is never past, always lives in them as a blessing or as a burden: and that though we may cherish a joyful confidence that "He who hath begun a good work in them will perform it," then only have we a right to cherish it, when we are doing our part towards fulfilling it.

(PS 3:298–300, "Infant Baptism")

82. The Church Invisible

When a child is brought for Baptism, the Church invisible claims it, begs it of God, receives it, and extends to it, as God's instrument, her own sanctity. When we praise God in Holy Communion, we praise Him with the angels and Archangels, who are the guards, and with the Saints, who are the citizens of the City of God. When we offer our Sacrifice of praise and thanksgiving, or partake of the sacred elements so offered, we solemnly eat and drink of the powers of the world to come. When we read the Psalms, we use before many witnesses the very words on which those witnesses themselves—I mean, all successive generations of that holy company—have sustained themselves in their own day, for thousands of years past, during their pilgrimage heavenward. When we profess the Creed, it is no self-willed, arbitrary sense, but in the presence of those innumerable Saints who well remember what its words mean, and are witnesses of it before God, in spite of the heresy or indifference of this or that day. When we stand over their graves, we are in the very vestibule of that dwelling which is "all-glorious within," full of light and purity, and of voices crying, "Lord, how long?" When we pray in private, we are not solitary; others "are gathered together" with us "in Christ's Name," though we see them not, with Christ in the midst of them. When we approach the Ministry which He has ordained, we approach the steps of His throne. When we approach the Bishops, who are the centres of that Ministry, what have we before us but the Twelve apostles, present but invisible? When we use the sacred Name of Jesus, or the sign given us in Baptism, what do we but bid defiance to devils and evil men, and gain strength to resist them? When we protest, or confess, or suffer in the Name of Christ, what are we but ourselves types and symbols of the Cross of Christ, and of the strength of Him who died on it? When we are called to battle for the Lord, what are we who are seen, but mere outposts, the advanced guard of a mighty host, ourselves few in number and despicable, but bold beyond our numbers, because supported by chariots of fire and horses of fire round about the Mountain of the Lord of Hosts under which we stand?

(PS 4:176–77, "The Communion of Saints")

83. God's Universe

And thus we are led on to consider, how different are the character and effect of the Scripture notices of the structure of the physical world, from those which philosophers deliver. I am not deciding whether or not the one and the other are reconcileable; I merely say their respective *effect* is different. And when we have deduced what we deduce by our reason from the study of visible nature, and then read what we read in His inspired word, and find the two apparently discordant, *this* is the feeling I think we ought to have on our minds—not an impatience to do what is beyond our powers, to weigh evidence, sum up, balance, decide, and reconcile, to arbitrate between the two voices of God, but a sense of the utter nothingness of worms such as we are; of our plain and absolute incapacity to contemplate things *as they really are*; a perception of our emptiness, before the great Vision of God; of our "comeliness being turned into corruption, and our retaining no strength;" a conviction, that what is put before us, in nature or in grace, though true in such a full sense that we dare not tamper with it, yet is but an intimation useful for particular purposes, useful for practice, useful in its department, "until the daybreak and the shadows flee away," useful in such a way that both the one and the other representation may at once be used, as two languages, as two separate approximations towards the Awful Unknown Truth, such as will not mislead us in their respective provinces. And thus while we use the language of science, without jealousy, for scientific purposes, we may confine it to these; and repel and reprove its upholders, should they attempt to exalt it and to "stretch it beyond its measure." In its own limited round it has its use, nay, may be made to fill a higher ministry, and stand as a proselyte under the shadow of the temple; but it must not dare profane the inner courts, in which the ladder of Angels is fixed for ever, reaching even to the Throne of God, and "Jesus standing on the right hand of God." . . .

But faith, without asking for one ray of light more than is given, muses over the wonderful system of Providence, as seen in this world, which is ever connecting events, between which man sees no necessary bond. The whole system of what is called cause and effect, is one of mystery; and this instance, if it may be called one, supplies abundant matter of praise and adoration to a pious mind. It suggests to us, equally with the topics which have already come before us, how very much our knowledge of God's ways is but on the surface. What are those deep hidden reasons why Christ went and the spirit came? Marvelous and glorious, beyond our understanding! Let us worship in silence; meanwhile, let us jealously maintain this, and every other portion of our Creed, lest, by dropping jot or tittle, we suffer the truths concealed therein to escape from us.

(PS 2:208–9, 212–13, "Mysteries in Religion")

84. The Mind of God

Mysteries in religion are measured by the proud according to their own comprehension, by the humble, according to the power of God; the humble glorify God for them, the proud exalt themselves against them. . . .

Let a man consider how hardly he is able and how circuitously he is forced to describe the commonest objects of nature, when he attempts to substitute reason for sight, how difficult it is to define things, how impracticable it is to convey to another any complicated, or any deep or refined feeling, how inconsistent and self-contradictory his own feelings seem, when put into words, how he subjects himself in consequence to misunderstanding, or ridicule, or triumphant criticism; and he will not wonder at the impossibility of duly delineating in earthly words the first Cause of all thought, the Father of spirits, the One Eternal Mind, the King of kings and Lord of lords, who only hath immortality, dwelling in light unapproachable, whom no man hath seen nor can see, the incomprehensible infinite God.

. . . Is God obliged to take us into counsel, and explain to us the reason for every thing He does; or is it our plain duty to take what is given us, and feed upon it in faith? And to those who do thus receive the blessed doctrine under consideration, it will be found to produce special and singular practical effects on them, on the very ground of its mysteriousness. . . . The temper of true faith is described in the text,—"Marvelous are Thy works; and that my soul knoweth right well." A religious mind is ever marveling, and irreligious men laugh and scoff at it because it marvels. A religious mind is ever looking out of itself, is ever pondering God's words, is ever "looking into" them with the angels, is ever realizing to itself Him on whom it depends, and who is the centre of all truth and good. Carnal and proud minds are contented with self; they like to remain at home; when they hear of mysteries, they have no devout curiosity to go and see the great sight, though it be ever so little out of their way; and when it actually falls in their path, they stumble at it. As great then as is the difference between hanging upon the thought of God and resting in ourselves, lifting up the heart to God and bringing all things in heaven and earth down to ourselves, exalting God and exalting reason, measuring things by God's power and measuring them by our own ignorance, so great is the difference between him who believes in the Christian mysteries and him who does not. And were there no other reason for the revelation of them, but this gracious one, of raising us, refining us, making us reverent, making us expectant and devout, surely this would be more than a sufficient one.

(PS 4:283, 291–93, "The Mysteriousness of Our Present Being")

85. The Paradox of the Second Coming

We too are looking out for Christ's coming—we are bid look out; we are bid pray for it; and yet it is to be a time of judgement. . . . how can we pray that Christ would come, that the day of judgement would hasten, that His Kingdom would come, that His kingdom may be at once, may come on us this day or tomorrow, when by so coming He would be shortening the time of our present life, and cut off those precious years given us for conversion, amendment, repentance and sanctification? Is there not an inconsistency in professing to wish our Judge already come, when we do not feel ourselves ready for Him? In what sense can we really and heartily pray that He would cut short the time, when our conscience tells us that, even were our life longer, we should have much to do in a few years?

I do not deny that there is some difficulty in the question, but surely not more so than there is on every side of us in religious matters. Religion has (as it were) its very life in what are paradoxes and contradictions in the eye of reason. It is a seeming inconsistency how we can pray for Christ's coming, yet wish time to "work out our salvation," and "make our calling and election sure." It was a seeming contradiction, how good men were to desire His first coming, yet be unable to abide it; how the Apostles feared, yet rejoiced after His resurrection. And so it is a paradox how the Christian should in all things be sorrowful yet always rejoicing, and dying yet living, and having nothing yet possessing all things. Such seeming contradictions arise from the want of depth in our minds to master the whole truth. We have not eyes keen enough to follow out the lines of God's providence and will, which meet at length, though at first sight they seem parallel.

(PS 5:47–48, "Shrinking from Christ's Coming")

86. God's Providence

Such is God's rule in Scripture, to dispense His blessings, silently and secretly; so that we do not discern them at the time except by faith, afterwards only. Of which, as I have said, we have two special instances in the very outline of the Gospel history; the mission of our Saviour, who was not understood till afterwards to be the Son of God Most High, and the mission of the Holy Ghost, which was still more laden with spiritual benefits, and is still more secret. Flesh and blood could not discern the Son of God, even when He wrought visible miracles; the natural man still less discerns the things of the Spirit of God. . . .

Now consider how parallel this is to what takes place in the providences of daily life. Events happen to us pleasant or painful; we do not know at the time the meaning of them, we do not see God's hand in them. . . . We see nothing. We see not why things come, or whither they tend. . . .

Wonderful providence indeed, which is so silent, yet so efficacious, so constant, so unerring! This is what baffles the power of Satan. He cannot discern the Hand of God in what goes on; and though he would fain meet it and encounter it, in his mad and blasphemous rebellion against heaven, he cannot find it. Crafty and penetrating as he is, yet his thousand eyes and his many instruments avail him nothing against the majestic serene silence, the holy imperturbable calm which reigns through the providences of God. Crafty and experienced as he is, he appears like a child or a fool, like one made sport of, whose daily bread is but failure and mockery, before the deep and secret wisdom of the Divine Counsels. He makes a guess here, or does a bold act there, but all in the dark. He knew not of Gabriel's coming, and the miraculous conception of the Virgin, or what was meant by that Holy Thing which was to be born, being called the son of God. He tried to kill Him, and he made martyrs of the innocent children; he tempted the Lord of all with hunger and with ambitious prospects; he sifted the Apostles, and got none but one who already bore his own name, and had been already given over as a devil. He rose against his God in his full strength, in the hour and power of darkness, and then he seemed to conquer; but with his utmost effort, and as his greatest achievement, he did no more than "whatsoever Thy hand and Thy counsel determined before to be done." (Acts 4: 28) He brought into the world the very salvation which he feared and hated. He accomplished the Atonement of that world, whose misery He was plotting. Wonderfully silent, yet resistless course of God's providence! . . . [A]nd if even devils, sagacious as they are, spirits by nature and experienced in evil, cannot detect His hand, while He works, how can we hope to see it except by that way which the devils cannot take, by a loving faith? how can we see it except afterwards as a reward to our faith, beholding the cloud of glory in the distance, which when present was too rare and impalpable for mortal sense?

And so, again, in a number of other occurrences, not striking, not grievous, not pleasant, but ordinary, we are able afterwards to discern that He has been with us, and, like Moses, to worship Him. Let a person who trusts he is on the whole serving God acceptably, look back upon his past life, and he will find how critical were moments and acts, which at the time seemed the most indifferent: as for instance, the school he was sent to as a child, the occasion of his falling in with those persons who have most benefited him, the accidents which determined his calling or prospects whatever they were. God's hand is ever over His own, and He leads them forward by a way they know not of. The utmost they can do is to believe, what they cannot see now, why they shall see hereafter; and as believing, to act together with God towards it.

. . . Let us profit by what every day and hour teaches us, as it flies. What is dark while it is meeting us, reflects the Sun of Righteousness when it is past. Let us profit by this in future, so far as this, to have *faith in what* we cannot see. The world seems to go on as usual. There is nothing of heaven in the face of society; in the news of the day there is nothing of heaven; in the faces of the many, or of the great, or of the rich, or of the busy there is nothing of heaven; in the words of the eloquent, or the deeds of the powerful, or the counsels of the wise, or the resolves of the lordly, or the pomps of the wealthy, there is nothing of heaven. And yet the Ever-blessed Spirit of God is here the Presence of the Eternal Son, ten times more glorious, more powerful than when He trod the earth in our flesh, is with us. Let us ever bear in mind this divine truth—the more secret God's hand is, the more powerful—the more silent, the more awful. . . . If He could work miracles in the days of His flesh, how much more can He work miracles now? And if His visible miracles were full of power, how much more His miracles invisible? Let us beg of Him grace wherewith to enter into the depth of our privileges, to enjoy what we possess, to believe in, to use, to improve, to glory in our present gifts as "members of Christ, children of God, and inheritors of the kingdom of heaven."

(PS 4:257–61, 365–66, "Christ Manifested in Remembrance")

87. The Deposit of Faith

[O]pen the Missal, read the minute directions given for the celebration of Mass—what are the fit dispositions under which the Priest prepares for it, how he is to arrange his every action, movement, gesture, utterance, during the course of it, and what is to be done in case of a variety of supposable accidents. What a mockery would all this be, if the rite meant nothing! But if it be a fact that God the Son is there offered up in human flesh and blood by the hands of man, why, it is plain that no rite whatever, however anxious and elaborate, is equal to the depth of the overwhelming thoughts which are borne in upon the mind by such an action. Thus the usages and ordinances of the Church do not exist for their own sake; they do not stand of themselves; they are not sufficient for themselves; they do not fight against the State their own battle; they are not appointed as ultimate ends; but they are dependent on an inward substance; they protect a mystery; they defend a dogma; they represent an idea; they preach good tidings; they are the channels of grace. They are the outward shape of an inward reality or fact, which no Catholic doubts, which is assumed as a first principle, which is not an inference of reason, but the object of a spiritual sense.

Herein is the strength of the Church. . . . She professes to be built upon facts, not opinions; on objective truths, not on variable sentiments; on immemorial testimony, not on private judgement;

on convictions or perceptions, not on conclusions. None else but she can make this profession. She makes high claims against the temporal power, but she has that within her which justifies her. She merely acts out what she says she is. She does no more than she reasonably should do. . . . She is the organ and oracle, and nothing else, of a supernatural doctrine, which is independent of individuals, given to her once for all, coming down from the first ages, and so deeply and intimately embosomed in her, that it cannot be clean torn out of her, even if you should try; which gradually and majestically comes forth into dogmatic shape, as time goes on and need requires, still by no private judgement, but at the will of its Giver, and by the infallible elaboration of the whole body—and which is simply necessary for the salvation of every one of us. It is not a philosophy, of literature, cognisable and attainable at once by those who cast their eyes that way; but it is a sacred deposit and tradition, a mystery or secret, as Scripture calls it, sufficient to arrest and occupy the whole intellect, and unlike anything else; and hence requiring, from the nature of the case, organs special to itself, made for the purpose, whether for entering into its fulness, or carrying it out in deed.

(Diff. 1:215–18, "The Movement Not in the Direction of a Sect")

88. The Mass *

"I declare . . . to me nothing is so consoling, so piercing, so thrilling, so overcoming, as the Mass, said as it is among us. I could attend Masses forever and not be tired. It is not a mere form of words—it is a great action, the greatest action that can be on earth. It is, not the invocation merely, but, if I dare use the word, the evocation of the Eternal. He becomes present on the altar in flesh and blood, before whom angels bow and devils tremble. This is that awful event which is the scope, and is the interpretation, of every part of the solemnity. Words are necessary, but as means, not as ends; they are not mere addresses to the throne of grace, they are instruments of what is far higher, of consecration, of sac-

---

* In Newman's novel *Loss and Gain*, Willis, a convert, describes the Mass.

rifice. They hurry on as if impatient to fulfil their mission. Quickly they go, the whole is quick; for they are all parts of one integral action. Quickly they go; for they are awful words of sacrifice, they are a work too great to delay upon; as when it was said in the beginning: 'What thou does, do quickly'. Quickly they pass; for the Lord Jesus goes with them, as He passed along the lake in the days of His flesh, quickly calling first one and then another. Quickly they pass; because as the lightning which shineth from one part of heaven unto the other, so is the coming of the Son of Man. Quickly they pass; for they are as the words of Moses, when the Lord came down in the cloud, calling on the Name of the Lord as He passed by, 'the Lord, the Lord God, merciful and gracious, long-suffering, and abundant in goodness and truth'. And as Moses on the mountain, so we too 'make haste and bow our heads to the earth, and adore'. So we, all around, each in his place, look out for the great Advent, 'waiting for the moving of the water'. Each in his place, with his own heart, with his own wants, with his own thoughts, with his own intention, with his own prayers, separate but concordant, watching what is going on, watching its progress, uniting in its consummation—not painfully and hopelessly following a hard form of prayer from beginning to end, but, like a concert of musical instruments, each different, but concurring in a sweet harmony, we take our part with God's priest, supporting him, yet guided by him. There are little children there, and old men, and simple labourers, and students in seminaries, priests preparing for Mass, priests making their thanksgiving; there are innocent maidens, and there are penitent sinners; but out of these many minds rises one eucharistic hymn, and the great Action is the measure and scope of it. . . .

(LG, 327–29)

89. Time and Eternity

[W]hen we contemplate human life in itself, in however small a portion of it, we see implied in it the presence of a soul, the energy of a spiritual existence, of an accountable being; consciousness tells us this concerning it every moment. But when we look back on it in memory, we view it but externally, as a mere lapse of time, as a mere earthly history. And the longest duration of this external world is as dust and weighs nothing, against one moment's life of the world within. Thus we are ever expecting great things from life, from our internal consciousness every moment of our having souls; and we are ever being disappointed, on considering what we have gained from time past, or can hope from time to come. And life is ever promising and never fulfilling; and hence, however long it be, our days are few and evil. . . .

Our earthly life then gives promise of what it does not accomplish. It promises immortality, yet it is mortal; it contains life in death and eternity in time; and it attracts us by beginnings which faith alone brings to an end. I mean, when we take into account the powers with which our souls are gifted as Christians, the very consciousness of these fills us with a certainty that they must last beyond this life; that is in the case of good and holy men, whose present state I say, is to them who know them well, an earnest of immortality. The greatness of their gifts, contrasted with their scanty time for exercising them, forces the mind forward to the thought of another life, as almost the necessary counterpart and consequence of this life, and certainly implied in this life, provided there be a righteous Governor of the world who does not make man for nought.

Such being the unprofitableness of this life, viewed in itself, it is plain how we should regard it while we go through it. We should remember that it is scarcely more than an accident of our being— that it is no part of ourselves, who are immortal; that we are immortal spirits, independent of time and space, and that this life is but a sort of outward stage, on which we act for a time, and which is only sufficient and only intended to answer the purpose of trying whether we will serve God or no. We should consider ourselves to be in this world in no fuller sense than players in any game are in the game; and life to be a sort of dream, as detached and as different from our real eternal existence, as a dream differs from waking; a serious dream, indeed, as affording a means of judging us, yet in itself a kind of shadow without substance, a scene set before us, in which we seem to be, and in which it is our duty to act just as if all we saw had a truth and reality, because all that meets us influences us and our destiny. The regenerate soul is taken into communion with Saints and angels, and its "life is hid with Christ in God;" (Col 3: 3) it has a place in God's court, and is not of this world. . . .

Let us then thus account of our present state: it is precious as revealing to us, amid shadows and figures, the existence and attributes of Almighty God and His elect people: it is precious, because it enables us to hold intercourse with immortal souls who are on their trial as we are. It is momentous, as being the scene and means of our trial; but beyond this it has no claims upon us. "Vanity of vanities, says the Preacher, all is vanity." We may be poor or rich, young or old, honoured or slighted, and it ought to affect us no more, neither to elate us nor depress us, than if we were actors in a play, who know that the characters they represent are not their own, and that though they may appear to be superior one to another, to be kings or to be peasants, they are in reality all on a level. The one desire which should move us should be, first of all, that of seeing Him face to face, who is now hid from us; and next of enjoying eternal and direct communion, in and through Him, with our friends around us, whom at present we know only through the medium of sense, by precarious and partial channels, which give us little insight into their hearts.

These are suitable feelings towards this attractive but deceitful world. What have we to do with its gifts and honours, who, having been already baptized into the world to come, are no longer citizens of this? Why should we be anxious for a long life, or wealth, or credit, or comfort, who know that the next world will be everything which our hearts can wish, and that not in appearance only, but truly and everlastingly? Why should we rest in this world, when it is the token and promise of another? Why should we be content with its surface, instead of appropriating what is stored beneath it? To those who live by faith, every thing they see speaks of that future world; the very glories of nature, the sun, moon, and stars, and the richness and the beauty of the earth, are as types and figures witnessing and teaching the invisible things of God. All that we see is destined one day to burst forth into a heavenly bloom, and to be transfigured into immortal glory. Heaven at present is out of sight, but in due time, as snow melts and discovers what it lay upon, so will this visible creation fade away before those greater splendours which are behind it, and on which at present it depends. In that day shadows will retire, and the substance show itself. The sun will grow pale and be lost in the sky, but it will be before the radiance of Him whom it does but image, the Sun of Righteousness, with healing on His wings, who will come forth in visible form, as a bridegroom out of his chamber, while His perishable type decays. The stars which surround it will be replaced by Saints and Angels circling His throne. Above and below, the clouds of the air, the trees of the field, the waters of the great deep will be found impregnated with the forms of everlasting spirits, the servants of God which do His pleasure. And our own mortal bodies will then be found in like manner to contain within them an inner man, which will then receive its due proportions, as the soul's harmonious organ, instead of that gross mass of flesh and blood which sight and touch are sensible of. For this glorious manifestation the whole creation is at present in travail, earnestly desiring that it may be accomplished in its season.

These are thoughts to make us eagerly and devoutly say, "Come, Lord Jesus, to end the time of waiting, of darkness, of turbulence, of disputing, of sorrow, of care." These are thoughts to lead us to rejoice in every day and hour that passes, as bringing us nearer the time of His appearing, and the termination of sin and misery. They are thoughts which ought thus to affect us; and so they would, were it not for the load of guilt which weighs upon us, for sins committed against light and grace. O that it were otherwise with us! O that we were fitted duly to receive this lesson which the world gives us, and had so improved the gifts of life, that while we felt it to be perishing, we might rejoice in it as precious! . . .

(PS 4:215–16, 221–25, "The Greatness and Littleness of Human Life")

90. Devotion to Saints

Whence is this devotion to St. John Chrysostom, which leads me to dwell upon the thought of him, and makes me kindle at his name, when so many other great Saints, as the year brings round their festivals, command indeed my veneration, but exert no personal claim upon my heart? Many holy men have died in exile, many holy men have been successful preachers; and what more can we write upon St. Chrysostom's monument than this, that he was eloquent and that he suffered persecution? He is not an Athanasius, expounding a sacred dogma with a luminousness which is almost an inspiration; nor is he Athanasius, again, in his romantic lifelong adventures, in his sublime solitariness, in his ascendency over all classes of men, in his series of triumphs over material force and civil tyranny. Nor, except by the contrast, does he remind us of that Ambrose who kept his ground obstinately in an imperial city, and fortified himself against the heresy of a court by the living rampart of a devoted population. Nor is he Gregory or Basil, rich in the literature and philosophy of Greece, and embellishing the Church with the spoils of heathenism. Again, he is not an Augustine, devoting long years to one masterpiece of thought, and laying, in successive controversies, the foundations of theology. Nor is he a Jerome, so dead to the world that he can imitate the point and wit of its writers without danger to himself or scandal to his brethren. He has not trampled upon heresy, nor smitten emperors, nor beautified the house or the service of God, nor knit together the portions of Christendom, nor founded a religious order, nor built up the framework of doctrine, nor expounded the science of the Saints; yet I love him, as I love David or St. Paul.

I consider St. Chrysostom's charm to lie in his intimate sympathy and compassionateness for the whole world, not only in its strength, but in its weakness; in the lively regard with which he views everything that comes before him, taken in the concrete, whether as made after its own kind or as gifted with a nature higher than its own. . . . [W]hat he had special to himself; and this specialty, I conceive, is the interest which he takes in all things, not so far as God has made them alike, but as He has made them different from each other. I speak of the discriminating affectionateness with which he accepts every one for what is personal in him and unlike others. I speak of his versatile recognition of men, one by one, for the sake of that portion of good, be it more or less, of a lower order or a higher, which has severally been lodged in them; his eager contemplation of the many things they do, effect, or produce, of all their great works, as nations or as states. . . . I speak of the kindly spirit and the genial temper with which he looks round at all things which this wonderful world contains; of the graphic fidelity with which he notes them down upon the tablets of his mind, and of the promptitude and propriety with which he calls them up as arguments or illustrations in the course of his teaching as the occasion requires. Possessed though he be by the fire of divine charity, he has not lost one fibre, he does not miss one vibration, of the complicated whole of human sentiment and affection; like the miraculous bush in the desert, which, for all the flame that wrapt it round, was not thereby consumed.

. . . In him I recognize a special pattern of that very gift of discrimination. He may indeed be said in some sense to have a devotion of his own for every one who comes across him, for persons, ranks, classes, callings, societies, considered as divine works and the subjects of his good offices or good will, and therefore I have a devotion for him.

(HS 2:284–88, "The Death")

91. The End Time

[I]t is not unprofitable to bear in mind that we are still under what may be called a miraculous system. I do not mean to maintain that literal miracles are taking place now every day, but that our present state is a portion of a providential course, which began in miracle, and, at least at the end of the world, if not before, will end in miracle. The particular expectations above detailed may be right or wrong; yet an Antichrist, whoever and whatever he be, is to come; marvels are to come; the old Roman Empire is not extinct; Satan, if bound, is bound but for a season; the contest of good and evil is not ended. I repeat it, in the present state of things, when the great object of education is supposed to be the getting rid of things supernatural, when we are bid to laugh and jeer at believing everything we do not see, are told to account for everything by things known and ascertained, and to assay every statement by the touchstone of experience, I must think that this vision of Antichrist, as a supernatural power to come, is a great providential gain, as being a counterpoise to the evil tendencies of the age.

And next, it must surely be profitable for our thoughts to be sent backward and forward to the beginning and the end of the Gospel times, to the first and the second coming of Christ. What we want, is to understand that we are in the place in which the early Christians were, with the same covenant, ministry, sacraments, and duties—to realize a state of things long past away; to feel that we are in a sinful world, a world lying in wickedness; to discern our position in it, that we are witnesses in it, that reproach and suffering are our portion, so that we must not "think it strange" if they come upon us, but a kind of gracious exception if they do not; to have our hearts awake, as if we had seen Christ and His Apostles, and seen their miracles, awake to the hope and waiting of His second coming, looking out for it, nay, desiring to see the tokens of it; thinking often and much of the judgement to come, dwelling on and adequately entering into the thought, that we individually shall be judged. All these surely are acts of true and saving faith; and this is one substantial use of the Book of Revelation, and other prophetical parts of Scripture, quite distinct from our knowing their real interpretation, viz., to take the veil from our eyes, to lift up the covering which lies over the face of the world, and make us see day by day, as we go in and out, as we get up and lie down, as we labour, and walk, and rest, and recreate ourselves, the Throne of God set up in the midst of us, His majesty and His judgements, His Son's continual intercession for the elect, their trials, and their victory. . . .

We are warned against sharing in her sins and in her punishment, against being found, when the end comes, mere children of this world and of its great cities; with tastes, opinions, habits, such as are found in its cities; with a heart dependent on human society, and a reason moulded by it; against finding ourselves at the last day before our Judge, with all the low feelings, principles, and aims which the world encourages; with our thoughts wandering (if that be possible then), wandering after vanities; with thoughts which rise no higher than the consideration of our own comforts,

or our gains; with a haughty contempt for the Church, her ministers, her lowly people; a love of rank and station, an admiration of
the splendour and the fashions of the world, an affectation of refinement, a dependence upon our powers of reason, an habitual
self-esteem, and an utter ignorance of the number and the hei-
nousness of the sins which lie against us. If we are found thus,
when the end comes, where, when the judgement is over, and the
saints have gone up to heaven, and there is silence and darkness
where all was so full of life and expectation, where shall we find
ourselves then? And what good could the great Babylon do us
then, though it were as immortal as we are immortal ourselves?

(DA 75–76, 92, "The Patristical Idea of Antichrist")

92. The Unseen

[W]e are, in all times of the Gospel, brought close to His Cross.
We stand, as it were, under it, and receive its blessings fresh from
it; only that since, historically speaking, time has gone on, and the
Holy One is away, certain outward forms are necessary, by way of
bringing us again under His shadow; and we enjoy those blessings
through a mystery, or sacramentally, in order to enjoy them really. All this witnesses to the duty both of remembering and of
looking out for Christ, teaching us to neglect the present, to rely
on no plans, to form no expectations, for the future, but so to live
in faith, as if He had not left us, so in hope, as if He had returned
to us. We must try to live as if the Apostles were living, and we
must try to muse upon our Lord's life in the gospels, not as a
history, but as if a recollection. . . .

. . . Always since the first, Christians have been looking out for
the Christ *in* the signs of the natural and moral world. If they have
been poor and uneducated, strange sights in the sky, or tremblings
of the ground, storms, failure of harvest, or disease, or any thing
monstrous and unnatural, has made them think that He was at
hand. If they were in a way to take a view of the social and political
world, then the troubles of states—wars, revolutions, and the
like,—have been additional circumstances which served to impress them, and kept their hearts awake for Christ. . . . We may be

wrong in the particulars we rest upon, and may show our ignorance in doing so; but there is nothing ridiculous or contemptible in our ignorance, and there is much that is religious in our watching. It is better to be wrong in our watching, than not to watch at all. . . .

. . . How then, it may be asked, can this world have upon it tokens of His presence, or bring us near to Him? Yet certainly so it is, that in spite of the world's evil, after all, He is in it and speaks through it, though not loudly. When He came in the flesh "He was in the world, and world was made by Him, and the world knew Him not." Nor did He strive nor cry, nor lift up His voice in the streets. So it is now. He still is here; He still whispers to us, He still makes signs to us. But His voice is so low, and the world's din is so loud, and His signs are so covert, and world is so restless, that it is difficult to determine when He addresses us, and what He says. Religious men cannot but feel, in various ways, that His providence is guiding them and blessing them personally, on the whole; yet when they attempt to put their finger upon the times and places, the traces of His presence disappear. . . . All this being so, and the vastness and mystery of the world being borne in upon us, we may well begin to think that there is nothing here below, but, for what we know has a connection with every thing else; the most distant events may yet be united, the meanest and highest may be parts of one; and God may be teaching us and offering us knowledge of His ways, if we will but open our eyes, in all the ordinary matters of the day. This is what thoughtful persons come to believe, and they begin to have a sort of faith in the Divine meaning of the accidents (as they are called) of life, and a readiness to take impressions from them, which may easily become excessive, and which, whether excessive or not, is sure to be ridiculed by the world at large as superstition. Yet, considering Scripture tells us that the very hairs of our head are all numbered by God, that all things are ours, and that all things work together for our good, it does certainly encourage us in thus looking out for His presence in every thing that happens, however trivial, and in holding that to religious ears even the bad world prophesies of Him.

. . . God does not so speak to us through the occurrences of life, that you can persuade others that He speaks. He does not act upon such explicit laws, that you can speak of them with certainty. He gives us sufficient tokens of Himself to raise our minds in awe towards Him; but He seems so frequently to undo what He has done, and to suffer counterfeits of His tokens, that a conviction of His wonder-working presence can but exist in the individual himself. It is not a truth that can be taught and recognized in the face of men; it is not of a nature to be urged upon the world at large, nay, even on religious persons, as a principle. God gives us enough to make us inquire and hope; not enough to make us insist and argue.

And if [the Christian] looks out into the world to seek, it is not to seek what he does not know, but what he does. He does not seek a Lord and Saviour. He has "found the Messias" long since; and he is looking out for *Him*. His Lord Himself has *bid* him look for Him in the signs of the world, and therefore he looks out. His Lord Himself has shown him, in the Old Testament, how He, the Lord of Glory, condescends to humble Himself to the things of heaven and earth. He knows that God's Angels are about the earth. He knows that once they were even used to come in human shape. He knows that the Son of God, ere now, has come on earth. He knows that He promised to His Church the presence of a miraculous agency, and has never recalled His promise. Again, he reads, in the Book of the Revelation, quite enough, not to show him what is coming, but to show him that now, as heretofore, a secret supernatural system is going on *under* this visible scene. And therefore he looks out for Christ, for His present providences, and for His coming; and though often deceived in his expectation, and fancying wonderful things are coming on the earth, when they still delay, he uses, and comforts him with the Prophet's words, "I will stand upon my watch, and set me upon the tower, and will watch to see what He will say unto me. . . ."

(PS 6:242–43, 245–46, 248–50, 253–54, "Waiting for Christ")

93. The Kingdom of God

Now, let this be observed. Persons commonly speak as if the other world did not exist now, but would after death. No: it exists now, though we see it not. It is among us and around us. Jacob was shown this in his dream. Angels were all about him, though he knew it not. And what Jacob saw in his sleep, that Elisha's servant saw as if with his eyes; and the shepherds, at the time of the Nativity, not only saw, but heard. They heard the voices of those blessed spirits who praise God day and night, and whom we, in our lower state of being, are allowed to copy and assist.

We are then in a world of spirits, as well as in a world of sense, and we hold communion with it, and take part in it, though we are not conscious of doing so. . . .

The world of spirits then, though unseen, is present; present, not future, not distant. It is not above the sky, it is not beyond the grave; it is now and here; the kingdom of God is among us. Of this the text speaks; "We look," says St. Paul, "not at the things which are seen, but at the things which are not seen; for the things which are seen are temporal, but the things which are not seen are eternal." You see he regarded it as a practical truth, which was to influence our conduct. Not only does he speak of the world invisible, but of the duty of "looking at" it; not only does he contrast the things of time with it, but says that their belonging to time is a reason, not for looking at, but for looking off them. Eternity was not distant because it reached to the future; nor the unseen state without its influence on us, because it was impalpable. . . .

Such is the hidden kingdom of God; and, as it is now hiding, so in due season it shall be revealed. Men think that they are lords of the world, and may do as they will. They think this earth their property, and its movements in their power; whereas it has other lords besides them, and is the scene of a higher conflict than they are capable of conceiving. It contains Christ's little ones whom they despise, and His Angels whom they disbelieve; and these at length shall take possession of it and be manifested. . . .

. . . The earth that we see does not satisfy us; it is but a beginning; it is but a promise of something beyond it; even when it is gayest, with all its blossoms on, and shows most touchingly what lies hid in it, yet it is not enough. We know much more lies hid in it than we see. A world of Saints and Angels, a glorious world, the palace of God, the mountain of the Lord of Hosts, the heavenly Jerusalem, the throne of God and Christ, all these wonders, everlasting, all-precious, mysterious, and incomprehensible, lie hid in what we see. What we see is the outward shell of an eternal kingdom; and on that kingdom we fix the eyes of our faith. . . . Bright as is the sun, and the sky, and the clouds; green as are the leaves and the fields; sweet as is the singing of the birds; we know that they are not all, and we will not take up with a part for the whole. They proceed from a centre of love and goodness, which is God himself; but they are not His fulness; they speak of heaven, but they are not heaven; they are but as stray beams and dim reflections of His Image; they are but crumbs from the table. We are looking for the coming of the day of God, when all this outward world, fair though it be, shall perish; when the heavens shall be burnt, and the earth melt away. We can bear the loss, for we know it will be but the removing of a veil. We know that to remove the world which is seen, will be the manifestation of the world which is not seen. We know that what we see is as a screen hiding from us God and Christ, and His Saints and Angels. And we earnestly desire and pray for the dissolution of all that we see, from our longing after that which we do not see.

(PS 6:205, 207–08, 210–11, "The Invisible World")

94. Divine Dispensations

[A]ll God's dealings with His creatures have two aspects, one external, one internal. What one of the earliest Fathers says of its highest ordinance, is true of it altogether, and of all other divine dispensations: they are twofold, "having one part heavenly, and one part earthly." This is the law of Providence here below; it works beneath a veil, and what is visible in its course does but shadow out at most, and sometimes obscures and disguises what is invisible. The world in which we are placed has its own system of laws and principles, which, as far as our knowledge of it goes, is, when once set in motion, sufficient to account for itself,—as complete and independent as if there was nothing beyond it. Ordinarily speaking, nothing happens, nothing goes on in the world, but may be satisfactorily traced to some other event or fact in it, or has a sufficient result in other events or facts in it, without the necessity of our following it into a higher system of things in order to explain its existence, or to give it a meaning. . . . Men grow to maturity, then decay, and die. Moreover, they form into society, and society has its principles. Nations move forward by laws which act as a kind of destiny over them and which are as vigorous now as a thousand years ago. And these laws of the social and political world run into the physical, making all that is seen one and one only system; a horse stumbles, and an oppressed people is rid of their tyrant; a volcano changes populous cities into a dull lake; a gorge has of old time opened, and the river rolls on, bearing on its bosom the destined site of some great mart, which else had never been. We cannot set limits either to the extent or to the minuteness of this wonderful web of causes and effects, in which all we see is involved. It reaches to the skies; it penetrates into our very thoughts, habits, and will.

Such is confessedly the world in which our Almighty Creator has placed us. If then He is still actively present with His own work, present with nations and with individuals, He must be acting by means of its ordinary system, or by quickening, or as it were, stimulating its powers, or by superseding or interrupting it; in other words, by means of what is called nature, or by miracle. . . . He is acting through, with, and beneath those physical, social, and moral laws, of which our experience informs us. Now it has ever been a firm article of Christian faith, that His Providence is in fact not general merely, but is, on the contrary, thus particular and personal; and that, as there is a particular Providence, so of necessity that Providence is secretly concurring and cooperating with that system which meets the eye, and which is commonly recognized among men as existing. It is not too much to say that this is the one great rule on which the Divine Dispensations with mankind have been and are conducted, that the visible world is the instrument, yet the veil, of the world invisible—the veil, yet still partially the symbol and index, so that all that exists or happens visibly, conceals and yet suggests, and above all subserves, a system of persons, facts, and events beyond itself.

Thus the course of things has a natural termination as well as a natural origin: it tends towards final causes while it springs from physical; it is ever issuing from things which we see round about us; it is ever passing on into what is matter of faith, not of sight. What is called and seems to be cause and effect is rather an order of sequence, and does not preclude, nay, perhaps implies, the presence of unseen spiritual agency as its real author. This is the animating principle both of the Church's ritual and of Scripture interpretation; in the latter it is the basis of the theory of the double sense; in the former it makes ceremonies and observances to be signs, seals, means, and pledges of supernatural grace. It is the mystical principle in the one, it is the sacramental in the other. All that is seen—the world, the Bible, the Church, the civil polity, and man himself, are types, and, in their degree and place, representatives and organs of an unseen world, truer and higher than themselves. The only difference between them is that some things bear their supernatural character upon their surface, are historically creations of the supernatural system, or are perceptibly instrumental, or obviously symbolical: while others rather seem to be complete in themselves, or run counter to the unseen system which they really subserve, and thereby make demands upon our faith.

. . . When Providence would make a Revelation, He does not begin anew, but uses the existing system; He does not visibly send an Angel, but He commissions or inspires one of our own fellows. When He would bless us, He makes a man His priest. When He would consecrate or quicken us, He takes the elements of this world as the means of real but unseen spiritual influences. When He would set up a divine polity, He takes a polity which already is, or one in course of forming. Nor does He interfere with its natural growth, development, or dependence on things visible. He does not shut it up in a desert, and there supply it with institutions unlike those which might naturally come to it from the contact and intercourse of the external world. He does but modify, quicken, or direct the powers of nature or the laws of society. Or if He works miracles, still it is without superseding the ordinary course of things. He multiplies the flocks or the descendants of Jacob, or in due season He may work signal or public miracles for their deliverance from Egypt; but still the operation of ordinary causes, the influence of political arrangements, and what is called the march of events, are seen in such providences as truly, and can be pointed out as convincingly, as if an Angel and a pillar of a cloud were not with them.

Thus the great characteristic of Revelation is addition, substitution. Things look the same as before, though not an invisible power has taken hold upon them. This power does not unclothe the creature, but clothes it. Men dream everywhere: it gives visions. Men journey everywhere: it sends "the Angels of God to meet them." Men may elsewhere be hospitable to their brethren: now they entertain Angels. Men carry on a work; but it is a blessing from some ancestor that is breathing on and through it unseen. A nation migrates and seizes on a country; but all along its proceedings are hallowed by prophecy, and promise, and providence beforehand, and used for religious ends afterwards. . . .

(Ess. 2:190–95, "Milman's View of Christianity")

INDEX

Christian life *(cont.)*
  Christ and, 76–82
  conscience and, 59–60
  Divine Law and, 82–84
  earthly goods and, 74–76
  faith and, 12, 41
  fasting and feasting and, 91–92
  fear and love and, 69–70
  God's gift and, 47–49
  Gospel and, 67–68
  gradual awakening and, 51–53
  happiness and, 54–56
  holiness and, 12, 14–15
  love and, 101–4
  obedience and, 96–97, 99–101
  prayer and, 46, 57–59, 65–66, 78–79, 97–98
  private judgment and, 84–86
  Scripture and, 45–47
  self-examination and, 99–101
  self-surrender and, 63–65
  serving God in youth and, 47–48
  sin and, 60–61
  suffering and, 86–88
  temper and, 92–94
  union of high and low and, 56–57
  virtue and, 94–96
Christians, true vs. professing, 61–63
Church. *See* Catholic Church
Church Fathers, 15, 20
Church Invisible, 162–63
Clement, St., 14
conscience
  Christian life and, 59–60
  following of, 19
  of man, 129
  obedience to, 43
  religion of world and, 136, 138
consolation, 126–27
contemplation, 56–57
continual prayer, 57–59, 148
conversion, continual, 17–18, 32–34
Creed
  Holy Trinity and, 30
  truth and, 29

Cross of Christ
  Christianity and, 25–26
  Christian life and, 80–82
  faith and, 24–26
  Gospel and, 26
  religion and, 25
  suffering and, 50
  See also Christian life

David, 36, 85, 175
death, 72–74
Devil. *See* Satan
devotion
  doubt and, 147–48
  intellect and, 70
  to saints, 174–76
Dives, 50
divine calls
  duties of, 43–44
  faith and, 37–39
  temptation and, 39
Divine Law
  Christian life and, 82–84
  conscience and, 59–60
Divine Ordinance, 161–62
Divine Voice, faith and, 23–24
doubt
  deferred rewards and, 151–54
  devotion and intellect and, 147–48
  Enlightenment and, 12
  faith and, 148–51
  hidden God and, 143–44
  Holy Spirit and, 158–60
  knowledge and, 144–47
  prayer and, 148
  religion and, 156–58
  Scripture and, 154–56

Easter, 89, 91
education, 11, 18, 44
Egypt, 184
Eli, 102
Elijah, 81
Elisha, 37, 181
English Oratorian Movement, 14

Nicene Creed, 153

obedience
  Christian life and, 96–97, 99–101
  to conscience, 43
  faith and, 96–97
  Scripture and, 57–58
  truth and, 29
Oriel College, 13, 15
Oxford Movement, 11, 13
Oxford University, Newman at, 12–13
Oxford University Sermons (Newman), 17, 18, 20

Parochial and Plain Sermons (Newman), 11, 12, 17, 19–20
Paul, St., 121
  call of, 38, 82
  Christianity and, 144–45
  Christian temper and, 93
  conformity to Christ and, 108
  devotion to saints and, 175
  doubt and, 149, 151
  kingdom of God and, 181
  reason and, 141
  Resurrection and, 52
  simplicity and, 140
  virtue and, 95
  doubt and, 151
  love and faith and, 104
penitence. *See* repentance
Pentecost, 67, 131
Peter, St., 37, 47, 67, 82, 99, 149
Pharisees, 62–63, 72, 108, 129–30
Pontius Pilate, 97, 108
prayer
  Christianity and, 66
  Christian life and, 46, 57–59, 65–66, 78–79, 97–98
  continual, 57–59
  doubt and, 148
  faith and, 28
  Holy Spirit and, 58
  intercession and, 65–66

religion and, 66
  truth and, 29
private judgment
  Christian life and, 84–86
  faith and, 23–24
  religion and, 18
Prophets, 44
Providence, 53, 167–69, 181–85
Psalms, 66
Pusey, E. B., 13

reason
  faith and, 18, 19
  highest, 29
  inventions of, 140–41
  mysteries and, 32
Redemption, 12, 95
religion
  beauty and severity and, 18, 88
  cheerfulness and, 18, 88–89
  continual conversion and, 32
  Cross of Christ and, 25
  faith and, 102
  freedom and, 70
  grace and, 30
  individuals and, 18
  knowledge and, 114–15
  love and, 76
  mysteries in, 156–58, 164–65
  of natural man, 129–30
  prayer and, 66
  private judgment and, 18
  self-knowledge and, 109–10
  work and, 14–15
  of the world, 18, 135–38
repentance
  God's law and, 65
  love and, 86, 116–17
  self-surrender and, 64
Revelation, 29, 60, 177, 180, 184–85
reverence, 27–28
Romanticism, 12
Ruskin, John, 12

sacramentalism, 13

JOHN HENRY NEWMAN

John Henry Newman was born in 1801, the son of a London banker, and was educated at Ealing School and at Trinity College, Oxford. Elected Fellow at Oriel College in 1822, he became vicar of the university church of St. Mary's in 1828, where he preached and lectured until 1843. In 1833, he began *Tracts for the Times* and became leader of the Oxford Movement. After publishing his controversial *Tract 90* in 1841, which interpreted the Anglican Thirty-nine Articles in a Catholic sense, he retired from Oxford to the nearby village of Littlemore in 1842. His *Essay on the Development of Christian Doctrine*, never completed, moved him closer to conversion. He was received into the Roman Catholic Church in 1845. Ordained a priest in 1847, he founded the Birmingham Oratory in 1848, his home for the rest of his life. He founded the Catholic University of Ireland and was its rector from 1851 to 1858. His Dublin lectures were published as *Idea of a University*. His autobiography, *Apologia pro Vita Sua*, published in 1864, was a response to a public attack by the novelist Charles Kingsley. In 1870, he completed his philosophical treatise on faith, *An Essay in Aid of a Grammar of Assent*. Created a cardinal in 1879 by Pope Leo XIII, he died in 1890. In 1991, he was declared "venerable."

ACKNOWLEDGMENTS

I would like to thank my wife for all the support and love during so many difficult times. My pets for all the snuggles and unconditional love. My family: mother, father, brothers and extended family, including my Sardinian "daughter." My chosen family that keeps me grounded in Dallas, my soul family in Austin that helped me to shift in my heart and my global family in the keto, paleo, biohacking, supplements, wellness and entrepreneurship world.

My closest business partners. Team Shawn Wells with this book and the Ingredientologist brand...thank you!

My mentors, life team and "soul fam," thank you for taking the time and pouring your energy into me. I am now proud of myself and love myself and that took a lot of work—work that led to this book in your hand.

Most importantly, I appreciate YOU and would like to thank you for reading this right now and taking the first step to a healthier and more energetic life. It takes courage and willingness to do that. I am proud of you.

—Shawn

DEDICATION

This book is dedicated to those who feel lost,
alone, depressed, sick, in pain, hurting, less than, judged,
falling short, overworked, underappreciated...
I SEE YOU. I LOVE YOU. I GOT YOU.

"Passion is energy! Feel the power that comes from focusing on what excites you!"

–Oprah Winfrey

PREFACE

I started writing this book two years before the pandemic, but once that happened, it changed everything. The virus being politicized, confusion over how to protect yourself and scientific misconceptions spread by many "gurus" were creating a lot of fear. Meanwhile, one word kept ringing in my head: resilience.

Resilience is a state of being tougher and "anti-fragile" but more than that, it means living an optimized and fulfilling life. This is an opportunity to heal and make people stronger—physically and mentally. We're living in a new world that will never look the same. So, I went back to my rough draft and started looking through a new lens—that's when the word "energy" became the acronym and took on new meaning. ENERGY: Experimentation, Nutrition, Exercise, Routines, Growth and Your Tribe. It fell into place, as did my heart and mind.

Days later, I got the news that my brother-in-law had passed away in his sleep at the age of 44 from mixed causes, some of which were a long-in-remission cancer and excessive weight. Within 24 hours of that, one of my two brothers (who is in his early 50's) had a massive heart attack and nearly died. At 46, I am between their ages. Life got very real for me over the course of that one day.

Doing Byron Katie style therapy with Kathryn Dixon and stepping outside of my victimization stories so that I could begin reframing my life started a massive shift during this "down time" of the pandemic; I found myself taking further steps to deep inner-work and understanding the journey and consciousness space with Tah and Kole Whitty, as well as friends Keith and Michelle Norris. Then I found it logical to bring body work in step with all of this soul work, so I began working with concierge medicine including biofeedback, biologics, genetics and peptides with Drs. Daniel Stickler and Mickra Hamilton (Apeiron Center for Human Performance). I struck up a give-and-take mentor relationship and friendship with an awesome 'Keto Coach,' Stephanie Foster. The plant medicine journeys I have taken, created profound shifts in my consciousness and warped my progress in ways I could have never imagined. These are things I never allowed myself time for or may have been scared to even face.

Pre-pandemic, I was working 80 hours a week. I was supposed to travel 300 days in 2020. I now realize that although I can't help but be passionate about my work and about helping others so deeply, I need to grant myself more time and space for proper self-care.

The pandemic was the greatest blessing for me because it allowed me to work on me...deeply. It has allowed me to reconnect with what truly matters, to get past pain and escapism and to live my authentic truth. It also led to a full rewrite of this book, which I'm excited about. I hope it connects with you as well.

This is as much your story as it is mine.

TABLE OF CONTENTS

INTRODUCTION

"The difference between one man and another is not mere ability . . . it is energy."

—Thomas Arnold

Everything in life—the relationships we hold dear, our jobs, our passions, even our fears—is fueled by energy. We need it to get out of bed in the morning, we need it to interact with the people we love and we need it at work. In fact, if you ask anyone what they truly need, they will likely reply, "More energy."

The standard definition of energy is the strength and vitality required for sustained physical or mental activity, but the one word that stands out to me in that definition is *sustained*. We are living in a world of short-term gains—online followers, superficial relationships, fleeting fads—and those things did not fade away with the pandemic. In fact, if you look at the boom in TikTok dances or the emerging market for fashionable masks, you could say that trend has only increased. Even so, these fly-by-night trends are not built to last. They are not sustainable—and what makes us human, what connects us to our deepest values and our deepest power, is our ability to see beyond the short term and to sustain.

As I was deciding on the best word to describe my work, I kept coming back to that concept of energy. From my personal life to the biohacks I've offered others as a formulator, dietitian and biochemist, I recognized that more than anything, all my work with the novel ingredients that I have patented and groundbreaking formulas I've conceived has been to help people build and achieve real, sustainable energy.

More and more, that is the one thing we all crave.

We live in an overwhelming world. From the news we consume to the hours we work to the endless to-do lists that keep us unavailable to the people we love, we are over-stressed and over-stimulated. We wake up exhausted and we go to bed exhausted. Often, this fatigue leads to real and chronic issues in our life, including auto-immune conditions, mental health challenges and chronic pain. In response, we try to find short-term comforts to deal with the pain. We medicate through food, prescription drugs, shopping or alcohol, but even more commonly, we medicate through numbing out. We medicate by giving up.

The pandemic of 2020 didn't make any of that easier. Fears, both real and imagined, have threatened us at an accelerated pace unknown to previous generations. Fear of disease. Fear of death. Fear of economic collapse. Fear of depression, addiction and isolation. This has all been added to our already overloaded lives. In some cases, these compound stresses can even evolve into traumas. The bottom line is fear makes us less resilient; it makes us more susceptible and more easily compromised.

It is just like Yoda says: "Fear is the path to the dark side. Fear leads to anger; anger leads to hate; hate leads to suffering."

When we give in to stress and imbalance, we lose whatever motivation we had and fail to generate the energy we need to create the rich, full and beautiful lives we're all meant to lead. Conversely, we can come back to a place of balance and rediscover the inspiration we have long been lacking—the inspiration to build resilience, which my friend Keith Norris describes as "becoming harder to kill." Resilience is a type of toughness or psychological elasticity that is a core component of the growth mindset, and a foundation upon which we can build a seemingly unending supply of energy.

The stress and the burnout many of us experience is understandable. We were not built for this modern life. Most of our busy world—the news on TV, the apps on our phones, the 10 hours a day we spend sitting at our desks—is new to the human experience. For centuries, we used to rise with the sun, move our bodies continuously throughout the day and eat an early and modest dinner with our families before retiring for the night.

Until the last century, this was our daily routine, shared by humans across the world. Now, instead of long meals with our families, we find ourselves driving down the freeway with the radio at full blast, shoveling down fast food and checking email between bites while

honking at the car in front of us. We bury ourselves in our work and then we race home. We squeeze in time with our family between whatever's on TV and the incessant texts and emails on our computers and phones. We lie in bed only to scroll through more news and shop on Amazon before the Ambien kicks in so we can finally sleep. And we wonder why we are exhausted!

We are living in a time of chronic bad news which divides us, scares us and tells us that the world is a terrifying place—and every day it feels harder and harder to get up and face it. I get it. I lived like that for a long time, and the irony of it all was that I was supposed to be one of the "healthy" ones!

The bottom line is fear makes us *less* resilient; it makes us *more* susceptible and more easily compromised.

I have made my career and my name as something of a health and fitness guru. I am a recognized dietitian, sports nutritionist and biochemist. I'm a supplement formulator who has patented more than 10 novel ingredients and been involved in more than 500 different supplements and cosmeceuticals. I work out almost daily, I diet, I fast and I know all about mindset, meditation and other performance-enhancing strategies to get the most out of every waking moment. But what most people did not know about me until very recently are the health problems I've gone through—problems like Epstein-Barr virus, chronic fatigue, fibromyalgia, depression, insomnia, obesity, anorexia and a pituitary tumor. For a long time, I was totally falling apart.

If I have any authority to speak on health, performance and energy, it's not because of my technical qualifications or supplements I've made; it's because I know what's true and what's not in the world of health and fitness, and I know how many of us are being lied to. I know because for a long time, I believed some of the same lies myself.

Formulator's Corner
How to Buy a Good Supplement

Things to look for when searching for a quality supplement that works:

Trusted Brands: I like brands that have stood the test of time, with consumers and third party testing. They have a name that has been built on consistent quality. Brands like NOW, Jarrow, Doctor's Best, Nordic Naturals, Thorne, Life Extension, Pure Encapsulations, Designs for Health and many more (There is a longer list later in the book).

Proprietary Blends: Flat out, I am not a fan of any proprietary blends. The companies behind them might say they are trying to protect their ideas, but in truth this is a way for them to avoid testing costs (it's far more expensive to be fully transparent) as well as raw ingredient costs. Perhaps more importantly, it's also a marketing ploy. An example of just how scammy this can get—imagine a label with 700mg of the "focus blend" and a total of 20 ingredients listed. The ingredients must be put in order of descending mass (i.e., weight) and so legally, they can put 681mg of the first ingredient and 1mg of the other 19 ingredients combined (a practice known as "fairy dusting"). Think you might be getting ripped off there? You're right. This is a way to list a lot of ingredients but have very few of them at any consequential level in terms of effect for you or cost for them. When people say supplements don't work, this is the biggest reason why. Do not buy anything with proprietary blends.

How to Buy a Good Supplement (continuation)

Full Transparency Labeling: You should be able to see the genus and species, part of the plant used, standardization percentage and compound standardized for, as well as its level in the product. For example: Rhodiola Rosea (root) standardized for 3% rosavins and 1% salidroside) at a 500mg dose. With that information, you can do a literature search to confirm if that is an efficacious dose that is backed by research. A great resource for this is Examine.com. They have exhaustive scientific summaries on ingredients.

Kitchen Sink: Watch out for "kitchen sink formulas" which contain too many ingredients. This usually goes hand-in-hand with proprietary blends. A good formula typically has 3-6 ingredients as they should have complementary mechanisms of action at the right dose and in the right forms. It should make sense why each one is in the formula. This is where a professional formulator makes all the difference. Less is definitely more here. Pick the best ingredient with the best data, then pick another ingredient that synergizes with it and so on.

Right Part of the Plant: Certain plants, such as ginseng or rhodiola, are studied for their efficacy from the root. Given that the root would therefore be more expensive, the rest of the plant (whole plant, stem, leaf, or flower) may be discarded or sold at a much cheaper price. Disreputable companies might use these cheaper parts so that it appears the correct herb is present, but it is not the right part nor standardized for the right compound.

Expiration Date: Generally 12 to 24 months after manufacturing is the typical shelf life or "best by" date. Make sure it is not out of date or won't go out of date by the time you use it. By law, companies must do stability testing and put in overages so that a product meets the label claims for the stated shelf-life of the product (both at the time of manufacturing and at 24 months out).

How to Buy a Good Supplement (continuation)

Structure Function Claims: The claims must be based on the entire product, meaning the product needs to have gone through a placebo-controlled, double-blind, trial with healthy individuals. The claims must be based on statistically significant findings from that study and the study must be publicly available. Claims around a single ingredient are valid as long as it is clear they are not referring to the entire formula (e.g. "An active ingredient in X formula has been shown to increase performance by 23% when taken for 8 weeks"). Additionally, be wary of any large number claims, such as "880% more testosterone," as statistics can be manipulated to come up with outlandish numbers. If you see unbelievable claims, don't believe them...and don't buy the product.

Quality Control: By law, you can call a company and get the testing results for a product's manufacturing lot that you have purchased. If they say they don't have that information, they are either hiding something (meaning it didn't test out), they don't have quality control testing at all (that's a problem) or they keep very poor records/document control. All of these would be huge issues with the FDA and it should be a big red flag for you if they cannot quickly provide you these answers.

Little Things: Good packaging that keeps light out, a good seal to keep air out, a desiccant packet or barrel to keep air down even after opening, cotton to keep the capsules from bouncing around, etc. These things add cost, but attention to detail matters; they can help you discern the companies that care from those that don't.

After everything I've been through, I've learned that it's not one biohack or one magic bullet ingredient that can change our lives and boost our energy. Those elements do play a role and can help us get those final percentage points of improvement, but real energy is much more foundational—and it has as much to do with our psychology and our spirit as it does with our supplements.

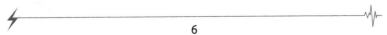

The human body is amazing, and we don't always have the perspective to understand the lessons it teaches us. It will tell us when we've run out of gas by stalling us on the side of the road whether we like it or not; the issue comes when we interpret that as just needing to add a new chemical compound to our morning routine. Sometimes those breakdowns show us that we need to go back to the drawing board entirely and rethink the people in our lives, our routines and our purpose. I know because I've been through that humbling process myself.

When I got sick...again...with my brain tumor as well as my two cervical disc replacements, I had to start looking at how I was living my life. I had to figure out why my life's "formula" wasn't working, which was tough to square with my ego considering my title of "World's Greatest Formulator." Even so, I knew I had to do some inner work to change, and I began to look for new sources of energy. As a supplement formulator, I knew there were thousands of ingredients out there that could enhance energy and long-term health, but I already had stacks and routines that maximized my performance that way. What I came to realize was that energy wasn't as finite a concept as I thought. Energy wasn't a "sum" that got added or subtracted; it was the result of how we negotiated and transformed our body's resources and how we negotiated and transformed the world around us. The second part of that formula was the path to the truly sustainable energy that I craved.

Having more energy isn't ultimately about having better supplements; it's about becoming a better person.

As I learned firsthand, having more energy isn't about having better supplements; it's about becoming a better person. Over time I came to realize that life was more than just sand passing through an hourglass, winding away until it was all gone; it was an open field with endless opportunities for connection and abundance. Still, it took exhausting the old path (many times, as it turned out) to finally put myself on the right one.

The result of my many rebounds from near-death health struggles and the life epiphanies that resulted from them is *The ENERGY Formula*—a book that marries more than two decades of technical experience of biochemistry and nutrition science with an honest, human approach to life, family, friends, society and self. My hope is that *The ENERGY Formula* will not just make you more focused, more powerful or more productive; it will make you more compassionate and caring, more grounded, more relaxed and more purposeful. It will make you a better listener and a better friend.

The ENERGY Formula is simple. It is based on six "ingredients" which will help you unleash your limitless potential (**and that's a life-changing promise, not just a subtitle**):

Experiment—Our lives are the great experiment. By determining the best inputs, we can establish what we need most to thrive and to create the lives we deserve.

Nutrition—Nutrition isn't just about the food we eat but how we eat it. By building a nutritional strategy that helps us eat mindfully, we can strengthen immunity, extend our healthspan and maximize energy.

Exercise—Our bodies are reflections of how we use them. If our bodies don't reflect our highest self, exercise can offer a reset button, giving us the opportunity to restore, rebuild and rejuvenate.

Routine—From how we begin our days upon waking to how we ease ourselves to sleep, building routines that minimize stress and enhance productivity is essential to living a life of vitality.

Growth—Reaching our potential not only requires that we embrace a growth mindset, but also that we connect with the people, tools, supplements and strategies we need to realize our highest selves.

Your Tribe—We don't do any of this alone. By identifying and investing in our communities, we find that energy isn't an individual, fixed sum—it's communal, and it can grow exponentially.

THE ENERGY FORMULA

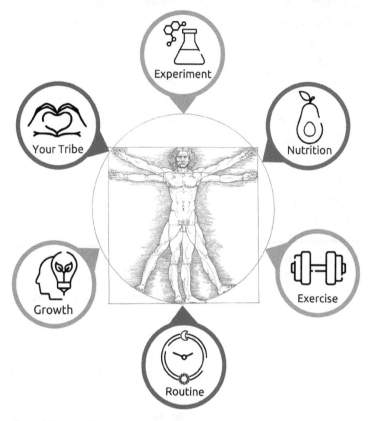

Graphic 1 – The Six "Ingredients" of The Energy Formula

At no other time in human history has the choice been clearer: We can either succumb to fear or we can engage with our highest selves. My hope for you is that it's not the former, for as Brazilian novelist Paulo Coelho, best known for his novel *The Alchemist*, said, "Don't give in to your fears. If you do, you won't be able to talk to your heart." We must finally stop and ask, "Is this the life I want for myself?" Bio-hacking is about developing shortcuts to reach our full potential, but perhaps the biggest biohack of all is *learning to love yourself*, and I don't mean that in some flippant, inspirational way. I mean truly honoring, respecting and rewarding yourself for your unique purpose on this planet. When we know our *why*, we can start developing the *how*. Surprisingly, that is how self-love really originates—and it's a process the biohacking community has sometimes gotten backwards.

When we live in commitment to our highest ideals of self-love, love for our communities and for the world, we truly build resilience. Instead of feeling disappointment, defeat or failure when we face obstacles, we lean into our strength and resolve to overcome them. When we are optimizing ourselves—showing self-love through nutrition, exercise and healthy routines and then sharing that with our tribe—we even end up strengthening our immunity and our biology. We have the energy and momentum to challenge ourselves more physically and mentally.

You will not change everything overnight. But slowly, you will begin to **EXPERIMENT** with your body and biology. You will start to change how you prioritize **NUTRITION** and **EXERCISE** and you will build a **ROUTINE** which promotes rest, recovery and resiliency. You will move into a **GROWTH** mindset supported by the elements you most need for enhancement and you will find **YOUR TRIBE**, the people who best support your growth. Through it all, you will begin to live with true **ENERGY**.

With all this in mind, I invite you to try The ENERGY Formula. Take it one piece at a time. Instead of an all-or-nothing approach, embrace an "always something" mindset. We cannot create change without action, and it is consistent, daily action that accumulates like compound interest, leading to monumental transformations. We start to slow down enough so that we can all begin to breathe a bit more easily, moving out of the fight, flight or freeze of survival and into the wide, systemic flow of how we work, live and celebrate this short but miraculous time on Earth. Now more than ever, we can make that change. In fact, it might be necessary for our survival.

We all deserve to get this life "right." We all deserve the same grace we so easily offer others, and we all have the opportunity right now to hit the reset button and begin to live the lives we know are out there waiting for us. So, let's get started.

Resource Hacks
How to Get the Most Out of This Book

Use This Book as a Guide. Throughout the book, I'll share tactical energy-building strategies with you along with the science and theories behind them. Use these tips to create a program that will improve your life. Add new habits and routines, starting with one thing at a time—and don't overwhelm yourself. Build your first habit for 30 days and then start tackling another (the goal of this book is to create more energy, not more stress). As you read, you will find many distinct elements to support your progress. Go to **EnergyFormulaBook.com** to get all of these tools in print, along with a hidden chapter, recipes and much more.

Fill Out the Surveys. At the beginning of each chapter, you'll have the chance to assess your baseline in each area, which will help you determine exactly how much you need to do to improve that part of your life. After each quiz, create three to-dos to help support your own ENERGY formula.

Learn the Science with Formulator's Corners. Throughout this book, I will share the supplements I've used to optimize particular areas of my life. You can experiment with these various supplements to build your own "stacks" as you like. At the end of the book, you will find my key supplements—those I think are most important—listed in one place as well.

How to Get the Most Out of This Book
(continuation)

Think Holistically with Resource Hacks. At the end of each chapter, I will share how I hack my body and environment to optimize my health in ways that go beyond supplements. You will learn about all the tools and techniques I use to develop my own ENERGY formula.

Disclosure of Conflicts of Interest with Recommended Products: I have worked for many supplement companies as a consultant, and I now work with the ingredient supplier NNB Nutrition, which produces some of the ingredients mentioned here. While I have worked on the marketing and science of those ingredients, I do not receive royalties or revenue from their sales. No products mentioned here result in additional revenue for me. As of this printing, I receive no affiliate codes and no royalties from those products; they are the ones I like to use. I receive a small amount of royalties from the sales of products with Tea-Crine or Dynamine because I am a co-owner and co-patent holder of those ingredients.

Disclaimer: Nothing in this book is intended to be medical advice, and any changes to your own health routines should be discussed with a physician.

For live links, updated content, bonus graphics and a hidden chapter, go to EnergyFormulaBook.com

EXPERIMENT SURVEY

How seriously do you take your health and wellness?		
I consciously make decisions daily to optimize my health. I work out, eat healthily and focus on self-care.	(3)	
I occasionally make decisions to be healthier. But really, I do not know exactly what healthy is.	(2)	
To be honest, I never think about my health!	(1)	
When did you last have a full blood panel done?		
I have one done at least once a year.	(3)	
More than a year ago.	(2)	
Never.	(1)	
How well do you know your body?		
I can tell when something doesn't work for me. My body feels different and I can tell when I feel a little "off.	(3)	
I can sense when I am coming down with a cold or the flu, but that is it.	(2)	
I feel like my body is completely foreign to me— I cannot tell what it needs.	(1)	
How often do you try something new around your nutrition, fitness or self-care routine?		
I often experiment with new things, like cutting sugar, trying yoga or red-light therapy.	(3)	
I have tried a few things to lose some weight, but never really stuck to any.	(2)	
I am not sure of the last time I tried to change my nutrition or follow any workout routine! I do not think much about self-care.	(1)	

Do you feel like you have control of your health?		
Yes. I know that I can make changes in my life to improve my health. It's just a matter of when I decide to do it.	(3)	
Kind of. I find it difficult to commit to some of the things I try to do.	(2)	
Not at all. I struggle to maintain my health.	(1)	
How experienced would you say you are at biohacking your body with things like supplements to enhance your life?		
I know ALL about the supplements I use and what my blood markers mean, so I know what goal I am trying to achieve.	(3)	
I often use supplements but am not sure if they are working or what they're doing in my body.	(2)	
I do not take many supplements or try to control my biology. My body is on its own mission!	(1)	
When was the last time you felt truly aligned with your body, mind and spirit?		
I feel better than ever! I am happy with the lifestyle I lead.	(3)	
I really desire to feel this way, but things have not lined up yet. I am looking for more ways to start feeling in tune with myself.	(2)	
I have never really felt this way. (	(1)	
YOUR TOTAL		

7-11 points: You have got some work to do! This book is a great place to start!

12-16 points: You are heading in the right direction! Keep at it!

17-21 points: You are really on the ball! Only small tweaks are needed to be your best self!

Chapter 1: Experiment: Discovering the Baseline for You and Your Potential

"Knowledge is a function of being. When there is a change in the being of the knower, there is a corresponding change in the nature and amount of knowing."

—Aldous Huxley

Growing up in the small town of Lenox, Massachusetts, as the son of a divorced mother and an enlisted Navy father on a paltry salary, I often felt like I was on the outside looking in. Lenox was a suburban tourist destination in the Berkshires for the wealthy and beautiful elite; prosperous New Yorkers would visit to listen to the symphony at Tanglewood, watch plays at the Berkshire Performing Arts Center, hike at Canyon Ranch and eat dessert at Cheesecake Charlie's. Lenox had an air of affluence...heck, our school team name was even pretentious—the "Lenox Millionaires" —and I kid you not, our mascot was the Monopoly guy.

To make matters worse, I was the "fat kid."

I was pretty smart, but when it came to playing team sports, I was usually picked last. Girls never passed me letters, exchanged looks with me or whispered to other girls about asking me out; nope, instead they would whisper the types of things to each other that made them laugh. And, of course, the popular boys would join in.

I remember waiting at the school bus stop, dreading what the day would bring and the cruel things they would say, like "You fat f#ck" or "Sit down, fat ass." Even teachers would point out my weight and laugh—encouraging, if not instigating, the bullying.

I felt ugly. I struggled to find any self-worth. I was not the alpha male like Glenn Hoff, who killed it at every sport. I was not the boy who the girls hoped would ask them to dance or to the movies—that was Ryan Thomas, the tall, handsome soccer star *and* salutatorian.

One thing I had going for me was that I was funny. Maybe that was my way of coping and deflecting the bullying. I got good at making people laugh, but there was a cost: I learned to make fun of myself —before others could. It was my way of surviving and, in a strange way, connecting.

Deep down, I lived with pain. I didn't take drugs, watch porn or drink alcohol to soothe my pain. Instead, I self-medicated with soda, candy, chips, junk food and video games. And to no surprise, my struggles with obesity only got worse. Any short-term relief was fleeting, compounding the depression.

I was living with a major lack of love, for myself and from others. As I learned over time, the opposite of love isn't hate; it's fear. I lived in constant fear—fear of other kids, fear of school, fear of looking in the mirror and seeing that chubby kid looking back.

When I say I struggled with my weight, let me make something clear: I wasn't just fat; I also had a large rear end—*fat ass*, as they called me. Scientifically, it is known as a "gynoid fat distribution," a pear shape that's more common among females than males. But that was me. Skinny up top, disproportionately fat in the butt and legs— so much so, in fact, that my legs would rub together. The short shorts they gave me for gym class…well, they took the laughter from snickers to unabashed heckling. Added to that, my life at home was chaotic with both of my brothers running away. One was a model and one was a star athlete, both of which I looked up to, but fell short of. On top of all that, I also had lots of acne, so as you could imagine, I wasn't brimming over with self-esteem, especially next to my "rock star" brothers.

Despite my lack of self-confidence, crappy nutrition and the relentless bullying I endured, I managed to make it through high school with good grades—but I knew I had to change. I didn't want to be the fat kid or the bullied kid for the rest of my life. Just as I'd found ways to be funny to make up for whatever I lacked, I knew I'd find a way to fix everything else, too.

In 1992, I decided I would study business at Babson College, the number one ranked business specialty school by U.S. News and World Report. It was in Wellesley, Massachusetts, outside of Boston. Meanwhile, I'd started reading *Muscle Media 2000* and *Muscular Development* magazines to get to work on changing my body. There were pictures of guys who were absolutely shredded with huge muscles—but there were also example workouts and supplements to try to help you build muscle.

I'd known about supplements since I was really young, because my mom was one of the first people I knew who touted the use of high-dose (orthomolecular) vitamins. She made me and my brothers take vitamin C when we were young and she kept up with various health trends. Even though I knew from a young age that vitamins could be highly effective, discovering creatine was something entirely different—it gave me real, serious energy and helped me power through my workouts. After tinkering and experimenting with different exercises, supplements and proteins, I started finding out what worked for me. My clothes became looser and I put on 10 pounds of muscle in a month. *This is really working*, I thought.

In 1993, everyone was talking about a book called *Optimum Sports Nutrition* by Dr. Michael Colgan, which contained all kinds of stacks with supplements and dietary tricks to enhance athletic performance used by the Olympic athletes he was working with. I absolutely devoured it, reading it probably 100 times through.

Another book that made an impact on me was *Sports Supplement Review* by Bill Phillips. He went through different supplements and rated them, and I couldn't wait try some of them for myself. *Creatine, Vanadyl Sulfate, Glutamine*...the doses, stacks, timing, ratings...I was learning so much and felt a sense of hope and enthusiasm that was new to me. The idea was planted in my mind that this was something I could dedicate my life to—I could be a sports nutritionist or an ingredient formulator myself and share my discoveries with the world!

Before enrolling in school each year, students were required to get a routine physical—and in 1994, before my junior year, I made an appointment to see Dr. Daniel Johnson, my physician in Boston. When I got there, I started rambling on to Dr. Johnson about some supplements I had been using and how helpful they'd been. I was telling him all about the difference I was seeing with creatine, as well as whey protein isolate. As I told him back then, "Someday, I believe people will rely more on supplements and diet than medication." Instead of scoffing and being dismissive like most doctors would have been (and can still be), Dr. Johnson listened as I shared my passion. What he did next not only stunned me but changed my life.

He quietly turned away, grabbed a piece of paper and drew a line on it with two hash marks on each end, one at 20 (my age at the time) and one at 80. "Why not be happy between here and here?" he said, referring to the 60-year span, or "dash" between those two points. I was looking towards a future when my passion would be appreciated, but Dr. Johnson was suggesting something radical: why not work towards pursuing my passion *right now*, day in and day out? I was dumbfounded. Did he just give me permission to pursue my dream? A dream I didn't even know I had until it poured out of me?

During that brief visit, it became clear to both of us that I wasn't as thrilled about business school as I was about nutrition and supplements. At that time, no one around me was encouraging me to "chase my dreams." Yet here was my doctor, telling me I could be happy right now. I could embrace the "dash" between birth and death which is where life is lived. That day radically changed my career path; a formerly fat-reared, bullied kid began to dream of becoming the best supplement formulator in the world. I dreamt of creating the world's most effective, cutting-edge, talked-about supplements that were not only rooted in good science, but that more importantly, changed lives.

For some reason, Dr. Johnson's opinion and encouragement were all that mattered and all I needed to start pursuing my dream. What he shared with me that day and the way he shared it made sense. My brain and heart would not let it go—and I would experiment as much as I had to make that dream a reality.

As I realized early in my health and fitness journey, there are no concrete answers that fit everybody. We all have our own bio-individuality, and we all have our own personality quirks. Methods that work for one person don't always work for another, and before we can find out what does work, we need to know where we stand when we start experimenting.

Before we can build the nutritional, fitness and daily routines that promote vibrant energy, radiant health, steadfast resilience, bulletproof immunity and peak quality of life, we must first answer one question: Where are we right now? What is our baseline? Where do we want to go from there? We need to figure out where the starting and finishing lines are in order to run the race—and it is no different in life.

I know that where I have been and where I am now are vastly different and I still have goals and experiments ahead of me too. I have spent most of my life in the majority. This is not the "in crowd" you want to be in though. Only 1 in 10 Americans is currently achieving optimal metabolic health.[1] This has serious implications for our longevity and energy since poor metabolic health leaves people more vulnerable to developing type 2 diabetes, cardiovascular disease and other serious health issues. It is now the aberration or exception to be "fit". Together we will go through all the secrets, research, tricks and tips I have learned in my health journey so we can all be on the healthier side of those statistics.

Before we begin, please note: *I am not a medical physician; I have spent the better part of two decades of my life as a biochemist, a sports nutritionist and dietitian. Before starting any new health, fitness or nutrition program, you should always consult with your doctor.* Nonetheless, one thing I've learned personally in two decades of professional scientific work is that the human experience is all about experimentation.

ESTABLISHING YOUR BASELINE

Assessing your baseline can be complex, as there are many factors that can affect your energy levels. Whether it's work, over-exercise, one-sided relationships, poor nutrition, travel, poor sleep or stimulants, many things can cause our "normal baseline" to be less than optimal and lead to low energy and fatigue. In this state, we are merely functioning, living to get through the day as opposed to thriving.

Our energy levels are tied to how well our mitochondria are functioning. Mitochondria are known as the "power plants" of all living things, which includes human beings. In fact, the mitochondria produce about 95 percent of the body's energy. To put this in perspective, it is estimated that there are over 30 trillion cells in the human body and each cell may have up to 5000 of these mitochondrion (though they are especially prevalent in the brain, heart and muscles). Both mitochondria number and function are critical, and in the absence of a dense network of efficient mitochondria, our ability to live, breathe, move, be energetic and live life to the fullest is severely compromised.

YOUR BODY IS FILLED WITH BILLIONS OF CELLS

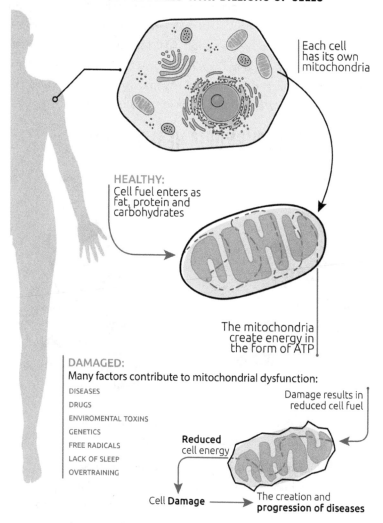

Each cell has its own mitochondria

HEALTHY:
Cell fuel enters as fat, protein and carbohydrates

The mitochondria create energy in the form of ATP

DAMAGED:
Many factors contribute to mitochondrial dysfunction:

DISEASES
DRUGS
ENVIROMENTAL TOXINS
GENETICS
FREE RADICALS
LACK OF SLEEP
OVERTRAINING

Damage results in reduced cell fuel

Reduced cell energy

Cell **Damage** ———> The creation and **progression of diseases**

Graphic 2 – The Importance of Mitochondrial Function for Healthy Cells

Mitochondria produce **ATP (Adenosine Triphosphate)**—the energy "currency" our bodies use to function—and the less ATP they produce, the more fatigued you feel. This makes mitochondrial function the ultimate marker of energy levels. If your mitochondria are small and weak and you have few of them, their output of ATP will be lower; on the other hand, having many mitochondria that are big and robust will lead to more abundant ATP—meaning more energy!

When we don't produce enough ATP for our body to move and function, we are in a state in research known as "ICE," or Insufficient Cellular Energy. This shortage of energy makes us feel tired and inefficient and is a state we call *mitochondrial dysfunction*.

MITOCHONDRIA HEALTH STATUS

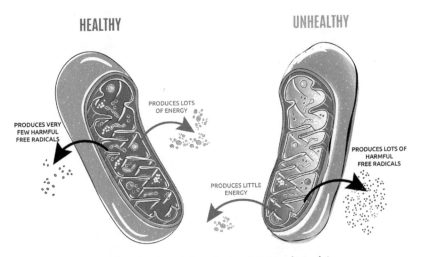

Graphic 3 – Healthy, Robust Mitochondria
vs Weak Mitochondria[2]

Using the power plant metaphor, mitochondrial dysfunction comes from a reduction in our number of power plants, from "transportation" issues that make it difficult for cellular raw materials to get to those power plants, or from problems with the "assembly line" inside our power plants (i.e., insufficient "workers" or helper chemicals, such as having inadequate levels of CoQ10 or PQQ). Mitochondrial dysfunction can result from any of these issues, or from many of them at once.

No discussion of the mitochondria or energy production would be complete without mentioning the important healthspan molecule, NAD (nicotinamide adenine dinucleotide). While it serves many functions in the body, NAD plays a critical role in energy metabolism by helping to turn food into usable energy. It also helps certain enzymes involved in vital cellular functions, such as cellular repair and cellular defense. NAD has also been referred to as a fundamental housekeeping molecule, a key modulator of cell signaling and survival pathways and a modulator of longevity and health.

Case in point, NAD is the key cellular fuel for the sirtuins, the gatekeepers of key longevity and resilience pathways in the body. For example, sirtuins are thought to be responsible, in large part, for the cardiometabolic benefits of fasting/calorie restriction, high-intensity exercise and cold exposure, and when upregulated, can delay key aspects of aging. For example, sirtuins regulate the activity of genes involved in mitochondrial biogenesis and stress resistance. As such, sirtuins have been regarded as toughness genes. In addition, sirtuins serve many other roles, including DNA repair, tissue regeneration, inflammation reduction, circadian rhythms and more.[3] That being said, sirtuins are NAD-dependent, which means their activity is limited by the availability of this all-important cellular fuel.

Unfortunately, our NAD levels drop with age, and what's more, chronic inflammation causes a reduction in NAD levels, as does excess alcohol consumption, excess UV exposure, inadequate sleep, poor diet, viral infections and a sedentary lifestyle. To make matters worse, we also experience a rise in CD38, which is involved in our body's processes of limiting and breaking down NAD. In short: as we get older, our bodies make less NAD, and it disappears faster than when we were young. By the time we hit 50, our NAD levels are half of what they were in our youth. While we know that inflammation causes lower levels of NAD, we also know that lower NAD levels increases inflammation (a term known as "inflammaging") for a seemingly downward spiral of energy and longevity.[4] No wonder we struggle so much with our energy levels!

Formulator's Corner
Mitochondrial Health Supplements

Since mitochondrial health is so important, here are my top supplements to support mitochondrial health and function as well as healthy aging:

Nicotinamide Mononucleotide (NMN): NMN supports multiple functions of mitochondria, such as helping regulate cellular energy and delaying aging. The dosage is often 250-500mg/day, but some data suggests larger doses of 1000-2000mg/day, which can get pricey. Some people try Nicotinamide Riboside (NR) and oral NAD or NADH supplements instead, but these are less effective than NMN based on data, testing and my experience. While oral supplementation can be good, NAD+ IV therapy seems to be the most effective way to raise levels (500-1500 mg slow drip). While the data is still lacking, NAD+ nasal spray (dose matters) could be the best option in lieu of IV therapy.

PQQ: Pyrroloquinoline quinone may help increase the number of mitochondria through mitochondrial biogenesis, which is associated with benefits like increased longevity and energy levels; PQQ accomplishes this by acting as a cofactor in the redox (reduction-oxidation) process. I prefer a fermented form of PQQ called BioPQQ with a dose of 10-20 mg taken twice a day.

Mitochondrial Health Supplements (continuation)

CoQ10: Ubiquinone is a key cofactor in the mitochondrial electron transport chain. It is one of the most widely recognized and used mitochondrial support supplements. Co-Q10 and PQQ may have synergy. Common dosing ranges between 50-600 mg a day (preferably in the ubiquinol form). Another interesting form is MitoQ, which could potentially be a superior formulation (though more data is needed to confirm that).

Polyphenols: There's a long list of plant-based phytochemicals with strong bioactive properties—some of which include antioxidant, anti-inflammatory and anti-aging benefits. Some of the top choices include resveratrol (make sure it is the trans-resveratrol form), EGCG, quercetin, fisetin, pterostilbene, sulforaphane and curcumin. Many of these benefit from containing phytosomes and liposomes, which enhance their bioavailability.

L-Ergothioneine: This rare amino acid found primarily in mushrooms is a powerful antioxidant. Unusually concentrated in the mitochondria, it may be one of the most powerful ways to rev up the mitochondria. A good dose seems to be 5-10 mg twice daily.

The good news is there are things we can do to naturally raise our NAD levels and reduce the activity of CD38—leading to more robust energy. Fasting and exercise are known to increase NAD levels; in particular, high-intensity interval training (HIIT) is especially effective at combating the age-related reduction of NAD levels. There are also two bioactive dietary flavonoids that are especially effective when it comes to inhibiting CD38, namely apigenin (found in parsley, chamomile, oregano and celery) and quercetin (found in apples, red onions, cherries, red grapes and raspberries).

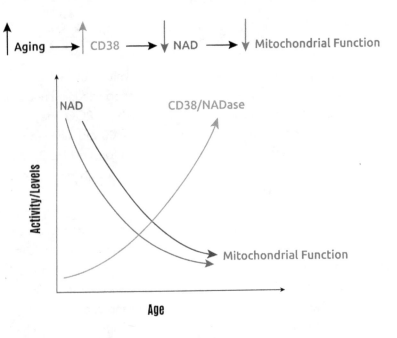

CD38/NADase increases during aging, and causes NAD decline and subsequent mitochondrial dysfunction.

Graphic 4 – NAD Boosting Strategies[5]

Without doing a muscle biopsy or a cellular respiration test in a lab, it's difficult to measure our exact levels of mitochondrial function; still, we can roughly gauge it through some observational and biological markers. Even if the most accurate testing methods aren't an option for you, there are three important blood biomarkers that everyone should get tested in order to get a good idea of how well their mitochondria are functioning:

- **hsCRP** (high-sensitivity C-Reactive Protein): For healthy levels of inflammation, hsCRP should be lower than 3.0mg/L. Too much inflammation can impair mitochondrial function, and that subsequent mitochondrial dysfunction can give rise to even less healthy levels of inflammation. It's a vicious cycle we should all do our best to avoid.

- **HbA1c**: Although this is very individualized to the person, HbA1c can give us an idea of our glycation, or blood sugar damage. HbA1c is optimal between 4.0-6.0 percent. In essence, this biomarker is a three-month snapshot of your blood glucose levels. Poor glycemic control is one of the primary variables contributing to mitochondrial dysfunction, as dysfunctional mitochondria may have an impaired ability to use glucose for fuel (leading to "transportation" and "assembly line" issues). The ketogenic diet, which is a very-low-carb and high-fat diet, can help with this, as it results in significant reductions in blood sugar levels and improvements in glycemic control. Ketones, produced through ketosis or taken exogenously as a supplement, can serve as an alternate energy source for damaged mitochondria.

- **oxLDL** (oxidized low-density lipoprotein): This biomarker relates to a more chronic condition of mitochondrial dysfunction, namely oxidation. The more oxidation, the more damaged your mitochondria will be. Oxidized LDL is one of the strongest markers in the potential development of heart disease via inflammation of the arteries—less than 2.3mg/dl is optimal.

Although some of these concepts may seem new to people, mitochondrial resilience is such an underrated and unappreciated part of our health. It will be a major focus in the future, as nearly every disease and almost all biological aging can be tied back to mitochondrial health—and conversely, the feeling of having enough energy is directly related to robust mitochondrial health. We will soon see a major commercial rise in "mito" supplements. Mark my words: "mito" is the next keto!

3 ESSENTIAL BIOMARKERS
TO ASSESS YOUR BASELINE MITOCHONDRIAL FUNCTION:

	LOW RISK	MODERATE RISK	HIGH RISK
hsCRP (Inflammation)	<1.0 MG/L	1-3	>3
HbA1c (Glycation)	<5.7%	5.7-6.4	>6.4
oxLDL (Oxidation)	<60 U/L	60-69	>70

Graphic 5 – Three Essential Biomarkers to
Assess Your Baseline Mitochondrial Function

Other biomarker tests you can take to better understand your energy baseline include **Vitamin D3 levels** (often measured by testing for 25(OH)D), **iron and ferritin levels** (oxygen is required to produce energy, and iron levels determine your oxygen-carrying capacity) and **thyroid function.** According to recent research findings presented at the 2020 European Congress of Endocrinology meeting, vitamin D deficiency is highly predictive of "all-cause mortality," otherwise known as death from all causes. In fact, researchers found that men with the lowest free 25(OH)D levels had a 91 percent increased risk for death from all causes compared to those with the highest levels of these vitamin D metabolites.[6]

When it comes to thyroid function, I recommend seeing a functional medicine doctor who is experienced with thyroid markers because the blood tests can easily be misread. Other tests include those that assess **adrenal function** by looking at DHEA (the precursor to testosterone and estrogen) and cortisol levels, both of which can lead to problems with blood glucose control, poor energy levels and sleep challenges when levels are too high or too low. Measuring your waking temperature three days in a row is also a straightforward way to track thyroid issues; if your temperature is chronically below normal, you may have an issue with **CBC** (complete blood count). What is normal? According to Stanford researchers in 2020, the "new normal" has decreased from 98.6 degrees to 97.9 degrees Fahrenheit. This could be related to the population having a slower metabolism, but seeing where you're at consistently is the most important data point here.

In order to determine your biological baseline, work with your doctor to get the proper test results or find a functional medicine doctor who can manage such testing. A useful practice is to create an Excel spreadsheet where you track your blood work. Once you get retested, you can compare your before and after results in an easy and structured way. Without drawing blood or sending in a stool sample, there are even simpler ways to examine your energy baseline. Ask yourself:

- How do you feel when you wake up? Are you wide awake or is it a struggle to get out of bed?

- Do you have energy towards the end of the day?

- How difficult are daily tasks such as walking your dog, carrying groceries and taking the stairs? Are they harder than they were in the past?

- What is your emotional state? Are you less emotive or interactive? Are you avoiding social interaction and/or pushing people away?

- Do you get sugar, caffeine or other stimulant cravings regularly?

- Do you have any addictive behaviors? Do you crave dopamine hits?

- Is your hair healthy and are your eyes bright?

- How is your circulation in your hands and feet?

Answering these questions can help you establish a baseline for self-experimentation—and you can ask yourself these questions periodically to assess your improvements. Sometimes the most important biomarkers are the ones we can see ourselves —the trick is to begin paying attention to our health and energy with the same level of care as a lab scientist examining a patient. After all, we are by far the best observers of our own health.

Formulator's Corner
Mitochondrial Dysregulation Supplements

We can promote healthy mitochondrial function—and robust energy levels—through nutritional support that helps combat excessive and unhealthy levels of inflammation, oxidation and glycation. Here are some of my favorite supplements for this:

Curcumin: Curcumin is the powerful polyphenol that is thought to be responsible for many of the benefits associated with turmeric, including profound anti-inflammatory effects and a potent ability to support the body's antioxidant and detoxification systems.

Because of curcumin's poor solubility and absorption, I prefer liposomal curcumin or CurcuWIN (an optimized curcumin preparation), with a dose ranging between 500–1,000 mg a day. A new form called tetrahydrocurcumin may even be superior to curcumin for inflammation, antioxidant activity and bioavailability—for this, I recommend 200 mg of CurcuPrime twice a day.

Mitochondrial Dysregulation Supplements (continuation)

CBD: Hemp-derived CBD has numerous health benefits, including support for healthy levels of inflammation. In some cases, full-spectrum hemp extracts can provide the best results, as the complementary phytocannabinoids and terpenes in hemp may work synergistically with CBD (though these can also be taken on their own).

For this approach, a good starting point for most people is 30 mg once or twice daily. Conversely, pure synthetic CBD allows for a consistent, predictable and clean version of the compound without any THC present even in small amounts. Depending on your goals, one may be preferable over the other.

Boswellia Serrata: Boswellia is another botanical traditionally used to support a healthy inflammatory response. My preferred preparation is 100 mg of AprèsFlex taken twice daily.

Berberine: This may be one of my favorite supplements. Often referred to as a glucose disposal agent, berberine helps lower blood sugar levels. It offers powerful support for glycation and also has a host of properties that make it popular for anti-aging and mitochondrial support. I recommend 500 mg of berberine three times daily. Even better yet, 150 mg of dihydroberberine/ GlucoVantage (a berberine derivative) can be taken twice daily.

Vitamin C: Vitamin C is a potent yet often overlooked antioxidant that promotes healthy mitochondria, which require high levels of vitamin C to support a healthy antioxidant status and redox balance. I like liposomal preparations of vitamin C, taking 2-5 grams a day.

Glutathione: Glutathione is known as the body's master antioxidant, and it plays a powerful role in detoxification and supporting healthy mitochondria. Liposomal glutathione seems to be best absorbed, and I like a daily dose of 1-2 grams.

THE N OF 1

In science experiments, N refers to the "number" of participants. A real-life "case study" where there is only one individual is often referred to as N of 1, and in this case, you are the N. You are the participant, and your unique set of characteristics sets you apart from every other human being on earth. I've done many experiments with compounds yet to be released and patented (sometimes before anyone in the world has even tried them). In doing so, I monitor how I feel, get blood tests, run myself through a workout, take my temperature, look at ketones, check blood glucose and track my sleep quality to see what all the effects are.

I have learned through my own N of 1 experiments and I continue to learn through them, as they are an ongoing, evolving process. When I was formulating BioTRUST IC-5, I did an experiment using 500 mg of berberine, which is a potent glucose disposal agent among other things (meaning it helps shuttle carbs out of the bloodstream). To test how well berberine could "dispose" of sugar, I did a "carbohydrate challenge" which involved eating fun and unhealthy sugar-laden foods—five Double Stuff Oreos and two frosted Pop-Tarts (about 75 grams or so of sugar)—and testing my blood sugar to see the results impact. To establish a "placebo" baseline, I ate the high-sugar foods without any berberine. My blood glucose started out at 65 (a great fasting blood sugar). Before the sugar set in I felt clear, not hungry and happy—but over the next two hours, that feeling changed. I was checking my blood glucose every 30 minutes, and at the two-hour mark, it had risen to 199 and wasn't coming down. I felt irritable, inflamed, hungry and cognitively less sharp.

A week later I did the same experiment, but this time I added the 500 mg of berberine. I started with a fasting blood glucose level of around 65 again, and within an hour of starting the carbohydrate challenge, I reached 100, but it never climbed higher. After two hours, I was essentially back to baseline. I never felt "off," hungry or inflamed. I was truly in awe of what berberine could do and have been taking the supplement every day since (and more recently, the even more powerful dihydroberberine). It is not only a potent glucose disposal agent, but also the most powerful anti-aging, pro-longevity compound I know of that exists legally, often compared to the longevity and diabetes drug metformin (that's had recent recall issues due to being tainted). That's saying a lot because metformin is considered one of the most potent anti-aging drugs for humans; in fact, in a recent trial, metformin, as part of an anti-aging cocktail along with DHEA and growth hormone, *reversed* aging (by 1.5 years) in humans, as measured by highly sophisticated and validated epigenetic "clocks". What that means is that berberine is a powerful candidate to slow aging, especially considering the safety concerns surrounding metformin (e.g., elevated homocysteine levels, B12 deficiency), not to mention that much of the world's supply is tainted. To me, that makes berberine hands-down a smart, reliable choice. Because berberine has antioxidant and antimicrobial properties and can help support healthy levels of inflammation, it is also extremely useful for helping support a healthy, robust immune system.

When we talk about bio-individuality, we are saying each of us is an individual combination of genetics, body size, gender and other biological markers. We are unique individuals given a unique set of genes that make us who we are. But what makes each of us even more distinct is the concept of epigenetics, which is basically how our environment (things like our diet, exercise, stress, sleep, gut microbiome, viruses, medications, toxins and more) has influenced or changed the way our genes are expressed. What originally may have been ABC is now read by our cells as BCA, which results in a different protein. This may seem like a small change, but even minor changes like this can lead to eventual diseases or disorders.

When we talk about bio-individuality, we are saying that each of us is an individual combination of genetics, epigenetics, body sizes, genders, environmental consequences and biological profiles.

One reader could be a 190-pound male with a propensity for cancer and perfect cholesterol while another could be a 120-pound female with an extreme iron deficiency and clinical depression.

We each come to the table with our own sets of strengths and weaknesses. But in order to develop a formula which responds to your specific qualities, you must become a study with only one participant.

We do that by controlling for *all* factors.

The great inventor Thomas Edison was once asked if he thought his failed experiments counted for nothing. His reply was: "Negative results are just what I want. They are just as valuable to me as positive results. I can never find the thing that does the job best until I find the ones that don't."

Just as Edison explained, experimentation is so critical to our success. We must figure out what works for us through a process of trial and error, because there is no such thing as true failure. That process is there to show us what works or how we can make something work better.

I know a lot of people who try to change their diet and when it doesn't work, they believe they have "failed." In reality, they are just experimenting with one of many methods, some of which will surely work better than others. When faced with an obstacle, you can either throw your hands in the air and give up or you can examine the specifics to see where you got closer at developing a successful diet. You can measure your wins and where you still struggled to make lasting and important change.

The essence of biohacking is realizing that we are all just experiments. Unlocking your perfect energy formula is about experimenting with different inputs (independent variables) and seeing how they affect you (dependent variable), ultimately finding what works best for you. Christopher Columbus once stated, "You can never cross an ocean until you have courage to lose sight of the shore" and at the heart of being an experimenter is also being adventurous and explorative!

To be innovative, you need to be ahead of the data.

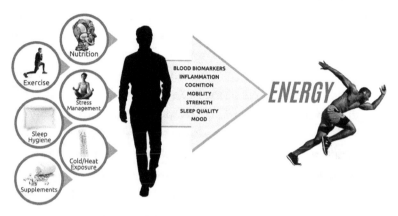

Graphic 6 – Independent Variables + YOU
(dependent variable) = Finding What Works Best for You

To be innovative, you need to be ahead of the data. Most research is still 20 years in the making, but you can still experiment on yourself and your limits. In order to be a successful scientist, you must keep an open mind. I often think back to the Socratic method. Socrates did not engage in dialogue presuming he knew the answer. Instead, he asked the right questions to reach philosophical conclusions.

Likewise, to achieve a robust study, we need to ask the right questions. We need to read the studies and talk to our doctors. We need to listen to what people who have been successful have to say on the subject. At the same time, part of experimentation is understanding that the same interventions do not work the same for everyone. Some may have side effects; some may do nothing. You might need to adjust dosage or frequency. It is not about assuming that you know the conclusion, but that you are open to whatever the answer might be.

BIO-RESILIENCE

Just as we talk about bio-individuality, we must also talk about bio-resilience: our strength and flexibility in responding to external forces. The concept of bio-resilience was developed in the 1800s by biologist Alexander von Humboldt. He noticed that the higher up a mountain he went, the greater the decrease in biodiversity; in other words, there were more species at the base of a mountain than at its peak. Though fewer in number, these species had more flexibility—more abilities to withstand, recover and adapt from the environmental shocks. They had greater resilience due to the robustness required to live in the conditions at the top of the mountain. As our world swiftly changes around us, our challenge is the same—but the great and miraculous difference for humans is that we have a choice in the ascent.

Bio-experimentation teaches us how we react to different stressors and how our bodies can adapt to resistance, which is what allows us to increase and enhance our energy. The same goes for all elements of our mind and body. As we increase resilience, we increase our ability to manage external stress and we develop a more robust immune system that can better and more appropriately handle the many threats thrown its way.

The amount of stress on the mind and body is known as **allostatic load, of which we have different individual capacities for**. In a way, our allostatic load can be thought of like a bucket—we can only carry so much water (stress) in the bucket before it overflows and becomes counterproductive; when it is too heavy, we end up having to carry the bucket differently, stressing different muscles in order to manage the burden.

By controlling our variables and inputs so the body can function efficiently, we can better adapt to stressful situations. For the many sources of stress that are outside our control, we can also build resilience through how we perceive and manage stressful situations by **allostasis**, a process of increasing load without breaking down the body. Through this practice, we improve our ability to respond calmly and evenly to

the daily stressors of living—from the honking cars in traffic to the endless news cycle and all the other trials and challenges in our lives.

Stress can come from many sources in life but when it compounds, it can cause your body more harm than good. This is where it's easy to get **hormesis** and our usual idea of stress confused. The idea behind hormesis is to impose small amounts of stress on the body (like cold showers/baths, sauna or exercise) and then to remove that stress for recovery afterwards. Fasting is another example; while it can be counterproductive if done too much or for too long, it is an otherwise healthy practice—a hormetic stressor. We need to employ these sorts of hormetic events intermittently and be careful not to do them too often when our bodies are exposed to stressors we cannot control—like work, relationship issues, poor nutrition, poor sleep and pandemics (particularly when those stressors are persistent and long-lasting).

Hormesis is quite literally the path to unshakable resilience. It teaches the body how to cope with and bounce back from stress bigger, better and stronger than before—and with more energy, vigor and vitality. Hormesis enhances our resilience to normal aging and protects against a broad spectrum of neurodegenerative and cardiovascular diseases, as well as trauma and other threats to health and well-being.

Believe it or not, even the food we eat benefits from hormesis. Plant-based foods produce important compounds which turn out to be quite beneficial when they face stress. In other words, when plants struggle with stressors like starvation, dehydration, UV radiation, insects and so on, they protect themselves by producing antioxidants, most notably a category of compounds called polyphenols, or what many now refer to as plant stress molecules. While there are hundreds of examples, some of the most recognizable are resveratrol, EGCG, anthocyanins and quercetin. The amazing thing, believe it or not, is that when we consume plant-based foods containing these polyphenols, they activate our own longevity, repair and stress resistance enzymes and pathways, such as the sirtuins. This is a process known as *xenohormesis*, which essentially means a protective response induced by a mild stress from a stranger. Pretty cool, right?

While intermittent "good" stress can help enhance immunity, too much stress—a bucket that's overflowing—can suppress our immune system and weaken the body's ability to deal with immune challenges robustly and appropriately.

Hormesis, when done in the right amount, does not "fill up" the stress bucket. Instead, it triggers certain biochemical pathways and physiological adaptations that make us more resilient towards future stressors. To reach our peak potential, we must become resilient to the diverse elements along the climb.

If we let life happen to us and externalize everything, we will not make it up the mountain. However, if we can find the proper internal responses to external stressors, finding the space where we take responsibility for ourselves, we can become robust despite the elements. It is easy to blame bullies and nay-sayers for our problems, but that doesn't change our situation. If anything, it only solidifies our position at the bottom of the mountain.

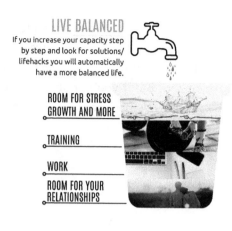

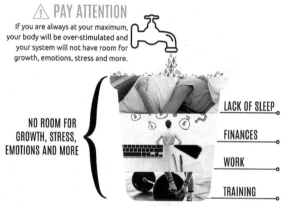

Graphic 7 – Allostatic Load or "Stress Bucket"

We must get honest about what role we play in our failures and how we can do things differently (changing our inputs) to get a different result (a better output). We cannot live truly energized lives if we are not living authentic ones.

Before getting into what supplements, diets or exercise routine is right for you, spend some time with yourself in front of the mirror. Get honest about who you are and where you are in life because that's the foundation that everything else is built on. As Thomas Jefferson put it, "Do you want to know who you are? Don't ask. Act! Action will delineate and define you." You have to be willing to do the work. Unless you are willing to identify your goals, take the time to put your gym bag by the front door and get rid of the easy excuses and self-pity, you will not be able to take the actions that lead to your fullest potential. If your inputs are caffeine, sugar, carbohydrates and too many hours at the office (even the home office!), it shouldn't surprise you if your outputs are disappointing. But if you're putting in meditation, healthy foods, long walks and a well-managed workload, guess what?

You are going to like the results!

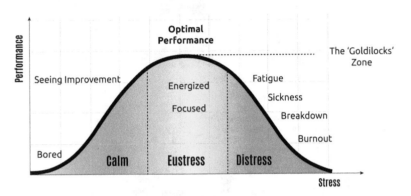

Graphic 8 – The Inverted-U Relationship Between Stress
(i.e., pressure or anxiety) and Performance

When I was taking computer programming classes at Babson, there was a term called GIGO, meaning Garbage In, Garbage Out. It meant that if the code going in was no good, the resulting program wouldn't run well either. The same is true for your body. Experimentation needs to start with the choice of becoming present and conscious in our choices so we can decide which ones make sense for us. We can't figure out what's working if we're not aware of the consequences of our behaviors. Part of becoming your own scientist means you need to evaluate your decisions and see how they are leading you up the mountain—or keeping you stuck at the bottom. Another way of saying that is that mindfulness—of yourself and your attitudes, actions, behaviors and decisions—plays a pivotal role in the ENERGY formula. Awareness is the first step in going from where you are to where you want to be: a place of vibrant energy, radiant health and unshakable resilience.

HUSTLE & FLOW

The reason most people feel like they are working from a deficit is that they set their expectations too high but don't put the systems in place to meet them. Research suggests that in an eight-hour day, the average worker is only productive for two hours and 53 minutes.[7] Since many of us work for eight to 10 hours a day, we end up grinding away and only "flowing" for a small portion of it. It has been no better during the pandemic, which has imposed many novel challenges on our productivity. According to data from the Institute of Corporate Productivity, during the pandemic, 96 percent of US-based organizations reported that their productivity was negatively impacted, with 41 percent of businesses saying that the pandemic hit their productivity to a *high* or *very high* extent.[8]

We all know how good it feels when you're in a groove: your juices are flowing, work is humming and you feel like you're energized. It's what many scientists and psychologists call a "flow state." Even if we don't all get to choose when we work, we can choose how to manage that time.

Too many people end up spending their time grinding away with extraordinarily little time spent in their flow. As I see it, we can either hustle and grind or we can hustle and flow. Grinding is about heat, friction and watching things break down and break off. It is about keeping your head down and pushing through, and it often leads to damage.

The Autonomic Nervous System (ANS) regulates many body processes, and as its name suggests, it works automatically and without conscious effort. It is made up of two divisions, sympathetic ("fight, flight or freeze") and parasympathetic ("rest and digest"), which are physiologically absolutely opposed. The sympathetic nervous system comes online during the hustle, but never goes offline in the grind. There needs to be some degree of balance. Hustle and grind is a sympathetic process with little room for the parasympathetic. Again, sympathetic is when we're living in fight-or-flight, where all we can do is force ourselves through the next task, heads down through the mental grinder of anguish.

AUTONOMIC NERVOUS SYSTEM BREAKDOWN

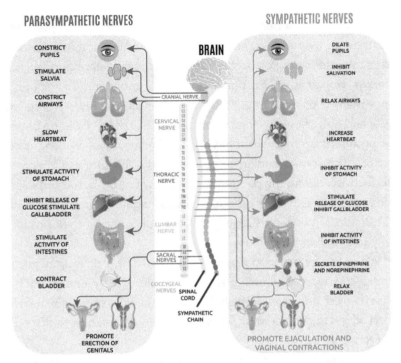

Graphic 9 – Autonomic Nervous System[9]

Humans have developed their sympathetic nervous system over millions of years as a result of living in a predatorial world. For example, imagine you are walking through the woods in the dark. You hear a branch crunch behind you and suddenly your heartbeat changes and your blood flow is shunted as it drains from your brain and prepares to go to your muscles so you can run from whatever lurks in the dark. This is why in moments of great stress, we feel lightheaded and our pulse quickens.

Our limbic system, the old part of our brain, is wired to support this type of autonomic response—even if the threats in our environment are totally different. We may no longer be chased by tigers, but we still live out the same kind of

From the violence on TV to the over-stimulation from our phones, we are constantly fueled by fight-or-flight energy.

fight-or-flight response when we have to break a piece of particularly bad news to someone, for example. When we're in a state like that, our prefrontal cortex—the home of logic and reason—goes offline. We're not producing brilliant solutions or rationally thinking things through. In our brains, we're running for our lives.

Speaking generally, the sympathetic nervous system developed in a way that it would only be activated intermittently in times of stress or danger, in balance with the parasympathetic system for times of rest, digestion and other low-stress situations. Today, our sympathetic nervous system is almost chronically overactive.

In today's world, most of what we see, hear and do—and often more importantly, how we *perceive*—drives us into that sympathetic state. From the violence on TV to the over-stimulation from our phones, we are constantly fueled by fight-or-flight energy.

It's true that sometimes we do need that extra sympathetic boost to chase things in life, but we don't always need to destroy ourselves in the process. We can achieve our goals through a flow state with our sympathetic and parasympathetic systems in balance. It's in the flow state where we find joy in what we're doing—we are "lit up," "on fire" and "in the zone." We are stimulated but at ease, with true elation and fulfilled purpose.

Rather than only focusing on "the grind," we should focus on the flow.

The flow is where we achieve our greatest success, where things seem to come to us without even trying. When Michael Jordan plays his best game or Elon Musk comes up with SpaceX, they're not in a frantic, over-stimulated state. They're in a flow, hitting shots or having breakthroughs.

The term "flow," as originally conceptualized by Hungarian-American psychologist Mihaly Csikszentmihalyi, refers to a state in which people are so involved in an activity that nothing else seems to matter.[10] You can only get into this state under the right conditions —by avoiding sympathetic nervous system dominance and moving into a parasympathetic state. When we experience psychological flow, we capture the positive mental state of being completely absorbed, focused and involved in our activities for some period of time as well as an additional level of enjoyment from that complete immersion. When we're in flow, hours can pass in what seem like seconds. The problem is that while we know flow states are good, we rarely prioritize seeking them out.

Even so, there are techniques we can use to help us get into flow.

In a recent study published in the Proceedings of the National Academy of Sciences, researchers from Columbia University School of Engineering and Applied Science showed that they could use online neurofeedback to modify an individual's state of arousal to improve their performance on demanding sensory motor tasks, such as flying a plane or driving in suboptimal conditions.[11]

The subjects in the study were immersed in a virtual reality game where they had to navigate an airplane through rectangular boundaries (this is known as a "boundary avoidance task" and is commonly used in cognitive tests). The experimenters made the boxes narrower every 30 seconds to escalate participants' arousal, which quickly resulted in task failure—missing or crashing into the boundary. When the researchers used neurofeedback—in this case, the sound of a slow heartbeat that was played louder when participants were more stressed—the subjects did better and were able to fly longer.

As the study showed, neurofeedback is one way to pull ourselves out of our sympathetic mind and into a parasympathetic one to improve performance—but the same principle can be applied in simpler ways as well. For one thing, we can practice mindfulness throughout the day and do meditation to train ourselves to be less reactive. In the middle of a difficult task, we can take a deep breath, separate ourselves from the problem, remind ourselves what we're there to do and get back to it.

The process of backing away from a hard problem to allow a subconscious or spontaneous breakthrough is what's known in academia and scientific literature as an "incubation period," a tool to enhance creative performance. Think about it like this: have you ever tried to "grind" your way through a creative obstacle like writer's block? How did that work for you? Chances are you were left spinning your wheels and wasting valuable time and energy for longer than you care to admit.

On the other hand, how many times have you stepped away from a project only to have a creative breakthrough in the interim? Whenever I notice that I'm stalling, I might take a walk outside (as much of a "nature walk" as possible), meditate or seek out a captivating conversation with a friend—three enormously powerful activities when it comes to engaging the parasympathetic nervous system. When I come back to whatever I'm working on, I'm typically able to complete it with renewed enthusiasm, creativity and perspective—in less time and in a more well-rounded way than if I had tried to "grind" my way through.

Though we know it's good to slow down and view things from a calmer perspective, we rarely make the time for activities like meditation and grounding that help us do those things. We don't watch TV that calms our mind or read news that puts us in a parasympathetic state. We are not giving ourselves a chance to live in that flow. Instead, we are addicted to the frazzled sympathetic mind, where we have less capacity to deal with stress—whether it's physical, mental, emotional or microbial. We are constantly adding to our allostatic load and then wondering why we're running on empty.

If there's one major takeaway from all of this, it's that there are no awards for grinding—just medical bills, failed relationships and an early grave. Overworking and burning yourself out makes you more likely to get sick—and when you do, it's with more severe symptoms and longer recovery time. While the interaction between the sympathetic nervous system and immune system is complex, just know that when you are always grinding—when your sympathetic nervous system is consistently asked to be "on"—it inhibits many aspects of the body's natural immune response, making you more susceptible to external threats of all kinds. Remarkable success, energy, resilience and health, meanwhile, come from the flow.

STRESS VS. EUSTRESS

Our ability to make optimal decisions, judgments and actions in dynamic environments—that is, out in the real world—hinges on our level of arousal. Being too aroused leads to us feeling overly stressed or distracted, whereas being too unaroused can mean feeling tired or uninterested—either situation can significantly hamper our decision-making. On the other hand, just the right amount of arousal—being "in the zone" or in a flow state—can improve our decision-making abilities significantly. It takes practice to get into a resilient zone between fatigue and recovery—and frequently, people swing like a pendulum between hyperactivity and depression or malaise. Experimentation here is key, but another factor is how we perceive the stressors in our lives.

Eustress supports bio-resilience, offering constructive pressure that can ultimately boost your energy. Distress, or negative stress, does the opposite, leading to anxiety or an inability to perform, which lowers your energy.

The relationship between pressure and performance is a lot like the story of *Goldilocks and The Three Bears*: optimal performance occurs when the amount of pressure we're under falls within a certain range rather than stretching to the extremes. For that very reason, that relationship is commonly called "the Goldilocks principle"—our relationship of stress to performance can either be too much, too little or just right. Even so, keep in mind that "just right" is a dynamic zone, not a static one. There may be times when your curve shifts to the left or to the right, and the shift may result from factors beyond your control. The pandemic is an odd but relevant example which has shifted most people's curves to the left; in other words, their ability to take on added stressors has decreased (if they want to stay healthy, at least).

THE GOLDILOCKS PRINCIPLE

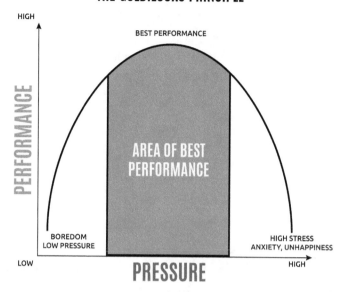

Graphic 10 – The Goldilocks Principle[12]

Stress always gets a negative perception, right? But stress is how we survive, adapt and grow. Stress makes us pursue things: it pushes us to become better at our jobs, to be more competitive at the gym and to become better parents, partners and friends. Stress in balance creates the resilient individual. While chronic, persistent stress suppresses the immune system, in the short-term, a healthy dose of stress (or hormetic stressors, as discussed) can boost the immune system.

When stressors are considered positive, they are referred to as *eustress* (as opposed to *distress*). Eustress supports bio-resilience, offering constructive pressure that can ultimately boost your energy. Distress, or negative stress, does the opposite, leading to anxiety or an inability to perform, which lowers your energy.

Generally speaking, "good stress" is short-lived, infrequent and over quickly; it inspires you to action and helps build you up. Exercise is a fitting example. "Bad stress," on the other hand, is chronic, long-lasting, negative, depressing and demoralizing. It de-motivates and paralyzes you. It breaks you down, leaving you worse off than you were before.

A key feature that distinguishes good stress from bad is how well the stressor matches your ability to recover from it—otherwise known as your resilience. Still, beauty is in the eye of the beholder to some degree when it comes to stress; in other words, our perception of a stressor also influences if it's "good" or "bad."

Formulator's Corner
Stress Reduction Supplements

People frequently ask me about the most important categories of supplements they should take to reduce their stress levels. Though these vary by individual, these are the ones I usually advise:

Magnesium (e.g., Glycinate, Citrate and Threonate): This has a calming effect and impacts the HPA axis, promoting a healthy stress response and easing feelings of tension and anxiety. I particularly like it in the evening, at a dose of 200-400 mg. I prefer magnesium in glycinate or bisglycinate form (i.e., bound to the amino acid glycine), as glycine is an inhibitory neurotransmitter that can help ease stress and promote feelings of calmness in its own right.

Adaptogens (e.g., Sensoril and RhodioPrime): The adaptogens Ashwagandha and Rhodiola help normalize numerous systems and functions in the body, including the adrenals and the body's stress response.

Magnolia Bark/Honokiol (e.g., Relora): A potent anxiolytic that in lighter doses is a good de-stressor and in larger doses can aid in sleep. 500 mg taken once per day in the evening or 250 mg taken twice daily (once in the morning and once in the evening) can reduce stress and cortisol levels while improving mood.

Stress Reduction Supplements (continuation)

Lion's Mane (Standardized for Polysaccharides): This is an adaptogenic mushroom that can improve neuroplasticity and resilience. Dosages can vary considerably, but a good starting point is 500-1,000 mg.

GABA (e.g., PharmaGABA): GABA is an inhibitory neurotransmitter that impacts our ability to calm the body and brain. GABA acts like a "brake" on stress, promotes a calm sense of focus and can help support restful sleep. 100-250 mg taken one to three times daily, particularly when you're feeling stressed, anxious, overwhelmed or distracted and/or before bed, seems to work best.

CBD: I prefer a pure and predictable synthetic or highly isolated version. At 10-100 mg, CBD is a critical player in the ECS (endocannabinoid system), though it requires experimentation for optimal dosing.

L-Theanine (e.g., SunTheanine): A dose of 100-200 mg increases inhibitory neurotransmitter levels and blocks the overproduction of excitatory neurotransmitters. L-theanine supports a healthy stress response and relaxation, and it also promotes a calm, centered attentiveness.

Coenzymated B Complex (e.g., Methylcobalamin, 5-MTHF and P5P): This is excellent for combatting stress since stress uses more B-vitamins; I prefer the active (i.e., coenzyme) forms.

Phosphatidylserine (e.g., SerinAid): A dose of 100-800 mg phospholipid is key to brain health and has been shown to reduce anxiety, improve memory and in higher doses, lower cortisol. For example, phosphatidylserine has been shown to reduce the body's cortisol response to acute physical and mental stress, and it has also been shown to improve mood and learning.

Stress is inherently neutral. It is how we perceive it and respond to it—what lens we view the event through, what we do for stress management, how we manage and integrate our reactions—that makes it eustress or distress.

That is what makes our current environment so unique. We are facing a global stressor that is long-term and negative, which means we need to be even more diligent in the world outside our front door. On the other hand, when we come to grips with the fact that the only things we have full control over are our actions, attitudes and effort, in the short-term, the situation offers us myriad opportunities to positively adapt.

Because we are in the throes of "more" stress, we have a grand opportunity to experiment with new stress management techniques. We need a robust immune system now as much as ever, and we have a choice to experiment with strategies that can support a healthier immune response.

Life often teaches us that what feels like a terrible outcome is often a set-up for something miraculous. This is why you need to practice backing up and reframing situations—because with the right management techniques, stress can be healthy—and unexpected events don't have to seem so bad. Instead of looking down the road, you might need to focus on the choices you are making right now. Maybe you are in an abusive relationship, or maybe you're in a financial situation where you are overextended. Maybe you are struggling in school or with your health. When you first notice these things, it might feel like the world is ending—but then you realize, "Wait, I have a choice here!"

You can start making decisions to improve your situation or you can lose yourself to the fear of something that hasn't happened yet. But you can always reframe. You can say, "Yes, I potentially have cancer. But you know what? I am going to address it and I'm going to grow stronger as a result of it. I am going to educate others around me on it. I'm going to get healthier in my relationships, exercise routines and nutrition. I am going to grow closer to my family. And when I come out on the other side, it is going to be my greatest story. It is going to be something that defines me and my strengths. I am going to appreciate the relationships I have and the people that supported me through this process. I would have never known the strength of those relationships unless this had happened."

Instead of immediately reacting and then regretting whatever comes out of your mouth, you can step back, take six deep breaths and list all the positives that could come out of any given negative. It is all about reframing. When we experiment with our choices, we are able to create new responses. As Carnegie Melon University computer science professor Randy Pausch famously said, "We cannot change the cards we are dealt, just how we play the hand."

When we are in a state of distress, we feel like life is happening to us, but when we are in a flow state, we realize we are making the decisions for ourselves. We are designing our lives. That power is within us. When we can manage our stress, we say, **Life often teaches us that what feels like a terrible outcome is often a set-up for something miraculous.** "I'm on a path and no one's stopping me from being on it. And yes, something has come into my path, but it's here for a reason and I'm going to grow from it."

Instead of being chased by an imaginary wolf, we can stop and go for a walk in the woods. We can develop a new response—beyond freezing, fleeing or fighting. We can look at whatever we might have considered terrifying and recognize it for what it is: a part of life. When we feel frustrated or in the midst of chaos, it's hard to recognize that we are our own choice makers. We get lost in self-victimization and forget that success comes from a place of empowerment and experimentation. Fortunately, we can always take a step back when we put our minds to it.

DEFINING THE FINISH LINE

Maybe the biggest question we can ask ourselves is, "Why am I here?" Personally, I was always greatly inspired by the drive of Kobe Bryant, whose "Mamba Mentality" I emulate in my own life. In a way, many professional athletes have it easy—they are born with such an obvious gift. They often make the logical choice to commit the time and energy to reaching their potential.

But most of us are not born with the ability to knock down three-pointers like Kobe did. Instead, we have to spend our whole lives figuring out our talents and abilities. But having purpose can drive us to that finish line. It is why so many people retire and then suddenly find that their health falls off a cliff. Once they lose their purpose, they lose their will to live—or, at the very least, they lose their way.

Along with purpose, you must have passion. Passion is what keeps us in an engaged flow and out of the grind. The old saying that if you love what you do, you will never work a day in your life is true—when we are working from our passion and driven by our purpose, we find that flow states are much easier to achieve. It's not about simply working hard for the sake of hard work. We only stay on our path if we feel like we're actually *going* somewhere.

The first step is to figure out where that place is. Here are some questions you can ask yourself to find out:

- Are you the type of person who believes your skills and abilities are finite and "you are where you are" or do you believe you have limitless potential?

- Are you the type of person who sees failure as disheartening or as an opportunity to learn and adapt?

- Are you the type of person who believes there are many things you will never be good at, or do you believe that you can learn to do anything you want?

- Are you the type of person who sticks to what you know or tries new things?

- Are you the type of person who takes feedback and criticism personally, or do you consider it to be constructive and collaborative?

Your answers to these questions shed light on whether you embrace a fixed mindset or a growth mindset, and this can have a powerful impact on motivation, productivity, relationships and more. There is a famous Henry Ford quote that comes to mind: "Whether you think you can or you think you can't, you're right." You are what you believe. You project your reality, so if you want positive things, amazing things, limitless things…you need to think that way.

That does not—and should not—happen overnight.

With experimentation, it's all about using the scientific method. You try one thing to make sure it works, tweak it if necessary, then you try something else. You stay committed long enough to make something part of your routine so you feel the difference and you benefit from it—but you don't do everything at once. It is important to do one thing at a time, spend a few weeks doing it, evaluate it and decide if it really works for you.

I wish I could just say, "Do this and you will be healed." But the journey is part of the process. It might take a little longer to get it right, but over time, the correct choices will start leading to greater flow and you will begin to feel what it means to live in the parasympathetic state—grounded, focused, resilient and filled with energy. That contributes to an appropriately balanced nervous system. This is also important when it comes to promoting a healthy, robust and properly responsive immune system, as the parasympathetic nervous system can help control inflammation in a healthy way by acting as an anti-inflammatory neural circuit.

FLOW SUPPORTS IMMUNITY

Without an immune system, our bodies would be open to attack from microscopic threats like bacteria, viruses and parasites. Involving many types of cells, organs and proteins, this system's job is to distinguish our tissue from foreign tissue. If the immune system encounters an antigen (a pathogen, bacterium, virus, parasite, etc.) it triggers an inflammatory cascade and a subsequent immune response, and the body fights to dispose of this foreign invader.

Now more than ever, our habits are critical to our health, and the best way to promote a healthy, balanced and proper immune response is to improve overall well-being. Ask yourself: Are you eating whole, nutrient-dense foods? Are you getting enough sleep and fresh air? What is your overall stress level? Are you moving your body in healthy ways regularly? Are you nourishing your relationships and fostering social connectedness as opposed to being socially isolated, leaving the door open to feelings of loneliness? We now know that there are many things which weaken the immune system and make us more susceptible to all kind of disease, including COVID-19. These include:

- Poor diet (sugar-rich, processed foods with additives)
- Smoking
- Excessive alcohol intake
- Sleep deprivation
- Dehydration
- Obesity
- Stress
- Antibiotics
- Not maintaining regular exercise
- Social isolation and loneliness
- Not spending time outdoors

No one wants to get sick or aid the spread of this virus, which means we need to focus on the habits that can build and sustain a strong immune system. If your immune system is weak or overall unhealthy, your body's ability to fight antigens will be weaker and you will be more vulnerable to getting sick and developing severe symptoms. What do we do during viral seasons? We load up on vitamins, medications and disinfectants. While I am not downplaying the importance of these things, it is important to remember:

Healthy immunity starts with a healthy you!

Every time life changes, we must adjust. We never end up "perfect," and we're all thrown curveballs—a child gets sick, a parent dies, we get laid off or we quit our job. A pandemic strikes and life as we know it is thrown upside down.

The thing is, we know how to deal with the big things more calmly than the little things. It is the little things that often take us out. We need to choose how and where we focus our time and attention because much

We are not that busy; we are just distracted.

like the tree reaching for the light, whatever we focus on will grow.

If we focus on stress and fear, they will consume us.

If we instead focus on our passions, families and friends, they will grow in abundance.

The better you take care of yourself, the better you can take care of other people. Here is the real secret: we are energized when we show up for other's lives. Working with patients and families and residents in nursing homes changed my life. I learned to appreciate life. I saw that we all bleed, we all cry, we all want to be happy and acknowledged. I learned true empathy as I saw myself in others. When you put yourself in the service of others and see the pain in others, it changes you.

I saw so many in the nursing homes experiencing spiritual and emotional pain, not just physical ailments. They felt lonely, abandoned, regretful, ashamed, sad, tired and scared often and I was there to listen, to be a smiling face, or a mirror they needed. I also saw their joy and laughter and deep connections. It was all beautiful. It was all a teacher for me on how to be present for those around me. Their resilience against all odds often inspired me. What do I really have to complain about?

The one resident I got closest to, however, was not elderly. He was barely out of high school. His mother had just died of cancer, his father was a deadbeat dad and Matthew had Osteogenesis Imperfecta (brittle bone disease). He couldn't walk, looked disfigured from so many fractures and was in an electric wheelchair. He lived in a nursing home with an 85-year-old roommate and needed someone to help him to the bathroom. He became a dear friend during my time there. I bought him cell phones, video games and consoles. He felt like a son or a brother to me and it gave me so much perspective to see him be happy despite these circumstances. He loved life and—good news—he eventually got his own place, found love and has two children. Anything is possible. I gave him things, but he gave me so much more: perspective and gratitude for what I have. We are still great friends and we make time to talk to this day.

We are not that busy; we are just distracted. I will tell you right now, "busy" is not an excuse. Never before have more people used "busy" as a high-minded reason not to participate in life. We have plenty of time to scroll through our phones, to look at pictures of our high school sweetheart on vacation or to follow some silly spat on Twitter. I recognize there is a time and place for social media—it has its benefits, no doubt—but it has also become an enormous time suck. When we get too "busy," we fail to show up for the communities we're a part of and for the people we love.

Changing your life starts with your experimentation. It starts with the choices you make first thing in the morning and ends with the choices you make right before you go to bed. Your choices are a direct reflection of your priorities. This is not meant to overwhelm you. This isn't about getting from Maine to California like Forrest Gump; this is about getting to the end of the block.

So start now. Instead of wasting time and energy staring into other people's lives and avoiding your own, you can start to focus on the great experiment of you. Forget about what you've been told before—about all those diets and workouts. I am not here to overwhelm you with a whole new plan or routine; I'm here to give you the tools to find the energy you need to get the results you deserve.

EXPERIMENT SUMMARY

- We all have our own bio-individuality; what works for one person may not work for another so before we can make changes, we need to understand our foundation. We cannot live truly energized lives if we are not living authentic ones. Get real about who you are and where you are in life.

- One of the biggest factors in our energy levels is our mitochondrial functioning, as mitochondria are the powerhouses of our cells. We can test our mitochondrial health through the following three blood biomarkers: hsCRP, HbA1c and OxLDL.

- Hormesis, when done in the right amount, triggers certain biochemical pathways and physiological adaptations that make us more resilient when facing future stressors. When done too much or for too long, however, they can become a stress on the body, adding to our "stress bucket." The greater your allostatic load, the less likely you are to respond positively to hormesis and the worse off you are. On the other hand, positive stressors, known as eustress, support bio-resilience, strengthening activity and energy. Distress does the opposite and leads to a lack of energy.

- Psychological flow means being completely absorbed, focused and involved in whatever you are doing and deriving enjoyment from being fully immersed in that activity. Flow, when we are in alignment with our creativity and our joy, is what we should seek and where we achieve the greatest success.

- Much of our stress comes from being distracted. Practice mindfulness by focusing on one thing at a time and staying fully present. Reframing stressful situations can allow us to find focus and choose the elements over which we have control, creating a new response. Begin experimenting with meditation, exercise, nutrition and breathing to create an environment which supports parasympathetic dominance. This takes time to achieve.

- Along with purpose, you must have passion; passion keeps us in our flow and purpose gives us our "why." We also need to see where that "why" not only serves our needs and goals, but also helps our families, communities and the world beyond our front door. The true secret to feeling energized is to be of service and show up for other people.

- Changing your life starts with experimentation, starting with the choices you make first thing in the morning and ending with the last decision you make before bed. When you experiment, change one thing at a time and evaluate the outcome. Take your time. If you "shotgun" a lot of changes, you will have no idea what's working and what's not. If something doesn't work, tweak or move onto the next hack.

Resource Hacks

Experimentation in Action

My Ultimate Blood Panel: I get blood tests every three to six months, and my must-have labs check for oxLDL, HbA1c, hsCRP, CBC, iron, ferritin, thyroid panel, cortisol, testosterone, lipids and 25-hydroxy vitamin D. LabCorp or Quest Diagnostics are two great labs to get this done.

MyChon: This is the first complete functional at-home mitochondria test tracker that accurately uncovers your mitochondrial health and function, though it is still in beta (you can sign up on the website). They are developing a testing technology that will make it easy and convenient for anyone to access, understand and improve their cellular health with the goal of improved energy, optimal wellness, increased healthspan and longevity.

Genova Diagnostics: This one is super extensive—probably the ultimate test—but you don't have to do it just yet. Start with the basics. I suggest the NutrEval test for in-depth nutrient deficiency analysis and the GI Effects for gut health. Consider working with a functional doctor to analyze these results.

23AndMe and Ancestry for Genetic Testing: These are used to test your DNA for any genetic susceptibilities to certain disease states or other vulnerabilities, but you can't have the same company give genetic testing and interpret the data. You can use the following for the second part:

Experimentation in Action (continuation)

SelfHacked: Owned by Joe Cohen, this company has a great evaluation/analyzation package called SelfDecode.

Found My Fitness: Rhonda Patrick's **Genetic Report** is a great place to start as well. This company, run by longevity influencer and host of a popular life-extension podcast Dr. Rhonda Patrick, offers a third-party analysis of genetic data from both 23andMe and AncestryDNA.

Viome: Analyzes the gut microbiome to understand how to dial in your nutrition optimally. This analysis used to be controversial. The science is not exact, but it's all part of the data collection that can help you understand your body.

Record Your Data: I like to plot my results in an Excel spreadsheet and date the tests. This allows me to compare and see my progress on my journey so I can adjust my strategies. Heads Up Health is more advanced and offers a dashboard you and your physician can look at. It syncs with wearables like Biostrap and Oura.

*For live links, updated content, bonus graphics
and a hidden chapter, go to
EnergyFormulaBook.com*

NUTRITION SURVEY

How well do you prioritize good nutrition on a daily basis?		
I am conscious of the food choices I make and the foods that go into my body.	(3)	
I have a basic understanding of nutrition but still feel there is a lot I don't know.	(2)	
I really don't know what to eat or how to use food to achieve my health goals.	(1)	
What is your past experience with research-backed diets and healthy eating?		
I have tried a few and experimented to know what works best for me and what my body runs on optimally.	(3)	
I've tried various research-backed diets and learned a little but am still not sure of the best way to eat for my body.	(2)	
I have done every diet ever made. I lose weight and gain it back and never make any sustained progress.	(1)	
How would you rate your knowledge of the keto lifestyle?		
I'm an expert! I know a lot about the keto lifestyle and have used it to improve my health and nutrition.	(3)	
I've heard of keto, but still don't fully understand it.	(2)	
I don't really know anything about keto!	(1)	
How would you rate your current relationship with food?		
I have a great relationship with food. I eat when I'm hungry and stop when I'm full and don't rely on emotional cues to eat.	(3)	
My eating is often emotion-driven where I tend to make poor food choices and overeat.	(2)	
I have a poor relationship with food and make choices that leave me frustrated with how I feel about my body and self.	(1)	

When it comes to eating mindfully, how well do you do?		
I am tuned in and paying attention when I eat. I savor each bite and check in with myself for satisfaction and fullness throughout the meal.	(3)	
I'm often distracted while eating, either by the TV or other things going on, so it's easy to eat too much and not focus on food quality.	(2)	
My meals are mostly eaten on-the-go and are convenience or fast-food type meals.	(1)	
How familiar are you with tracking calories or macronutrients?		
I'm very familiar with tracking calories or macros and have used it successfully to know how much I'm eating.	(3)	
I have tracked a little here and there, but not consistently and I don't know my current intake	(2)	
I've never tracked calories or macros and I wouldn't know where to start!	(1)	
When it comes to gut health, how do you feel you are doing?		
My gut health and digestion are excellent; I don't have any unusual or outstanding issues.	(3)	
My gut health needs some work, but overall, I feel okay most of the time.	(2)	
My gut health is horrible. I suffer from fatigue, brain fog, poor sleep quality, skin issues, hormone imbalances, joint discomfort, allergies, cravings and/or difficulty with weight management.	(1)	
YOUR TOTAL		

7-11 points: You have got some work to do! This book is a great place to start!

12-16 points: You are heading in the right direction! Keep at it!

17-21 points: You are really on the ball! Only small tweaks are needed to be your best self!

Chapter 2: Nutrition: Nourish Your Body, Eat Whole Foods

"The food you eat can be either the safest and most powerful form of medicine or the slowest form of poison."

—Ann Wigmore

I studied hard at Babson College and double-majored in Marketing and Information Technology. I figured I would learn the raw skills behind computers and entrepreneurship and marry them to my passion for health and supplements. Meanwhile, I was still transforming my body through supplements, exercise and nutrition—but my routines were starting to get a little extreme, even if I didn't notice at the time.

I'd had some early success with creatine and weightlifting, but I was still dissatisfied with how I looked. Growing up, my two brothers looked like models. My brother Randy in particular had an incredible physique. He was a Minor League baseball player and an all-around great athlete. Meanwhile, my brother Russell exercised all the time and had a great body throughout high school as well. Growing up, beautiful girls lined up to see them or to go on dates. On any given weekend at the mall, you were liable to see my two ripped brothers, their hot girlfriends (who were constantly rotating) and me tagging along, clearly the odd one out. I was still jealous as the obese kid with acne and had no dates or attention from girls even at Babson.

During my time there, I was sick of being what felt like fat and ugly. Tired of being the "beta male." So I started working out and taking supplementation to the next level using ephedrine and caffeine stacks. Creatine had been good, but the ephedrine and caffeine combination was *unbelievable* for energy—to this day, nothing comes close to it (though full disclosure, the FDA has cracked down on ephedrine supplements for some very real health risks that it poses—but at the time, the jury was still out). It was an incredible fat burner and combined with playing with amino acid supplements and the rest of my routine, my body was changing drastically. I could feel my dreams taking shape, and I knew I had to go back and get my Master's in nutrition to take the next step.

My parents had moved from Massachusetts to North Carolina while I was at Babson, and I knew that if I believed in this dream, I would have to fund it and achieve it myself. My top choice was UNC-Chapel Hill, the best of the best. To be accepted there, I would need two straight years of sciences as prerequisites, which led me to UNC-Greensboro, where I visited a guidance counselor. Let's call him Mr. Smith (I have honestly blocked his name out, but not his face). I told him with unrepressed zeal about my dream of becoming a sports nutritionist, a clinical dietitian and a supplement formulator. But before I even finished saying Chapel Hill, he stopped me.

"You would need 26 credit hours of straight sciences a semester —with labs," he said dismissively. "This is not doable, especially for a business student. Why don't you pick something more realistic? You're not even that fit, if I am being honest."

I couldn't believe what I heard—after all the progress I'd made, it seemed I was still the person I feared I'd always be. Devastated, hurt and angry, I stormed out of his office with tears streaming down my face.

For two days straight, I contemplated suicide. I looked at bottles of Tylenol and aspirin and thought, "I'll just take all of this, wash it down with some Pepe Lopez tequila and slip out of this world. No one will miss me. I am the fat-ass with a stupid, unrealistic dream."

I was in a new city with no family, no friends and certainly no girlfriends. But in that moment, I heard Dr. Johnson's voice again in the back of my mind: *Why not be happy between here and here?* I decided I didn't care what the counselor said. I would try. If I failed, I would revisit the idea of ending my life—but in the meantime, I decided to take the risk. I would try to be happy.

The next morning, I went into the office at UNC-Greensboro and put an additional full semester's worth of classes on my credit card: Chemistry 1 & 2, Biology 1 & 2, Human Biochemistry, Plant Biochemistry, Nutrition, Genetics and more. For most students in those days, that was more like three or four semesters' worth of classes. The prerequisites to get into Chapel Hill were lengthy and the difficulty curve was steep. I didn't just need to take the classes; I needed to ace them.

In addition to my huge workload, I was also pushing my body to the limit—more than I ever had before. Hearing that UNC-Greensboro guidance counselor's voice still ringing in my ears, I decided I was still too close to the "fat kid" I'd always been. I needed to be even slimmer. In truth, I had secretly been fighting with my body issues behind the scenes for years.

Early on, my goal was to shed as many pounds as I could. I cut my fat intake to nearly zero (ironic for someone who later would be known as "the keto guy") and before I knew it, I was on the other side of a 150-pound swing—I'd gone from morbidly obese to rail thin, and now friends and gym buddies were calling me "Skeletor." They were poking fun at me—and in retrospect, maybe it was their way of showing concern for my health without really asking me what was going on. The truth was I was fully anorexic—which seemed supremely ironic for someone interested in nutrition. I wasn't giving my own body the fuel it needed and it was affecting my energy and my health. I felt as alone as ever—after all, how many men suffered from anorexia? (That was my immature thought at the time—the truth, of course, is that men can suffer from eating disorders just like women can).

After I started getting self-conscious about being too skinny instead of being too fat, I went the other way and changed my diet, adding in more protein. I started exercising four hours a day while taking supplements, and my weight went back up to 215 or 220 pounds. This time, I was all muscle—but the way I'd gotten there had not been healthy. I had traded anorexia for orthorexia, and I still felt trapped in my relationship with my body.

In 1999, I made good on my promise to myself. I finished at UNC-Greensboro with exemplary grades and got accepted at Chapel Hill. The whole time, I was elated that my dream was coming true. I was going to learn all about nutrition, and I was going to add it to my repertoire of skills to become a more perfect person and to share that wisdom with the rest of the world. Despite my success, I still wondered if maybe the bullies and nay-sayers were right about me. Maybe I wasn't fit enough or smart enough for all this. I shook the thoughts out of my mind and pushed on—if I couldn't exorcise my demons, I'd just have to outrun them.

In 2001, I had nearly wrapped up my Master's degree at Chapel Hill. I had only two-and-a-half months to go. I was getting offers to work in hospitals as the Chief Clinical Dietitian, a position usually reserved for a clinician with 20 years of experience. But the crazy thing is throughout my life, it seems like every time I've had a taste of success or overcome an obstacle, life has hit back with another hurdle, another test. This time, it was mononucleosis—better known as "mono"— which is caused by the Epstein-Barr virus. While many know mono as "the kissing disease," they don't know that Epstein-Barr can play a role in the development of autoimmune disease. That's what it was doing to me, right as I was on the verge of finishing my degree. My body was beginning to shut down.

An autoimmune disease—and there are many of them—is when your immune system attacks your own body. The role of the immune system is to identify and attack foreign invaders like bacteria, viruses, parasites and toxins—but in my case, my overactive immune system was mistakenly mounting an attack against the healthy cells in my body. In a lot of the "traditional wisdom" I'd heard up to that point on the topic, once you developed an autoimmune disease, it was with you for life—and that scared me.

AUTOIMMUNE DISEASE

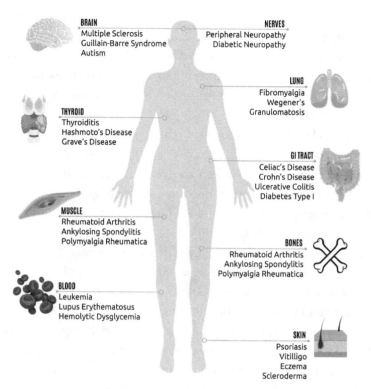

BRAIN
Multiple Sclerosis
Guillain-Barre Syndrome
Autism

NERVES
Peripheral Neuropathy
Diabetic Neuropathy

LUNG
Fibromyalgia
Wegener's
Granulomatosis

THYROID
Thyroiditis
Hashmoto's Disease
Grave's Disease

GI TRACT
Celiac's Disease
Crohn's Disease
Ulcerative Colitis
Diabetes Type I

MUSCLE
Rheumatoid Arthritis
Ankylosing Spondylitis
Polymyalgia Rheumatica

BONES
Rheumatoid Arthritis
Ankylosing Spondylitis
Polymyalgia Rheumatica

BLOOD
Leukemia
Lupus Erythematosus
Hemolytic Dysglycemia

SKIN
Psoriasis
Vitilligo
Eczema
Scleroderma

Graphic 11 – Autoimmune Disease

My liver was swollen and pushing on my ribs. I was sleeping 23 hours a day. My throat was swollen shut. I could only drink liquids. I felt like I was dying. My depression flared back up with a vengeance and I wasn't sure I was going to make it. Brain fog, fatigue, extreme fevers and shivering went on for days, then weeks. Although I have never gone through it myself, I suspect it was similar to what it might feel like to go through extreme withdrawal from alcohol.

I was missing classes, but as much as I wanted to finish my degree and step into the life I'd always wanted, that wasn't my most pressing worry anymore. I wasn't sure I would even be alive another month. I couldn't muster the energy to leave my apartment. I wasn't eating and I was barely drinking anything.

The best I could do was get online (on dial-up, no less), and it's a damn good thing I did. In my search for innovative ideas and solutions, I began reading about a diet called the *ketogenic* diet. From what I read, a keto diet could help with autoimmune issues and inflammation—at least according to a few trailblazers on the message boards. It sounded like my autoimmune issues didn't have to hinder me my entire life. They didn't have to be a death sentence, and there might be some hope.

As I was finally starting to heal from mono, I knew I had to make a change. I couldn't keep bouncing back and forth between undernourished and skinny to overworked and way too ripped. It was tearing my body down. I needed to boost my immune system, to turn my health around so I could live the life I wanted. I decided to give this high-fat, very-low-carb approach a shot. I stopped buying processed foods—even the so-called healthy stuff like whole wheat breads, cereals, pastas and the like. I kept to the outside ring of the grocery store where the whole, real food was.

I continued to experiment with keto, on and off from 2001 through 2003, and every time I stuck to it, it seemed to help. In fact, as my body adapted and I became more active, I felt like I could see myself through this new normal of life with an autoimmune condition—and I did.

Through the keto diet, I went from spending my days in and out of the hospital and doctor's offices as a patient to building a life and career focused on diet and nutrition. I discovered that what I put in my body ultimately determined the trajectory of my life—and whether my body was filled with energy or illness. I was living proof that nutrition could have a profound influence on inflammation and the immune system. In fact, nutrition would change my entire life.

Before we move forward into the wonderful and wild world of nutrition, I want us to discard one terribly negative word: diet. Scientifically, a diet is what you eat, but many people associate the word with restrictions. They think that a diet is a fast fix to a long-term problem, but the fact is people don't get unhealthy in a short period of time so they can't recover from it quickly either. Diets might offer a quick outcome, but crash diets are physically and emotionally unhealthy.

And taking your time while shifting nutrition means it's also going to be far more long lasting and impactful.

A better word than diet—and the one I would like us to agree to use moving forward—is lifestyle. You are not going on a diet—temporary, restrictive, reversible. You are adopting a new lifestyle—permanent, gradual, transformative.

The thing about treating food like a lifestyle and not a diet is that you have room to be flexible. If you have one salad a week and you eat fast food junk the rest of the time, you're not going to get healthy. It is not all or nothing. If we are healthy 90 percent of the time, we can decide how we want to spend the other 10 percent. Fair warning though: the healthier you become, the less appetizing other options become. (Except for McDonald's fries—man, those still taste so good!)

Today, I plan my food choices around my lifestyle. The reason a lifestyle is so different from a diet is that you are agreeing to make choices for the long run. One of the things I enjoy about paleo and keto is that it empowers us to make decisions outside of the norm. Most cultures tell us that we need to have bread on the table and eat three times a day, but by simply questioning that status quo, we begin to develop more conscious choice-making. We get comfortable breaking social norms in order to make healthier choices; just imagine how that quality can show up in other areas of our lives! We not only become healthier in this new lifestyle, but we also become empowered.

DIET VS. LIFESTYLE

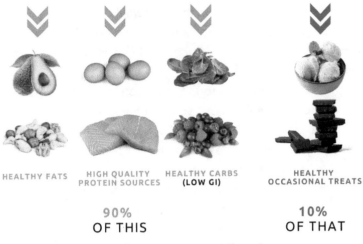

| HEALTHY FATS | HIGH QUALITY PROTEIN SOURCES | HEALTHY CARBS (LOW GI) | HEALTHY OCCASIONAL TREATS |

90%
OF THIS

10%
OF THAT

Graphic 12 – Diet vs Lifestyle

This isn't only true when it comes to food. When we start deciding how we'll eat and commit to going to the gym, we begin to look at our other life choices. Maybe we are taking part in unhealthy sexual behaviors or drinking too much alcohol. Maybe we are "checking out" in other areas of our lives. Now that our consciousness is raised around food and nutrition, we begin to question behavior that we may have taken for granted before. We begin expecting more not just from ourselves, but also from the people and communities around us.

I like to think if we are conscious about what we put in our bodies, we will be more conscious about other decisions in our world too.

When we embrace the idea of a lifestyle practice, we are truly taking our health, longevity and energy levels into our own hands. Recent research, for example, provides clear and convincing evidence that adopting a healthy lifestyle can help you live longer and stronger and reverse aging. According to leading anti-aging expert Dr. David Sinclair, "We now know from studying twins that 80% of your health in old age is up to you, how you live your life." Along those lines, a recent study published in the journal *Circulation* found that people who consistently practiced five low-risk lifestyle factors—never smoking, maintaining a healthy weight, exercising moderately/ vigorously regularly, not drinking alcohol excessively and eating a healthy diet—lived 12-14 years longerz than those folks who didn't do any of those things routinely.[13] Dr. Sinclair, meanwhile, would add that fasting and getting a good night's sleep can also help you live longer and more energetically.

For example, when we are eating better, we are less tired. When we are less tired, we drink more water and less coffee. When we drink more water, we have more energy. When we have more energy, we go to the gym. When we go to the gym, we eat better... and so on and so on.

On the other end of the spectrum, we can also end up in an unhealthy spiral: we wake up tired and don't make it to the gym, and then because we are tired, we have coffee and M&Ms before lunch—and then we figure, "Screw it, the day is already ruined, so why not have pizza for lunch?" Then instead of water, we have another cup of coffee and then we can't sleep at night so we wake up tired —and the vicious, self-defeating, energy-draining cycle repeats.

You are not going on a diet—temporary, restrictive, reversible. You are adopting a new lifestyle—permanent, gradual, transformative.

To take control of our health, we need to start by defining what each part of our health means. We need an understanding of how cholesterol and fat work in the body, and what we mean when we say "healthy."

THE CHOLESTEROL QUESTION

Many of the dietary changes I'll suggest lead to raising fat and cholesterol in your diet...but when you hear or see the word "cholesterol," what comes to mind? There is a good chance you are not thinking about sunshine and rainbows. For decades, cholesterol has been demonized and vilified as the poster child for heart disease. But what is the truth about cholesterol? Why do we need it? What are the different types of cholesterol? What causes elevated levels, and can foods like eggs really contribute to increased cholesterol? Let's set the record straight on this poorly understood molecule.

In modern humans, cholesterol accumulates in deposits in the arterial walls. Considering that heart disease is the number one killer in middle-aged and older people, cardiologists have been pointing to cholesterol as the bad guy and primary cause of heart disease. However, cholesterol may simply be guilty by association, as research shows that it is being sent there to "patch up" or repair damage to the arterial wall. If it is repairing damage, what is causing that damage in the first place?

The answer is inflammation. Doctors have known for a long time that inflammation is associated with heart disease. This is why the primary test for your cardiovascular disease risk is CRP (C-reactive protein)—the key inflammatory marker.

We're also realizing that saturated fat isn't as much of a culprit either. We can see that eating foods that are rich in trans-fatty acids, an overabundance of processed omega-6 fats (skewed heavily over dietary omega-3s) and sugars, are causing systemic inflammation and disease. But it's all about ratio. Ultimately, we need to establish a healthier ratio between our omega-6 and omega-3 fats. By balancing those, we can improve our CRP levels.

Certainly, eating higher fat can potentially raise cholesterol, but on diets like the ketogenic diet or Mediterranean diet, our HDL will rise as well, which is protective. In some cases, high-fat diets can raise LDL, but they typically raise the large "fluffy" particles of LDL, which are actually healthy.

The bottom line is this: cholesterol is vital to health and function. It is so important that the body produces it. Yes, you read that correctly. The liver produces about two grams of cholesterol daily, accounting for about 80 percent of the cholesterol needed.14

In addition, cholesterol is a critical part of your steroid hormones —including estrogen and testosterone—and make up a large part of our brain matter. There are Eskimos who have cholesterol levels of 600, but they have no evidence of heart disease.

Contrary to what most people *still* believe, dietary cholesterol only contributes a fraction of our total cholesterol. Even America's ultra-conservative nutrition advisory panel, the Dietary Guidelines Advisory Committee (DGAC), recently stated: "Available evidence shows no appreciable relationship between consumption of dietary cholesterol and [blood] cholesterol."[15]

Conversely, you may be wondering how to lower bad cholesterol or what foods can help reduce cholesterol. Without question, lifestyle modification is the first step in reducing cholesterol levels and cardiovascular risk.[16] Of course, there are non-modifiable risk factors such as age, genetics and gender. Modifiable risk factors include smoking, high blood pressure, diabetes and obesity. In other words, eating more real, whole foods, moving your body in a variety of healthy ways every day and losing weight (which is typically a by-product of the former two behaviors) are all known to be effective.

WHAT IS FAT?

Fat molecules are simple in structure. They have a head and a tail—the glycerol molecule and fatty acid chain, respectively. Their structure depicts their stability, and the stability of a fat depends on its number of "open binding sites." The fewer binding sites, the more stable they are—meaning they are less likely to let free radicals oxidize them, which can lead to aging, inflammation and many diseases.

There are three main types of fats (from most to least stable):

- Saturated Fats (SFA): All binding sites are filled/ saturated — they have NO double bonds and are solid at room temperature (e.g., butter).

- Monounsaturated Fats (MUFA): These are relatively stable, but not as stable as saturated fats. Mono means that there is one double bond in the tail—there is one open site that a free radical could oxidize (e.g., olive oil).

- Polyunsaturated Fats (PUFA): These are the least stable fats, as they have many ("poly") open binding sites for oxidation to take place (e.g., soybean oil (omega-6) or krill oil (omega-3)).

Just because the fats are less stable does not necessarily mean they are bad for you—it only means you must be more careful in buying and preparing foods with them to ensure they do not oxidize. So, we need to avoid processed fats and "vegetable oils" like soybean, corn, safflower, canola, sunflower and cottonseed, which are high in PUFAs—as exposing them to high heats and chemicals makes them rancid and carcinogenic. On top of that, most of their nutrients have been ripped out in the refining process. Therefore, they are *cheap* and used in almost all restaurants and foods across the US—even in "healthy" protein bars and health snacks. They are oxidized, highly inflammatory and often void of nutrients no matter where or how they are used.

WHAT IS HEALTHY?

We all must find our own definition of healthy. Although I will offer my definition here, it is imperative that you find your own.

Healthy does not mean the same thing for everyone and even on an individual basis, your definition of healthy will likely change over time—like seasons—and that's absolutely okay. It can be about weight loss management and body composition, or it can be about diet quality. It can be defined by certain health markers like blood cholesterol, triglycerides, blood sugar, insulin and inflammatory markers. Or it can be defined by a hard end point like death.

The truth is that any of these examples—and a litany of others — may be relevant and important to you depending on where you are (and where you want to be) on your health and wellness journey. As I experimented with different food plans, I could tell that by removing sugar, increasing my intake of high-quality proteins and increasing fats, I just "felt" different. I felt more engaged and energized and had greater clarity and resilience.

I began to discover I not only felt better from the diet, but my body performed better as well. As I like to say, you are not what you eat, you *burn* what you eat. At the end of the day, food is simply fuel for energy—and the more dynamic the fuel, the more energy we will have.

Keto is beneficial to many people for assorted reasons, and it can be customized to fit your bio-individuality. There are three main factors that led me to sticking to the keto diet: it cuts out all nutrient-deficient foods, it helps me to feel full and satisfied and it has cognitive-enhancing effects. Even so, there are several major alternate food pyramids worth considering and experimenting with as you overhaul your own nutrition plan.

KETO FOOD PYRAMID

CARBOHYDRATES	0-10%
PROTEIN	20-25%
FATS	65-75%

Graphic 13 – The Keto Food Pyramid

In a review of 23 weight-loss trials published in the *American Journal of Epidemiology*, researchers from Tulane University found that both low-carb and low-fat diets led to weight loss, reduced waist circumference and improved metabolic risk factors with no significant differences between diets. They concluded: "These findings suggest that low-carbohydrate diets are at least as effective as low-fat diets in reducing weight and improving metabolic risk factors. Low-carbohydrate diets could be recommended to obese persons with abnormal metabolic risk factors for the purpose of weight loss."[17]

One of the best and most reliable examples is the A TO Z Weight Loss Study, a randomized trial conducted by a group of Stanford researchers led by Dr. Christopher Gardner. In the trial, the researchers compared four popular weight-loss diets—Atkins (low-carb *and* high-fat), LEARN (low-fat), Ornish (low-fat) and Zone (technically considered lower carb)—and they found that women following the Atkins diet lost more weight and experienced more favorable metabolic effects after 12 months compared to the other diets.[18]

At the end of the day, food is simply fuel for energy—and the more dynamic the fuel, the more energy we will have.

In another recent study published in the *Journal of the American Medical Association*—the DIETFITS clinical trial, which randomized 609 overweight or obese adults to a healthy low-fat or a healthy low-carb diet for 12 months—both diets led to similar weight loss and metabolic health improvement (e.g., reduced fasting glucose and insulin).

Notably, the low-carb diet led to more favorable improvements in HDL cholesterol and triglycerides.[19]

One of my favorite aspects of the DIETFITS trial was the emphasis on diet quality. The lead physician Dr. Gardner and his team put a tremendous emphasis on high dietary quality for both groups, which is important because traditional low-fat diets often lead to reduced diet quality due to the low-nutrient density of heavily processed, convenient, pre-packaged low-fat foods (e.g., refined grains, added sugar).

Now, if you want to know how healthy a low-carb diet can be, you don't have to look any further than two of the most popular approaches to eating: Mediterranean and paleo-style diets, which consistently rank highly for diet quality and beneficial health outcomes.

MEDITERRANEAN FOOD PYRAMID

MEATS & SWEETS   10%

POULTRY & EGGS   10%

FISH & SEAFOOD   10%

VEGETABLES
& FATS   70%

Graphic 14 – The Mediterranean Food Pyramid[20]

Recently, these nutritional strategies have also been gaining popularity as the Whole 30 diet, which essentially is a marriage of keto and paleo with more targeted marketing.

Truth be told, neither Mediterranean nor paleo diets have specific macronutrient targets. (That's what makes both perfect partners for keto, which does have specific requirements for carbohydrate, fat and protein intake yet doesn't traditionally have the same emphasis on diet quality.) However, studies estimate that for paleo-style diets, carbohydrate intake is roughly 35-40 percent (ranging as high as 65 percent), while total fat intake may be as high as 35 percent (or as low as 20 percent). While Mediterranean-style diet composition can vary significantly across regions and time of year, researchers estimate that about 37 percent of calories come from fat and 43 percent of calories come from carbohydrates.[21]

Whether we are talking about Mediterranean or paleo diets, the commonalities are fairly simple. The most important aspect to healthy eating is a focus on whole foods—whether our diet is carnivorous or herbivorous. It is about choosing healthy, natural, non-processed food products, which are usually not sold far from where they are farmed.

PALEO **FOOD PYRAMID**

NUTS & BERRIES   15%

FRUITS (LOW GI)   15%

MEAT & SEAFOOD   30%

VEGETABLES   40%

Graphic 15 – The Paleo Food Pyramid[22]

That means going to farmer's markets and buying from local butchers. It means getting to know your food and where it comes from. One of the reasons Italy is so renowned for its meals is that most of the ingredients used are from neighborhood farms. The longer a piece of meat or produce lingers in shipping, the higher the likelihood that it is being treated with preservatives and that the nutrients are being reduced.

But nowadays, you can find similar whole foods, keto and paleo options at your local grocery store or even at Costco. As someone who has been doing this a long time, it has been encouraging to see how the movement has grown and become more accessible to more people.

When we eat clean, we feel clean—we feel that clear, pure energy that guides us through our day and into our potential.

On the contrary, if you are eating "dirty keto," where you're in ketosis with the right macros, but eating ultraprocessed foods and decadent desserts and snacks, then you are not going to tap into all the benefits and it's highly unlikely that you'll have consistent, vibrant energy levels. You can be vegan and survive on Oreos and chips, just like you can be keto and be "compliant" on processed keto snacks, but neither one is ideal.

Eating whole foods and unprocessed foods is what elevates how we eat, how we prioritize our health and ultimately, how we develop and experience energized lives.

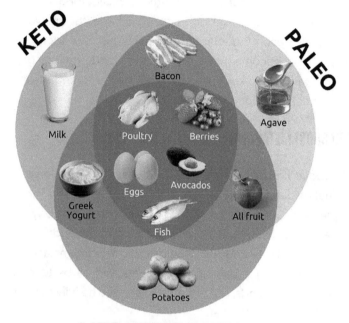

MEDITERRANEAN

Graphic 16 – The Overlap of Keto,
Mediterranean and Paleo

There are two extremely popular dietary philosophies out there right now with a lot of hype around them: the vegan diet (all plant-based) and the carnivore diet (all animal-based). People get confused because they see others thriving on each of these food plans. This is where bio-individuality is so key. People *can* thrive on completely different types of diets and when they do, they often believe their diet is right for everyone, creating a very polarizing environment where each side becomes extremely dogmatic and narrow-minded.

This is not the healthy, open-minded or scientific way to have this discussion; unfortunately, in fact, it ends up being a non-conversation. If we can realize that each person may thrive on a unique diet, we can find agreement. What I've always said is we didn't get sick from eating plants, animals or a combination thereof. It was when we started to have ultra-processed foods with long lists of addictive ingredients—a lot of which compose our Standard American Diet (or SAD)—that we saw our health decline, our bodies change shape (for the worse), our energy levels become depleted, our brains become foggy, our immune systems become more susceptible...and the list goes on. Eating whole foods is key —whether that means eating meat, vegetables or a combination of the two.

HOW TO BOOST METABOLIC FLEXIBILITY: EASY AS 1, 2, 3...

Metabolic flexibility refers to "the capacity for the organism to adapt fuel oxidation to fuel availability." Pretty straightforward, right? In simple terms, metabolic flexibility means that your body can efficiently and effectively switch between using carbs and fats for fuel based on availability and need. Under normal circumstances, most people are burning a combination of fats and carbs to meet the body's energy demands, but this is often skewed heavily towards carb reliance due to the SAD diet.

The ability to switch back and forth between fuel sources makes a great deal of sense from an evolutionary standpoint; a flexible metabolism was necessary for the human species to adapt its energy needs to various climates, seasons and vegetation conditions. In simple terms, metabolic flexibility safeguarded human survival independent of food availability. At a fundamental level, the human metabolism (and metabolic flexibility) has been shaped by a wide range of different food sources (biodiversity) and abundant daily exercise often under fasted conditions (foraging behaviors), as well as an unpredictable food supply (intermittent fasting).

A metabolically flexible individual is one who has the remarkable ability to adapt fuel selection based on supply and demand. Metabolically inflexible individuals (who are usually fueled mostly by glucose), however, are not able to adequately adapt to metabolic challenges. Mitochondria play a crucial role in determining metabolic flexibility.

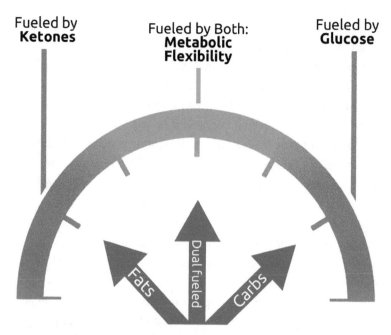

Graphic 17 – Metabolic Flexibility Meter

At the extreme end of unhealthy metabolic flexibility—that is, metabolic inflexibility—lies disease, including metabolic disorders like type 2 diabetes, obesity, cardiovascular disease, hypertension, dyslipidemia (e.g., high triglycerides), Alzheimer's disease, non-alcoholic fatty liver disease, certain types of cancer and more.23 But even before things get that "ugly," the path to metabolic inflexibility may manifest as:

- Feeling tired and fatigued
- Battling brain fog
- Lacking energy to exercise
- Not having the stamina to complete physically demanding tasks
- Dealing with cravings and hunger
- Difficulty with weight loss
- Struggling to manage blood sugar levels

Simply put, metabolic flexibility is a key to looking, feeling and performing your best and living your most energized life. So how do you know where you sit on the metabolic flexibility continuum?

Ask yourself: Do I feel tired, exhausted and have low energy when I fast? This is a sign that your body has a challenging time "switching" over to burning fat for fuel (i.e., you're a sugar burner), you haven't activated fat-metabolizing enzymes and pathways and you don't use ketones well for fuel. You may have guessed by now that markers of blood sugar management and insulin sensitivity are considered surrogate markers of metabolic flexibility. Along those lines, fasting blood sugar, tests for insulin resistance (e.g., HOMA-IR) and oral glucose tolerance may all show signs of metabolic flexibility (or a lack thereof). However, these metabolic snapshots do not really tell you how metabolically flexible you are.

Keep in mind that the concept of metabolic flexibility is all about the body's ability to adapt its fuel selection based on availability and need, whether it's glucose from carbs or ketones from fat. Along these lines, more sophisticated tests for metabolic flexibility assess the difference in fuel use in fasting versus fed states *and* during exercise (compared to rest).

Researchers believe that healthy mitochondria number and function play a critical role in metabolic flexibility. To that end, the very things we need to be doing to boost metabolic flexibility are amazingly effective at improving insulin sensitivity and enhancing mitochondrial number and function.

Of course, *how much* and *what* you do (and don't) put into your mouth also influences metabolic flexibility. On one hand, excessive caloric intake drives metabolic inflexibility; on the other hand, caloric restriction (e.g., intermittent fasting) and/or equilibrium promotes metabolic flexibility. Not surprisingly, the typical Western-style diet and its reliance on processed foods (fortified with high-glycemic, refined carbohydrates and poor-quality, inflammatory oils) pushes the body toward metabolic inflexibility. On the other hand, a diet founded on whole foods (particularly diets rich in plant-based polyphenols and healthy fats) that has minimally-processed, low-glycemic carbohydrates in proper amounts for activity levels and body type is a dependable recipe to boost metabolic flexibility. *Why?* Because if you're feeding your body carbohydrates, you are never allowing it to start burning fat. You need periods of fasting or carb restriction to activate fat-burning enzymes and to improve metabolic flexibility.

Like many things in life, the right amount of discomfort leads to learning and growth—and the same holds true for boosting metabolic flexibility. In order to improve metabolic flexibility, you have to expose your body to the right types and amounts of metabolic stress, which require the body to adapt in healthy ways. Just as we discussed with external stressors, exposing ourselves to a healthy level of metabolic stress can be another case of hormetic stress, which puts us in the "Goldilocks" zone—our bodies are neither too comfortable nor too hard-pressed to convert any energy source into fuel. Simply put, if you want to boost metabolic flexibility, which should be important to virtually everyone, then you may need to step outside your comfort zone. After all, that is where the magic happens.

Formulator's Corner
Blood Sugar and Glycemic Control Supplements

Berberine: Berberine hydrochloride or berberine sulfate are the most common forms.

Dihydroberberine (GlucoVantage) has been shown to be more effective and more bioavailable.

L-BAIBA (MitoBurn): An exercise mimetic, this supplement can give you more reps or more steps during exercise, along with impacting AMPK.

Blood Sugar and Glycemic Control Supplements (continuation)

Apple Cider Vinegar: Though the mechanism is not clear, the acetic acid, a short-chain fatty acid, may have a favorable impact on gut microbiota, which influences our insulin and glucose. For this, I personally love Bragg's.

Ceylon Cinnamon: Rich in blood sugar-optimizing polyphenols, this has long been a tool for glycemic control. Also worth noting is that other cinnamons are not actually cinnamon, so be sure to buy the real thing.

Optimized Preparations of Chromium (Chromax): This is a critical trace mineral often deficient in those less-insulin sensitive. It may aid in improving blood sugar.

HOW WE EAT

What is the best diet? What should you eat? What are the "good" foods you should be eating more of? What are the "bad" foods you should be avoiding? How much should you be eating? While relevant and important, prioritizing these questions may mean overlooking the most important variable of good nutrition. You see, *how* we eat is just as important as *what* we eat, and this is often the missing link when it comes to achieving health and weight-loss goals.

I can tell you all the details of ketones and metabolic flexibility and the upsides of intermittent fasting, but unless you are willing to look at what defines your relationship to food, it is all just a bunch of mumbo jumbo. Culturally, we are being manipulated every day into consuming. Whether it's those chips that are designed to never fill us up or two-day shipping, we are being programmed to buy things with the belief that they will make us happy and feel fulfilled (or at the very least, full). The marketing is created to make us believe we need something outside of ourselves to feel good, and food has become the easy "feel-good" sell.

Emotions drive so many of our food choices. Stress distracts us from paying attention to what and how much we are eating. Anger or sadness can drive us to over or under eat. Then of course, food becomes a source of comfort-seeking. I think that's why people eat so much around the holidays. They are stressed out, trying to get through seeing family and balancing work and so many other expectations. Combined with all those cookies and cakes and other carbs, it's a perfect storm. Those foods from the holidays only come around twice a year so we overindulge; we tell ourselves that we'll rectify things in the new year. When was the last time you upheld a New Year's resolution? Or even remember one that you made?

We connect food to emotional comfort throughout the rest of the year too, except it's no longer homemade cookies or mashed potatoes but store-bought cookies and potato chips. If I gave you a handful of almonds, you would eat 10 of them; if I roasted them, you would eat more. If I put some oil and salt on them, you would eat a handful. If I put honey and habanero on them, watch out!

Foods have many different characteristics that trigger pleasure in our brains. If you walk into a convenience store, you're really walking in a store of addiction triggers: each one is filled with caffeine, sugar, alcohol and bright colors. If that same store were filled with cucumbers, broccoli and water, I don't think they would sell as much (and the system is built on selling).

Food engineers work on drinks and foods to create a "once you pop, you can't stop" mentality for the people who eat and drink them. They all have great flavor on the front end, but then you need more on the backend. This is the science of addiction. They are engineering products to make you need more.

You are very likely to go through withdrawals getting off of these foods.

It is not your fault!

Have you watched the documentary *Fed Up*? If so, you have learned that processed food has been engineered to make us addicted. But there is a reason that all these foods have this level of oiliness and crispness and crunch. Why do we like bacon? Why do we like certain foods that are just so amazing and addictive?

It is because of something quite literally called the *bliss point*.[24]

In the book *The Dorito Effect*, the author Mark Schautzer reviews the history of flavoring and how flavor chemists extract molecules from certain foods that they then replicate in the lab, adding them to other foods to make them taste addictively good. These engineered flavors release dopamine and serotonin into our system, making us crave them more and more.

It's important to realize that sugar and fat don't occur together in nature. Food scientists combine them in processed foods, which override our systems and make us crave more. We end up chasing a result that we can never achieve.

The human body has evolved to favor foods delivering these tastes. The brain responds with a "reward" in the form of a jolt of *endorphins*, remembers what we did to get that reward and makes us want to do it again—an effect run by *dopamine*. For our hunter-gatherer ancestors who didn't know where their next meal was coming from, this makes a whole lot of sense—it's the brain saying to stock up now! Since today we have continuous access to food—and generally "junk" food—this is no longer an advantage but a weakness.

Sugar and fat don't occur together in nature. Food scientists combine them in processed foods, which override our systems and make us crave more.

Combinations of sugar, fat and salt act *synergistically* and are more rewarding than any one alone. In food product optimization, the goal is to include two or three of these nutrients at their bliss point.[25] And if you're living a life where you're overworked, disconnected, short on sleep and out of balance—or where you're in a lot of physical or emotional pain—something that can instantly give you a feeling of bliss can be very seductive. Before I became Shawn Wells, a biochemist, sports nutritionist, dietitian and the world's greatest formulator, I was trapped in a deep place of pain, using video games and food to self-medicate. In other words: I know what it's like to be ensnared by the bliss point and fall deep into the downward spiral of obesity, inflammation, fatigue, depression and brain fog.

When we are seeking the bliss point, we're usually engaging in "recreational eating" or reward-induced eating, which the scientific community refers to as "hedonic" eating. We are not eating out of real hunger or metabolic need.[26] Instead, we are motivated to eat by internal and external triggers, which contribute to automatic, inattentive and unnecessary food consumption. Some of these "triggers" include:

- Stress and anxiety
- Emotions (sadness or happiness can both apply)
- Boredom
- Environment (e.g., if trigger foods are around, we're likely to eat them)
- People we surround ourselves with
- Social gatherings
- Rewards/celebrations
- Lack of sleep

When it comes to eating for fat loss and improving overall health, everyone wants to know "what" and "how much" to eat. These are important questions, no doubt, as certain foods will fuel your goals better than others. Portion control is a key player in regulating energy balance as well, and we all know that typically, we must eat less to lose more.

For some, however, this is not the best strategy for optimizing health or increasing energy. Many young women and some men are already chronic dieters who may have been under-eating and nutritionally deficient for years. Their metabolic rate drops and they are now existing on too few calories and not enough nutrition. In those cases, cutting calories will only threaten their health, energy and vitality. Instead, they will actually benefit from increasing food, allowing their body to get back to a healthier metabolic state. This is why experimentation and bio-individuality are so key to developing a unique and effective nutritional plan.

No matter your plan, let's be honest: counting calories is annoying and time-consuming—and measuring and weighing foods can be even worse. In the short-term, these can be very useful tools to give you a better idea of exactly what you're putting in your body, but they are unsustainable actions, which means they don't often last. It is also not healthy, mentally or physically, to be a chronic dieter. When you look for a new lifestyle of eating, you must ask yourself: "Is this sustainable? Is this something I can keep up over the long-term? Ultimately, does this food lifestyle make me feel better or worse?"

Are you present while you eat? Even when we understand the reasons "why" we eat, we very infrequently talk about "how." What does your *how* look like?

- Do you eat quickly?

- Do you eat while watching TV or checking your email?

- Do you count the number of times you chew before you swallow?

- Do you think about where your food originated?

- Do you take the time to prepare your food?

Believe it or not, recent research shows that *how* we eat can either aid or impede our progress toward fat loss and overall health goals. Some of the latest findings in the science of nutrition and behavior change suggests that "mindful eating" and "eating attentively" may be among the most valuable tools in winning the battle of the bulge.

Recent research published in the journal *Physiology & Behavior*, for example, found that participants consumed 15 percent more calories when using a smartphone or reading a magazine compared to eating without distractions.[27] Meanwhile, a meta-analysis (the highest level of scientific scrutiny) published in the *American Journal of Clinical Nutrition* found that attentive eating influences food intake in a healthy way and "provides a novel approach to aid weight loss and maintenance without the need for conscious calorie counting."[28]

When we are present to the act of eating, we no longer treat it as an unconscious habit. We are forced to reckon with our choices, and in the process, we are liberated from falling victim to the bliss point. At last, we begin to gain control of what we put into our body and how.

WHAT IS MINDFUL EATING?

As the name suggests, mindful eating has roots in mindfulness, a practice based on Zen Buddhism. As the Buddhist teacher Jon Kabat-Zinn once described mindfulness, it is "paying attention in a particular way, on purpose, in the present moment and non-judgmentally." Mindful eating similarly encourages us to gain awareness of our eating experiences.

While there is a psychosomatic connection between stress and unhealthy foods, there can also be a connection between what makes us happy and what makes us healthy. We begin to associate healthier foods with healthier times. There is also a true bliss point in healthy eating.

In turn, mindful eating involves paying attention to our food, on purpose, moment by moment and without judgment. It is an approach to food that focuses on sensual awareness and the experience of the food. It is about bringing a full and deep awareness to each plate or bite of food. It begins with the first thought of food and lasts until the final bite is swallowed. Mindful eating is not just about what is on your plate, but also about how it made its way there.

At its very core, mindful eating raises awareness and attention. It helps us cultivate awareness of both internal and external eating triggers, and helps us interrupt automatic eating so we eat in response to natural physiological cues of hunger and satiety. Through practice, eating mindfully helps us regulate our food choices.

Unlike diets and most nutritional guidance which focuses on the "rules" of eating, mindful eating has little to do with carbs, fats or protein. It's not about what to eat or how much to eat. Rather than rules and restrictions, mindful eating encourages you to appreciate eating attentively and in a non-judgmental, self-accepting way. While "diets" have "short-term" written all over them (which typically results in long-term failure), mindful eating is about behavior changes.[29]

One common mindful eating exercise is to eat a single raisin mindfully, as if for the first time. This exercise helps us to notice the appearance, color, texture and smell of the raisin before placing it in our mouth and then chewing it with deliberate attention to taste and sensory stimuli. By eating a raisin without impulse, distraction or emotional interference, we begin to break the automatic cycle of eating.[30]

You can also create a healthy "bliss point" of your own, where your mind and body associate healthy foods with moments of clarity by engaging your parasympathetic state. Just as we can grind our way through work, we often do the same with food. Instead, we can try to create a flow in the way we eat, developing practices that bring focus and clarity around eating.

Here are some helpful tips to increase your attentiveness while eating and put mindful eating practices to use right away:

- **Remove Distractions.** Distractions can cause you to eat more. Turn off the TV, shut down the computer and set your phone in another room. As a matter of fact, sit at the table and take the time to enjoy your meal.

- **Use Smaller Plates.** Appearances can be deceiving. A smaller plate that's full is much more satisfying than a large plate that is half empty, because it gives the impression that there is a more abundant amount of food.

- **Take Your Time.** Cara Stewart, Registered Dietitian and member of the Penn Metabolic and Bariatric Surgery team, says that it takes approximately 20 minutes for your brain and stomach to register fullness. I don't know about you, but I can put a lot of food down in 20 minutes. Taking your time allows you to better gauge your level of fullness and satiety.

- **Chew Your Food.** Experts have a lot to say about chewing. One common piece of advice is to chew your food an estimated 32 times before swallowing, approximately two minutes between each swallow. It takes fewer chews to break down soft and water-filled food. Not only does increased chewing suppress appetite, but it also increases feelings of fullness.

  Note: I don't count how many times I chew my food, but this is an excellent experiment to try that forces us to slow down and be present at mealtimes. Try this as one of your "N of 1" experiments.

- **"Hara Hachi Bu."** This ancient Confucian adage means "Eat until you are eight parts full" or "belly 80 percent full." Practice this wise teaching when you eat by stopping your meal when you are almost full—not stuffed.

- **Take Smaller Bites.** Cut your food into smaller pieces, which will help increase the duration of the meal. You could use baby utensils to help decrease the size of each bite. This will also help you feel like you have eaten more.

- **Put Your Fork Down.** Remember, your fork is not a shovel. You can set it down between bites, which will help you focus on the taste, look, smell and feel of your meal and help you to slow down your pace.

- **Have a Conversation.** *Gasp!* Yep, I mean actually talk to someone while you are eating. You're already sitting at the table; you might as well ask your partner and children how their days were. If you have any manners, you won't talk and chew at the same time, so this will slow down your eating, as well as enhance the memory of the meal.

- **Eat with Your Non-Dominant Hand.** Michael Jordan once said that one of the reasons he is the greatest basketball player of all time is that everything that he did with his right hand he also did with his left—from dribbling a basketball to brushing his teeth. Not only will doing this develop your dexterity, but the awkwardness of this task will also force you to slow down and take smaller bites.

- **Set a Timer.** Start with 15 minutes per meal as a basic goal. Work up to 20 or even 30 minutes.

- **Break Out the Journal.** The food journal, that is. While I don't think it's necessary to measure, weigh and record everything you eat indefinitely, food journaling can be a useful tool to raise awareness of what (and how much) you're putting into your mouth.

- **Practice Mini-Meditations.** Focus on your breath and become aware of the bodily sensations of hunger and satiety before and during meals and snacks.

How we eat can be just as important as what we eat, but we all know that inputs ultimately produce outputs. As such, what we put into our systems will ultimately influence how much energy we bring to the world.

Now, with all these different elements of "what" and "how" in place, we can get a little more specific about choosing a nutrition lifestyle that's right for our needs.

THE KETOGENIC LIFESTYLE

Keto, just like any other lifestyle, is about finding what works for you. There is no "one size fits all," because lifestyle choices are like a compass—they might point you where you need to go, but you have to continually tune into your internal and external environment to get there. The one argument for Paleolithic Ketogenic Diet (PKD) that has always felt particularly authentic is that it is based on how humans have eaten for centuries.

If you were to look at a historical Native American society, you would probably find that they had a largely carbohydrate-driven diet in the summer months. Even in the times of higher carbohydrate consumption, it was not ultraprocessed carbs or genetically modified fruits higher in sugars at the peak of ripeness. Those "ancient carbohydrates" might not have been keto, but they were far different than the carbs of today, being higher in fiber and resistant starch as well as lower glycemic. For most of the year, these tribes would have a ketogenic diet. During the summer months, they might have consumed more carbohydrates just based on the crops, but for most of fall, winter and spring, they ate animals and often went days without eating while trying to track down food.

Over time, as food availability increased, we began to develop this notion of three meals a day, which was based on the industrialized work schedule. Lunch was developed so upper-class men could network with greater ease. In fact, in European society, it was considered proper etiquette to take part in breakfast, lunch and dinner.

Then in the 1900s, people began to look once again at the value of fasting. In one instance, doctors started to realize that fasting was the best way to treat epilepsy. After about two or three days of fasting, seizures subsided in people who had epilepsy. Nobody really understood why that was happening, but they noticed that this fasting was having a positive effect.[31]

What they found was that the body was shifting away from burning carbohydrates for fuel and instead relying on fat and byproducts of fat. Over the 20th century, two things occurred: carbs were mistakenly touted as the body's preferred source of energy, and fats were mistakenly decried as harmful to one's health. It was not until the 1970s and 1980s that low-carb diets like Atkins began gaining some popularity and reversing that idea.

In the 1990s, another case began to catch attention in its use of ketogenic therapy. Eleven-month-old Charlie Abrahams had a version of epilepsy that could not be treated with drugs. His parents read about the ketogenic diet and within a week of implementing it, Charlie's seizures were gone. Charlie was on the diet for five years, but even when he came off it, his seizures never returned. It signified that keto was not just therapeutic but could also be curative.

The ketogenic diet is more than just a weight loss diet; it is a life-style choice for an energized life.

When I stumbled into keto after getting extremely sick with Epstein-Barr, I started reading two books, *The Body Opus* and *The Ketogenic Diet for the Practitioner*. One was from a clinical perspective and one was a bodybuilding book. That's when I started researching online message boards (before the days of Facebook or even Myspace) to find people who had been struggling with similar conditions and who had also been using keto.

I was in an uphill battle against chronic fatigue syndrome, brain fog, depression and fibromyalgia. The more I researched the ketogenic diet, nutritional ketosis and ketone bodies, the more convinced I became that this was the solution to my health woes. I was turning the corner and for once, it seemed the flames were fanned by the positive reinforcement around me. People who knew me online and in real life were inspired by my turnaround, which was like a shot in the arm to me. Ultimately this encouragement gave me greater drive to get better so I could improve lives—including my own.

Many people think that low-carb diets are all the same. However, keto is significantly different from just your ordinary "I'm going to cut back on carbs" diet. We can talk more about percentages, but to put it in perspective, "low carb" can mean anything from one percent of your calories to up to fifty percent. In the latter case, we're talking about 100-200 grams of carbs, which is quite a lot. By comparison, keto is typically less than 20 grams of carbs per day, and just as a general idea of how much fat we're talking about when we say "high-fat," it can be up to 80 percent of our caloric intake—maybe even more, depending on how keto is designed for you. No matter the details, keto is defined as a very-low-carbohydrate and high-fat diet with a moderate amount of protein.[32]

The whole point of a ketogenic diet is to shift into a powerful metabolic state during which the body is burning primarily fat (as ketones are derived from fats). It's becoming increasingly clear that elevated ketones have an array of important signaling functions (e.g., regulating inflammation and gene expression) and the metabolic shift to increased ketone use may be the secret behind most of the benefits of the ketogenic diet.[33]

Ketones, which are often called the "brain's preferred source of fuel," appear to support brain health and enhance cognitive function.[34] In fact, most keto disciples rave about the cognitive clarity, energy and up-shift in brain processing speed they enjoy while in a deep state of ketosis. What's more, ketones are thought to have a direct effect on appetite regulation.

Keto is a powerful tool for easy weight loss—by crushing cravings, creating boundless energy, clearing through brain fog, supporting a healthy immune system, building unwavering resilience and much, much more.

Although much of the attention placed on keto focuses on weight management, energy and cognitive function, the underappreciated aspect may be the role it plays in immunity. Recent research has provided evidence that the ketogenic diet may modulate inflammation and help the immune system in beneficial ways. One recent study published in the journal *Science Immunology* showed that the ketogenic diet protected mice against the influenza virus infection through T-cell expansion and metabolic adaptation. More specifically, keto increased the number of T-cells in the respiratory tract, and those T-cells were able to kill off influenza-infected cells.[35]

Another great aspect of a keto diet is that it's going to make you back off the sugar, starches and the processed carbohydrate foods that fill the center of every grocery store in bags and boxes. If you follow my lead and recommendations, you are going to get more into *whole foods* and you'll begin to break yourself of that sugar addiction. Unfortunately, with keto's rise in popularity, there's been tremendous interest for food manufacturers to come up with convenient processed foods that can be marketed as keto-friendly—many of which use copious amounts of sugar substitutes and marketing tactics like "net carbs." As a result, there is an increasing trend toward the "dirty" keto I mentioned earlier, which doesn't discriminate between highly-processed, packaged foods and the real, whole foods I suggest.

MY TOP 9 KETO PRODUCTS

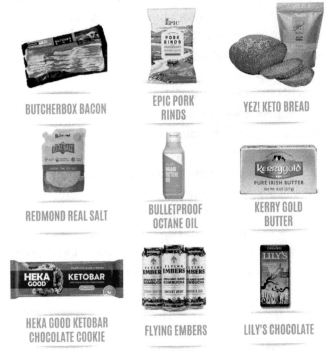

BUTCHERBOX BACON	EPIC PORK RINDS	YEZ! KETO BREAD
REDMOND REAL SALT	BULLETPROOF OCTANE OIL	KERRY GOLD BUTTER
HEKA GOOD KETOBAR CHOCOLATE COOKIE	FLYING EMBERS	LILY'S CHOCOLATE

Graphic 18 – Ready to Go Keto "Fast Foods"

How we consume and break down sugar not only dictates how healthy and energetic we are right now, but also our quality of life in the future. Glucose is stored in your liver and released as needed for energy. However, after carb intake has been extremely low for one to two days, these glucose stores become depleted. Your liver will then make glucose as necessary from amino acids in the protein you eat via a process known as gluconeogenesis, but not nearly enough to meet the needs of your brain—which requires a constant fuel supply.

Fortunately, ketosis can provide an alternate source of energy. In ketosis, your body produces ketones at an accelerated rate. Ketones, or ketone bodies, are made by your liver from fat—both fat that you eat as well as your own body fat. The three ketone bodies are beta-hydroxybutyrate (BHB), acetoacetate and acetone (although acetone is technically a breakdown product of acetoacetate). Your liver produces ketones on a regular basis even when eating a higher-carb diet. This happens mainly overnight while you sleep, though usually only in tiny amounts. However, when glucose and insulin levels decrease, such as when you're on a carb-restricted diet, the liver ramps up its production of ketones in order to provide energy for your brain.

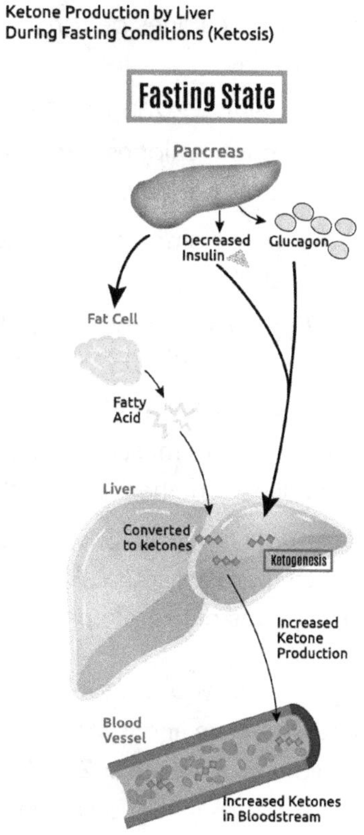

Ketone Production by Liver
During Fasting Conditions (Ketosis)

Fasting State

Pancreas

Decreased Insulin   Glucagon

Fat Cell

Fatty Acid

Liver

Converted to ketones   Ketogenesis

Increased Ketone Production

Blood Vessel

Increased Ketones in Bloodstream

Graphic 19 – Endogenous Ketone Production[36]

Once the level of ketones in your blood reaches a certain threshold, you are in nutritional ketosis. According to leading ketogenic diet researchers Dr. Steve Phinney and Dr. Jeff Volek, the threshold for nutritional ketosis is a minimum of 0.5 mmol/L of BHB (the ketone body measured in blood). A well-formulated ketogenic diet is typically:

- Very high in fat (70-80 percent of calories)

- Very low in carbohydrates (5 percent of calories or ≤ 20 grams per day)

- Adequate in protein (15-20 percent of calories)

What does that translate to? Here is what the ketogenic diet would look like on a traditional 2,000-calorie diet:

- **Fat** (75 percent of calories): 2000 * 0.75 = 1500 calories from fat. Since there are nine calories per gram, this means about 165 grams of fat per day.

- **Carbs** (5 percent of calories): 2000 * 0.05 = 100 calories from carbs. Since there are four calories per gram, this means about 25 grams of carbs per day.

  o Please note, I do recommend keeping carbs < 20 grams per day the first 90 days.

  o More than 20 grams of carbs can be fine after the first 90 days if they are mostly from fiber and/or lower glycemic carbohydrates.

  o Those that have more muscle mass or are active have a higher tolerance for higher carbs and protein.

- **Protein** (20 percent of calories): 2000 * 0.20 = 400 calories from protein. Since there are four calories per gram, this means about 100 grams of protein per day.

Practically speaking, let's say you're a six-foot, 200-pound, 40-year-old male who's moderately active and is looking to drop weight. Your typical day with keto might look like this: 2,118 calories, 165g of fat, 132g of protein and 20g of carbs (although again, I would recommend keeping those carbs less than 20 grams for the first 90 days). Meanwhile, if you're a five-foot six-inch, 160-pound, 50-year-old female who's lightly active and wants to lose weight, your keto diet might look more like this: 1,373 calories, 107g of fat, 86g of protein and 17g of carbs.

What's really important is finding what's optimal for *you*, and that can vary from person to person; it can also take time to figure that out. When you have established a ketogenic state, you are likely to feel

what many describe as a "euphoric" state—with increased energy, mental clarity and increased cognitive performance. To help give you a greater state of awareness, you need to be tracking your ketones through urine, breath or blood.

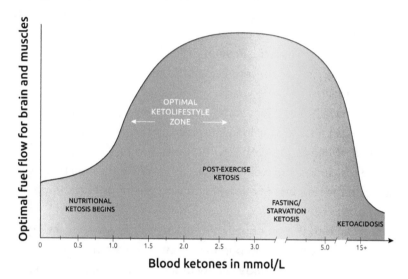

Graphic 20 – Blood Ketone Levels

The truth is just because virtually everyone under the sun is talking about keto does not make it right for everyone. Just as with any new nutritional program, you need to experiment with it to see if it's appropriate for you, consult with your physician and then build the ketogenic lifestyle that works for you.

KETO BASICS

So how do you get started on keto? *Should* you get started on keto? What do you need to know? What should your macros be? How do you know when you are in ketosis? If you are ready to jump on the keto bandwagon, let's talk about how to make your plan.

By definition, keto is a high-fat, very-low-carbohydrate diet and that leads us to keto's number one rule: **limit carbs to 20 grams or fewer per day.** Write that down on the back of your hand with a

Sharpie®. Put it up on Post-it® Notes on every refrigerator and pantry door. If you nail that consistently, you'll be most of the way there.

Now, that brings us to the all-important question: *How do I figure out how many calories I should be eating?* Ideally, you would have some baseline established. In other words, you should already have a good idea of how many calories you typically consume to maintain your weight. Check out the Resources Hack at the end of this chapter for some suggestions on keto calculators, which can help you calculate your macros.

If you have been weight-stable (neither gaining nor losing weight), then you can track your caloric intake for a couple of weeks to gather this data. While this is probably the most accurate method, it does require measuring and weighing your food. While that can be a pain, it is worth the few days of effort in order to gain long-term knowledge and get results.

You can also use an equation or calculator designed to estimate daily caloric needs, but keep in mind that these are not error-proof. For starters, there are a wide variety of them and generally speaking, the simpler they are, the greater their margin of error. I prefer one that takes into account fat-free mass, activity levels, exercise activity, height, weight, age and gender.

Arguably the most robust and comprehensive online tool to estimate caloric intake is the **NIH's Body Weight Planner**, which allows you to set your goal weight, when you'd like to achieve it and how much you plan to increase your activity level to do so. This, along with My Fitness Pal, is an excellent tool, as it provides calorie estimates for weight maintenance and weight-management goals.

Keep in mind that there are many factors that go into deciding what the "best" caloric intake is—such as your goals, body composition, weight history, physical activity, exercise levels and more. Even the most reliable and scientifically-validated methods have a margin of error. These are not bullseye recommendations; they are simply meant to get you in the ballpark.

At the end of the day (or week or month), just ask yourself a simple question: "How's that working for you?"

Especially early on, you will need to be diligent about tracking your intake, assessing dependent variables (e.g., subjective and objective outcomes) and adjusting accordingly. Remember, this is the great experiment of you. We are controlling for variables to find out what works best for your bio-individuality. If your goal is to lose weight and the scale isn't budging (or it's going up), then after a few weeks, it may be time to try something else (although there could be other variables at play).

Below are some keto food basics to start you thinking about the foods to focus on and which ones to avoid:

EAT FATTY FISH AND SEAFOOD THREE TIMES PER WEEK.

There are good reasons health organizations like the American Heart Association urge folks to eat fatty fish at least twice a week: they're the best dietary sources of the key omega-3 fats DHA and EPA. The best fish and seafood (which also tend to be the best dietary sources of vitamin D) that meet these criteria include: **wild salmon, fish roe, Pacific sardines, mussels, Rainbow trout, Atlantic mackerel, oysters, anchovies and herring.**

FOCUS ON HEALTHY FATS.

We can also add to our list **avocados, olives and extra virgin olive oil**, the hallmark of the Mediterranean diet, to the list of "healthy fats." Speaking of olive oil, very recent research has shown that it may, at the present, be the most powerful anti-aging food we have available to us—yes, even more so than red wine. More specifically, olive oil is a rich source of the monounsaturated fatty acid oleic acid, which a landmark study published in the journal *Molecular Cell* found to be a potent activator of the longevity sirtuin enzyme SIRT1—and does so in the same way that resveratrol does.[37] In fact, the study's authors suggest that this (olive oil/oleic acid) may explain many of the health benefits of the Mediterranean diet. The researchers do caution, however, that consuming more olive oil is not enough; to optimize the anti-aging benefits, olive oil should be incorporated with fasting, limiting caloric intake and exercise, which help release the oleic acid so it can, in turn, activate the SIRT1 signaling pathway.

Meanwhile, you will want to limit your intake of industrially-produced vegetable and seed oils (soybean, corn, canola, safflower, sunflower and cottonseed oils), which are rife with omega-6 fats and other inflammation-promoting compounds. An easy life hack here is to sniff for metallic, bitter or soapy aromas to determine whether there are omega-6 compounds in your foods.

Remember, there are three main types of dietary fat, categorized by their number of double bonds:

- Saturated (no double bonds)

- Monounsaturated (one double bond)

- Polyunsaturated (more than one double bond).

When it comes to fatty acids, stability refers to susceptibility to oxidation, which takes place when a double bond breaks and an oxygen molecule attaches. Along those lines, saturated fats are the most stable while polyunsaturated fats are the least.

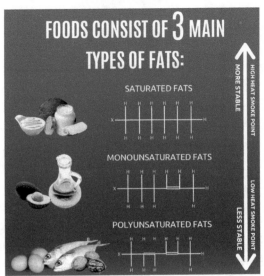

Graphic 21 – Foods Consist of Three Main Types of Fats

As I mentioned before, the ratio between omega-3 and omega-6 is what really matters. We need both, but most of us get enough omega-6 from our diets without even trying because of its abundance in the Standard American Diet. Research has shown that the imbalance between omega-3 and omega-6 is associated with many, if not all, non-communicable and chronic diseases.[38] This is mainly because omega-6s are pro-inflammatory while omega-3s are anti-inflammatory.[39] Chronic inflammation is the root cause of many chronic diseases and health issues, so we need to focus on optimizing omega-3 intake to balance it out. That is why supplementing with an excellent quality, high DHA fish oil is so critical. To that end, three types of omega-3 include:

- Eicosatetraenoic acid (EPA): This 20-carbon fatty acid's main function is to produce chemicals called eicosanoids, which help reduce inflammation.

- Docosahexaenoic acid (DHA): A 22-carbon fatty acid, DHA makes up about eight percent of brain weight.

- Alpha-linolenic acid (ALA): This 18-carbon fatty acid can be converted into EPA and DHA, although the process is not very efficient. ALA is mainly used by the body for energy.

Sources of omega-3s include wild salmon, grass-fed beef, algae oils, sardines, eggs, walnuts and flaxseeds. Fish oil is definitely a critical supplement in my book. Plant-based diets are extremely poor in omega-3s as they only provide ALA. The only plant source of DHA/EPA is micro algae (which is what the fish eat and how we can get these PUFAs from fish).

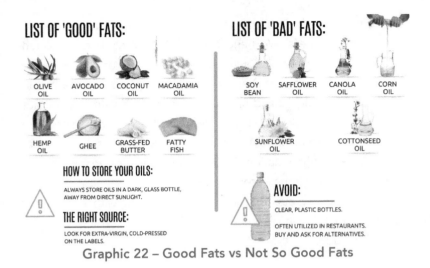

Graphic 22 – Good Fats vs Not So Good Fats

GO THE EXTRA MILE FOR PASTURE-RAISED, ORGANIC MEAT, DAIRY AND EGGS.

One of the greatest advantages of **meat, dairy and eggs from pasture-raised, naturally-fed animals** is that their fatty acid profile has more omega-3 fats, a better omega-6 to omega-3 ratio and more Conjugated Linoleic Acid (CLA). What you are not getting when you go the extra mile matters, too. Your investment means no GMO ingredients, no antibiotics, no added hormones and no persistent pesticides. Even your big box grocery stores now sell much better options.

Though humans were not made to consume cow's milk, the broad recommendation for everyone to completely avoid dairy seems impractical and unnecessary. Some fermented dairies (such as **yogurt** and **kefir**) may be key in anti-inflammatory support because they contain probiotics, which play a principal role in the immune system and support a healthy inflammatory response.[40]

LOAD UP ON VEGGIES.

There may be heated debate around the carnivore diet but it holds promise for some people, some of the time. For example, I have used the carnivore diet, which is a highly restrictive approach that involves eating ONLY animal products (primarily meat), in short spurts (e.g., one month) to help address gut microbiome imbalance and autoimmune flareups, as well as for an energy reset. A somewhat similar approach can be used with the Paleo Autoimmune Protocol (AIP), although AIP is an elimination-style diet that can be (and often is) followed for a longer period of time, particularly after personalized reintroduction.

Still, I am a fan of variety—particularly when it comes to a class of antioxidants called polyphenols and certainly in regard to the vitamin content of vegetables.[41] I shoot for **four to five-and-a-half cups of a variety of colorful veggies a day**. Below are some of the most nutritious fruits and vegetables based on the nutrients offered:

- **β-carotene**: Carrots, pumpkin, sweet potatoes, mangos, papaya, cantaloupe, dark leafy greens, bok choy, bell peppers and broccoli.

- **Vitamin C**: Oranges, grapefruit, clementines, tangerines, bell peppers, bok choy, broccoli, Brussels sprouts, strawberries, pineapples, kiwis, cauliflower, dark leafy greens and cabbage.

- **Vitamin E**: Dark leafy greens (such as spinach, kale, mustard greens, collard greens, turnip greens and Swiss chard), avocado, asparagus, broccoli, bell peppers, mangos and kiwi.

Though fruits should be reserved for dessert, some lower glycemic options can be eaten to satisfy that ever-craving sweet tooth. Just be mindful of how much fruit you consume. Berries tend to be lower glycemic and when eaten in small portions can still be enjoyed on a well-designed healthy diet.

WATCH WHAT YOU DRINK.

While moderate alcohol consumption (e.g., a four-ounce glass of a dry red wine) may be a good thing, keep in mind that excessive alcohol has the opposite effect. As with eating, it is not always about what you drink but how you drink. Be mindful of how and why you consume alcohol. Just as we experiment with our food and exercise, so we should experiment with our alcohol intake.

Previously, I mentioned that not drinking alcohol excessively was one of five pillars (or low-risk lifestyle factors) that have been shown to help people live up to 14 years longer. Indeed, although it's a controversial topic, recent research has shown that light-to-moderate alcohol consumption may have anti-aging benefits, effectively helping you live longer. For instance, the recent 90+ Study, which is an observational study of folks age 90 and older, found that consuming about two beers or glasses of wine daily was associated with an 18 percent reduction in premature death compared to abstainers.[42] According to the study's lead author Claudia Kawas, "That's been shown all over the world. I have no explanation for it, but I do firmly believe modest drinking is associated with longevity."

KETO FOOD LIST

FRUIT

Strawberries, Blueberries, Raspberries, Blackberries, Cherries, Avocados

VEGETABLES

Lettuce, Kale, Spinach, Swiss Chard, Bok Choy, Celery, Asparagus, Cauliflower, Broccoli, Cabbage, Cucumber, Radishes, Endives, Chives, Brussel Sprouts

NUTS

Macadamia nuts, Pecans, Brazil nuts, Hazelnuts, Walnuts, Pine Nuts, Almonds, Pili Nuts

DAIRY

Hard Cheeses (Parmesan, Swiss, Feta and Cheddar), Soft Cheeses (Brie, Mozzarella, Monterey Jack and Blue Cheese), Cream Cheese, Sour Cream, Full-fat Yogurt, Mayonnaise, Cottage Cheese, Heavy Cream

PROTEIN

Beef, Poultry, Pork, Lamb, Goat, Organs, Bacon, Eggs

FATS

Butter, Ghee, Olive Oil, Coconut Oil, Lard, Duck Fat, Avocado, Macadamia Nuts, MCTs

BEVERAGES

Water, Broth, Flavored Water, Flavored Carbonated Water, Tea, Coffee

Graphic 23 – Keto Food List

With alcohol, it does seem to be a case where the dose makes the poison...or the remedy... as previous studies have also shown that light-to-moderate alcohol intake is associated with decreased risk of premature death, as well decreased risk of type 2 diabetes, heart attack and stroke, which may relate to beneficial effects on circulation (e.g., endothelial function), inflammation, blood pressure and feelings of stress and anxiety.[43] Be that as it may, how and what you drink are important factors to consider.

For instance, I envision enjoying a glass of dry red wine (like Dry Farms Wine, which curates low-sugar, organic, sustainable, lower alcohol wines) around a dinner table with family and friends in a safe, fun and relaxing environment as the ultimate way to incorporate alcohol into your lifestyle in a healthy way that promotes longevity. Lastly, if you don't currently drink alcohol, I don't believe this is grounds to start.

Obviously, there are plenty of books out there with recipes galore, but you should work to find those that work for your lifestyle and routine. What you want to avoid is falling into the habit of eating "dirty keto" or "lazy keto," where we replace healthy meals with poor quality processed meats and fats as well as keto "treats" or "snacks," most of which are highly processed, artificially sweetened and colored.

Further, these low-carb treats can be loaded with sugar alcohols and short-chain "fibers" that can have a glycemic shock, affecting the GI system and causing gas and bloating. So be careful—not all "net carbs" are equal.

If you have the time to make two big keto meals where you get to prepare your food, sit down and enjoy, that's great! But if you don't have the time to sit down for two meals a day, plan for what will fit into your schedule. You need to find the food choices that are right for your lifestyle. When I travel, it looks a lot different than when I'm home, for example. On the road I most often fast in the morning, do a protein bar and high fat decaf coffee with heavy cream and MCTs for lunch and enjoy a bigger dinner.

KETO IN ACTION

I know that it's great to imagine your life on keto—to feel the renewed energy of eating clean whole foods and of being free of sugar addiction—but I also know that imagining the keto life and adopting it can be two vastly different things.

I am a firm believer that nothing needs to be done perfectly. Even I can get thrown off my diet when life gets crazy or I get too busy or I find myself in an airport with only 40 minutes between flights.

For me, it works to skip breakfast because I've already been fasting during sleep. If you are doing intermittent fasting (more on that shortly), you can keep your fast going or even make it past lunch. If I am going to eat breakfast, I usually go for eggs, bacon and decaf coffee with some collagen and fats.

Most days though, I just wait until lunch, where I eat a low-carb, high-fat lunch. I might have a steak or grilled chicken with a big bowl of veggies, or I might have an omelet. I find that if I just shift the time that I eat breakfast, I can still get the convenience of eating relatively cheap and easy high-fat, low-carb breakfast foods, just later in the day.

Dinner can be anything—I usually have meat for dinner (especially if I had breakfast for lunch) with either a big bowl of greens and vinegar, coleslaw, broccoli with butter, asparagus and olive oil, or a full-fat cheese on cauliflower.

But what about between meals? Because I travel so much, I don't always get a solid keto meal all the time. Instead, I have learned how to make keto snacks using nuts and seeds like macadamias, walnuts and pili nuts. Cacao nibs are also a fantastic way to get fiber. I try to bring along cut-up, non-sweet veggies like cucumber, broccoli or cauliflower.

Another great fast snack is dehydrated meat—just make sure you know where your jerky is being sourced. I like to buy from local butchers or stores like Sprouts Farmers Market, where I know what kind of meat I'm eating.

You need to find the food choices that fit your lifestyle, because your food choices are your lifestyle.

Of course, we can't forget about cheese but make sure you are getting a full-fat, high-quality cheese. Usually a block is better, where you can cut off pieces for yourself. I like using a food processor to shred blocks into the perfectly portioned amount needed for recipes.

Many people in the paleo community are opposed to dairy—and for good reason. For centuries, we have consumed human milk through the first two years of our lives. The ratios of protein in human versus cow's milk can create complications when humans over-consume cow dairy, which is likely why we are seeing so many dairy allergies. We consume cow dairy now more than ever in history, and the milk we drink is ultra-processed and over-homogenized. There is an argument for consuming raw milk, but in lieu of more extreme options, the best cow dairy is high-fat, organic and grass-fed with no hormones. The closer you can get to buying it from a local dairy, the better.

If you are comfortable including dairy or dairy-like options in your diet, you can add yogurts, kefirs and cheese to your snack list. Full-fat Greek yogurt with no added sugars is a great snack and also high in probiotics.

WAYS TO MAXIMIZE KETOSIS

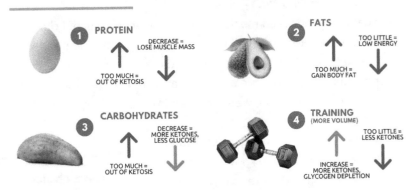

PROTEIN
1
DECREASE = LOSE MUSCLE MASS
TOO MUCH = OUT OF KETOSIS

FATS
2
TOO LITTLE = LOW ENERGY
TOO MUCH = GAIN BODY FAT

CARBOHYDRATES
3
DECREASE = MORE KETONES, LESS GLUCOSE
TOO MUCH = OUT OF KETOSIS

TRAINING (MORE VOLUME)
4
TOO LITTLE = LESS KETONES
INCREASE = MORE KETONES, GLYCOGEN DEPLETION

Graphic 24 – The Sweet Spot for Ketosis

Now, the one question that often pops up when people start keto is: can I cheat? The thing is, I don't like the word cheat. You are not doing something that you need to cheat on. You are simply creating a lifestyle which best supports the most optimized, energized version of yourself. But humans love boundaries, and we love to test those boundaries almost as much.

The short answer is, yes, you can have a "cheat" meal or "cheat" day and it will not cancel out the benefits, completely derail you or ruin all your hard work. But like I said, it is not about cheating on your diet; it is about planning ahead for what works for your lifestyle.

If you want some carbs, plan them into your lifestyle and enjoy them. That is not "cheating" and it is not a bad thing. Carbs are not necessary, but they are a tool. Plan it out (e.g., one meal a week or so), enjoy it and then get back to your energized keto lifestyle.

Moral of the story: If you are keto and just want to be able to have an occasional meal or treat with carbs, there is no problem with that. In fact, it is likely a strategy that can help improve your results and performance.

For most people, the Standard Ketogenic Diet, where you are keeping carbs to 20g a day, is going to be the baseline of your success. However, if you are looking to increase carbs at certain times, below are some approaches that can also be used by a non-athlete, but perhaps with a little less leeway when on your standard keto diet (please note, you should not incorporate the two techniques below until at least 90 days of following a strict SKD):

Targeted Ketogenic Diet (TKD) involves eating carbs around workout times (usually 30-60 minutes before) and following the standard ketogenic diet at all other times. It only takes around 20 grams of high-glycemic carbs to get the benefits of TKD.

Cyclical Ketogenic Diet (CKD) combines carb-loading day(s) with the standard ketogenic diet. Those who do high-intensity exercise (bodybuilders and athletes) implement carbohydrate refeeding days once or twice a week to fully replenish glycogen stores. The CKD provides us with a simple way to maintain high-intensity exercise performance and promote glycogen replenishment. Again, this involves following the SKD—usually around 20g carbs—for five to six days, followed by one to two days of higher-carb refeeds. These refeeds are important for anyone on a keto diet because they also allow your body to "remember" how to burn carbs. Adhering to strict SKD for too long can hinder your body's ability to burn carbs via glycolysis—so turning on carb-burning pathways every now and then is useful to maintain your metabolic flexibility.

CHOOSING A KETOGENIC DIET

1 STANDARD KETOGENIC DIET (SKD)

Want to lose fat quickly and you only do low to moderate intensity activities (e.g., walking, cycling, yoga, and light weightlifting). **Less than 20g carbs a day.**

2 CYCLICAL KETOGENIC DIET (CKD)

Combines carb loading day(s) with the standard ketogenic diet. Implement carbohydrate refeeding days once or twice a week to fully replenish glycogen stores and aid in long term adherence by allowing diet variability and metabolic flexibility.

3 TARGETED KETOGENIC DIET (TKD)

Eating carbs around workout times (usually 30-60 min before) and following the SKD at all other times. The TKD provides us with a simple way to maintain high-intensity exercise performance and promote glycogen replenishment. **An additional 20g carbs pre-workout.**

Graphic 25 – The 3 Traditional Variations of the Ketogenic Diet[44]

I think it's a good idea to wait until you have established your baseline and adapted to keto before you start playing with carbohydrate intake. I recommend committing to a strict keto diet for 90 days first, then allowing yourself the flexibility to schedule a carbohydrate refeed. I prefer phrasing like "free meal," "diet break" or "refeed" to the word "cheat." Although it may seem like a matter of semantics, choosing the right terminology can be a useful reframing tool, helping you to get back on track faster.

Once you get comfortable on keto, you are going to find that keeping carbs to 20 grams or below is what makes you experience the benefits of ketosis. But first you are going to start shedding those carbs, one bad habit at a time. Once you are down to a strict keto diet, you can start adding some things back in, like fiber or small amounts of non-fibrous carbs. The key is scheduling and dissociating the notion of guilt since this is a strategic carb timing approach to improve your metabolic flexibility or performance.

THE KETO FLU

So, you are really going to do it! You are going to take the plunge and give keto a shot. Why not? It seems like everyone else is doing it—from your family and friends to celebrities and sports stars. More importantly, keto seems to be working for quite a few people (in some cases, quite impressively). You have cleaned out all the processed garbage from your pantry. You've done your keto grocery shopping. So far, you haven't violated the cardinal rule of keto and have done a killer job of keeping your carbs to under 20 grams per day. In just the first couple days, you are already getting some positive feedback from your body, the scale and the people around you. Winning!

Then bam.

Seemingly out of nowhere, you run into a brick wall. You feel like poor ol' Wile E. Coyote. You are tired (and wired), trying to navigate through a brain fog denser than the air off the coast of Newfoundland, the foggiest place in the world. Your energy levels …what energy?

And your cravings? Let's just say that you've imagined that your co-workers' heads look like pizza, bread and chocolate.

The keto flu refers to a constellation of issues (literally, flu-like symptoms) that some but not all people experience when embarking on a ketogenic or other low-carb diet. In addition to brain fog, these include headaches, nausea, muscle cramps, increased heart rate, fatigue, dizziness, sugar cravings, difficulty sleeping, digestive discomfort and constipation.

This can be especially stressful when we are scared of getting sick, which is why it's important to take the keto plunge when you know you're healthy and can distinguish between keto flu and other flu-like symptoms.

Fewer than five percent of people experience the "keto flu," but if you're transitioning from a lifestyle that has been sugar and carb-dependent, you are more likely to experience it. After all, if you think about coming off any drug that you're addicted to, it probably feels like a mild flu.[45]

For some, the symptoms of the keto flu are the consequences of not getting into ketosis fast enough. Though you might be craving more food or feeling lethargic, the solution might be as simple as adding in intermittent fasting or some high-intensity interval training to get into ketosis faster.

KETO FLU

SYMPTOMS

Sugar cravings

Dizziness

Brain fog

Irritability

Poor focus

Poor concentration

Stomach pains

Nausea

Cramping

Confusion

Muscle soreness

Insomnia

REMEDIES

Drink more water

Increase your intake of sodium, potassium, and magnesium

Eat more fat (especially MCTs)

Go for a walk every morning

Meditate every day

Make sleep a top priority

> **Minerals/Electrolytes as a treatment**
> Recommended Doses:
>
> **Sodium** - 5 to 7 grams of unrefined salt per day
>
> **Potassium** - 3,500 mg per day for people ages 16 and up
>
> **Magnesium**
> For men: ~400 mg per day
> For women: ~310 mg per day

**Graphic 26 - Common Symptoms
of Keto Flu and Best Remedies**

If you get muscular cramps, it may be related to not hydrating enough. But if you are hydrating well and adding back in electrolytes, you can minimize the effect by taking magnesium every day. In fact, I recommend magnesium whether you are doing the keto lifestyle or not; you will feel better and have more strength and better heart health.[46]

Formulator's Corner
Magnesium Supplements

Amino Acid Chelates (AACs):

Glycinate: Magnesium bound to glycine, very cost effective.

Taurinate: Bound to taurine.

Threonate: Bound to threonine with some data on improving cognitive function.

Citric Acid Cycle (the Krebs Cycle) Intermediates:

Citrate: Commonly used in OTC products for improving bowel movement.

Malate: Good overall form and cost effective, this form has data with muscle soreness and function.

Avoid These Inferior Forms with Low Absorption/Bioavailability:

Oxide: Poor absorption, but probably the cheapest and therefore most common form.

Carbonate: Another cheap and common form that is not worth using.

Women can have a harder time transitioning to keto, often because they traditionally consume more carbohydrates than men. It has also been argued that for hormonal balance, women might physiologically need more carbohydrates than men. Energy requirements are greater at certain times related to fertility and potentially for maintaining pregnancy. Also, women often consume less protein, which can make switching to a moderate-protein, low-carb diet more challenging.

The more muscle mass you have, the more carb-tolerant you are, and because men tend to have larger muscle mass, they can stay in ketosis longer, which makes the transition less challenging.

Women can also be more sensitive to dietary changes and to any sort of calorie restriction. Women often try to adopt a keto diet and still keep their high-paced schedule, even when they are not feeling well. The fasting and keto turn from being hormetic stressors into full-on stress.

In addition, diet affects hormonal fluctuations, which can create an energy imbalance when women try to adopt a keto diet too strictly or too quickly. Since cholesterol is a precursor to steroid hormones such as testosterone, estrogen and progesterone, the changes in those hormones can be felt more significantly in women. If your allostatic load is high, hold off! Look at your lifestyle as a whole and see where you can begin to make incremental changes, starting with whole foods. Give yourself plenty of grace and self-love and be honest with yourself as you explore the changes that make sense for *you*.

Though the risk of keto flu varies from person to person, most who do experience it will have symptoms within **the first weeks of starting keto.** While some folks find that the flu-like symptoms can linger into the second week—perhaps even the third or fourth—most turn the corner very quickly (or mitigate the keto flu altogether) with a well-formulated ketogenic diet and some of the remedies shared below.

- **Eat enough fat.** Remember, keto is a high-fat diet—with 70-80 percent of calories coming from fat. Quite often, folks who have been brainwashed to believe that fat is bad don't eat enough fat, which you need to help you feel full and satisfied and to provide energy as your body adapts.

- **Eat enough calories.** For most people, keto means elimination. It means getting rid of junk food and foods that contain processed carbs. While there is no question those are positive dietary moves, it often leads to people not eating enough. Yes, if weight loss is the goal, then you need to eat fewer calories than you burn. However, cutting calories too much too fast can be a big contributor to many of the keto flu symptoms.

- **Go easy on the protein.** Keep in mind that keto is a moderate-protein diet—with roughly 15-30 percent of calories coming from protein. Eating too much protein can be problematic for a couple of reasons. The satiating power of protein may keep you from eating enough fat and calories overall; additionally, too much protein may impair the body's ability to make ketones through ketogenesis.

- **Drink up.** With keto, your body initially runs through and reduces its stored form of carbohydrate (called glycogen), along with quite a bit of water (for every gram of glycogen, the body stores four grams of water). Plus, the kidneys tend to excrete more water when insulin and blood glucose levels drop like they do during carbohydrate restriction. Make sure you are drinking plenty of water; after all, even mild dehydration can explain nearly every one of the symptoms of keto flu.

- **Get salty.** Salt, like fat, is not the demon that we have been led to believe. When you are on keto, you are going to need to pay particularly close attention to your sodium intake. On one hand, the cardinal keto rule (20 grams of carbs) leads to eliminating most processed foods, which are the major source of dietary sodium. Plus, carbohydrate restriction results in the kidneys excreting more sodium and other electrolytes (such as potassium, magnesium, calcium and chloride) because of a drop in insulin. If you're exercising regularly, which I strongly recommend, then you should be getting three to five grams of sodium (about one teaspoon) and two to three grams of potassium a day. For magnesium, 300-500mg is a good target.

- **Get moving (if you can).** *Exercise? Are you kidding me?* Believe me, I know how it feels. If you are not used to exercising regularly, that may be the *last* thing on your mind. If you do typically work out, then you are likely to feel like it seems your body has been taken over—your legs feel like lead and like you're moving at a snail's pace. The truth is that all the activity and exercise you can muster may help in accelerating the adaptation period by depleting your carbohydrate stores and ramping up your body's shift to burning fat.

- **Easy on the booze.** You don't have to completely abstain from alcohol on the ketogenic diet. However, it may be a good idea to limit alcohol when you're first getting started. After adaptation, a glass of dry red wine or the keto favorite "Ranch Water"—tequila, carbonated water and lime—should not be a problem.

- **Stick with it.** While this admittedly isn't the most original advice, remember that this too shall pass. Generally speaking, after climbing the adaptation mountain, many people enjoy a bounty of benefits with keto. Stick with it and make sure you can check off all the boxes above and listen to your body. If you are still not feeling well, consult with your physician and make sure keto is appropriate for you.

Over the last several years, keto has taken the world by storm. It is easily one of the top health and wellness trends and it's not showing any signs of losing steam. In fact, it seems to be gaining momentum—and let's face it, a major reason for its popularity is that it's such an effective tool for weight loss. But more than that, it is one of the primary tools for an energized life.

Formulator's Corner
Ketogenic Diet Supplements

Beyond the standard keto shopping list, there are a handful of dietary supplements that can help you get all the nutrients you need to thrive on a keto diet:

Electrolytes: The main electrolyte you need on keto (and in general) is sodium. Potassium, magnesium, calcium and chloride are also useful electrolytes. I use Redmond Real Salt or LMNT Recharge's ready-to-mix flavored powders, which taste amazing.

Magnesium: Even if you are supplementing your keto diet with a multivitamin and electrolytes, you may need some additional magnesium, not only because it alleviates that "tired but wired" feeling but also because it helps with muscle cramping and spasms. Look for one with magnesium glycinate or other chelates for optimal bioavailability and tolerance mentioned in other sections.

Exogenous Ketones: D-BHB/R-BHB is the active isomer of the key blood ketone BHB and is, in my experience, two to three times more effective. The sodium form is about 30 percent better than the other salts, which helps meet the increased sodium needs of the ketogenic diet. I like five grams of D-BHB sodium before a workout or when I am hungry.

C8 MCTs: More ketogenic than standard MCTs and far more ketogenic than coconut oil, C8 MCT is great to cook with or add to shakes. Bulletproof Brain Octane is a great liquid and C8Vantage is great as a powder. I add a teaspoon or two to my morning (decaf) coffee or shake.

Ketogenic Diet Supplements (continuation)

Dihydroberberine/Berberine: Anti-glycation is crucial in lowering Advanced Glycation End-products (AGEs), decreasing blood glucose/HgbA1c, increasing AMPK, lowering triglycerides and inflammation and providing positive hormetic stress to mitochondria. This could be the most powerful thing I recommend when it comes to battling aging and disease and promoting wellness and DHB is the more bioavailable version. I use 150 mg twice a day.

High DHA Omega-3: The most recent research reinforces the long-standing message that omega-3 supplements are foundational for virtually everyone, keto or not. And while some may contend that the research is not conclusive on omega-3 supplements, the counterargument is that it's becoming increasingly clear that we need even more omega-3s than previously thought to drive up the omega-3 index. I prefer a DHA-rich formula that provides omega-3s in natural triglyceride form, and I also like to choose a brand verified through IFOS.

Vitamin D3/K2: A vitamin D supplement, in addition to time in the great outdoors, helps make up for the fact that few food sources contain it. Make sure you choose one that is paired with its partner, vitamin K, but not just any K will do—you want vitamin K2, preferably the MK-7 form.

Probiotics + Prebiotics: A high-fat, low-carbohydrate diet like keto can have a profound impact on the makeup of the gut microbiome. At some point, preferably sooner than later, you will likely need to support the diversity and composition of your gut microbiome. While there are many probiotics out there, there's no one-size-fits-all option so you may have to do some experimentation. I tend to lean toward formulas containing soil-based organisms or spore form since there's solid evidence that they are more stable and can help support a healthy balance of gut bacteria.

Ketogenic Diet Supplements (continuation)

Polyphenols: Most people think about various fermentable fibers when they think of prebiotics. While those certainly fit the bill, polyphenols—which are found in various plant-based foods like vegetables, fruits, herbs and spices—pass undigested into the large intestine, where they can help control opportunistic microbes and serve as prebiotic fuel for healthy bacteria. I am a big fan of green powders that combine prebiotics with polyphenol-rich superfoods such as chlorella, spirulina, turmeric, reishi and berries.

Of course, keto isn't the only trendy diet out there. Let's move on to discussing some others.

WHAT IS THE PALEO DIET?

Evolved from the Primal diet, paleo encourages eating whole, minimally-processed foods that you could hunt or forage in their most natural forms, as opposed to the standard Western-style diet characterized by the overconsumption of heavily processed and refined foods. In other words, the paleo diet may be summed up with slogans such as "eat real food" or "don't eat processed garbage."

Paleo first came into consciousness in 1985, when Drs. Stanley Boyd Eaton and Melvin Konner from the Department of Anthropology and Program in Neuroscience and Behavioral Biology at Emory University published a seminal article titled "Paleolithic Nutrition: A Consideration of Its Nature and Current Implications" in the Journal of the American Medical Association. In the paper, they argued for the "Evolutionary Discordance" hypothesis, which states that "our genome evolved to adapt to conditions that no longer exist, that the change has occurred too rapidly for adequate genetic adaptation and that the resulting mismatch helps to cause some common chronic diseases," or "diseases of civilization"—including cardiovascular disease (e.g., atherosclerosis), type 2 diabetes, chronic obstructive pulmonary disease, lung and colon cancers, hypertension, obesity, diverticulitis and dental caries (cavities).[47]

As a fundamental basis for Evolutionary Discordance, they found that there is "surprisingly little overlap" between foods of the Paleolithic era, which spans from approximately 2.6 million to 10,000 years ago and the current era, which began with the introduction of agriculture and animal husbandry 10,000 years ago.[48] While 10,000 years may seem like a long time, it's just a drop in the bucket in the grand scheme of things.

Generally speaking, ancestral diets were characterized by much lower levels of refined carbohydrates and sodium and much higher levels of fiber and protein. Currently, most people get the majority of their calories from grains, refined vegetable and seed oils, domesticated livestock, dairy products and refined sugars. On the other hand, hunter-gatherers ate naturally occurring plant foods (fruits, vegetables, nuts and seeds), wild game and fish.

Just like with all nutrition lifestyle options, there is no "one-size-fits-all" approach to the paleo diet. In fact, one of the greatest criticisms (and there are many) is that there is simply no blanket prescription of an evolutionarily appropriate diet. Having said that, the following are typically considered staples of the paleo lifestyle:

- Unprocessed lean meats, including beef, chicken, turkey, bison, lamb, pork and wild game, from pasture-raised or wild animals when possible

- Fish and shellfish, wild-caught when possible

- Eggs, from local, pasture-raised hens when possible

- Most fresh vegetables (including root vegetables and various forms of squash), local and in-season when possible

- Most fresh fruits, local and in-season when possible

- Nuts and seeds

- Fresh and dried herbs and spices

- Liberal amounts of honey, molasses and agave for flavoring

- Healthful unrefined fats and oils, including lard, tallow, ghee, butter and olive, walnut, flaxseed, coconut, avocado and macadamia oils

- Water, water and more water—natural, local spring water when possible

Just like with keto, paleo is a way of life. Still, both approaches share a number of important similarities—they help you to reduce your sugar intake, they support eating whole foods and they are focused on practicing mindful eating. Ultimately, they are about adopting a lifestyle where there is more movement, energy and conscious choice-making—in short, more life!

At the end of the day, the paleo promise extends not just to where you are at right now, but where you will be in 20, 30 and 40 years. Because both keto and paleo offer long-term benefits, they make you less prone to disease and more likely to live a long, healthy and energized life.

Before moving on, I want to mention the Paleo Autoimmune Protocol (AIP for short), which is an elimination-style diet that's rooted within the paleo lifestyle, albeit considerably stricter. The goal of AIP is to promote a healthy lifestyle—with an emphasis on diet—to help calm down unhealthy levels of inflammation and an overactive immune system, which may stem from a leaky gut, gut dysbiosis and/or food sensitivities. The aim of AIP is to provide the body with nutritional resources required for immune regulation, gut health, hormonal regulation and tissue healing while removing inflammatory stimuli from both diet and lifestyle.

Like the standard paleo diet, AIP avoids processed and refined foods and empty calories, dairy, legumes, grains and pseudograins, and it also eliminates foods that have compounds that may stimulate the immune system or harm the gut environment, including nightshades (like tomatoes and peppers), eggs, nuts, seeds and alcohol. As an elimination-style diet strategy, AIP ultimately allows for the reintroduction of certain foods that are initially off limits. As such, AIP is a toolbox of sorts to help you understand how your body responds to food, and ultimately, to help you personalize your diet. Although it can be difficult to stick to consistently, AIP can be a very powerful and effective tool for dealing with unhealthy levels of inflammation, an overactive immune system and poor gut health (and all the symptoms associated with them, from brain fog and lackluster energy levels to skin issues to hormonal imbalances to mood issues to joint problems and more).

AUTO-IMMUNE PROTOCOL (AIP) OF PALEO

EAT	ELIMINATE	REINTRODUCE
Coconut	Alcohol	
Herbs	Cocoa	Alcohol
Spices	Coffee	Cocoa
Fermented Foods	Dairy	Coffee
Fruit	Eggs	Eggs
Bone Broth	Grains	Grass-fed Dairy
Meat and Poultry	Legumes	Legumes
Vegetables	Nightshades	Nightshades
Healthy Fats and Oils	NSAIDS	Nut & Seeds oils
Fish	Nut and Seed Oils	Nuts
	Nuts	Seeds
	Processed Oils	Spices*
	Refined Sugars	*(Derived from Berries and Seeds)
	Soy	
	Seeds	
	Spices*	
	*(Derived from Berries and Seeds)	

Graphic 27 – Auto-Immune Protocol of Paleo (AIP)

WHEN TO EAT

Although intermittent fasting (IF) has garnered a lot of attention over the last decade or so, it has been around for a long time. In fact, periods of **voluntary fasting**—which is a key distinction from starvation—have been practiced since early antiquity by people around the globe.

Intermittent fasting is a broad term that refers to dietary approaches where people go extended periods of time (typically 12-48 hours) with little to no caloric intake, with intervening periods of normal intake, on a recurring basis. Although that definition is fairly clear-cut, there is still quite a bit of confusion when it comes to IF because it encompasses several different eating patterns or subclasses.

You may be thinking that this whole fasting thing sounds difficult and slightly crazy! Well, it helps to remember the difference between *starvation* and *fasting*. Fasting is deliberate and voluntary; starvation is forced upon us and happens without our control. Your body is starving when it is deprived of nutrients, but when you are fasting, your body creates those nutrients from endogenous fuel sources in a controlled and efficient way. The body prevents starvation by entering a state of nutritional ketosis—a state where you use fat for energy and you feel amazing!

We will discuss how you can incorporate intermittent fasting in greater detail in the Growth chapter, but as you begin to build your routine, think about how you can establish a more structured routine around when you eat—and how.

GUT HEALTH

Of course, nutrition is not just a matter of what you are putting into your body or how you are consuming it, but how you are digesting those foods. Over the last 10-15 years, gut health and the gut microbiome have been the subject of intense scientific scrutiny. They've become such popular terms, in fact, that they're colloquially thrown around in day-to-day conversations—though many using them don't have the necessary appreciation for their far-reaching implications. In fact, many people I talk to still use terms like these synonymously with digestion and digestive health when they are only part of the story.

The gut microbiome is essentially our second brain. All of the neurotransmitters that are in the brain are in the gut, which is why similar disorders can be rooted in the microbiome. Depression can be rooted in poor gut health and an imbalanced gut microbiome, as can brain fog and obesity. Of course, there is a strong, intimate connection between the gut and the immune system. For example, 70-80 percent of the immune system resides in the gut and relies on a healthy gut for optimal immunity. So yes, immune system challenges and vulnerability to pathogens can be rooted in poor gut health.

Simply put, poor gut health goes well beyond the digestive tract. It can lead to fatigue, brain fog, poor sleep quality, skin issues, hormone imbalances, joint discomfort, allergies, cravings and difficulty with weight management. Surely, you have experienced some of these issues—in fact, they may be the very reasons you're reading this book. Along those lines, there is no question that improving gut health and digestion involves centering your diet on what you eat and don't eat. But first, let's look at some healthy options for optimal gut health.

Formulator's Corner
Gut Health Supplements

Digestive Enzymes: When it comes to certain intolerances and sensitivities, a broad-spectrum enzyme can be good diet insurance, especially when it comes to hidden ingredients that may be present when you're eating out. Bioptimizers Masszymes is a great product for this.

Gut Environment/Flora: Use prebiotics, probiotics and postbiotics (butyrate). See information throughout the book and other Formulator's Corners about these.

Antimicrobials: Ingredients such as black walnut, oregano oil and silver are helpful when dysbiosis is pronounced and you need to get your gut back in line (to encourage probiosis).

Acid Reflux: Licorice may help reduce the acidic burn some experience after a meal.

Digestive Soothing: Mallow root and slippery elm are go-to herbs.

Gut Repair: Zinc carnosine helps to stabilize the gut and stimulate gut repair while collagen helps feed, nourish and improve the gut lining and resilience.

Reducing Allergic Histamines: Quercetin is a potent antihistamine that can help quell allergic triggers. Liposomes (also called phytosomes) can greatly improve bioavailability and efficacy.

Gut Health Supplements (continuation)

Digestive Bitters: While often used in stiff drinks after dinner, I say skip the alcohol and just use the bitters—such as angelica, dandelion, ginger and citrus peel—as they can enhance digestive function by stimulating stomach acid, bile and digestive enzymes to break down food and absorb nutrients better. I like Dr. Shade's Bitters No. 9 by Quicksilver Scientific.

Glutamine: This is a key amino acid heavily present in the gut lining, keeping the tight junctions tight, improving the absorption of the nutrients you want absorbed and keeping the other leaky gut toxins out. Take 5-10g as tolerated.

As we age, many of us lose the ability to digest foods properly. Over time, as we produce fewer enzymes with which to break down food, we further compromise our gut health. We compound that by drinking too much with our food at meals (and not drinking water consistently throughout the day) and by not chewing our food enough. That said, there are some foods that are definitely not good for gut health:

Sugar. Just like healthy bacteria use *prebiotics* to thrive and proliferate, "bad" bacteria also require food for their survival. Not surprisingly, these pathogenic bacteria tend to thrive on "unhealthy" compounds like sugar. Sugar cravings and overeating junk food can be signs that your gut microflora is out of balance—and some researchers believe that microbes can act as "puppet masters," hijacking key neurotransmitters that impact appetite.[49]

Artificial Sweeteners. Many studies provide evidence that artificial sweeteners have a negative impact on the gut microbiome (examples include acesulfame potassium, sucralose, aspartame and saccharin). In one study, Duke University researchers found that consumption of sucralose for 12 weeks altered the gut microbiome in rats by significantly reducing the number of good bacteria —which didn't even fully recover after 12 weeks.[50] Though we might use them from time to time, the more we can avoid artificial sweeteners, the better for our gut health.

THE BEST LOW CARB
SWEETENERS

 **SWERVE ©**
SWEETENER

 **ERYTHRITOL**

 **MONK FRUIT**
EXTRACT

 **XYLITOL**

  STEVIA EXTRACT

 **ALLULOSE**

Graphic 28 – The Best Low Carb Sweeteners[51]

Food Coloring. There are more than 100 different food colorings used in food and currently, fewer than 10 are considered safe in the US food supply. In fact, in other parts of the world, most of these ingredients are banned for human (or even animal) consumption. But food companies are trying to sell things and make people addicted to them, and the cheapest way to do that is through artificial coloring. If your Pepsi or Gatorade is clear, you're not as attracted to it. Unfortunately, the three most widely used culprits—Yellow 5, Yellow 6 and Red 40—contain compounds like benzidine and 4-aminobiphenyl that have been linked to cancer. Research has also associated food dyes with problems in children—including allergies, hyperactivity, learning impairment, irritability and aggressiveness.[52]

Omega-6 Fats. Due to overconsumption of refined vegetable oils (e.g., soybean, corn, safflower, sunflower, cottonseed, canola) in processed foods and products from animals fed corn and soy, most people consume far too many omega-6 fats which are pro-inflammatory, especially in relationship to more anti-inflammatory omega-3 fats.

An omega-3 deficient diet also increases small intestinal bacterial overgrowth (SIBO).[53] This is an important finding, as there are a number of adverse outcomes common with SIBO, including bloating, diarrhea, abdominal discomfort, malabsorption, malnutrition and difficulty with weight management. SIBO is also a hallmark of several gut-related issues, including IBS and IBD.

Alcohol. The thinking around alcohol consumption isn't as cut-and-dried as it is around artificial sweeteners. For example, in a recent study published in the *American Journal of Clinical Nutrition*, researchers from Spain found that daily consumption of red wine for four weeks significantly increased the number of beneficial microbes in healthy human participants—an effect likely due to the prebiotic-like effects of the polyphenols found in wine.[54] Similar findings have been reported with beer, which contains polyphenols (e.g., xanthohumol) that may stimulate the growth of beneficial bacteria and inhibit pathogen bacteria, exerting prebiotic-like effects.[55]

Food Sensitivities. Gluten and FODMAP-containing foods are both common "trigger foods" for digestive complaints, but they are far from the only ones. In fact, there's a slew of probable suspects, including milk products, wheat and other grains, corn, soy, fish and seafood, eggs, nuts, nightshades (such as tomatoes), histamine-releasing foods, spicy foods, fried foods and caffeine.

FODMAP-Containing Foods. FODMAPs (fermentable oligo-, di-, monosaccharides and polyols) are carbohydrates (such as fructose, lactose and sugar alcohols like sorbitol, maltitol, mannitol, xylitol, isomalt, fructans and galectins) that are found in a wide range of foods, including cereal grains, dairy, legumes, vegetables and fruits. Undigested in the small intestine, these poorly absorbed FODMAPs draw water into the large intestine via the osmotic effect where they are fermented by gut bacteria. Many people with digestive complaints do particularly well when they consume a diet with reduced FODMAPs, as these carbs can lead to gas, bloating and digestive discomfort. For gluten haters, FODMAPs such as fructans found in gluten-containing foods may actually be responsible for the digestive discomfort that some folks experience when eating these foods—*not* gluten. That's not to say, however, that gluten can't be traced back to gut-related issues, such as leaky gut.

> **It's most important to tune into how food makes you feel and if you find a "probable suspect," experiment with it.**

LOW FODMAP DIET

	EAT	AVOID
VEGETABLES	Lettuce, Carrot, Cucumbers & more	Garlic, Beans, Onion & more
FRUITS	Strawberries, Pineapple, Grapes & more	Blackberries, Watermelon, Peaches & more
PROTEINS	Chicken, Eggs, Tofu & more	Sausages, Battered Fish, Breaded Meats & more
FATS	Oils, Butter, Peanuts & more	Almonds, Avocado, Pistachios & more
STARCHES, CEREALS & GRAINS	Potatos, Tortilla Chips, Popcorn & more	Beans, Gluten-based Bread, Muffins & more

Graphic 29 – Low FODMAP Diet[56]

Of course, it's most important to tune into how food makes you feel and if you find a "probable suspect," experiment with it. It is not at all uncommon for some people to have a negative physiological reaction to foods that are typically considered "good" and "healthy," so rule number one is to build your diet around foods that make you feel good and drop the ones that don't.

As much as some foods might lead to gastrointestinal disorders, others can alleviate them. Below are some foods which can help restore gut health and your health overall:

Fermented Foods. These foods contain probiotics, which are beneficial microbes (including strains from the *Lactobacillus, Streptococcus, Enterococcus, Lactococcus, Bifidobacterium* and *Saccharomyces* families) and can have a wide variety of health benefits, including aiding in digestion and nutrient absorption. A handful of the most common fermented foods include yogurt, kefir, kombucha, sauerkraut, pickles, kimchi, natto, miso and yes, even wine (I prefer a dry red for the health benefits and low sugar).

Coconut Oil and other MCTs. Compared to other fats and oils, coconut oil and to a lesser extent, butter and ghee (also known as clarified butter) are relatively high in medium-chain triglycerides (MCTs), which are easier to digest than more common long-chain triglycerides such as stearic acid. Even better, grass-fed butter or ghee are good dietary sources of the easy-digesting short-chain triglyceride butyric acid, which may have beneficial effects on digestion, the gut microbiota, inflammation and immunity.

Bone Broth. Broth is all the rage these days and while some of this may be hype, bone broth is fantastic when it comes to digestion. It contains nutrients (e.g., gelatin, glycine and glutamine) that support the intestinal lining, promote healthy gut microbiota, aid in the production of stomach acid and bile (which both play critical roles in digestion), improve gut motility and more. These nutrients also support a healthy immune system. For instance, glutamine is considered "fuel for the immune system" because many cells of the immune system rely heavily on glutamine as their *primary* source of fuel.

NUTRITION AND IMMUNITY

As many are now aware, 70-80 percent of your immune tissue is situated in your digestive tract. What many don't know is that our intestines form a protective barrier between our bloodstream and the external world. Our gut is truly its own system, managing the pathogens of everything we ingest throughout the day, which is why it needs its own immune system to prevent illness. This is why it is so important to have "good" bacteria in the gut in order to maintain balance and strengthen the gut microbiome against intruders.

When the integrity of the gut is compromised, it can lead to a "leaky gut," which means that the body is no longer protected against these invaders—which can lead to autoimmune conditions and other problems. Leaky gut also makes way for undigested food particles to enter circulation. A classic example is gluten, although that is just one on a laundry list of probable suspects when it comes to food sensitivities. When these undigested food particles enter our circulation (a place they shouldn't be), they set off an immune response—an inflammatory cascade followed by a massive defense effort by immune cells. The result is an overactive, dysfunctional immune system that is overworked, confused and distracted—one that ultimately is less capable of providing protection from the real foreign invaders it's designed to attack.

The bottom line is that the healthier our food, the stronger our gut health, which boosts our immune system and helps us fight off infection from the common cold and far more dangerous pathogens. While probiotics, prebiotics and the foods listed above are all important, the optimal way to support a healthy immune system is to clean up our diet—which means ditching the processed, nutrient-sparse junk food and eating abundant amounts of healthful, nutrient-dense foods. In terms of nourishing our immune system by eating more real, whole foods, a robust, properly responsive immune system is one that has all the vitamin C (e.g., citrus fruits, cruciferous veggies, bell peppers, tomatoes), vitamin D (e.g., eggs, mushrooms, fatty fish), vitamin E (e.g., dark leafy greens), vitamin A (e.g., sweet potatoes, carrots), zinc (e.g., beef, pumpkin seeds) and selenium (e.g., Brazil nuts, sardines) it needs.

Formulator's Corner
Pre, Pro & Post Biotics…Synbiotics

Prebiotics: These short-chain fibers are fermentable and used for fuel by the bacteria in the gut, though make sure you resolve any dysbiosis before using. My favorites are FOS, GOS and a phage called Pre-ForPro.

Probiotics: This is the good bacteria in your gut, where not only your digestion happens but also about 80 percent of your immunity. Your neurotransmitters, the brain-gut axis and many diseases are linked to dysbiosis (bacteria skewed negative over positive). I prefer stable pro-biotics in spore form or that are microencapsulated and my favorite strain that is gaining great data is lactobacillus plantarum.

Postbiotics: Butyrate is one of the key short fatty acids that probiotics produce and it's pivotal in our overall health. Tributyrin is the triglyc-eride form and is better absorbed over the free fatty acid.

Synbiotics: When combined, pre, pro and postbiotics are known as synbiotics, which means they are working together.

It's understandable that COVID-19 has motivated many to priori-tize their health more than ever before and search for new ways to boost immunity. Vitamin C sales have surged and manufacturers are struggling to meet demands for hand sanitizer, as our communities transition to online work and outdoor gatherings for social events.

We all know that the number one defense against sickness is a strong immune system. Without an immune system, our bodies would be open to attack from microscopic threats like bacteria, viruses and parasites. Involving many types of cells, organs and proteins, this system's job is to distinguish our tissue from foreign tissue.

If the immune system encounters an antigen (like a pathogen or virus), it triggers an immune response and the body fights to dispose of this foreign invader. If your immune system is weak or unhealthy, your body will be less able to fight back and you will be more vulnerable to getting sick and developing severe symptoms. Research has revealed that a diet rich in whole, unprocessed foods will encourage the growth of good bacteria in the gut, helping to establish a strong immune system.[57] Beyond diet and supplementation, other factors that are critical to supporting a robust immune system that can respond to challenges are stress management (e.g., meditation, gratitude, prayer), regular (but not too much) exercise, proper sleep, time spent outdoors and a good sense of connection and social integration.

IMMUNE SYSTEM INGREDIENTS
A ROBUST, PROPERLY RESPONSIVE IMMUNE SYSTEM IS ONE
THAT HAS ALL THE INGREDIENTS IT NEEDS.

VITAMIN C (e.g., citrus fruits, cruciferous veggies, bell peppers, tomatoes)

VITAMIN D (e.g., eggs, mushrooms, fatty fish)

VITAMIN E (e.g., dark leafy greens)

VITAMIN A (e.g., carrots, sweet potatoes)

ZINC (e.g., pumpkin seeds, beef)

SELENIUM (e.g., Brazil nuts, sardines)

Graphic 30 – Foods for Immunity

Many people think of a diet rather superficially—a choice motivated by the number on the scale and not by a larger desire for truth and empowerment. Changing how we view, choose and consume food should go much deeper. How we eat affects every element of our health and our ability to function and thrive in the world.

Once you start peeling back the layers of your well-being, you realize just how deep you can go. Through the process of getting sick, fighting off autoimmune disease and taking my health back into my own hands through the food I was eating, I reworked my nutrition and changed my life—but that was just the beginning. Seeing the benefits of that shift gave me more energy and motivation to grow even more—and to see that I was doing it all to fully seize my life and connect with others. I decided a long time ago that I could be a passenger in a life of sickness or I could be the pilot making healthy choices every day. It has become my passion and my purpose.

Food reflects our deepest values and our ability to choose wisely in a world that overwhelms us with choice. Finding a system which offers both structure and flexibility, creating a lifestyle plan tailored to our life and biology and finding and using healthy foods and supplements to support our health journey ultimately leads to the best choices—and to an empowered and energized life.

Once you start peeling back the layers of your well-being, you realize just how deep you can go.

NUTRITION SUMMARY

- Most people think of a diet as something that's a short-term quick fix. That is why I prefer to use the word lifestyle, which connotes that you are agreeing to make choices for the long run. This allows us room to be flexible —because the concept of "healthy" is individual and variable, each of us must find a definition based on experimentation over time. A lifestyle is not all or nothing; it is tailored to meet your individual needs.

- There are three main factors that led me to sticking to the keto diet: it cuts out nutrient-deficient foods, helps me feel full and satisfied and has cognitive enhancing-effects. But both keto and paleo focus on whole foods, whether they are meats or vegetables. It is about choosing healthy, natural, non-processed food products, which are usually sold close to where they are farmed. Paleo is more than whole food, it is ultimately about adopting a lifestyle that focuses on more natural movement, less allergens, more conscious choices—that we are evolved for.

- Metabolic flexibility means your body can efficiently and effectively switch between using carbs and fats for fuel based on availability and need—and it is a key to looking, feeling and performing your best as well as living your most energized life. The goal of a ketogenic diet is to create a powerful metabolic state during which the body is primarily burning fat (since ketones are derived from fats). Following a paleo-keto diet means avoiding processed fats and oils like soybean, corn, safflower, canola, sunflower, cottonseed and palm, which are high in PUFA, since they've been exposed to high heats and chemicals that turn them rancid and carcinogenic. Nutrition is not just about what you are putting into your body and how, but also how you are digesting those foods. A diet rich in whole, unprocessed foods will encourage the growth of good bacteria in the gut, helping to establish a strong immune system.

- Mindful eating involves paying attention to our food on purpose, moment by moment and without judgment, and it focuses on our sensual awareness and experience of the food. When we are present to the act of eating, we can no longer treat it as an unconscious habit. We are forced to reckon with our choice-making and become liberated from the bliss point, gaining control over what we put into our body and how. Through practice, this helps interrupt habitual eating behaviors and provides greater regulation of food choice. Mindful eating is about behavior changes.

- Both keto and paleo offer long-term health benefits, making you less prone to disease and more likely to live a long, healthy and energized life. The goal is to eat mindfully and attentively. Intermittent fasting is a broad term referring to dietary approaches where individuals go extended periods of time with little or no caloric intake (typically 12-48 hours), with intervening periods of normal intake, on a recurring basis.

- Keto flu refers to a group of symptoms such as brain fog, headache, nausea, muscle cramps and more that some people may experience when starting a ketogenic or other low-carb diet. Fewer than five percent of people experience this but it's more likely for those transitioning from a lifestyle that is sugar and carb-dependent.

Resource Hacks

Nutrition

Favorite Cookbooks: *The Anti-Anxiety Diet* by Ali Miller, *The Primal Blueprint Cookbook* by Mark Sisson with Jennifer Meier, *The Keto Reset Diet Cookbook* by Mark Sisson with Lindsay Taylor, *Cali'flour Kitchen* by Amy Lacey, *Eating Well, Living Better* by Michael Fenster, *The Ketogenic Kitchen* by Domini Kemp and Patricia Daly, *Made Whole* and *Made Whole Made Simple* by Cristina Curp and *Simply Keto* by Suzanne Ryan. Side note: Robb Wolf's book series on the science and history of eating is a masterclass.

Places to Shop: Keto foods online from the Explorado Market, Thrive Market and Amazon. Favorite grocery stores are Costco, Aldi, Sprouts, Trader Joe's and Whole Foods.

Kitchen Equipment: Insta-pot, slow cooker, air-fryer and dehydrator (Emeril Lagasse sells one piece of equipment containing all four of these devices in one, which I use), bacon grease strainer, ceramic cookware and silicone tools. I also love a milk frother for coffee that's "biohacked" (with collagen, butter, heavy cream or MCTs). Also, a high-power immersion blender (e.g., stick blender) will change your life when it comes to protein shakes, soups and creams; it's super quick and easy to clean up, unlike a traditional blender. A solid food processor is helpful, too. My favorite knives are ceramic or a tempered 440 stainless steel and counterbalanced. My favorite style of knife for all-purpose use is a santoku—you almost do not need any other.

Recipes: My website and Instagram have Shelley's Cadillac Skinny Margarita, Keto Hard Chocolate Ice Cream Shell, Keto/Paleo Pancakes and much more.

Nutrition (continuation)

Fasting Apps: Simple and clean: Zero app. Best for Community: LIFE Fasting Tracker.

Favorite Products: I have a variety here—some treats, some regular foods, some snacks—and I keep them all in the rotation. Redmond Real Salt, Paleo Powder seasonings, Primal Kitchen sauces and dressings, Kerrygold butter, SuperFat nut butter, Yez! Keto Bread, EPIC bone broth and pork skins, Whisps dried cheese snacks, HighKey cereals and cookies, Visionary Foods Nutola unsweetened granola, Choc Zero syrup and chocolate chips, Lily's dark chocolate, Killer Creamery Ice Cream, Dry Farm Red Wine, FitVine Wine, Butcher Box, Crowd Cow, Nose to Tail and Slanker Grass-Fed Meat

Calorie Trackers: Overall: MyFitnessPal. For inspiration: SparkPeople. For keto: Carb Manager. For lots of cool features: LifeSum.

Ketone Tracking: There are three methods of tracking your ketosis:

Urine: Use strips that track acetone in the urine. This is the least exact method, but also the most inexpensive. Perfect Keto makes strips I like to use.

Breath: Breath acetone tests used to be inaccurate but have markedly improved. One of the best on the market is the Biosense: it uses patented technologies and advanced computational algorithms to get as close to blood glucometer testing as possible.

Blood: Blood glucometers can check ketones and blood glucose at a very reasonable price now. Keto Mojo and Keto Coach are my favorites in this area.

Adaptation: As you keto adapt, there will be fewer ketones excreted or hanging around in the blood plasma. More of them are being used as a fuel, so don't be concerned if the numbers aren't as high as you think they should be. You will get more adapted. The key metric here is how you feel—you should be less tired, have more energy, a lower appetite and fewer cravings.

For live links, updated content, bonus graphics
and a hidden chapter, go to
EnergyFormulaBook.com

EXERCISE SURVEY

How many times per week do you incorporate movement into your day?		
I move my body regularly 3-5x per week doing different exercises.	(3)	
I try to exercise regularly but often forget or run out of time to do it.	(2)	
I rarely move my body throughout the week and I feel the effects of that.	(1)	
Outside of my profession, I work out more than 20 hours a week.	(-1)	
What is your familiarity with resistance training?		
I regularly weight train and love incorporating resistance training into my routine!	(3)	
I am familiar with some resistance training and body-weight exercises and have done it here and there, but I don't feel confident in consistently doing them on my own.	(2)	
I never do resistance training. I would not know where to start!	(1)	
What do you feel your allostatic load (total stress load) is when it comes to adding in exercise?		
I have ample capacity to add in exercise and do not feel any negative effects from adding in 3-5 days per week of resistance or cardiovascular training.	(3)	
My allostatic load is moderate to high and adding in too much exercise sometimes causes me to feel worse.	(2)	
My allostatic load is high and I often don't even have the energy to get up off the couch to go exercise.	(1)	

Do you have any internal "resistance" when it comes to resistance training?		
No, I clearly see the benefits of resistance training and I regularly do it and enjoy it!	(3)	
I understand that there are benefits but I'm afraid of getting too bulky or not knowing what I'm doing.	(2)	
I just do not see the appeal and have a hard time getting excited about it.	(1)	
What is your familiarity with HIIT (high-intensity-interval-training)?		
I extensively use HIIT for various forms of cardio exercise and know how to use it effectively.	(3)	
I have heard of HIIT but don't really understand how to use it for myself.	(2)	
I have no idea what that means! Or how to use it!	(1)	
How often are you exposed to temperatures beyond a comfortable 70 degrees?		
Often! I take cold showers, ice baths and go outside in cold weather or purposefully set my thermostat lower.	(3)	
Not very often. But occasionally I will take a contrast shower or expose myself to cooler temperatures.	(2)	
Never. I like to keep my body temperature static!	(1)	
Have you experimented with Cold-Exposure therapies before?		
Yes, I know about the benefits and include these in my overall healthy-life strategy.	(3)	
Not really, but I have heard of them!	(2)	
I have no idea how to get started with cold exposure.	(1)	
YOUR TOTAL		

5-11 points: You have got some work to do! This book is a great place to start!
12-16 points: You are heading in the right direction! Keep at it!
17-21 points: You are really on the ball! Only small tweaks are needed to be your best self!

Chapter 3: Exercise: Move Your Body and Master Your Mind

"Motion creates emotion."

—Tony Robbins

After I finished my Master's, I got an offer to work in a nearby level 1 trauma hospital in North Carolina as Chief Clinical Dietitian—an amazing job for someone coming right out of school. On the outside, I was exercising five times a week, looking lean and fit, making good money and dressing sharp in ties and a lab coat. Girls were finally attracted to me, and I really looked the part. But behind the scenes, my energy was lower than ever.

The combination of orthorexic (i.e. workout addiction) burnout, malnutrition, pushing to be popular in college and going out all the time had nearly ruined me—and on top of it, I was now working strenuous hours at a demanding job with people looking to me for guidance. Though I'd achieved my goal of getting a graduate degree, my fatigue, muscle cramps, brain fog and depression remained close to unbearable—and would for the next few years.

At the very least, the keto diet was giving me some improvements. I was easing up on the extreme workouts I'd been pushing myself through, and instead of only taking supplements to make me stronger and faster in the short-term, I started experimenting with compounds to take for longevity and recovery—like an insurance policy for my health. Slowly but surely, my body was adapting and I was becoming more active again. I was putting my dream of formulating supplements on hold and giving myself time to adjust to real life, and to a baseline of health again.

I decided to move closer to my family and move away from the high level trauma environment I'd been working in to get a different clinical experience in a nursing home and rehabilitation facility. I've always had a deep connection to the elderly and loved the rehab environment. In some ways, I was getting a preview of the end result of various ways of living. More than anything else though, I felt more strongly than ever that I needed to use the skills and information I'd learned to help others.

I decided to stop telling the stories where I was the victim and start telling the stories where I was the hero.

While working at the skilled nursing facility and living out in the country in North Carolina, I would commute to Charlotte on a busy thoroughfare called US 74/Independence Blvd. This involved merging from another highway, I-485, at a stoplight-controlled intersection. Traffic coming off of 485 was fast and sometimes not ready for that red light. One day, as I waited at the crossing, I heard a screeching sound behind me. I looked in my rearview mirror to see piles of smoke and then —BOOOOOOM! In that instant, my life changed. Rear-ended at 70 MPH, my neck whipped back and forth like a rag doll and it seemed like a dream…a nightmare really. For the next several years, I did rehab five days a week, getting pain injections, burning nerves down (rhizotomies), chiropractic work and massage to deal with compressed and degenerating discs, chronic nerve pain, dizziness and extreme fatigue. Despite, yet again, feeling like life wouldn't let me get ahead and my depression being at an all-time high, I fought my way out of the darkness back into the light of existence. I eventually got to the gym and started working out with the frequency I was used to, five days a week after work.

With the pain mostly controlled, it allowed me to get into shape. After several months, I found a Russian trainer that was a former Olympic boxer and Spetsnaz (Special Forces). As someone who was used to dealing with extremes, this insanely fit and disciplined trainer pushed me…hard. He loved the Jim Rohn quote, "Take care of your body, it's the only place you have to live." Point blank, he would follow that up with (in his hard Russian accent), "So, do you choose to live or die today? You choose." To which I responded while exasperated and sweating, "Live. LIVE!" He had me doing functional mobility and metabolic conditioning, much like CrossFit, before that was popular. He was ahead of his time. When we trained, I was doing feats of endurance and strength that seemed impossible to nearly everyone in the gym, including the "me" who had just been doing rehab for 2 years straight. Eventually I did get two titanium discs put in my cervical spine largely due to that car accident, but what else I got along the way was discipline and hope. I started understanding that setbacks were going to come. Something was going to shake up my life health-wise every few years. Now, though, I felt empowered to endure it and even thrive. I was stronger inside because of the strengthening I was doing outside. I decided to stop telling the stories where I was the victim and start telling the stories where I was the hero. When you are in peak shape, life just feels better. I promise this is not hyperbole, but something that can transform your life too. Exercise can save you from a life of frailty—mentally, physically and medically.

Per Newton's First Law of Motion, a body at rest stays at rest. Likewise, a body in motion stays in motion. The more we move our bodies, the more energy we have to accomplish our goals and overcome obstacles.

I always tell people that exercise rarely starts in the gym. Movement is all about connecting once again to your body. Even people who are diehard fitness folks sometimes forget that. They think that by running 10 miles or lifting weights, they are connecting to themselves when really, they are just bringing their grind to the gym.

I always advise people who have been exceptionally sedentary to just start by walking—even the simple act of a morning or evening walk can promote circulation and increase energy, not to mention shift your mindset. Feel your body rise with the sun. Go for a walk in the brisk morning air. Notice how your legs move, how your shoulders feel; connect into the aches and pains, but also try to get a sense of where your body feels the energy and how the most basic movements can make you feel alive.

We need to start somewhere, and by setting the starting line in a place that's reasonable and comfortable for you, you're more likely to stick with your exercise routine as you increase your stress and stamina. This means that whether you walk or swim, whether you prefer a stationary bike or chair yoga, you should start where you are. Stick with it and I promise, you will progress.

You will build a fitness routine that offers a foundation for truly radiant energy. After all, perhaps the most noticeable, immediate and reliable benefits of regular physical activity are robust improvements in feelings of well-being and vitality—having physical and mental energy, a sense of enthusiasm, aliveness and feelings of vigor and calm energy. What's more, if you ever feel like you are running low on mental energy, exercise is the prescription to cut through brain fog and enhance mental clarity, as it can increase cerebral blood flow both acutely and with regular physical activity.

Before you embark on any fitness regimen, you should always first check with your physician. After you've been given the green light, you can start to figure out the best structure and style for you. The point is not to overwhelm yourself on day one. Again, we experiment with what works knowing there are no right answers—there's only what's right for us. By gently adding pieces to your routine, you can find out what does and doesn't work for your body. You don't want to go too hard too fast; not only do you risk burnout and frustration, but you also risk injury.

RESISTANCE TRAINING

If I were to ask you the key factors and predictors of living a long life, what kinds of things come to mind? Genetics? Sure, they play a role, but much less than you might think. So, what about *lifestyle* factors?

Is weight management—especially belly fat—on the tip of your tongue? Social support and connectedness? Exercise, especially good old cardio?

What about muscle strength? Was that even on your radar? Believe it or not, one of the single most important factors in dictating how long and well you live your life is muscular strength. Yes, you read that correctly.

A seminal review study published in the *British Medical Journal*, which involved 8,762 male participants who were followed for nearly 19 years, found that "muscular strength is inversely and independently associated with death from all causes and cancer." This was even after taking other confounding factors like cardiorespiratory fitness into consideration.[58]

I am not just talking about statistical significance; I am talking about *game-changing* significance. For example, men in the lowest third of muscle strength—which was quantified by bench press (upper body) and leg press (lower body) performance—had a 50 percent higher rate of death during the study period compared to men in the middle and upper thirds of muscular strength. What's more, low muscular strength was associated with an 83 percent increased risk of death from cardiovascular disease and a 45 percent increased risk of death from cancer compared to stronger men.

Yes, many of these studies have focused on men. Unfortunately, there have been far fewer studies on women, which is frustrating not only because of the hormonal differences between men and women, but also because there are often far more variables with women when it comes to weights. We hope to get more information on this, and perhaps the CrossFit community will provide it, but that science isn't there yet.

Even more evidence has highlighted the important connection between muscular strength and lifespan. For instance, a recent study published in the journal Medicine and Science in Sports and Exercise from the National Health and Nutrition Examination Survey—which included 4,449 participants (all older than 50)—found that death from all causes was 2.66 times higher in those with low muscle strength.[59] Another study has pointed to grip strength as one of the single best indicators of healthy aging and longevity.[60]

But here is something even more important: Muscular strength doesn't just increase **lifespan**; it also enhances healthspan.

What is **healthspan**? Great question.

Researchers define healthspan as "the period of life free of major chronic clinical diseases and disability." It is based on the premise that life can be roughly divided into two phases: a period of relatively

healthy aging (healthspan) and a period of age-associated disease and disability.

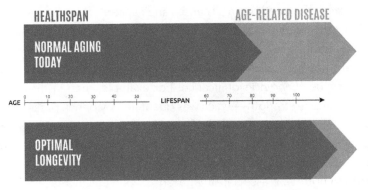

Graphic 31 – Lifespan vs. Healthspan[61]

Another way to think about healthspan is optimal longevity, which means living long with an even greater interest in living well. In other words, increasing healthspan is not just about surviving longer; it is about living longer. This is an important distinction to make. Even though medical advances have resulted in an increased average lifespan, many would argue that this is the result of folks surviving longer with age and lifestyle-associated diseases and disabilities rather than increasing healthspan.[62]

How does muscular strength enhance healthspan and optimize longevity? To answer that question, we need to look no further than the health-related benefits of resistance training—the most effective tool for enhancing muscular strength.

Lifting weights does more than simply increase strength and muscle mass. In other words, it's not just for athletes and bodybuilders. Resistance training is as much about training the mind as it is about training the body.

As a recent study showed, when we participate in high-intensity workouts, we also increase brain-derived neurotrophic factor (BDNF), which helps generate new neurons in the brain. Therefore, working out not only promotes youthfulness, but also creates more neuroplasticity in the brain, which increases our ability to learn new things. There are numerous studies which prove that exercise can increase your ability to learn, improve your mood and enhance your outlook on life. The researchers stated that "BDNF concentrations are increased after an acute bout of resistance exercise regardless of training paradigm, and are further increased during a 7-week training program in experienced lifters."[63]

Of course, many people who regularly engage in exercise, particularly strength training, are aware of the fact that it's a powerful tool to amplify resilience and bounce back from stress. This may be because physical exercise regularly activates the stress system, which in turn forces the body to adapt so it's then able to handle stress more effectively and with greater vigor. It is also possible that regular exercise reorganizes the brain so that its perception of stress (and subsequent response) is reduced. The enhanced resilience to stress may also relate to increased levels of feel-good chemicals (such as endorphins, neurotransmitters and galanin) that result from physical exercise. Although the link between working out and relieving stress isn't entirely understood by scientists, and researchers haven't quite pinned down how exercise modulates stress in the brain and the body, we know that regular exercise enhances and strengthens the brain and body's resilience to stress.[64]

TOP 7 BENEFITS OF RESISTANCE TRAINING

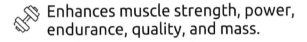 Enhances muscle strength, power, endurance, quality, and mass.

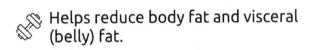 Helps reduce body fat and visceral (belly) fat.

Helps reduce fasting insulin levels, improve insulin sensitivity, and reduce the insulin response to help increase HDL, carbohydrates.

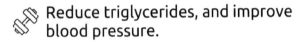 Reduce triglycerides, and improve blood pressure.

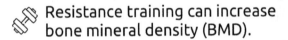 Resistance training can increase bone mineral density (BMD).

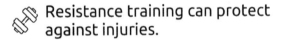 Resistance training can protect against injuries.

Train the brain while you train the body.

Graphic 32 – Top Seven Benefits of Resistance Training

As with allostatic load, each person has a "threshold level." While adding stress to an already full "stress bucket" causes overflow and health problems, adding the right level of stress helps you to learn, grow and increase energy. When resistance training is performed safely, appropriately and gradually, it leads to adaptations which make you stronger. It is important to note that it is not a matter of more being better but rather better being better. Let me put it in no uncertain terms: Resistance training is essential for *everyone*. Here are some ways it can help you live longer, better and more optimally:

Resistance training enhances muscle strength, power, endurance, quality and mass. This is well-known, but the health consequences of maintaining (and increasing) muscle strength, power and mass over the years can help protect you from physical disability, falling and even death. An ideal routine would include resistance training three times a week, HIIT twice a week and some moderate aerobic exercise twice a week. When it comes to aerobic activity, do whatever you enjoy, whether it is shooting hoops or playing volleyball or tennis, but also add some low-level physical activity like walking every day.

Resistance training helps reduce body fat and visceral (belly) fat. Even though weight lifting on its own may not lead to "weight loss" on the scale (i.e., a net reduction in body mass), it can radically change your body composition—meaning how you look and feel and how your clothes fit—since it helps you reduce body fat while increasing lean muscle. In fact, the more muscle mass you have, the more carbohydrates your body can handle. But perhaps most importantly, resistance training helps decrease abdominal fat (i.e., visceral or belly fat), which is associated with metabolic disorders, increased risk of type 2 diabetes and cardiovascular disease.

Resistance training can also reduce fasting insulin levels, improve insulin sensitivity and reduce the insulin response to carbohydrates. For starters, muscle is the primary site where the body uses and stores glucose (carbohydrates), and muscle contraction increases glucose uptake—improving insulin sensitivity, which helps promote glycemic balance and control. Essentially, the less muscle you have, the smaller your glucose reservoir, which is why every time you eat, the sugar in your bloodstream gets stored as fat. It is no wonder the American Diabetes Association recommends that all adults should engage in regular resistance training. Many people turn to the ketogenic diet to improve glycemic control, yet resistance training is also an overlooked and extremely powerful way to balance glucose. I would go as far as to say that resistance training may be the most reliable method for improving glycemic variability, which is one of the most important aspects of having radiant health and vibrant energy.

Resistance training can help increase HDL, reduce triglycerides and improve blood pressure. Low HDL, high triglycerides and high blood pressure (along with elevated waist circumference and fasting blood glucose) contribute to an elevated risk for metabolic syndrome. Muscle strength has been inversely associated with metabolic syndrome and there is some evidence that resistance training may improve HDL, triglycerides and blood pressure. In fact, one recent study found that just an hour per week of resistance training—even without aerobic exercise—was linked to a 29 percent lower risk of developing metabolic syndrome. The unfortunate reality is that many people turn to traditional slow-go cardio for this level of prevention. It seems, however, that the greatest benefits—in terms of preventing metabolic syndrome—come from a combination of resistance training and aerobic training.

Resistance training can increase bone mineral density (BMD). Long-term studies have shown that lifting weights can significantly increase bone mass in people of all ages. BMD is a tremendous concern, especially among women and especially as we get older, because it is intricately tied to osteoporosis and the risk for broken bones. So tell Grandma to get out those weights for a major biohack!

Train the brain while you train the body. The benefits of resistance training go beyond strong, healthy muscles. In a recent systematic review and meta-analysis involving 33 clinical trials including 1,877 participants, researchers found that resistance training significantly reduced depressive symptoms among adults.[65] Yep, lifting weights promotes a healthy brain, not just brawn, and emerging research shows that resistance training can improve cognitive function and quality of life in older folks.

Resistance training can protect against injuries. When you think about staying physically healthy and reducing your risk for injury, what type of exercise or activity usually comes to mind? If stretching activities are at the top of the list, it is time to reconsider. Though stretching might feel good and can hold other benefits, injury prevention isn't one of them. In fact, not only does research show that stretching has *no* beneficial impact on injury prevention, it also tells us that strength training reduces the risk of injuries by nearly 70 percent.[66] Quite ironically, when done incorrectly, stretching can create injuries. I sometimes do some basic movements to warm up and cool down before athletic activity, but I do not "stretch" in the traditional sense.

If all of the above doesn't get you excited about building muscle, I'm not sure what will. But here's the deal: As you get older, simply *maintaining* hard-earned muscle is an uphill battle. For instance, research shows that adults experience profound losses in muscle mass after reaching the age of 30.[67] Losses begin at about three to eight percent per decade and the rate accelerates to losses of one to two percent of muscle mass *each year* once folks hit their 50s. Ultimately, from the time you're 20 to the time you hit your 80s, it's likely that you'll lose between 35 and 40 percent of your muscle. *Yikes!*

Essentially, the older you get, the less efficient your body is at building muscle from the protein you eat. With age, you need more protein to get the same muscle protein synthesis (MPS) response as you do when you are younger, which is why eating quality protein (and enough protein) is essential as you age. Here are my recommendations:

- 25-30 grams of high-quality protein with each meal (if you are vegan, this may be much higher)

- 2-3 grams of leucine (the key amino in protein that is responsible for MPS) with each meal

- Protein spread out evenly throughout the day ideally

OPTIMIZING MUSCLE PROTEIN SYNTHESIS

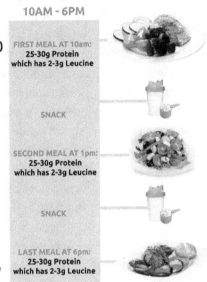

0.8 - 2.2 GRAMS
OF PROTEIN PER KG (LEAN MASS)

10AM - 6PM

FIRST MEAL AT 10am:
25-30g Protein
which has 2-3g Leucine

25-30 GRAMS
OF PROTEIN WITH EACH MEAL

SNACK

2-3 GRAMS
OF LEUCINE PER 3-4 HOURS

SECOND MEAL AT 1pm:
25-30g Protein
which has 2-3g Leucine

SNACK

MEAL TIMING:
SPREAD OUT EVENLY
THROUGHOUT THE DAY OR
IN A RESTRICTED TIME WINDOW

LAST MEAL AT 6pm:
25-30g Protein
which has 2-3g Leucine

Graphic 33 – Optimizing Muscle Protein

As we age, we might either maintain or put on more weight, but in either scenario, we are likely to increase fat mass and decrease our muscle mass, thereby decreasing our bone/muscle density. The more muscle we have, the stronger the bone needs to be to support the body. As you age and lose muscle mass, you also lose the bone mass needed to uphold it.

Resistance training strengthens the muscle, which requires that the bone remain strong. One secret training method you may not know of is blood flow restriction (BFR). As you get older, you cannot or don't want to lift extremely heavy weights all the time. The way we get stronger is by causing a certain amount of tension and stress (e.g., muscle cell swelling, metabolite-induced fatigue) within the muscle tissue when we lift weights. This stress provides a low oxygen nutrient supply to the muscle tissue. So, this stress can be mimicked or achieved by using BFR bands while lifting lighter weights, decreasing the blood supply to your muscle and tricking your body into perceiving a really heavy weight. By creating that same stress with a lighter load, you can still build muscle. As you increase muscle mass, you also increase bone density.[68]

I would encourage anyone getting started or returning to working out to hire a trainer to set up a program. This doesn't have to mean weekly workouts with a trainer—just an initial consultation followed by monthly check-ins. Trainers have made a massive difference in how I exercise—not because of the macho stuff but because they help me age healthily. My weights are dramatically lighter, but I am still getting great benefits.

Thanks to trainers, I'm employing techniques like drop sets and supersets, intra-set stretching and BFR (also called KAATSU). Intra-set stretching is different from stretching in the typical sense: If you are doing a set of curls, you flex your triceps as hard as you can in between sets and then go back to your set after a minute. The idea is to stay under constant muscle tension but with alternating groups. The harder you flex your triceps, the more the bicep is "stretched," fully exhausting the muscle. You don't need to do 10 sets. It is incredible how difficult this workout can be even though you're not lifting tremendous weight. You just have to keep more time under constant tension.

It's no longer about how big I can get, but about how much energy I can have. Sit down with your trainer and explain that it is not about what you want to look like (though that can be part of it) but about the kind of life you want to have. Find a trainer who understands your fitness goals as well as your life goals so you can create a plan to achieve both.

Formulator's Corner
Exercise Performance Supplements

Pre-Workout Supplement: For me, the name of the game here is boosting focus, enhancing mental energy and clarity and boosting the mind-muscle connection. Because I'm sensitive to caffeine, I prefer a non-caffeinated formulation, but that is up to you. My favorite product is Genius Preworkout. It has legitimate, branded and science-backed nootropics like alpha-GPC, taurine, huperzine A and tyrosine; citrulline and arginine for blood flow; HICA for muscle protein synthesis; betaine, ATP and beta-alanine for strength and power; and adaptogens like rhodiola. If you need the type of boost you can only get from stimulants, you can add caffeine or, better still, the ingredients I co-patented, TeaCrine and Dynamine. Genius Consciousness contains caffeine, Dynamine and eight other brain-boosting ingredients. Combined with Pre, it could be the ultimate pre-workout stack.

Electrolytes: Replacing electrolytes lost during intense exercise is just as important as rehydrating, and this may be even more important for folks on keto and other low-carbohydrate diets. I look for formulas that contain, at a minimum, sodium (as bicarbonate), potassium and magnesium. Onnit, Thorne and LMNT are all good choices.

Nootropics: I mentioned this above, but some of my favorite pre-workout nootropics are alpha-GPC, lion's mane, tyrosine, taurine, acetyl-L-carnitine, huperzine A and creatine.

Beta-Alanine: Beta-alanine is an amino acid that promotes and maintains muscle endurance and output and helps boost athletic performance. It can even enhance mental focus and may help build muscle faster. Look for the CarnoSyn brand of beta-alanine and use 3.2-6.4g daily.

Exercise Performance Supplements (continuation)

BAIBA: BAIBA is a myokine, also referred to as an "exercise factor" or "exercise mimetic." It plays a powerful role in the many benefits of regular exercise (e.g., increased glucose uptake and fatty acid oxidation), but it can also facilitate the "browning" of fat tissue, which can lead to increased metabolic rate and fat burning. Look for MitoBurn, the branded version of BAIBA. I use 750-2000 mg pre-workout.

Grains of Paradise (GOP): GOP has been shown to activate BAT, which is a unique type of fat tissue that burns extra calories to generate heat. Activating BAT can help increase metabolic rate, fat burning and glucose disposal. Look for CaloriBurn GP, the branded version of GOP. I use 40-80 mg twice a day.

Carbs: As a keto guy, I have found that consuming a small amount (~17 grams) of carbs before workouts can be tremendously helpful for performance and recovery. While there are some innovative ingredients (e.g., modified starches), something as simple as dextrose can get the job done. Even more interesting is data on "carb rinsing"—that is, swishing something like Gatorade in your mouth and spitting it out—which may have a benefit without consuming the sugar/carbs.

L-Citrulline: While arginine gets most of the love as a nitric oxide (NO) booster, l-citrulline is my go-to supplement when it comes to supporting NO production, blood flow and exercise performance. I prefer L-citrulline over citrulline malate and I usually look for a dose of six grams.

Nitrates: Speaking of NO production, dietary nitrates—such as those from beets and beetroot (300-500 mg)—can also help raise NO levels, maximize blood flow and improve athletic performance. Recent research shows that dietary nitrates from amaranth may also help increase NO and athletic performance.

HIIT - HIGH INTENSITY INTERVAL TRAINING

When it comes to cardio, there are many types to choose from: walking, jogging, running, rowing, climbing, playing (sports or games), circuit training, cycling, exercise classes and more. In addition to the type of cardio, you also have the option of choosing the frequency, duration and intensity of your sessions.

In one corner, you have moderate-intensity aerobic training, which is synonymous with the ol' "Slow-Go" cardio that has been a mainstay of exercise guidelines since the 1960s, when Dr. Kenneth Cooper literally wrote the book *Aerobics*. Slow-Go cardio—which is also referred to as moderate-intensity continuous training (MICT), steady-state exercise or endurance training—consists of 30 to 45 minutes (or longer) of continuous exercise.

In the other corner, you have the aforementioned "new kid on the block" of high-intensity interval training, which is often called HIIT or HIT for short. According to fitness researchers in the academic journal *Sports*, HIIT is "characterized by brief, intermittent bursts of vigorous activity, interspersed by periods of rest or low-intensity exercise."[69] Speaking generally, HIIT workouts typically last only 10 to 20 minutes (sometimes even less), with as little as one minute of that time comprised of "bursts" of vigorous activity.

Because "lack of time" is one of the most common reasons people give for not exercising regularly, the time-efficient nature of HIIT often fits more conveniently into people's busy schedules. The American College of Sports Medicine tells us that we need a minimum of 150 minutes per week of Slow-Go cardio to improve health and as much as 300 minutes a week if we're looking to lose weight. On the other hand, we can get the same health benefits from 75 minutes of HIIT weekly.[70]

In a recent study, a research group at McMaster University in Canada led by Martin Gibala, an authority on HIIT, found that HIIT programs that involved a mere 30 minutes a week (and only one minute of actual "work" per 10-minute session) resulted in similar health benefits (e.g., blood sugar management, insulin sensitivity) and physical adaptations (e.g., increases in mitochondria) as 150 minutes of steady-state cardio. That is 20 percent of the time commitment.[71] Wow!

The only ultimate HIIT product that used to be available was the Wingate Bike, which was only found in exercise physiology labs and cost tens of thousands of dollars. But now there is an AI-powered, home version called the C.A.R.O.L. AI bike. Workouts are two to five minutes and are some of the most difficult routines you can do. Most people are not used to maximal effort, but the results are impressive once you try.

I am not going to sugarcoat it; what HIIT lacks in time requirement, it more than makes up for with effort. In other words, to benefit from HIIT, you must push yourself—*hard*. If it feels easy, it is time to make it harder.

Since HIIT typically burns fewer calories during exercise, then what gives? Well, it's possible that HIIT may have a stronger appetite-suppressing effect than steady-state cardio and in turn, may result in reduced caloric intake. Along those lines, there is some evidence that high-intensity exercise can reduce levels of the hunger hormone ghrelin to a greater extent than moderate-intensity exercise.[72]

If it still sounds too intense, remember this: HIIT depends on you! If you're sedentary, it could mean a series of bouts of jogging to walking to jogging. If you have progressed, it might mean bouts of jogging, then sprinting, then jogging again. From there, you can increase duration or frequency as long as the intensity is high—near the maximum for *you*!

Can HIIT really help you live longer? According to the largest and longest randomized controlled exercise trial performed to date, the answer appears to be *yes*.[73] The Generation 100 Study, which involved over 1,500 adults, compared the effects of HIIT to steady-state cardio performed twice a week for five years. The results clearly showed that older adults who were able to keep up high physical activity levels had a much lower risk for premature death than what was expected for their age group. But here's the kicker: there were larger health benefits in the group that did the HIIT workouts; in fact, their rate of premature death was *half* that of the group that did traditional steady-state cardio.

Quite often, I've been greeted by enthusiastic folks who are under the impression that a few days of exercise a week will be the secret sauce for their weight loss goals. I can't blame them—that kind of thinking is the norm among the general population and even among medical professionals and fitness coaches.

I hate to be a Debbie Downer, but exercise by itself is a pretty futile tool for *weight loss*. I mean, we are talking about *maybe* dropping three to four pounds over the course of a year—with a strong likelihood of gaining it all back (and then some) after two years. That is a substantial investment of time and sweat with very little return (well, at least when it comes to *weight loss*).

Notice that I have highlighted "weight loss" multiple times. What I am referring to here is a number on the scale, or to be more scientifically accurate, a net change in body mass. Outside of weight loss, there are many health benefits associated with regular exercise, including what I like to call *quality weight loss*, which reflects changes in *body composition*. In other words, exercise can accelerate *fat loss* while preserving or increasing *lean muscle*. These changes are often not captured by a number on the scale—meaning it only provides quantitative, and not qualitative, feedback.

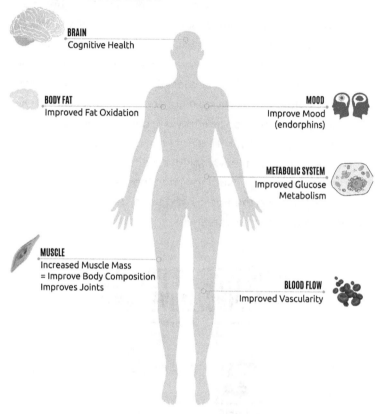

WEIGHT LOSS **IS OFTEN THE ULTIMATE GOAL, BUT YOU ALSO ACHIEVE:**

BRAIN
Cognitive Health

BODY FAT
Improved Fat Oxidation

MOOD
Improve Mood
(endorphins)

METABOLIC SYSTEM
Improved Glucose
Metabolism

MUSCLE
Increased Muscle Mass
= Improve Body Composition
Improves Joints

BLOOD FLOW
Improved Vascularity

Graphic 34 – Whole Body Benefits of Weight Loss

Having said all that, regardless of whether *weight loss* or *quality weight loss* is your goal, both scientific research and real-world experience unequivocally tell us that regular exercise plus nutrition (as part of a behavioral weight management program) is more effective than either alone.[74]

Nevertheless, as a health and fitness professional as well as an avid exercise and science geek, I have zero hesitation insisting that structured exercise (as well as regular physical activity and spontaneous movement throughout the day) is a cornerstone of any healthy lifestyle and weight management program. When it comes to the types of exercise that make up an effective program, I concur with professional health organizations like the American College of Sports Medicine (ACSM) and American Diabetes Association, which suggest a combination of strength (i.e., weight training) and cardiorespiratory training (i.e., "cardio"), not to mention flexibility and balance training every week.

Even more importantly, HIIT is not just about aesthetics or athletic performance; it is about developing a routine that promotes both healthy aging and energy. Nutrition and fitness are not the ends; they are the means to have the energy you need to reach your peak potential and live the life that you envision for yourself.

MAIN TYPES OF PHYSICAL TRAINING/MOVEMENT:

RESISTANCE TRAINING
2-3X WEEK
(30-60 MINS)

Eg: 4 x 6-15 reps of bench press, row, deadlift, squat, lunge with moderate to heavy weights

AEROBIC (GO-SLOW)
2-3X WEEK
(30-60 MINS)

Eg: Mountain hike, steady 60 min cycle (maintain low heart rate)

HIIT
2-3X WEEK
(15-45 MINS)

Eg: Tabata (4 mins of 20 sec exercise, 10 sec rest)

MOBILITY WORK
(2-3X WEEK)

Eg: yoga class, stretching

*Can combine the above methods together, eg HIIT + yoga in same day

Graphic 35 – Main Types of Physical Training and Movement

NEAT: NON-EXERCISE ACTIVITY THERMOGENESIS

As I alluded to above, I'm a bit of a "gym rat" these days, and I'm a staunch believer that structured exercise—particularly resistance training and HIIT—is a pillar for building radiant health, vibrant energy and unshakable resilience. Having said that, I also know that exercise alone is not enough. It's not enough to combat an otherwise sedentary lifestyle, and it's not enough to optimize healthspan.

We also need to accumulate plenty of low-level physical activity throughout the day. The research is clear that prolonged sitting and sedentary time increases the risk of obesity, weight gain, diabetes, some cancers, muscle loss, high blood pressure, cardiovascular disease and mental health problems...and you're not necessarily protected even if you get your 30-60 minutes of exercise daily. In other words, we need to exercise, sit less and move more.

Basically, the idea here is to increase a key component of metabolism called "non-exercise activity thermogenesis, or NEAT for short. Some also refer to this as non-exercise physical activity, or NEPA, but I think NEAT is a pretty nifty and catchy acronym, as in, a NEAT way to get and stay lean and healthy. Essentially, this component of metabolism accounts for all calories burned throughout the day during non-scheduled exercise activity, and it includes things like taking the stairs, doing chores, taking a walk, getting up and moving around and fidgeting.

In general, research shows that people who tend to have an easier time staying lean burn more calories via NEAT on a daily basis compared to those folks who struggle with their weight. In fact, NEAT can vary between individuals (of similar size) by as many as 2,000 calories per day! Along those lines, NEAT is the most variable component of daily energy expenditure, and to that end, it's the component of metabolic rate over which we have the most control.

This is why researchers consider NEAT such an important piece of the puzzle for weight control, but that's really just the tip of the iceberg. Properly timed low-level physical activity can also be a highly effective tool for blood sugar management. For example, research shows that a 10- or 15-minute walk after a meal is more effective for lowering post-meal blood sugar than a single 30- or 45-minute continuous bout of walking during the day.[75] Low-level physical activity, microworkouts and exercise snacks may also help improve pain management, markers of cardiovascular health (e.g., blood pressure, cholesterol, resting heart rate), mood, self-efficacy, quality of life, cardiorespiratory fitness, energy levels, cognitive function, creativity and more.

Unfortunately, because so many of us work sedentary jobs, sit during our commutes, and sit when we are home, we often have to "schedule" more NEAT and low-level physical activity into our days —that is, until the practice becomes a habit. Ultimately, the idea is to make your days more active by baking in more physical activity. Along those lines, you might set a timer for every 30-60 minutes throughout the day, and when it goes off, you might go for a walk, do some chores, take the stairs, do some rearranging, move some boxes, dance to some music, do some bodyweight exercises and so on.

CHILL OUT (THE BENEFITS OF COLD EXPOSURE)

One of the upsides of modern life is that we are able to create environments of comfort. It is not just that we seek shelter, but also that we are able to engineer our homes (and even cars!) to warm us up when it's cold outside and cool us down when it's too hot. The only problem is we weren't built for such well-regulated temperatures. We keep our bodies at a chronic 70 degrees, which shields us from building the appropriate resistance to temperature that our biological systems have adapted to regulate. Once again, it goes back to allostatic load. We need to challenge our bodies to adapt or they will respond in maladaptive ways.

On the contrary, when we expose ourselves to heat, we increase something called heat shock proteins, which propagate growth hormones—supporting anti-aging and recovery processes. Additionally, because we are constantly inflamed when exposed to heat, these anabolic and growth factors also decrease inflammation. That is why moving from hot to cold exposure is so beneficial (more on cold therapy in a bit.)

IMPORTANCE OF RECOVERY

WHY?	HOW?
Muscle repair	Cold therapy
Avoid overtraining	Heat therapy
Avoid hormonal fatigue	Lymphatic drainage (NormaTec® boots)
Activate PNS	Epsom salts bath
Lower SNS activity	Meditation
	Sleep

Graphic 36 – Importance of Recovery

Cryotherapy—which involves exposing the body to vapors that reach ultra-low temperatures ranging from -200 to -300°F—has become a trendy way for people to boost their metabolism and growth hormones while reducing inflammation. They are experiencing the delta between the two, which provides an even greater effect.

Stress is the impetus for adaptation and resilience.

I remember one of the first mornings I walked into the house from the near-freezing 34°F-degree frigid outdoors, wearing only my underwear. My wife looked at me, rolled her eyes and asked, "Are you crazy?!"

While I'm sure my wife could make a case for me being insane from time to time, I was just trying to take advantage of the *many* benefits of short-term cold exposure. As I've said, stress has a negative reputation, but it's not inherently bad. In fact, stress has more than the potential to be good—it is absolutely necessary If you want to get better in any domain in life.

Cold exposure is a notable example of hormetic stress. While long-term exposure to the extreme cold can have obvious repercussions (such as hypothermia), stepping outside your thermoregulated zone —that 72-or-so degree comfort zone—can have a tremendous upside. (And, yes, adjusting the thermostat can also be highly beneficial.)

Stress is the impetus for adaptation and resilience.

Maybe you've heard the saying "what doesn't kill you makes you stronger." While the phrase is a bit hyperbolic—not to mention a top hit from Kelly Clarkson—it's relevant when it comes to describing the *hormetic stress* that can increase our allostatic capacity. It is all about resilience, or as my friend Keith likes to say, being "harder to kill." There is no growth, in any domain, without hormetic doses of stress.

Graphic 37 – Nine Benefits of Cold Exposure

I know the idea of exposing your body to colder air or water may not be all that compelling, but that's the idea behind hormetic stress —stepping outside your comfort zone. After you discover the lengthy list of benefits that mild cold exposure can offer, I think you'll be willing to at least dip your toe in the water—figuratively and literally. Here are a few:

Increased metabolic rate. One of the greatest benefits of cold exposure is an increase in energy expenditure, which happens because of the activation of brown adipose tissue (BAT), a metabolically active thermogenic tissue designed to generate heat and help regulate body temperature. Activation of BAT is an "energy-wasting" process that results in an increased metabolic rate. We are essentially burning fuel to produce heat. It is a survival mechanism, but also a great way to promote fat loss! Speaking of...

Increased fat burning and fat utilization. If boosting metabolic rate is not sexy enough for you, how about increased fat burning? In order to stay warm, the body increases rates of both fat breakdown and utilization, which are necessary to fuel the increased metabolic rate.

Improved insulin sensitivity and glycemic control. Researchers also view cold exposure as a tool to combat type 2 diabetes, thanks to its potential impact on insulin sensitivity and metabolic health.[76] In other words, cold exposure may not only have an anti-obesity effect, but it may also have an anti-diabetic effect.

Reduced inflammation and pain. This is probably one of the more well-known benefits of cold exposure, yet research is beginning to question its validity. For instance, cold-water immersion is a common post-exercise recovery treatment because it is believed to reduce muscle fatigue and soreness. However, the results of cold therapy on muscle soreness are mixed and while some studies have shown that it can reduce exercise-related soreness, there is some evidence to suggest it may make the pain worse.[77]

Improved mood. Believe it or not, cold exposure may also boost mood and feelings of well-being. In one study, researchers found that 15 whole-body cryotherapy sessions over a period of three weeks led to significant reductions in depression and anxiety scores in patients ages 18-65. Researchers believe these beneficial effects may be tied to cold exposure starting an endocrine response and increasing hormones like epinephrine, norepinephrine, adrenocorticotropic hormone (ACTH), cortisone, pro-opiomelanocortin (POMC), β-endorphins and perhaps even testosterone. While depression is multifactorial, one neurobiological hypothesis is dysregulation of many of these hormones just mentioned. On top of that, cold exposure may activate the endogenous opioid system responsible for pain control, which may also be beneficial in the treatment of mental disorders.[78]

Improved quality of sleep. You've probably heard that it's a good idea to turn down the thermostat at night to ensure a good night's sleep. The rationale is that a cooler bedroom (between 60-67°F) helps reduce core temperature, which in turn helps sleep. Not surprisingly, body temperature is a strong driver of circadian rhythms. In fact, like light, temperature is one of the so-called *zeitgebers* able to reset the body's circadian clocks. While lowering the thermostat is one way to facilitate a lower core body temperature, taking a cold or contrast shower at night may also support improved quality of sleep.

Increased alertness and focus. This may seem like an odd benefit riding on the coattails of better sleep quality, but there's no debating the fact that a cold shower can wake you and your body up and promote a higher state of alertness. The cold also stimulates deeper breathing, helping increase oxygenation of the body's tissues. In the aftermath of the literal wake-up call—activation of the body's sympathetic nervous system (the "fight-or-flight" response)—cold exposure actually results in an increase in parasympathetic nervous system activity (the "rest and digest" response), which ultimately promotes relaxation.[79]

Considering the hormonal benefits and the enhancement in resilience, it may not surprise you that cold exposure can also be good for the brain and lead to better brain function. One recent study showed that people with mild cognitive impairment showed improvements in tests for memory after whole-body cryotherapy.

Enhanced resilience and stress tolerance. Along these lines, repeated cold exposure "hardens" the body and prepares it for similar "threats." In a nutshell, this is what hormetic stress is all about—exposure to small, transient stress that leads to adaptation. For example, while acute cold exposure increases sympathetic nervous system activity, that stress response is blunted after repeated exposure (i.e., cold acclimation). On the other hand, parasympathetic activity, which initially only increases to a minor degree, is enhanced after cold acclimation. In other words, cold acclimation lowers sympathetic activation and results in a shift toward increased parasympathetic activity.

The amazing thing about cold exposure is that this improved stress tolerance can carry over to other areas of life, enhancing your resilience and helping you remain cool-headed in other stressful situations. There is no denying the fact that cold exposure takes a strong mind to endure, but regularly incorporating cold exposure into your routine will likely increase your willpower to adapt and overcome.

As you may have gleaned from the benefits of short-term cold exposure, there are multiple ways to implement this potentially useful tool and they basically come down to the two different environments of cold air and cold water:

- Hot and cold contrast showers
- Cold-water immersion (e.g., cold pools, ice baths)
- Whole-body cryotherapy
- Turning down the thermostat
- Going outside in cold temperatures (e.g., shiver walks)

METHODS TO PRACTICE
COLD EXPOSURE

HOT AND COLD CONTRAST SHOWERS   **COLD-WATER IMMERSION**   **WHOLE-BODY CRYOTHERAPY**

TURNING DOWN THE THERMOSTAT   **GOING OUTSIDE IN COLD TEMPERATURES**

Graphic 38 – Methods of Cold Exposure

While each of these methods is likely to serve as a probable hormetic stress—and potentially lead to various health benefits—my personal preference is to use the shower and take advantage of Mother Nature whenever possible.

Keep in mind that the cold air version of cold exposure doesn't work if you compensate by putting on extra clothing. Although you don't have to strip down to your skivvies, you'll want to limit your clothing to a t-shirt and shorts.

That said, if you go to the extreme by walking in below-freezing temperatures, you'll absolutely want to keep your extremities (hands, feet, head, ears, nose) covered, as they're most susceptible to negative consequences like frostbite.

However, some consequences of severe cold can be beneficial.

For example, shivering is a sign that your body is working to keep itself warm; after a period of shivering, you will likely notice that it subsides. That is actually an even better sign that non-shivering thermogenesis (activation of BAT) has kicked in. Truth be told, mild cold stress begins at about 60°F in the air and you do not need to go to extremes with water either. Cold stress probably begins around 80°F in water and many benefits can be achieved with water temperatures about 60°F.

The most effective way to take a cold shower is to step out after you've done everything you need to accomplish in your warm to hot water. Then turn the water to cold, get your mind right and go back in. Try to stay as relaxed as possible and focus on controlling your breathing. Start with as little as 15 seconds and work your way up to a minute or so. If you need more incentive to take the plunge, according to my wife, cold showers also help make your hair extra shiny by closing cuticle cells to lock in water as well as any conditioning ingredients (she recommends apple cider vinegar and coconut oil for extra moisture).

If you want to work in both extremes, contrast showers are also a great cold exposure tool—some would argue that they are even more effective because they represent a broader relative change in temperature signal hormetic stress. Former NASA Scientist Ray Cronise developed a popular contrast shower protocol, which involves alternating 10 seconds of warm/hot water with 20 seconds of cold water. That cycle is repeated 10 times, always ending on cold.

Formulator's Corner
Exercise Strength and Recovery Supplements

Grass-Fed Whey Protein: The name of the game in the post-workout period is optimizing recovery, and in my opinion, that centers on maximizing muscle protein synthesis (MPS). Halting muscle protein breakdown also helps promote a positive net protein balance, but this is usually a side effect of taking care of the MPS side of the equation. There's arguably no better choice for this purpose than whey protein or hydrolyzed whey protein. I prefer whey from grass-fed cows because it's the highest quality nutrition. A plant-based option is a combination of rice, pea and pumpkin seed protein, preferably with some added digestive enzymes which can significantly enhance protein quality. A dose of 20-40 grams of high-quality protein will get the job done.

Exercise Strength and Recovery Supplements (continuation)

Essential Amino Acids (EAAs): While leucine is the most noteworthy of the nine EAAs, the body needs all the EAAs present to synthesize and build new muscle. Although leucine can flip the MPS switch, the body can't build anything if it doesn't have the other materials (EAAs) handy. EAAs, particularly with some added leucine or dileucine, can be handy after training, especially if you're fasting or don't have access to protein. Kion Aminos is a great product here.

L-Ergothioneine: L-Ergothioneine is a powerful antioxidant that may help promote recovery from exercise and support mitochondrial health and function. Look for MitoPrime, a branded version of this ingredient.

Nucleotides: Nucleotides are complex molecules that form DNA and RNA, act as signaling molecules and form the body's energy-rich molecules, namely adenosine triphosphate (ATP). Although the body can make nucleotides, its demand increases dramatically during exercise. Supplementation can be highly beneficial for performance and recovery. Look for NucleoPrime, a branded version of this ingredient.

HMB Free Acid: There's impressive research on HMB free acid (HMB-FA) which shows that 12 weeks of supplementation (with three grams a day) led to significant increases in bench presses, squats and deadlifts, and sizeable increases in lean body mass (e.g., muscle) in trained individuals. HMB-FA has also been shown to have beneficial effects on markers of muscle damage and cortisol levels during heavy training.

Creatine: Creatine is one of the most studied sports nutrition supplements of all time, and it is backed by a tremendous amount of evidence—both in the lab and in the real world. In my opinion, it is one of those "no-brainer" supplements that everyone should try to see how it works for them. Many people will find that it helps improve performance, builds muscle and increases strength—and there may even be cognitive and detoxification benefits. For daily use, I recommend five grams of creatine monohydrate such as Creapure.

Exercise Strength and Recovery Supplements (continuation)

Collagen: Collagen protein, and more specifically hydrolyzed collagen peptides, contains an incredibly unique amino acid profile—significantly different than whey protein. Collagen is high in proline, hydroxyproline, glycine and arginine, which are the same building blocks that make up the collagen-containing tissues in your own body—such as your joint cartilage, tendons, ligaments and muscles. While high-quality protein like whey is important for building muscle, collagen protein is critical for promoting full-body recovery. I take up to 40 grams of collagen daily and many people will benefit from at least 10-20 grams a day. Usually, different types of collagen (e.g., I, II, III, V and X) work best to support the most robust array of full-body benefits.

CBD: Is there anything CBD cannot do? Not if you ask Google. In all seriousness, I look at CBD as a sort of adaptogen by helping to promote a healthy stress response. While we do not want to mute the body's stress response and cortisol levels, getting them under control (which CBD can do) can help with protein breakdown. CBD's anti-inflammatory properties may also come in handy, although we do not want to squash our inflammatory response to exercise, since it may serve as an important signal for adaptation. CBD is all about bringing the body into balance, which is why it's a helpful tool for recovery.

EXERCISE AND THE IMMUNE SYSTEM

Over the last four decades, many studies have investigated how exercise affects the immune system. In a 2018 study, doctors concluded that while exercise doesn't suppress immunity, it is actually critical for immune function. According to the study published in *Frontiers in Immunology*, in the short term, exercise can help the immune system deal with pathogens while in the long term, it slows down age-related changes, in turn reducing the risk of infections.[80]

In addition, they concluded that infections are more likely to be linked to inadequate diet, psychological stress, insufficient sleep, travel and, importantly, pathogen exposure at social gathering events like marathons—rather than the act of exercising itself.

Exercise not only builds up our immunity through strengthening our physical defenses, but also increases our mental stamina—giving us the resilience we need to overcome disease and disorders.

How we use our bodies ultimately impacts their short and long-term capabilities. Though weight loss might be what propels us into different nutrition and fitness choices, it's not what makes us maintain them. Once you begin to adopt healthier habits and routines, the number on the scale feels fairly insignificant when compared to the larger impact on your energy and life. That was a lesson that I had to learn the hard way.

Partly as a result of the mindset I had in my childhood, my initial approaches to transforming my body and exercise came from a misguided place. At the most unsustainable part of my anorexic cycle, playing basketball four to six hours a day, I got all the way down to 165 pounds (down from 300 pounds)—and I'm 6'2". Then I got up to 220 pounds, lean and muscular, but was still working out for four hours a day. Even after all that effort and physical, external transformation, I still didn't feel right in my body. I couldn't keep going the way I was—or listening to my self-destructive thoughts. Everything I did felt both "extreme" and never good enough. After doing some inner work, I started to re-examine my relationship with exercise and eating.

I had to learn that it was okay to eat the food I needed so my body could have the fuel it needed, and it was okay not to look like some airbrushed image in a magazine. With a lot of work and the love of the friends and family around me, I started focusing more on the mind-body connection and the *intention* behind my workouts. I focused on the process of each lift and less on how heavy the weights were, more on my energy levels and how I felt instead of just how I looked or what the scale said. The result was more balance and energy to bring to my life and my relationships.

Though not everyone will face the same mental and image-related challenges, it's something to keep in mind during any transformation process. When you start changing and looking into yourself, you never know what may come out. But just remember that every new day brings a new chance to experiment and change course.

Above all, remember that exercise isn't an end in itself but another tool in your toolbox to live your best life.

Above all, remember that exercise isn't an end in itself but another tool in your toolbox to live your best life.

From this perspective, we begin to care less about weight loss and more about healthspan. We begin to care less about the body we see in the mirror and more about the person inside. Fitness and nutrition stops being about the size of our body and more about our life goals.

The choice is yours: end up in a healthy spiral—where smart behaviors lead to even smarter behaviors—or end up in an unhealthy one.

I often tell people that the easiest way to get to the gym starts the night before. Pack your gym bag before you go to sleep and set it by your front door. This not only means you are ready to go in the morning (no excuses!) but also that you have mentally prepared yourself to work out. You have chosen your gear based on the exercise you plan to do, you have packed your headphones, thought about what album or podcast you might listen to and have started to get excited about how you're going to feel when you take that contrast shower, post-workout. You are excited for the next morning before you have even gone to bed.

When it comes to exercise, I am a bit biased toward lifting weights. But high-intensity exercise is for…well, everyone who wants to optimize longevity and enjoy a long life marked by good health, function, productivity and independence. Your exercise journey might start with a walk around the block. With increased endurance, you too can find out what happens when you increase positive stress to build resiliency and energy.

See you in the gym!

EXERCISE SUMMARY

- We all need to start somewhere. By making the starting line a place that is reasonable and comfortable, you are more likely to stick with your new habit as you increase the stress and stamina of your exercise routine. If you have been exceptionally sedentary, just start by walking—even the simple act of a morning or evening walk can promote circulation and increase energy, not to mention shift your mindset.

- One of the single most important factors dictating how long and well you live is muscular strength. Muscular strength doesn't just increase lifespan, it also enhances healthspan—the period of life free of major chronic clinical diseases and disability. It is based on the premise that life can be divided into two phases: a period of relatively healthy aging (healthspan) and a period of age-associated disease and disability. Another way to think about healthspan is optimal longevity, which means living long with an even greater interest in living well.

- Outside of weight loss, there are *many* health benefits associated with regular exercise, including what I like to call quality weight loss, which reflects changes in body composition. When resistance training is performed safely, appropriately and gradually, it causes adaptations which make you stronger. It is important to note that it is not a matter of "more is better" but rather "better is better." To put it plainly, resistance training is essential for *everyone*.

- Working out not only promotes youthfulness, but also creates more neuroplasticity in the brain, in turn improving our ability to learn new things and increasing brain-derived neurotrophic factor (BDNF), which helps generate new neurons in the brain. An ideal routine might include resistance training three times a week, HIIT twice a week and some low-level aerobic exercise three times a week that you enjoy (e.g., golf, basketball, tennis, biking).

- As with allostatic load, each person has a "threshold level." While adding stress to an already full "stress bucket" causes overflow and health problems, adding the right level of stress helps you to learn, grow and increase energy. The concept of hormetic stress (e.g., cold exposure) confirms the fact that mild, transient stress can be highly beneficial, lead to adaptation and promote resilience. This then carries over to other areas of life and helps you stay cool-headed in other stressful situations.

- Exercise not only builds up immunity through strengthening our physical defenses, but also increases our mental stamina, which helps us overcome disease and disorders.

Resource Hacks

Exercise

Advanced Weight Training Methods:

Blood Flow Restriction (BFR): Also called KAATSU training, BFR involves using bands/cuffs to train with a lower level of weight/resistance and still get tremendous results. This is great to use when reducing volume/intensity, recovering or while in rehabilitation.

High-Intensity Interval Training (HIIT): This beats out low-intensity steady state (LISS) when it comes to fast changes in performance and body composition in the least amount of time. Sprints on a treadmill are one option where you can easily raise and lower speed and keep track of time. Look at Tabata training as well.

Drop Sets, Supersets, Super Slow, Eccentric (Negatives), Forces Reps, Partials: These are all classic ways to continue stimulating the muscle for hypertrophy and strength gains. Bodybuilding.com has some great articles on these techniques.

Static Contraction: This is a unique way of lifting weights where you hold the weight in a peak position of contraction for as long as you can. It is a great way to finish off a set; it works great with biceps on a preacher curl.

Exercise (continuation)

Intra-Set Stretching: Holding a stretch instead of resting the muscle you just worked helps strengthen that muscle. Do this by contracting the opposing muscle group so the active group is stretched between sets.

Resistance Bands: These are great to use when on the road with limited options. Get different bands with different tensions. Also, you can combine weights with bands (or chains) with a trainer or spotter for some alterations in the resistance curves —which can lead to greater hypertrophy and strength gains.

Wearables: Try a Biostrap or Oura ring to access your workout and readiness.

Recovery:

NormaTec Boots: Air pressure massage that increases circulation.

Red Light Therapy: I use Joovv.

Hot/Cold Exposure: Expose yourself to heat followed by cold repeatedly. I use SunLighten Saunas and a cold shower—where I get my head and any sore muscle group thoroughly wet in order to promote alertness and reduce inflammation.

Theragun: A powerful handheld massage device ideal to use on any tight muscles.

Cold Laser: This is done at a rehab clinic, is expensive and requires training.

*For live links, updated content, bonus graphics
and a hidden chapter, go to
EnergyFormulaBook.com*

ROUTINE SURVEY

How would you rate your morning routine?		
It is solid. I go through my morning routine regularly and it starts my day off on the right foot.	(3)	
I have somewhat of a morning routine, but I don't always use it and mornings are still a bit crazy.	(2)	
I need morning routine help! My mornings are chaotic and I am always chasing the next to-do.	(1)	
How is your circadian rhythm functioning?		
Great! I feel alert in the mornings, tired at night before bed and have good, steady energy throughout the day.	(3)	
It could use some help. I feel groggy in the mornings and sometimes too awake at night.	(2)	
Horrible. My circadian rhythm is completely off and it is starting to affect my health.	(1)	
How would you rate your sleep hygiene?		
Excellent! I have a pre-bedtime routine that I stick to religiously, I avoid screens and blue light, fall asleep easily and sleep through the night.	(3)	
It could use some work. I try to wind down but often get caught up in a TV show and my sleep isn't always the best.	(2)	
What's sleep hygiene? I stay up late watching screens, snack late into the night and wake up feeling the effects.	(1)	

What ratio of artificial light/blue light to natural or sunlight are you getting each day?		
I get morning sunlight first thing most days and take time throughout the day to get outside for more sunshine. I wear blue light blocking glasses at night!	(3)	
I get some natural sunlight but not as much as I should. My daily routine makes this challenging.	(2)	
I'm on a mostly artificial light diet! I need resources to help me get natural light exposure throughout the day.	(1)	
Do you take time to map out your day using a planner, journal, or similar workbook?		
Yes. I take time at the beginning and end of my day to create a plan, make a list and review my goals.	(3)	
I have a running to-do list in my head, but I don't have a dedicated time or journal for this.	(2)	
No, I'm usually meeting the day's demands as they come without mapping out my day and have never employed these strategies.	(1)	
How often do you take time throughout your day for stillness, quiet, or meditation?		
Regularly. I make it a priority to sit still and meditate daily.	(3)	
Sometimes. Most days are hectic, so it doesn't always happen, but I try to pause now and then for some quiet.	(2)	
Never. I rarely have a quiet minute to myself and do not prioritize this.	(1)	
YOUR TOTAL		

7-11 points: You have got some work to do! This book is a great place to start!

12-16 points: You are heading in the right direction! Keep at it!

17-21 points: You are really on the ball! Only small tweaks are needed to be your best self!

Chapter 4: Routine: Align Your Circadian Rhythm and Start Every Day Right

"You will never change your life until you change something you do daily. The secret of your success is found in your daily routine."

—John C. Maxwell

Throughout graduate school, I'd been working at GNCs to learn more about supplements and in that time, I'd built up a reputation on message boards under the usernames "Androgenic" or "Neogenic," which I chose for the personal meaning they held: creating a new or better man. While I worked at the hospital or rehabs, any spare time I had went into posting on an anti-aging board called LongeCity, as well as on Bodybuilding.com. Over the years, I wrote thousands and thousands of posts about supplements and exercise topics—multiple books' worth of material that are likely lost to the digital sands of the internet by now.

My goal on those message boards was to be an outspoken advocate for the truth—to cut through the marketing hype and point people towards products that actually worked. At the time, there was a major authority gap in that area—a lot of noise and not a lot of signal, since thorough supplementation routines and biohacking communities were still in their infancy. As my authority grew online, I started getting offers from reputable nutrition companies to promote or review products on various websites. I was developing a noteworthy "second career," making some small steps towards my bigger dreams. Although I didn't get my Certified Sports Nutritionist (CISSN) credential through the International Society of Sports Nutrition until later, at work and in my spare time I was building momentum.

As the years passed, I worked on side projects in other nutritional companies, even helping to research and develop novel ingredients. Although I ended up being cut out of the profits of some of the ingredients I'd invented (I still wince just a little every time I pass a bottle of raspberry ketones), I was cutting my teeth in fascinating parts of the nutrition and supplement business.

But my passions were coming in conflict with my work.

One day while doing clinical rounds at a facility, I suggested putting one of the residents on creatine to protect lean muscle mass. The doctor on staff scoffed, "There's no data on that."

"There are 500+ studies on creatine," I told him. I added that there were a couple of studies on medications that were re-done several times just so they could show positive results and pass FDA scrutiny.

He was unmoved.

My daily conversations and experiences were increasingly frustrating.

I kept working my job for almost nine years, until 2011. Between all the work drama, day in and day out, I kept my energy and inner peace together through my daily workouts and positive routines. As I lifted weights, I thought about the situation I was in. It was clear I would need to go out on my own to make a greater impact, and more importantly, truly serve people. As a side note, I did eventually co-author a chapter on creatine in an academic textbook! My life is often full circle like this and I am proud of my ability to manifest incredible things. I feel I can focus on achieving my dreams and creating because I have dialed and organized routines that allow for serendipity and passion to be capitalized on during my days.

Those last six months, when I decided to start manifesting my new life of higher impact outside of my clinical roles, were amazing. Days after my heart committed, I got a call that changed everything. It was now seventeen years after the annual physical exam with Dr. Johnson that had given me the spark and belief in myself to do nutrition, performance and supplements as a career.

I was on lunch break at a rehab center, sitting in my car on a hot and hazy North Carolina summer day, when I got the call. On the other end of the phone, a recruiter said, "Shawn, I am looking to hire for this company in the Dallas-Fort Worth area called Dymatize. They need a Chief Science Officer there. It is a C-level executive position with a six-figure salary, equity in the company, high growth area, warm climate and state income tax...are you interested?"

I felt like a small stage actor getting a call for the lead role in a Steven Spielberg movie. This was my dream, fully manifested on the end of this phone—of course I was interested! In my head, I was already in Dallas.

Over the next three months, I went through nine rounds of interviews. During the final round, it was between me and a guy who had worked as a VP and C-level executive for companies like GNC and a slew of other massive supplement brands. He was a PhD published researcher and professor who had written book chapters and even been on TV. And then there was me, a guy who had also worked at GNC...at a retail register. I had my hospital and nursing home experiences and my message board reputation, sure, but I didn't have *his* level of respect.

I finally got the call from my recruiter. "Hey, Shawn," he said. "They decided to go with the other guy."

It made sense, given his resume—and I'll be the first to say he was an absolute rock star. Nevertheless, I was crushed. I was so close to finally fulfilling my dream, but somehow I'd tripped at the finish line. This was meant to be my job. There was no way it could end like this.

After a long pause, the recruiter continued. "I do have good news," he boomed. "They *do* have a multiple six-figure job waiting for you as Director of R&D doing all their formulations. You'd be working under the guy that just got the CSO role, but he could teach you the ropes and you can bring your brilliance on ingredients to the table. This job not only includes Dymatize's own products but they also do private label for companies like Smoothie King, Advocare, GNC and Vitamin Shoppe. Are you still interested?"

I was shaking. Holding back tears and laughing, I boomed back, "Yes, yes, I am!"

It was another life-changing moment. My wife Shelley and I packed up our things in North Carolina and moved to Texas to start this exciting new chapter of our lives.

Overnight, I went from formulating little known supplements like Ultima and Scorch, working online at nights with smaller companies like MAN Sports and Bodybuilding.com, gathering market research from sports nutrition shops like HealthNutz—to managing an R&D and product development team, learning from my one-time competitor and now mentor, Dr. Rob. I worked tirelessly at Dymatize, coming in at 7 am and leaving at 11 pm. I became Employee of the Year, got raises and established myself as an essential person in executive meetings, driving the formulations and directions of new products. Later, I became a fellow of the International Society of Sports Nutrition and an editor of their academic journal. I was a published author in academic textbooks and peer-reviewed journals, I presented research at conferences and I had award-winning supplements on the shelves of stores I used to work at.

Most importantly, I was learning how to make really great supplements—ones that were within budget, compliant with claims, tested in raw materials and created for a long shelf life. I learned how to be transparent in labeling and avoid proprietary blends. I was becoming an expert in how to make products that flat out *work*. But about two years into my job at Dymatize, my body turned against me once again. I got sick with the same nasty cast of characters—fatigue, brain fog and depression—and I wasn't sure why.

There was something different this time, however.

"These headaches are new," I told my doctor. "There's a pressure on my eyes that I can't deal with. I have insomnia that seems to be getting worse by the day, despite my fatigue. I have zero libido as well."

I ended up getting an MRI and some blood work done. When the results came back, it was bad news. "Son, you've got a pituitary adenoma, specifically a prolactinoma," my doctor said soberly. "It's a brain tumor. Even though it's not cancerous, the pituitary is critical for the health of your brain and body. Furthermore, your testosterone is basically non-existent and your estrogen is sky-high. I'll be honest and tell you that even though it's not cancerous now, you have a higher likelihood of developing cancer in the future."

Once again, the bottom had dropped out of my life.

Hadn't I figured everything out by now? I was a master formulator! I had a good exercise routine and a dream job! Shouldn't I be fixed by now? In truth, I had strayed from my "clean eating" and keto protocols for about a year because I'd been so busy with work and travel. Stress had become my norm, and I'd been working 80+ hour weeks for years and years on end, barely stopping to take a weekend off here and there. Even though I was a dietitian and sports nutritionist, I'm sad to say that I was living off of Subway subs, pizza, M&Ms, Diet Coke and a laundry list of processed, fast junk foods that are typical of the standard American diet.

I broke down and cried. It felt like every time I achieved something, something else got taken away. Even so, the truth was simpler than that: I'd let all my routines fall apart once again, and my health had gone down the tubes with them. Once again, I was at a crossroads with my health and my future.

I decided to go back on an extremely *strict* ketogenic diet, and I started eating Primal, which at the time was similar to paleo but included more fat than the original CrossFit version of paleo—focusing on whole, real foods. I got back on a regular gym routine, took my medication and got my energy back up. Before long, I was back to fighting shape and ready to work 16-hour days again.

At least, I would be until something else jumped in my path to stop me.

Over the last few years, there has already been a lot of focus on morning routines—and for good reason. In his book *Tools of Titans*, for example, Tim Ferriss, who has interviewed hundreds of world-class performers in all domains to extract their tactics, tools and routines, says that successful people have two things in common: 1. A solid morning routine and 2. They are experimenters (2 of my 6 pillars in this book).

When it comes to morning routines, we need to give them the respect and attention they deserve. Our mornings ultimately determine whether we're set up for success or stagnation. When we feel like we're waking up with our hair on fire and spending the rest of the day putting it out, we are mindlessly burning energy. Having routines are one of the most critical ways to enhance and sustain our energy throughout the day—but also throughout our lives.

"We make the world we live in and shape our own environment," said Dr. Orison Marden, back in 1897. Marden was the founder of *Success* magazine and he was right: the life we lead is because of the choices we make. We select our friends. We decide how to spend our time. We choose how to take care of ourselves—or whether to at all. It's also up to us to change if we're not happy with where we are in life. If you want to change your *life*, it starts by making the choice to change your *day*.

I know quarantine threw many people off their routines. But there is nothing healthier and more sustainable in a time of so many unknowns than creating routines to start and determine your day.

It's no surprise that highly successful people have very dialed-in morning routines, and that there are similarities among them such as gratitude journals, deep breathing, cold showers, blue light devices, relaxing podcasts, meditation, mantras/words of affirmation, vision boards and more. Those who practice these activities have found their lives transformed.

In order to get the most out of our lives, we need to set the tone each day, first thing in the morning.

Think about it: how do you start your day? We all want to grow and be successful—not just financially, but also in terms of spirituality, relationships and impact on the world around us. We only have so many revolutions around the sun, and in order to get the most out of our lives, we need to set the tone each day, first thing in the morning.

We can begin right now. The best way to start is by choosing one thing and trying it out for a couple of weeks. If it's something that works for you and adds benefit, include that element as part of that routine, build it into your life and stick with it. That's why now, my routine includes exercise. I started making my morning workout a non-negotiable in my life. I would wake up and go to the gym, working out with a trainer. Even when I had a tenth of the income I have now,

I hired a trainer because I knew being accountable to someone else would help me commit to the habit.

Once you've got your first thing down, like I did with exercise, add something else. For me, since I was already up early, I added a few minutes of meditation—nothing fancy, just a few minutes of silence and connecting to a peaceful place before my day got busy. Yet I only added this piece after I'd already grown used to exercising first thing. If you try everything at once, you have no idea what works for you. A good morning routine is founded on good habits, and that means finding a routine that fits your individual rhythm.

GETTING YOUR MORNING RIGHT

Ask yourself a simple question: "How do I wake up every morning?" By that, I mean, what do those first few moments of consciousness feel like?

Here is how I used to wake up. I would hear my typical alarm rousing—*beep, beep, beep*—and I would roll out of bed tired. Usually, I would've taken Ambien the night before and would feel slightly drowsy as a result. I would reach over and look at my phone and scroll through emails, news and social media—which was really just an extension of what I'd done right before going to bed, falling asleep to blue light in the dark. Sometimes I would spend too long on the internet and wouldn't even have time to shower; I'd roll out of bed, brush my teeth and throw on clothes. After getting some caffeine in and eating something sugary for breakfast, I would get in my car, fight traffic and get to work. I would be overwhelmed and behind before the day even began.

In short, I started the day at a deficit and was mentally exhausted by noon. At lunch, I would eat something with a lot of carbs and then move into the afternoon more tired than before. I would go down to the vending machine in the afternoon for some sugar and caffeine before leaving work with a longer list of to-dos than I started with that morning. After that, I would drive home sitting in traffic, mindlessly listening to music or talk radio and never thinking about what I was putting into my mind. I would get home and switch from radio to TV before heading to bed, scrolling through more emails, falling asleep and starting the next day the same way.

It's no wonder I lived in the cortisol-filled fight-or-flight mode; I was waking up in it every day. There was no mindfulness or peace, just deficit and chaos. I was living on autopilot, and that is not a good way to live.

Now, let's look at a vastly different morning.

You awake after seven to nine hours of sleep to light that comes in naturally and grows in intensity, all to the sound of chiming bells that gradually get louder. You take slow deep breaths with gratitude for the blessings in your life. You don't have your phone nearby so instead you spend the first few minutes upon waking in meditation. Maybe you even go outside and get grounded with your bare feet in the grass, greeting the day with lungs full of fresh air.

The craziest part is that entire routine only needs to take 10 minutes!

First thing is to set your mindset for the day—through affirmations and prayer, silent time and breath work, gratitude and movement, or anything that connects your mind and body to the morning. Build out some space to keep you from rushing into your day. Then you can plan for the day, maybe even listing what you're grateful for, what you intend to accomplish and what you need to let go of. As you decide how you want to move through your plans, try to work backward and think, "At the end of the day, what do I want to have accomplished?"

A lot of these concepts were inspired from Craig Ballantyne's "Perfect Day" formula (check it out on Amazon), which shares some practical and tactical ways to establish healthy morning routines to make the most out of every day.

Before taking a cold shower, you might take a walk or go to the gym. It's a great idea to get your exercise in before starting work. I always say that having a dog is a great biohack because you can walk your dog every morning, moving your body while connecting with something that loves you unconditionally—two birds, one stone! (Shout out to my Shih Tzu, Maya.)

For breakfast, maybe you have a protein shake if you've done some cardio or interval training. Otherwise, I suggest a cup of coffee (decaf for me—if you're adventurous, try some mushroom coffee like Laird Hamilton's), adaptogen tea (Four Sigmatic), bone broth (Epic or Fire and Kettle) or lemon water. If you prefer, you can also wait for lunch to break your fast. (As you become more consistent with your routine, you'll find you need coffee a lot less!) The more you commit to a new lifestyle and a new routine, the more you'll be able to listen to your body. If you've gone to the gym, perhaps try a cold plunge, a sauna or both for thermic contrast. After that, start your work.

If you have a commute, on the way to work, you might choose to listen to music that inspires you or puts you in a good mood, or maybe a podcast that gets you motivated to start your day. Once at work, tackle one big thing. As you might have noticed, nowhere have I said to check your email. There's no reason to check it until you are in the office. If something urgent comes up, you'll know—but more often, we take up our entire morning responding to group chats and debating what restaurant we should go to for Cindy's birthday on Friday. Instead, focus on getting your day's biggest task done and out of the way before you start going through your inbox. Even better, make sure you clean out your inbox the day before, so you start each day fresh. If you go straight to your email, you will go down the rabbit hole.

You want to own your day, not let your day own you.

At some point, you'll get to lunch, which should be a whole food-based meal that you might have packed the night before—something keto or paleo-ish, which will give you energy to spur you on through the rest of your day. As more and more of us begin to work from home, the need for a healthy and balanced routine becomes even more critical, helping us craft a day that allows us to find a flow rather than being forced into the grind.

I like to stack my phone calls in the afternoons when I'm not at my full energy levels. Usually, I'll go on a walk and do all my return calls during the stroll, gaining energy and taking care of business at the same time—but always have your calls after your creative time. Give yourself the space to use your most potent brain energy for the tasks that require it. You want to own your day, not let your day own you.

Although daily routines can be both effective and powerful, most people—including me—struggle to maintain them. I have periods of success and then I have times where I fall back into old routines, rushing into my day and failing to take time to prepare for it. What's important is to keep trying to build an improved life. Don't let a temporary slip-up stop you from striving.

The thing about morning routines is that even if the rest of the day is crazy, you still start off on the right foot. A strong morning routine offers you a foundation on which to build the rest of the day's plans, providing you the peace and grounding you need to achieve your goals, but also the ability to maintain your energy and flow throughout the day.

THE CIRCADIAN RHYTHM

The circadian rhythm exists in all living things. It is the body's internal clock, also known as the sleep/wake cycle, and there are a lot of variables that can affect its rhythm. When this clock becomes desynchronized, which is common, we see an increased risk for things like diabetes, obesity, neurodegenerative diseases and mood disorders. A good example of the results of a disrupted circadian clock is Seasonal Affective Disorder (SAD).

A major part of our circadian rhythm is controlled by the body's "master clock," called the suprachiasmatic nucleus (SCN). The key to a properly timed SCN is a group of photoreceptors in the eyes called photosensitive retinal ganglion receptors. These receptors send information to the master clock about the levels of brightness in your surroundings. I'll spare you the rest of the fascinating details, but what's important to appreciate is that light—or a lack thereof—is perhaps the most critical input for our circadian system.[81]

Graphic 39 – Circadian Rhythm[82]

While the SCN is the body's master clock, there are other smaller circadian "clocks" throughout the body which govern the behavior of our cells. In other words, taking light as its cue, our master clock signals the rest of our body when it's time for all the physiological processes and changes we experience throughout the day, such as:

- Body temperature

- Pulse rate and blood pressure

- Reaction time and performance

- The production of melatonin, serotonin and cortisol

- Intestinal activity

You can think of this system of clocks like those you might find in a school. Each classroom clock is bound to a "master clock." Obviously, this type of system is crucial for the school day to run efficiently, with classes starting and ending "on time." If any clock were "broken"—especially the master clock—you would expect chaos.

In much the same way, when the body's master clock is broken, it puts an extraordinary strain on the body. This strain increases the risk for several serious health issues including cancer, heart disease, type 2 diabetes, depression, Alzheimer's and other neurodegenerative diseases. In addition, a broken clock can have profound negative effects on your energy levels—affecting your ability to think clearly, your appetite and weight management to boot.[83]

While light and dark are the primary drivers of the body's circadian clock, many factors can disrupt circadian rhythms—including food, exercise, shift work, travel, jet lag, poor sleep hygiene, stress and more.

When it comes to fixing a broken circadian clock, there are obviously many variables—*zeitgebers*, which are external cues that influence your circadian rhythm. These typically involve light exposure, sleep and meal timing. That's why increasing your exposure to sunlight, reducing your exposure to artificial blue light in the evening, timing your meals appropriately and establishing healthy sleep hygiene habits are so important. Psychotherapy and mind-body connection therapies like relaxation techniques, meditation and art or music therapies can help as well.

These lifestyle choices can have tremendous bearing on nearly every aspect of your health. Outside of an extreme survival scenario, animals typically don't sacrifice sleep. When they need to rest, they rest. Humans, on the other hand, will rationalize sacrificing sleep for things like staying up for a Netflix marathon or powering through midnight for a party that starts at 10 pm. Then we wake up exhausted and go through the day consuming sugar, caffeine and whatever it is we need to have in order to power through. It is what my friend Tim calls "social jetlag," and it's one of the biggest reasons we dread Monday mornings!

Unsurprisingly, staying up late became one of many bad habits people developed during quarantine. They weren't able to adhere to a regular schedule and found themselves overwhelmed at night when they should have been relaxing. (Of course, it's hard to relax when you're surrounded by so much uncertainty.)

It is such an unnatural state. Your clock is telling you, "Look, you need sleep." And you're refusing to listen.

SLEEP HYGIENE

Quality of sleep determines quality of life. You can't be fully awake and alert if you haven't gotten proper sleep and it's not just about the number of hours you spend in bed, but also about the quality of your sleep while you're getting those zzz's. There is a natural detox and repair that's part of the circadian rhythm—your heart rate lowers; your breathing slows and your brain and digestive system are able to enter a parasympathetic state.

By definition, circadian rhythms refer to your wake/sleep cycles. In other words, sleep is both foundational to and a byproduct of circadian biology. Along those lines, healthy sleep hygiene habits are crucial when it comes to fixing your broken clock.

People with sleep disorders are missing the critical repair that sleep provides. If you have sleep apnea, you are basically sleeping in a trauma state—you're gasping for air, unable to repair and recover. Even folks who suffer from severe snoring shorten their life expectancy due to the quality of their sleep.[84]

Lack of sleep also leads to more superficial consequences. You look tired and have bags under your eyes, prompting people to ask you if you're feeling okay…and it's hard not to yawn in response. It's also hard to be in deep, connected, responsive relationships when you're exhausted. It's certainly not the mindset that's going to produce your best work.

Your sleep hygiene begins with how you prepare for sleep.[85] If you watch when a cat comes into the room, it finds the sunny spot, cleans itself and gets comfortable on the pillow. There are psychosomatic connections between sleep and these preparation activities, a rhythm to how we wind down. What kind of messages are you sending your body right before you go to sleep? How can you begin to wind down instead?

SLEEP HYGIENE

Graphic 40 – Sleep Hygiene

Block blue light in the evening. One of the biggest things disrupting our circadian rhythms in today's society is exposure to blue light from fluorescent light bulbs, cell phones, tablets, computer monitors, TV screens and more. It suppresses melatonin production, delaying feelings of sleepiness and the onset of our nighttime cycle. This disrupts circadian rhythms as well as sleep.[86] Try the following strategies two to three hours before bed:

- Avoid TV and computer screens
- Use the app f.lux if you must use your computer
- Use a similar app if you must use your smartphone (check out the Resource Hacks for more apps to help you sleep)
- Dim your lights

- Use amber-tinted light bulbs
- Wear amber-tinted, blue-light-blocking glasses

The simplest habit to develop is to put down the screens by removing them from your nightstand. You can put your phone at the other end of the room (or even better, in another room), but do not have it right next to your head while you sleep, waiting for you when you wake up. Instead, put things on your nightstand that you would like to engage with before bed—perhaps a book you have been wanting to read, meditation journals or even your own journal. If there are any relaxing rituals you like to do to help aid in the sleep process, include them in your routine—whether it's having your partner rub your back or maybe stroking your arm or neck. Don't go to bed wired; go to bed tired.

Take melatonin supplements. Melatonin is a hormone made by the pineal gland—that's a pea-sized gland found just above the middle of your brain. It helps your body know when it's time to sleep and wake up. Normally, your body makes more melatonin at night: your levels increase in the evening once the sun sets, and they drop in the morning when the sun comes up. The amount of light you get each day—plus your own body clock—set how much melatonin your body makes. For supplementation, start low at 0.3mg and work up to as much as 3mg, if needed. Fruits like cherries, pineapples, oranges, kiwifruit and bananas, have high levels of naturally occurring melatonin (which is also an antioxidant), and have been shown to elevate levels of melatonin in the body.

All of this is especially important when we are feeling overwhelmed by working from home, managing homeschooling for children and balancing out the fears and concerns about our current crisis. Science has begun to show the effects of reduced melatonin for various reasons. It can lead not only to poor sleep quality, but also an increased risk of numerous health conditions.

Red-light therapy. Just as blue light can play an important role in helping you wake up or preventing you from going to sleep, red light can help supplement the circadian rhythm. It promotes healing and reduces inflammation, but it also stimulates collagen and is known to increase testosterone. More and more, we are finding out about the power of light. Most of us are familiar with infrared saunas, but many biohackers use red-light panels that don't produce heat and can be used any time of day, unlike blue light. I have a SunLighten Infrared sauna that also incorporates chromotherapy.

Chromotherapy. It's not surprising that the more we learn about light's ability to heal, calm and energize, the more centers have popped up across the country with light saunas, which promote healing and help us stabilize our circadian rhythms. Over the last 30 years, there has been an enormous reduction in the amount of time spent outside. Perhaps the pandemic has helped shift some of that by forcing people outside and into nature, but for much of the last three decades, we have missed out on the significant benefits of the sun and the infrared wavelengths that echo from deep within the cosmos and the source of all creation. This is a shame, since they've been vital to human functioning since the beginning of time.

Cold laser therapy. Cold laser therapy uses infrared light to reduce inflammation, swelling and pain. The infrared light works at the cellular level, synchronizing continuous and pulsed emissions to generate anti-inflammatory effects without steroid injections. The laser does not suppress inflammation, but rather stimulates the body's cells to reduce inflammation, swelling and pain.

When you eat. Meal timing is actually one of the most important variables affecting circadian alignment. Timing can have meaningful effects on the body's circadian rhythms, which regulate appetite, gastrointestinal function, nutrient absorption, pancreatic insulin secretion and hepatic (liver) enzyme activity.[87] In fact, according to Dr. Satchin Panda, a biologist who specializes in circadian rhythms, "Mealtimes

have more effect on circadian rhythm than dark and light cycles." Conversely, circadian rhythms can have a substantial effect on how we metabolize the food we eat.

Just as research on circadian biology shows that carb tolerance and insulin sensitivity are greatest in the morning and decline over the course of the day, it has also shown that eating closer to bedtime (such as a late dinner or late-night snack) can have a negative effect on sleep quality. According to time-restricted feeding research conducted by Dr. Panda and others, it seems best to limit your "feeding window" to less than 12 hours each day with most (if not all) food intake during daylight hours whenever possible. Still, everyone works different hours, and it's important to find the schedule that best works for you.

What you drink. Research shows that consuming caffeine even six hours before bedtime can have a significantly disruptive effect on sleep, since caffeine consumption delays the release of melatonin. And while alcohol may help you fall asleep, it disrupts sleep quality and reduces REM sleep in a dose-dependent manner. In other words, the more you drink, the worse you sleep.

Speaking of caffeine, I previously mentioned that I am "sensitive" to caffeine, and this is worth unpacking a bit, especially considering that so many people turn to caffeine-containing beverages and supplements to help boost mental energy, clarity and focus. There's no denying that caffeine—which, believe it or not, has significant antioxidant effects—can increase alertness and energy levels, as well as mood, feelings of well-being, vigilance and cognitive function and performance.

However, individual differences most certainly apply, and as the saying goes, one man's meat is another man's poison. That is, some people (like myself), thanks to a variation of a gene (CYP1A2) are "slow" caffeine metabolizers, which makes them more prone to feel jittery, anxious and irritable when consuming caffeine. These same folks are also more likely to experience insomnia and high blood pressure in response to caffeine ingestion. On the other hand, you have "fast" metabolizers of caffeine, who are more likely to reap the benefits of caffeine and beverages (such as coffee) that contain it.

When it comes to caffeine, the bottom line is that you need to listen to and honor your body. Even if you do metabolize caffeine at a fast or normal rate, it is still best to avoid it within six hours of bedtime, as it literally "blocks" the body's ability to sense a molecule called adenosine, which essentially serves as a signal to tell the brain how tired you are. In other words, as adenosine naturally builds up, it increases "sleep pressure," causing sleepiness. In general, consuming caffeine too close to bedtime makes it harder to fall asleep, shortens total sleep time, increases awakenings and decreases the amount of time you spend in deep sleep.

Let's also take a moment to talk about the ol' elephant in the room: alcohol, which is often consumed in the evening, close to bedtime. Yes, alcohol acts as a sedative, and although it can help you fall asleep faster (which is certainly a reason why some people turn to alcohol), it also tends to disrupt sleep quality in the grand scheme of things. For example, alcohol disrupts REM sleep, which is the phase of sleep when learning takes place and memories are formed, in a dose-dependent manner. In other words, the more alcohol you drink, the worse you sleep. As alcohol "wears off," the second half of the night is riddled with increased wakefulness and light sleep, causing you to miss out on the all-important deep sleep, which is the phase of sleep you need to feel refreshed in the morning.[88]

Alcohol also messes with a variety of hormones, including the inhibition of one known as vasopressin (also called anti-diuretic hormone), which leads to the production of more urine and nighttime bathroom breaks. Because alcohol can have that type of diuretic effect, it's a good idea to make sure you're drinking plenty of water between drinks.

Alcohol is not all bad, and this isn't meant to scare you. It's intended to be a reminder that alcohol is *not* a sleep aid, and if you choose to consume it, be mindful and do so in moderation. Usually a drink or two isn't enough to disrupt sleep, so implement a two-drink maximum. It's also a smart move to try to consume alcohol earlier in the evening (and further away from bedtime) to allow the body ample time to metabolize it prior to going to bed to limit the effects on sleep quality.

What you watch. I think we can all agree that watching violent or hypersexual content (including porn) right before bed is not the best recipe for drifting off or counting sheep. The images and sounds that enter our psyche right before bed generally stay with us, and can produce restless sleep or intense, disturbing dreams. While all of us occasionally want to watch something in the evening to unwind, it's important to be conscious about the content. Find shows and movies that will aid in your sleep and keep away from anything that might distract from it.

While it can be easy enough to get into an hour-long conversation with a partner, family member or roommate right before bed, try not to. In fact, I strongly recommend setting a quiet zone at least 30 minutes to an hour before bedtime. Don't start any major discussions or try to finish the important conversation from dinner. Use this time instead to prepare yourself for sleep. The last words you should say to anyone at night—whether it's your spouse, your children, your dog, your cat or yourself—are "I love you."

Set your bedtime. Few people can get to bed when the sun actually goes down, so find a time that is reasonable for you. Figure out what works best and then back your night schedule out from there (in the army, they call that backwards planning—figuring out what you need to do, in the right order, with enough time to execute your intended goal). If you decide 10 pm is your bedtime, establish what time you need to have dinner, get ready for bed and do whatever else you need to—say, get your kids ready for bed—so you know when to turn out the lights and ensure you're asleep at 10 pm.

Staying asleep. Once you're asleep, you need to ensure your environment supports you staying there. The right bed, the right lighting (meaning none) and the right amount of white noise can make all the difference between restful and restless sleep. Make your room as dark as possible at night by using dark curtains and removing all sources of artificial light.

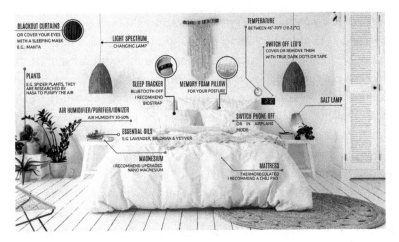

Graphic 41 – Optimal Sleep Environment

Rest is a critical component of energy. There is a term in sports training called over-training, but a different way to say that is under-recovering. In order to achieve the flow state, we need to offer ourselves appropriate focus and rest. **The Pomodoro Technique** suggests that for every 25 minutes of work, you take a five-minute break to look away from your screen, get up, stretch and walk around a bit.[89] Another technique called **Deep Work** has you intensely focus on a single task without distraction. There isn't really a hard and fast rule here, but to get started, you should set aside about a 90-minute chunk of time before switching to another task or project. Either technique can work for increased productivity, so try them both out! I often use both throughout the day. Two really large "Deep Work" blocks and the rest laser focus for twenty to thirty minutes with breaks between.

> The last words you should say to anyone at night—whether it's your spouse, your children, your dog, your cat or yourself—are "I love you."

Grinding does not just reduce our ability to get into a flow state, but also affects our rest state as well. Depression, weight gain and high blood pressure are some of the well-known health issues linked to insufficient sleep, but stress and sleep are also intricately related—and the connection is cyclical. Too much stress can cause you to sleep poorly, leading to mental and physical health issues which can cause stress in daily life, leading to even worse sleep.

In order to protect our rest and flow times, we need to set boundaries for where we work and where we relax. For example, it is best not to work from the bedroom; similarly, when you get home, have a protected period of time where you get to connect with loved ones or have dinner with friends. Now more than ever, we need to make the time to connect, to relax and have fun.

Recently, I've been building a new routine with less work. I recognized that I had an addictive relationship with my work and that if I wanted to enjoy my life more (and have more energy), I needed to create some space to connect, think, listen and get lost in my dreams—not just my workload.

WAKING UP

How we wake up in the morning can be one of the most significant biohacks, because it sets the tone for everything that follows. Perhaps by now, you're aspiring to have a healthier lifestyle around food and exercise; maybe you're figuring out your supplements and have started a training routine that works for your lifestyle and schedule. Possibly some of those initial morning ideas don't feel so out of reach anymore. You've started changing your life one choice at a time, and you're ready to embrace a morning routine that helps you starts every day energized. But what does that look like?

After preparing (is that gym bag packed?) and getting solid sleep the night before, we can set into our morning routine.

Formulator's Corner
Morning and Night Supplements

Morning Supplements: Greens, collagen, MCTs, chia seeds, alpha GPC, B12, CBD, mitochondrial health (CoQ10, PQQ, curcumin), fish oil, probiotics, nootropics, exogenous ketones and the first half of your multivitamin.

Brain and Metabolism Greens: I use BioTrust MetaboGreens. There's also a great metabolism product on Amazon called Genius Burn. If you are looking to burn extra fat, it also includes my energy ingredient, TeaCrine, as well as grains of paradise, which stimulates BAT (brown adipose tissue) and has no caffeine.

Night Supplements: Melatonin, 5-HTP, theanine, magnesium, alpha-GPC, B12, CBD, collagen and the second dose of your multivitamin. Chamomile, lavender and valerian are also good to calm the mind. They are known as the "sleepy time" teas.

One easy shift is to wake up slowly with bells and chimes that get progressively louder or even with a lamp that slowly lights up so you don't awaken too abruptly. It is so much better to wake up in the right brain wave state. There are alarm clocks and apps you can buy—even wearables that buzz more progressively.

Bright outdoor light in the morning. Exposing yourself to the sun — without sunglasses—within the first hour can have a substantial effect on how awake you feel during the day. That's because it fosters the natural rise in cortisol, suppresses melatonin and increases the melatonin precursor serotonin, which is converted to melatonin when it

gets dark. In other words, early-day exposure to sunlight, even if that just means opening the blinds in your house, sets the stage for melatonin production to peak at in the morning to simulate natural light and nighttime. If you can't expose yourself to natural light, use blue light stimulate your brain.

Consider bright light therapy. Bright artificial light (i.e., bright light therapy or full spectrum light), particularly in the morning, may also help re-establish the daily sleep/wake cycle, increase daytime alertness, improve sleep and improve mood. In fact, you might have heard about the use of bright light therapy to combat the "winter blues."

Generally speaking, bright light therapy consists of daily exposure to 10,000 lux of cool-white fluorescent light for 20-60 minutes. To put it into perspective, that is about 20 times the intensity of normal indoor lighting. By using bright light therapy, such as the Joovv light, you can increase the amount of light that comes into your house or office.

Check your nutrition. Food is an important driver of our circadian rhythm, which can make breakfast another good morning ritual (if you're not doing intermittent fasting, of course). Breakfast is especially powerful if you're away from home. When you're traveling across time zones, eating your first meal of the day at your regular time in the new time zone can really help maintain your circadian rhythm. If, on the other hand, you arrive somewhere and eat at midnight, you're telling your body that it's time to eat when it isn't, which means your circadian rhythm will be misaligned and you may experience jet lag. If you wait until the morning to eat at the usual breakfast time, you have both light and food as external cues that help get your circadian rhythm realigned to the new time zone.

From a circadian rhythm standpoint, food timing (in addition to light and temperature) is one of the major variables that impacts alignment. Along those lines, intermittent fasting regimens (such as time-restricted feeding) that limit food consumption to daytime/ light hours may be particularly effective at promoting metabolic health. In a recent study published in the journal *Cell Metabolism*, for instance, men with prediabetes were randomized to early time-restricted feeding (a form of IF that involved a 6-hour feeding period, with dinner before 3 pm, early in the day to be in alignment with circadian rhythms in metabolism) for 5 weeks and later crossed over to a "normal" (12-hour eating) schedule.[90] Early time-restricted feeding improved insulin sensitivity, pancreatic function (e.g., beta-cell responsiveness), blood pressure and oxidative stress and lowered the desire to eat in the evening. The effects were independent of weight loss, meaning that time-restricted feeding can improve health in the absence of weight loss, and meal timing may play a key role in promoting cardiometabolic benefits.

Be active. Regular exercise also seems to help regulate your circadian clock. In fact, there is some evidence that suggests the benefits of exercise may be maximized when it's done in the middle of the day (i.e., afternoon).[91] Not surprisingly, evening exercise can delay the normal release of melatonin, potentially disrupting circadian rhythms. As we have discussed, committing to a daily exercise routine, bringing in some High-Intensity Interval Training and introducing cold showers into your day can not only increase energy, but also extend your healthspan.

Practice stress management. Under ideal circumstances, cortisol levels are high early in the morning and low at the time of sleep. However, disturbances in normal cortisol rhythms are closely tied to disrupted circadian rhythms. Needless to say, stress management is an important tool when it comes to helping control evening spikes in cortisol, which would have obvious implications on circadian rhythms and sleep.

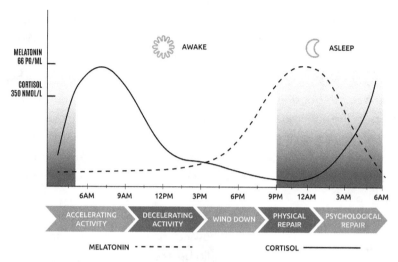

Graphic 42 – Cortisol and Melatonin Relationship[92]

While it's crucial to limit exposure to screens at night, during the day blue light can produce the effect we want by stimulating our brains and increasing energy. In fact, there are some great devices that can simulate blue light and are especially helpful for those prone to SAD (Seasonal Affective Disorder) like me.

In an optimized scenario, you would wake up with the sun every day and go outside for at least a few minutes. After that, you would maybe make yourself a cup of herbal tea, sit outside, breathe in the fresh air and expose yourself to the elements.

TAKE YOUR TIME

The reality is that for most of us, the mornings are just a blur of alarm clocks, fast showers, quickly-made lunches and rushed breakfasts before we run out the door. By waking up 30 minutes earlier usual, you can transform and energize your morning and your life.

Scripting the beginning and the end of your day is a great way to establish your goals, routine and commitment. Waking up at least 15 minutes earlier to do this or spending a few minutes at the end of the day can help you feel successful.

Plan your day with the 5-Minute Journal (either the app or book) to be more effective. Use the techniques in *The 4-Hour Work Week* by Tim Ferriss, who recognizes gratitude as a major part of greeting each day. Writing down what you are grateful for and planning what you need to get done will start you off at peace, as opposed to distracted and agitated. The next steps would be to work out, check your journal to see what you need to get done and knock out a big task within your first two hours. Between your morning workout and your first big accomplishment at work, you'll feel like you're killing it by 10 or 11 am.

By waking up 30 minutes earlier than usual, you can transform and energize your morning and your life.

You can also plan something for the following day to look forward to—it could be as simple as scheduling a haircut, setting time to go to the gym or planning lunch with a friend. No matter what it is, make it happen.

Healthy relationships are a huge key to a happy, successful life and are critical to well-being. Our lives are defined by the people we include in them and healthy relationships make us feel like we have a purpose on this planet. We get energized by the mentors around us—the people who are building us up while still offering constructive criticism to help us improve.

A gratitude adjacent activity you can include in your morning routine is writing a hand-written thank you note, email or text to someone to say how much you appreciate them. In an age of memes and emojis, taking the time to send a heartfelt message is more valuable than ever. Doing this in the morning can set a great tone to your day and can make someone else feel good at the same time.

Hugging or kissing someone you love is also a great morning ritual. Physical touch is so important, and a lack of it has been one of the hardest parts of 2020. If you're fortunate enough to live with someone that you love, make sure you tell them every day. Thank them for all they mean to you, and watch this one habit transform not only your morning but theirs as well. If not, and you don't already have a fur baby, consider adopting a pet!

While mornings are crucial, we need to build periods of rest throughout our day. Whether it's a mid-day power nap or meditation, we can recalibrate our days to be more focused, more relaxed and more energized.

Taking some time to think is so valuable—whether it's an hour in the afternoon or a few days off (meditation retreats are also great for this). When we go on vacation, we *really* need to take our vacations—leaving behind the work email, the laptop and the stress. Slowing down and focusing on what matters by prioritizing daily routines is key to a life of more energy.

BE HERE NOW

I am not a meditation expert, but I have found that even five minutes of silence can make a world of difference in how my day looks and feels. But quiet time is not just relegated to meditation—spending a few minutes in the middle of the day to daydream provides a little quiet in our otherwise busy lives. The key is to be *fully* present with whatever form of rest we're doing. When we commit to being present, it is easier to establish and maintain healthy routines.

Meditation can be intimidating at first, and it can feel far from quiet. All those voices in your head! All those thoughts and things you need to do! Where is the peace in that? Fortunately, I've found some easy techniques to get into a better meditative space:

Breathe. Just by practicing breathing techniques, you can quiet your pulse and mind. First, take a deep breath in and slowly exhale through pursed lips while letting your cheeks puff out. These slow exhales can activate the parasympathetic nervous system, moving you out of fight-or-flight. You can also practice some box breathing, where you inhale for a slow four count, hold your breath in for four counts, slowly exhale for four counts and hold your breath for another four counts. By focusing on counting, you can detach from your other thoughts and center on your breath.

Another great technique is called diaphragmatic breathing. Start by sitting comfortably in a chair or lying down with knees bent. Place your hand on your abdomen. Take a deep breath in and, as you inhale, let your belly expand into your hand as your ab muscles relax. Slowly release and allow your belly and hand to fall with a slight contraction of the abs as the lungs empty. This is also a great way to get yourself sleepy at night when you're lying down.

A quick and inexpensive "hack" I have incorporated into my morning routine is a simple saline nose rinse. Not only does this traditional Ayurvedic medicine practice help with allergies and keeping sinuses healthy but it also helps promote better nasal breathing, which offers benefits like better oxygenation to calm the body and mind.

Walk. Although we need sun more than ever, an increasing concern about skin cancer has us avoiding it more than ever. While sun protection is crucial, feeling the sun on our faces allows us to slow the world around us.

There is an activity now called "forest bathing," which really just means taking a very leisurely walk in nature. If you live in the city you may not have access to a forest, but the more greenery you surround yourself with, the more oxygen you'll be able to breathe. The more we are in nature—feeling the dirt, smelling the air—the lower our cortisol levels, and the more we can ground ourselves and feel more secure throughout the day.

Grounding. One more way to become more present and aware is to connect to the earth. Just like meditation (and frequently in collaboration with it), grounding gets us out of the clouds—or "the cloud" (the internet-based one)—and back on planet earth. After all, studies have shown that by walking around barefoot for 20 minutes a day, you can improve your health and increase your lifespan.[93]

When we feel the ground beneath our feet, the sun on our faces and oxygen in our lungs, we experience the world around us and reconnect with nature. We get out of the office and into the field for a moment.

How does grounding work? Glad you asked! Believe it or not, the Earth is teeming with an endless supply of energy (called free electrons) that we can absorb in our bodies when we "plug in" via grounding (this is also known as "earthing"). This energetic charge can help neutralize free radicals, normalize our circadian rhythms, increase circulation and more. Practically speaking, that means less pain and stiffness, lower inflammation and stress, better sleep, improved heart rate variability and blood pressure, and you guessed it, more *energy*!

When we feel the ground beneath our feet, the sun on our faces and the oxygen in our lungs, we experience the world around us and

So, go outside and take off your shoes—no, really, I'll wait.

Guided Meditation Session

Binaural Beats for Focus

HEART RATE VARIABILITY

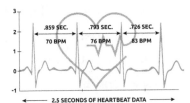

Graphic 43 – Heart Rate Variability

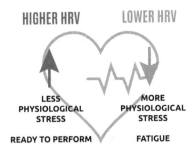

HIGHER HRV   LOWER HRV

LESS PHYSIOLOGICAL STRESS   MORE PHYSIOLOGICAL STRESS

READY TO PERFORM   FATIGUE

Graphic 44 – Higher HRV vs Lower HRV

SLEEP   FOOD

EMF

SPORT   STRESS

IT IS A REPRESENTATION OF HOW WELL RECOVERED YOU ARE.
HIGH HRV = GOOD = MORE PARASYMPATHETIC DOMINANT
LOW HRV = BAD = MORE SYMPATHETIC DOMINANT (STRESSED OUT!)

Graphic 45 – What Effects HRV

To measure the state of your autonomic nervous system (ANS), you can track your heart rate variability (HRV). HRV represents how well-rested and recovered you are, and a higher HRV indicates higher vagal tone and more Parasympathetic Nervous System (PNS) dominance; likewise, Sympathetic Nervous System (SNS) dominance causes lower HRV. You may find that after drinking alcohol, eating late at night or exercising very hard[94].

This is an indicator that you are not fully recovered yet and you should focus on things like yoga, easy walks, self-care and meditation.

There's a little experiment you can do on your own to see just how much you can control your HRV: sit still and upright and breathe. Deep, slow diaphragmatic breathing—during which you visualize filling up the lower part of your lungs just above your belly button like a balloon ("belly breathing")… then exhaling slowly.

As little as one short minute (though I recommend more) of diaphragmatic breathing a few times per day has been shown to have a positive effect on the cardiovascular and pulmonary system as well as enhance parasympathetic activation through something called "vagal tone." One of my favorite ways to stimulate vagus nerve through breathwork is the following: breath in to the count of five, pause, breath out for five, pause in, all while wearing a tracking device for biofeedback. You'll notice that your HRV increases, which shows that there's a connection between your brain and your heart that you can consciously control. This is a powerful area of potential for the human species.

The human body is a miraculous instrument that instinctively knows what it needs. Unfortunately, the human ego often drives us not to listen.

Forty-three percent of Americans admit to being tired more than three days a week and one million Americans experience chronic fatigue.[95] In other words, nearly half our country is exhausted!

Just as there are rhythms to retrograde motion and the pull of the heavenly bodies, our bodies also experience the weight of gravity and time. We're all affected by these rhythms, just as the tide reacts to the setting of the sun and the rising of the moon (after all, our body is primarily made of water). The body knows when to rest—and frequently, it rebels when we refuse to honor that knowledge.

> **The human body is a miraculous instrument that instinctively knows what it needs. Unfortunately, the human ego often drives us not to listen.**

REST AND THE IMMUNE SYSTEM

More sleep won't stop you from getting sick, but skipping rest can leave you a lot more susceptible. Without sufficient sleep, your body makes fewer cytokines, a type of protein that targets infection and inflammation. When we are sleep-deprived, we create immune disorders. Studies have shown that lack of sleep can even make flu vaccines less effective.

It's important to develop a healthy sleep schedule so you're not living in a deficit—even if that means taking naps, allowing yourself to sleep in and creating firm boundaries around your schedule so you're not burning the midnight oil. Sleep can also protect you against chronic health issues like heart disease, diabetes and obesity.

When we push ourselves through our exhaustion, we are pushing our adrenal system as our hormones, like cortisol and adrenaline, attempt to make something from nothing. Daily fatigue is not natural to any mammal on the planet, and it's definitely not natural to humans. How can anyone be expected to perform at their absolute best when they're running on empty? In order to return to an energized state, we need to realign ourselves with our deepest rhythms —but these can look different for men and women.

Men and women both run on a 24-hour rhythm of sunrise and sunset. Fertile women are of course affected by a monthly, cyclical rhythm in line with the lunar cycle. It follows that women may need to pay even closer attention to this and know that is it *normal* to not feel the same from day to day—some days and weeks may require more rest than others.

Sleep is the foundation of an energized life, supporting us to make healthy conscious choices. When we lack sleep, we often rely on caffeine and sugar to get us through the day…which only leads to more sleep disorders and a daily energy deficit. When we build a healthy routine, we can tap into a deep, parasympathetic rhythm which allows us to enhance and sustain our energy. By doing so, we not only increase our lifespan—but also deepen our relationships and increase the quality of our time on earth.

ROUTINE SUMMARY

- Our mornings ultimately determine whether we are set up for success or stagnation, which is why a strong morning routine offers you a foundation on which to build the rest of the day's plans—allowing you to stay grounded, achieve goals and maintain energy and flow throughout the day. The best way to start is by choosing one thing and trying it out for a couple of weeks. If it is something that works for you and benefits your life, then include it as part of your routine.

- When the circadian rhythm becomes de-synchronized, we see an increased risk for things like diabetes, obesity, neurodegenerative diseases and mood disorders. While light and dark are the primary drivers of the body's circadian clock, many factors can disrupt circadian rhythms—including what and when we eat and exercise, as well as work, travel, poor sleep hygiene, stress and more. Increased sunlight exposure, reduced artificial blue light in the evening, meal timing and healthy sleep hygiene habits can all go a long way in promoting circadian rhythms. Getting sunlight exposure first thing in the morning can have a substantial effect on setting the circadian clock to feel more awake during the day.

- Sleep is the foundation of an energized life—ultimately supporting us to make healthy conscious choices. Quality of sleep determines quality of life. It's not just about the number of hours you spend in bed, but about the quality of sleep while you're getting those zzz's.

- From a circadian rhythm standpoint, food timing (in addition to light and temperature) is one of the major variables that impacts circadian alignment. Intermittent Fasting regimens (such as TRF) that limit food consumption to daytime/light hours may be particularly effective at promoting metabolic health. According to time-restricted feeding research, it may be best to limit your "feeding window" to less than 12 hours each day with most—if not all—of your food intake during daylight hours.

- Men and women both run on a 24-hour rhythm with the earth's rotation and the sunrise and sunset. Fertile women are more clearly affected by a monthly/cyclical rhythm in line with the lunar cycle so women may need to pay even closer attention to this realignment process and know that it's normal to not feel the same from day to day. The more time we spend in nature, the lower our cortisol levels. This helps ground our nervous system and make us feel more secure as we move about our day.

- Scripting your day, both at the beginning and at the end, is a great way to establish your goals, routine and commitment. Waking up 15 minutes earlier to do this or spending a few minutes at the end of the day can help you feel successful. When we build a healthy routine, we tap into a deep, parasympathetic rhythm, which allows us to enhance and sustain our energy. We not only increase our lifespan, but also enhance our lives in ways we could have never imagined—deepening our relationships and increasing the quality of our time on earth.

Resource Hacks

Routine

Promoting Better Sleep:

Manta Sleep Mask: Blue light, LEDs from devices (including smoke detectors and TVs), outdoor light pollution at night and daylight can all prevent optimal sleep. Using a good sleep mask is a great way to protect your sleep routine.

White Noise App: Spotify has this available, but I also use some dedicated apps—find one that works best for you.

Ear Plugs: These are an option if noise is an issue when you travel (i.e., when you're on flights or in hotels).

ChiliPAD: This is a great product to keep your body at an optimal sleeping temperature in bed. The Ooler is my favorite.

Weighted Blanket: Data shows that these reduce anxiety and promote deeper sleep with feelings of security. ChiliPAD makes one of these as well.

F.lux App: If you need to use a device before bed, make sure you have F.lux downloaded to filter out the blue light from a screen.

EMF Blocker: Somavedic is a great EMF-blocking device.

Routine (continuation)

Red Light: Make sure a red light is the only source of light in your bedroom. This can be an incandescent bulb or a red-light therapy device such as Joovv.

Air Purifier: I use Molekule, which has an app, superior filtration and Bluetooth options.

TrueDark Dots: Put a "dot" over those pesky LEDs on nearly every device.

Sleep Tape: It could be the single best sleep hack you've never tried. Breathing through your mouth tends to be hypocapnic and therefore delivers less oxygen to the tissues. Even if you're not sleep apnic, you'll find drastically improved sleep by taping the mouth at night and forcing nasal breathing only. SomniFix Sleep Strips are my preferred brand.

Grounding:

Straps and Shoes: If you don't want to get your feet dirty, try using straps from Earthling or grounding shoes and sandals from Pluggz and Earthrunners.

Grounding and Sleep Mats: For around-the-clock grounding, you can buy therapy sleep mats and grounding mats to place under your desk—Ultimate Longevity has great products for these.

Sleep Tracking:

BioStrap: My preferred sleep tracking device. Other popular devices include Garmin, Oura and Whoop.

Routine (continuation)

Promoting Better Wakefulness:

Lumie Alarm Clock: This uses a gradual, artificial sunrise to wake you naturally and feeling refreshed. It has a sunrise duration of 15-90 minutes and your choice of final light intensity.

Philips goLITE BLU: Daylight is essential to well-being and to keeping fit and energized throughout the day. This portable blue light mimics the natural energizing power of daylight.

HumanCharger: A quick, effective and convenient way to get your daily dose of light. The creators of the device say a 12-minute session will increase energy levels, improve mood, increase mental alertness, reduce the effects of jet lag and keep winter blues at bay.

Work Productivity and Time Management Techniques:

Pomodoro Technique: This technique uses a timer to break down work into intervals, traditionally 25 minutes separated by breaks of five minutes. Using a timer can help you stay focused on the task at hand, preventing interruptions that disrupt workflow.

Deep Work (Cal Newport): This method suggests focusing on a cognitively demanding task for at least 90 uninterrupted minutes.

Top Apps:

Trello/Asana for project management.

Slack for communication related to work projects.

Routine (continuation)

Google Keep for notes.

Elevate for brain games.

Spotify for podcasts.

Blinkist for book summaries.

Headspace for meditation.

Audible for audiobooks.

*For live links, updated content, bonus graphics
and a hidden chapter, go to
EnergyFormulaBook.com*

GROWTH MINDSET SURVEY

Would you consider yourself someone with a growth mindset (you believe you can grow and improve) or a fixed mindset (the elements of your life are static and will not change much)?		
I definitely have a growth mindset and am always seeking to grow and learn in a variety of ways.	(3)	
Some of both—I want to change and grow but I doubt my ability to do so based on my past performance	(2)	
I have more of a fixed mindset. I question whether I can make significant changes in my life.	(1)	
Do you feel that you have a sense of purpose and a *why* for your life?		
Yes! I have a strong sense of purpose in life and I stay focused on my why, which helps me make the right decisions.	(3)	
I somewhat know what my purpose is but I still struggle with understanding it fully and connecting with my why for life.	(2)	
I am really struggling to find a sense of purpose and a strong why for my life.	(1)	
How would you rate your fear of failure and your willingness to step outside your comfort zone?		
I regularly step outside my comfort zone and try new things without a fear of failure.	(3)	
I have some fear of failure which keeps me from venturing outside my comfort zone and trying new things.	(2)	
I am scared to try new things and have a strong fear of failure. I want to step outside my comfort zone but cannot!	(1)	
Have you experimented with Nootropics?		
Yes, I extensively use nootropics in my daily supplement regimen for clarity, energy and enhanced health.	(3)	
I have heard of nootropics and tried a few, but do not use them regularly.	(2)	
"Noo"-what?! I've never heard that term before.	(1)	

Do you feel there are areas of your life that you need to grow in and that could be enhanced?		
I have a few areas that still need improvement (we all do!) but overall, I am happy and feel that I am on the right track.	(3)	
Yes, I have areas that I need to grow in and I am actively trying to improve them.	(2)	
Definitely. I have several areas in my life that need improvement and don't know where to start.	(1)	
Do you have someone in your life who can give you honest feedback when it comes to important life matters?		
Yes, I have this person and I do this for others as well.	(3)	
Somewhat but it is not something I consistently seek.	(2)	
No, I do not have someone that I trust to give me the honest feedback I need on important things.	(1)	
Have you ever committed to a time of deep self-work and experimentation to find what works for you in a diet and health regimen?		
Yes, I have used various methods such as looking inward, experimentation, research and trial/error to learn what works best for me and my health.	(3)	
I have experimented somewhat but not in a detailed way to really track my progress or my results.	(2)	
I have never done this and don't know where to start in committing to deep self-work and health experimentation.	(1)	
YOUR TOTAL		

7-11 points: You have got some work to do! This book is a great place to start!

12-16 points: You are heading in the right direction! Keep at it!

17-21 points: You are really on the ball! Only small tweaks are needed to be your best self!

Chapter 5: Growth: Live Your Life with Intention

"Everyone wants to live on top of the mountain, but all the happiness and growth occurs while you're climbing it."

—Andy Rooney

In 2017, I got a message on Facebook from a woman—let's call her Wendy—who said she'd been following me for years and loved the information I put out. I thanked her, but I could sense there was more to her message than just an acknowledgment of the information I put out there.

Wendy proceeded to tell me she had been taken off chemotherapy and radiation by her oncologist and told that she had six weeks to live with her glioblastoma multiforme (GBM), a deadly brain tumor. In her case, it had taken over about 40 to 50 percent of her brain.

"I will be buried in the ground in a little over a month," she said. "Can you help me?"

Having had my own brain tumor scare, I immediately related to her predicament. My own health issues had changed the way I looked at every single one of my routines and habits, and I wanted to pass on whatever wisdom I could.

"I'm not a doctor, so I can't give you medical advice," I told her. "I can tell you what I would do in your situation, but I also want to make sure you talk to your doctor."

This is what I suggested to Wendy:

Hyperbaric Oxygen Therapy (HBOT): This is shown to have tumor-inhibitory effects on certain cancer cells. This is thought to be because hypoxia (i.e., lack of oxygen) is a causative factor in cancer progression, as cancer cells and tumors seem to thrive in this type of environment. HBOT, which involves inhaling 100% oxygen at increased atmospheric pressure, has been used for centuries to treat conditions involving hypoxia by enhancing oxygen delivery to cells. This is really the tip of the iceberg when it comes to HBOT, which has a broad range of uses from athletic performance and recovery to anti-aging. In fact, in a recent clinical trial, HBOT was shown to not just slow or stop aging but actually *reverse* aging in humans. Specifically, the study showed that 60 HBOT sessions over 90 days resulted in lengthening of telomeres (by up to 38%), which are considered bi-omarkers of aging (with shorter telomeres reflecting accelerated aging), and a 37% decrease in old and malfunctioning cells (i.e., senescent cells).[96]

Strict Keto of Less Than 20 Grams of Total Carbohydrates a Day: In addition to helping regulate blood sugar levels, there is compelling evidence that a **keto** diet may lower a tumor's ability to produce growth signals.[97]

IV Vitamin C at 30-50g Twice a Week: In test studies, Vitamin C has been shown to slow the progression of cancer and even kill cancer cells.[98]

16-8 Time-Restricted Feeding/Fasting: This means 16-hour windows of not eating and an eight-hour window to eat. There's good reason to believe that short-term fasting may be both a powerful prevention tool as well as adjuvant therapy for cancer and the 16-8 form of intermittent fasting seems to be one of the most feasible means.[99]

Paleo: I suggested eating whole foods only, avoiding added sugar, refined grains and refined vegetable oils—in other words, abandoning processed foods and the typical Western-style diet, which is linked to increased risk for several types of cancer as well as increased tumor progression.[100]

Supplements for Inflammation, Mitochondrial Health and to Raise Ketones to Promote Growth of Healthy Cells: I suggested NMN, PQQ and CoQ10 for her mitochondrial health; creatine, methylcobalamin and 5-MTHF for methylation; and exogenous ketones, particularly the D- or R-BHB salt (which is an active isomer and more biologically active) and sodium for efficacy (over potassium, calcium or magnesium). I recommended C8 MCTs to raise ketone levels and Monolaurin to improve immune system along with AHCC. I suggested she start cooking with coconut oil and research berberine, or even better dihydroberberine, since cancer is typically a metabolic disease.

Wendy messaged me a few times telling me she told her doctor, but he didn't seem to care too much—almost as if it was all superfluous. After all, in his mind, none of it compared to drugs or radiation.

Six weeks later, Wendy had another brain scan.

"Shawn!" she said. "There was an 80-90 percent reduction in my tumor...I am supposed to be buried in the ground and I am living. I am *alive!"*

I was awe. It felt like a culmination of everything I'd been working so hard for in life.

After helping Dymatize through their acquisition to Post Foods as their Director of Research and Development, I was in a position to set up a scientific dream team—including Dr. Tim Ziegenfuss and Dr. Hector Lopez. We patented TeaCrine and Dynamine, two of the best-known and studied branded energy ingredients on the market. At the same time, I had BioTRUST Nutrition reach out to me to become their Chief Science Officer and lead R&D, Quality Control and Regulatory for the company. The company's co-founder, Josh Bezoni, called me personally to explain, "We want the best. I have one person on my list, and it's you." Joel Marion, the other co-founder, called me "the LeBron James of supplements." Both men are worth hundreds of millions of dollars, and they sought me out.

I own numerous companies and have been featured in numerous articles, podcasts, documentaries, radio and TV shows. I've made money doing what I love and fulfilled childhood dream after childhood dream. Even so, that experience with Wendy might have meant more to me than any of those others. It was the ultimate proof of my purpose in life, the one I'd told Dr. Johnson about so many years earlier. It was what spurred the creation of the book you're reading now.

Ironically perhaps, as I started writing this, I was working harder and longer than I ever had before, with numerous stops and starts. And then, of course, COVID-19 hit and shut everything down. Still, it happened at exactly the right time.

Before the pandemic, I was traveling 75 percent of the year, living on the road and having to rebuild my rhythm around airports and hotel rooms, jet lag and layovers. When I was at home, I had a set of routines and plans to ensure my success. I would wake up at the same time, fast during the day, eat a lunch and dinner that properly fueled my body and get off screens at night in order to spend time with family and protect my sleep. And then I would do it all over again.

Without the convenience and stability of home, my nutrition, exercise and sleep suffered. Everything went out of whack and not surprisingly, so did I. I was not living anything close to an energized life; I was back in survival mode. I was realizing yet again that something I was doing was "off." Things weren't going perfectly—but the answer wasn't a more perfect routine. It was more flexibility.

I realized I had to start being more open-minded and forgiving with my routine while still building in some constants—from how I woke up in the morning to making time for workouts. I had to focus on the essential parts of my ideal routine and make sure I did at least some of those parts every day to keep my energy levels high. Just as I was getting into a flow with that, the pandemic hit, which meant I once again had to renegotiate my routine (though then again, so has everyone else).

COVID-19 has thrown everyone's routines into disarray. For me, after finally adapting to being on the road, I had to readapt to being stuck at home and unable to go anywhere—including the gym. The tricky thing was in the pre-pandemic world, my highly-structured routines were empowering and gave me energy, and I mostly looked forward to completing them. What I didn't realize was that baked into those routines was the ability to use that energy they created to freely leave the house, go into the world and do what I wanted to do. As many of us discovered, once that ability disappeared, the routines became a little less attractive. I saw that mine needed to be adjusted.

I've come around to seeing the pandemic in some ways as an opportunity. It's tempting to think our routines give us the power to take on the whole world—meaning the external world—but sometimes we can use that energy to strengthen what's right in front of us. I learned I was "burnt out" at times, not from doing "too

Sometimes routines don't have to be about maximizing performance or going harder, better, faster and stronger.

much" but from not doing enough of the things I truly love. The "most important thing is to keep the most important things the most important thing," according to Jim Kwik.

For me, COVID-19 has meant slowing down, spending more time with my wife, adorable cat and loving dog, putting my feet in the grass and continually grounding myself for the challenges ahead. It has meant learning an important lesson:

We can design our routines to give us more energy (and we should), but we can also design them to give us more clarity, peace and appreciation for the things around us. After all, the answer to extreme stress is often not to hustle, scramble or speed up; sometimes we just need to take a breath, mindfully, and smile.

In that slow down, I realized that a lot of the "work" I'd been trying to do on myself over the years was designed to "fix" things from early in my life. I'd developed beliefs about myself as a child that had shaped everything that followed. But I was starting to wonder if the way this "work" was framed was even the right way to approach things at all. I was looking for healing, acceptance and connection in myself and with others, and to get to know my higher, authentic self beyond my programming. But thinking of it as arduous "work" set it up mentally as something I couldn't fully accomplish or enjoy. Very recently, I've been trying to think of it more in terms of "self-play."

When we're kids, we start off authentically ourselves before our experiences change us into our adult personas. But if we're trying to reclaim that innocence, how can we get there by using those false adult tools? We need to act like the inner child that we want to get in touch with. Subconsciously, I'd been approaching things from a "tragically flawed" angle (and in all honesty, I may still have healing to do on this part of myself). Lately I've been getting more in touch with the idea that I entered this world as a perfect spirit. The solution comes back to self-love as the foundation of growth. Trust me, the last conclusion I ever thought I would come to is that self-love is the ultimate "biohack." And yet, here we are.

To put it more concretely, we do not need to put microchips in our bodies to biohack ourselves. Maybe I don't have to grind myself into the ground year after year to feel totally fulfilled and like I'm giving life my all. (Okay, maybe I'm not quite that enlightened yet—but it's the thought that counts, right?)

As many people are realizing, we have been overtaken by the technology we thought would make our lives easier. Although some of that technology has been helpful, some of it has threatened to replace the human connections we crave and need. In order to enhance our lives, we need to enhance our minds. We can do that through new routines, external ingredients or by changing our perspective.

For me, fasting has become a powerful tool for mental clarity, but also for discipline and detoxification. Through fasting, you begin to realize that (1) you will survive without eating for 24-72 hours; (2) you don't have to eat when everyone else does and (3) you are incredibly strong and powerful. Fasting has helped me to develop a growth mindset, simply by choosing when I eat food throughout the day.

The beauty of the human mind is that we are ultimately its chief technology officer. Biohacking offers the skill set to master that process. As we recognize our own biological habits, we can begin to change them and feel better. In light of our improved lives and energy levels, we see that the fixed mindset is an illusion that we don't have to accept any longer. Instead, we can aim for growth each day.

THE POWER OF FASTING

Scientists now believe that many of the benefits of Intermittent Fasting (IF) are the result of flipping the metabolic switch—but what does that mean? Researchers define the metabolic switch as "the body's preferential shift from utilization of glucose to fatty acids and fatty-acid derived ketones."[101] In other words, IF turns off sugar burning and turns on fat burning and ketone production. That shift encourages weight loss and enhanced metabolic function, including increased insulin sensitivity and reduced levels of blood glucose, insulin and leptin. All of those increase heart health and longevity.

People invariably want to know if coffee and branched-chain amino acids (or BCAAs) break the fast. The short answer, I believe, is that anything other than water will break a fast. The better question is: does it matter? That depends. If you're trying to do a three-day fast to maximize cellular cleaning (known as autophagy), then it may not make sense to include anything besides water. Whenever we ingest anything, our body shifts from a focus on autophagy to a focus on dealing with whatever we just ingested. If you're doing daily time-restricted feeding for weight management and overall health, however, if coffee or BCAAs help you, they're probably not a big deal.

Graphic 46 – Extended Fasting Timeline

The fact that hunter-gatherers went extended periods of time without food doesn't fall under the umbrella of voluntary fasting but it does highlight the fact that humans are designed to withstand periods of abstinence. On top of that, we're markedly efficient at storing energy (e.g., body fat), and during periods of prolonged fasting and carbohydrate restriction, it's clear that we're wired to flip the metabolic switch to produce and use ketones, which some argue are the body's preferred fuel source.

Many wonder if they're supposed to take supplements during a fast, and there's a variety of opinions out there about it. Although many supplements are unlikely to "break your fast," some are absorbed best by the body when taken with food. In other words, taking them while fasting may be a waste of your time and money. To avoid unintentionally breaking your fast with supplements, let's break down how fasting affects our bodies.

The health benefits of fasting are a result of your body being in a post-absorptive state, where it can focus on maintenance and recovery instead of digesting and building. This shift from a fed to a fasted state is what I call the "metabolic switch." Through fasting, your body undergoes many metabolic changes, which include a drop in insulin levels and a rise in glucagon and growth hormone. These metabolic shifts allow fat to be broken down to produce ketones for energy and for autophagy.

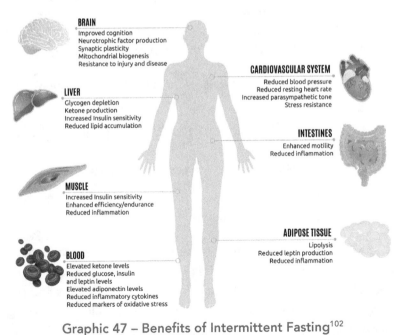

BRAIN
Improved cognition
Neurotrophic factor production
Synaptic plasticity
Mitochondrial biogenesis
Resistance to injury and disease

CARDIOVASCULAR SYSTEM
Reduced blood pressure
Reduced resting heart rate
Increased parasympathetic tone
Stress resistance

LIVER
Glycogen depletion
Ketone production
Increased Insulin sensitivity
Reduced lipid accumulation

INTESTINES
Enhanced motility
Reduced inflammation

MUSCLE
Increased Insulin sensitivity
Enhanced efficiency/endurance
Reduced inflammation

ADIPOSE TISSUE
Lipolysis
Reduced leptin production
Reduced inflammation

BLOOD
Elevated ketone levels
Reduced glucose, insulin
and leptin levels
Elevated adiponectin levels
Reduced inflammatory cytokines
Reduced markers of oxidative stress

Graphic 47 – Benefits of Intermittent Fasting[102]

When we eat, insulin is released from the pancreas into the blood. Carbohydrates cause the greatest rise in insulin, while fat causes little to no insulin response in the body. Unless we ingest a substantial number of fat calories all at once, fat generally has a marginal effect on insulin levels. So, when considering what you can eat during a fast, look at the ingredients carefully. Does the product contain artificial sweeteners, sugars, a lot of fat or any fillers? If so, it is likely going to break your fast and slow down the autophagy process. Ultimately, the most important thing to remember is not to have any sweetened or high-calorie supplements. Look at the ingredients carefully and make sure they are low to no-calorie and contain no sugar or artificial sweeteners. Ultimately, taking supplements during a fast is a personal preference, and I would suggest approaching the question with an open mind.

Here are some of the most common examples of intermittent fasting:

INTERMITTENT FASTING

- TIME RESTRICTED FEEDING (TRF)
- ALTERNATE-DAY FASTING (ADF)
- ALTERNATE-DAY MODIFIED FASTING (ADMF)
- PERIODIC FASTING (PF)
- FASTING MIMICKING DIETS (FMD)

Graphic 48 – Types of Intermittent Fasting

- **Time-Restricted Feeding (TRF).** This is the most popular form of IF, and it involves restricting food intake to specific time periods of the day—often referred to as "feeding windows" — which are typically no longer than eight hours (for example, one might fast for 16 hours followed by an eight-hour feeding window). *The Warrior Diet* is an example of TRF, as is the popular IF method Leangains.

- **Alternate-Day Fasting (ADF).** This involves alternating "fasting" days (no calories) with "feast" days (unrestricted food intake). In other words, eat nothing one day, then eat to your satisfaction the next.

- **Alternate-Day Modified Fasting (ADMF).** This variation of ADF restricts calories by about 75 percent of your baseline needs on "fasting" days (about 500 calories/day), which are alternated with unrestricted "feast" days (*ad libitum* food consumption, meaning you can eat as much as you want). *Every Other Day Diet* is an example of ADMF and is based on the research of Dr. Krista Varady (who is also the co-author). ADF and ADMF are the most studied forms of IF in humans.

- **Periodic Fasting (PF).** This IF eating pattern, which is sometimes referred to as "whole-day fasting," consists of one or two days of fasting along with *ad libitum* food consumption the other five or six days of the week. One popular example is Brad Pilon's *Eat Stop Eat* program. A modified version is the *2-Day Diet* (also known as the *5:2 Diet* or MPF), which involves two consecutive days of calorie restriction (about 500-700 calories/day) followed by five days of "normal" eating. PF can also include water fasts, which often last between two and five days.

- **Fasting Mimicking Diet (FMD).** As the name implies, FMD is designed to mimic the physiological state of fasting *and* provide many of its benefits—without actually fasting. FMD is based on research conducted by Dr. Valter Longo and colleagues and it hinges on a five-day period of calorie restriction within a monthly cycle. During this five-day period, you consume a very-low-calorie diet (about 34-54 percent of your normal intake, or 800-1100 calories per day) that's also very low in protein (about 10 percent of your normal intake). The rest of the month, you eat normally. This cycle is typically repeated at least three times. If you're interested in learning more about FMD, *The Longevity Diet* (by Dr. Longo) and ProLonFMD.com are excellent resources.

TIME RESTRICTED FEEDING (TRF)

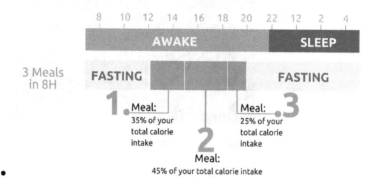

ALTERNATE-DAY FASTING (ADF)

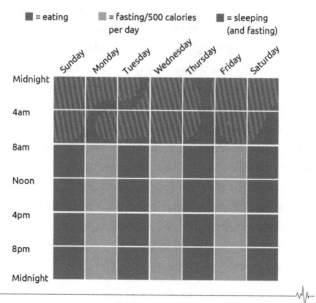

FASTING MIMICKING DIETS (FMD)

■ = Eating   ■ = Fasting   ■ = Sleeping (and fasting)

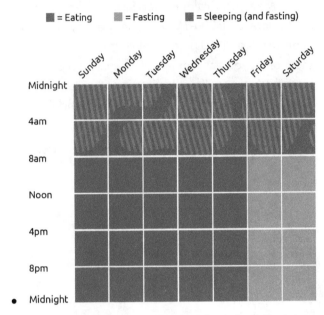

Graphic 49 – Intermittent Fasting Sample Schedules

Though it may seem unusual to those who haven't tried it, fasting has been a common practice across cultures for thousands of years. Medical practitioners across many different historical eras have used fasting for healing purposes—among them ancient Chinese, Greek and Roman physicians. Fasting has also been used in a religious context that continues today; Ramadan and Lent are two well-known periods of religious fasting for Muslims and Christians, respectively.

Fasting even has a history in early Colonial America: in fact, Benjamin Franklin, one of America's founding fathers, said, "The best of all medicines is resting and fasting." He was echoed into the next century by author Mark Twain, who wrote, "A little starvation can really do more for the average sick man than can the best medicines and the best doctors. I do not mean a restricted diet; I mean total abstention from food for one or two days." Even those who are unsure about fasting should experiment with it for its potentially life-changing effects—you'll be in good company!

Formulator's Corner
Fasting Supplements

Hydration: Drink plenty of water and get electrolytes. Add Redmond Real Salt to your water or drink LMNT packets. Consider taking magnesium glycinate for this as well if you are prone to cramping. I have used EPIC bone broth on some extended fasts.

Spare Muscle: Consider BCAAs (7 g of 2:1:1), EAAs (10 g), HMB free acid or L-HICA if you are considering working out while fasting. These can spare muscle (anti-catabolic).

Sleep Supplements: Magnesium (e.g., glycinate), L-theanine (100-200 mg) or melatonin (0.3-10 mg) can help if you struggle to sleep while undertaking longer fasts.

Detoxification Aids: Curcumin (liposomal or other high bioavailability form), N-acetylcysteine (NAC), liposomal glutathione and apple cider vinegar are all helpful. Acetic acid feeds the gut and the "mother" bacteria (the cloudy stuff in the bottle) does as well. For ACV, I prefer Bragg's Cider Vinegar.

Ketone Boosters: These aid in getting past hunger, brain fog and fatigue. Use C8 MCTs, exogenous ketones (the active isomer called D-BHB or R-BHB at 5-10 g per serving) and dihydroberberine (100-200 mg, twice a day).

INGREDIENTS FOR GROWTH

While growth begins from within, we can enhance that process from without. Though I recognize that supplements can help people live their best lives (after all, I help create them and use a ton of them myself), we must first create a foundation for growth before we can begin to enhance it.

Diet and exercise can take us incredibly far in our health journey, but supplements help us transcend the barriers that diet and exercise can't. The human body was not built for this modern world. Though we know a lot more about food than ever before, we've still been consuming nearly the same ingredients for centuries. Supplements can help us catch up to the modern age, but more importantly, they can help us live energized lives.

Unfortunately, an array of phony and dangerous products on the market have made many people skeptical about supplements.

Also, some people in the medical community dismiss what's going on in the health and supplement world while touting pharmaceuticals as the only answer—just as some in the health and supplements world promote food and experimental chemicals as the only way forward. Just like with everything else, it's all about creating balance and finding a tailored regimen that works for you.

Once you begin building a new foundation for living, you can begin to explore which supplements can help you go from good to great. In this chapter, I'd like to focus on three particular kinds of supplements that can forever revolutionize and energize your growth: nootropics, MCTs and CBDs.

NOOTROPICS

"Noo what?" you ask. In case you've never heard the term before, nootropics are one of today's most popular (and not to mention confusing and misunderstood) categories of supplements and chemicals that improve cognitive functions—including things like memory, creativity and motivation—in healthy individuals. This relatively new term differentiates chemicals and compounds that can give us benefits and improvements in healthy ways that strengthen our bodies without the negative effects of "drugs." As you'll see though, the lines between these categories can seem a little blurry, and there is ongoing research determining which substances are and aren't "nootropics."

As someone who's always searching for new ways to optimize both my mental and physical productivity, I've experimented plenty with nootropics—which are often referred to as "smart drugs," "brain boosters" and "cognitive enhancers." While those are sexy nicknames, what exactly are nootropics? What are they used for and how can they benefit you? Are they safe for everyone? Do they have negative side effects?

The first thing that comes to mind for many people when they think about nootropics is the movie *Limitless*, where Bradley Cooper plays someone who is able to access 100 percent of his brain abilities thanks to a mysterious pill. Indeed, most people interested in nootropics are usually eager to see how they can improve focus, concentration and energy. The fact that influential high performers like Tim Ferriss, along with other Silicon Valley entrepreneurs, use them more regularly are moving nootropics from "underground" to more mainstream.

The actual term nootropics was proposed in 1973 by Romanian psychologist and chemist Dr. Corneliu E. Giurgea, the so-called "founding father of nootropics." According to Giurgea, "The term 'nootrope' comes from the Greek words *noos* for 'mind' and *tropein* for 'towards' and is loosely translated as 'mind-turning.'" He coined the term after he demonstrated a positive effect of piracetam—a compound he created in 1964 which is widely considered the first nootropic—on cognitive improvement (including memory, learning and creativity).[103] Unlike Central Nervous System (CNS) stimulants (e.g., amphetamines) and other psychotropic drugs, piracetam offers cognitive benefits without negative side effects (such as dependence).

In addition to acutely enhancing cognitive function, nootropics can also protect or repair the brain. Different nootropics work via different mechanisms, but most work by modulating key neurotransmitters like dopamine, norepinephrine, acetylcholine and glutamate. (Acetylcholine and dopamine are central in improving cognitive function.)

When used carefully, thoughtfully and in conjunction with an overall healthy lifestyle, nootropics can be effective at boosting feelings of well-being and energy, promoting resilience and helping ease feelings of stress and anxiety.

The right nootropics can combat feelings of fatigue, cut through brain fog and help clear through mental clutter, which is why they are often used for studying, taking exams, public speaking, writing and other mentally demanding tasks. When used carefully, thoughtfully and in conjunction with an overall healthy lifestyle, nootropics can be effective at boosting feelings of well-being and energy, promoting resilience and helping ease feelings of stress and anxiety.

Many fitness fanatics, gym-goers and athletes are exploring nootropics to help them achieve record-setting and competition-winning performances. On top of that, certain nootropics (such as alpha glyceryl phosphorylcholine, or Alpha-GPC for short) have shown promise in increasing strength and power (i.e., explosive performance). By positively influencing the brain and CNS, nootropics may also improve reaction time—especially when you're fatigued.104 Of course, even the slightest improvements for a competitive athlete can be game-changing.

Nootropics have also become increasingly popular ingredients in pre-workout supplements, as they are said to enhance the mind-muscle connection, making us more conscious of our movements and enhancing our ability to gain muscle from strength training—all while increasing stamina and boosting resilience. Some nootropics also support brain health through various neuroprotective effects—for instance, by providing protection against excessive oxidative stress and free radical damage. Others may promote a process called neurogenesis, which stimulates the growth of new neurons.

Unfortunately, the medical community is still divided over the use of nootropics and their efficacy. Insurance and medical systems are not set up around proactive care and health optimization; since their goal is to treat disease and a large share of profits come from pharmaceuticals designed to treat symptoms of existing diseases, there's less incentive to invest in and study proactive or preemptive health modalities.

By and large, nootropics have a high degree of safety associated with their use. However, the definition of a nootropic remains somewhat murky. As a result, nootropics encompass a broad range of compounds.

Some continue to confuse smart drugs (prescriptions and research chemicals for brain boosting), which combine a range of potentially negative and positive effects, with nootropics. But the fact is that there is a limited amount of long-term research in humans on nootropic substances of all kinds. In other words, while nootropics have a high degree of perceived safety, we must still proceed with caution with any untested or unproven substances.

CATEGORIES OF NOOTROPICS:

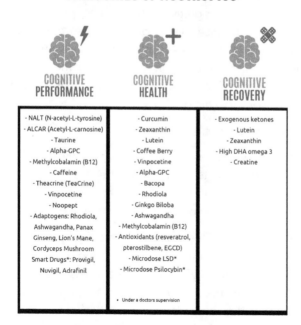

COGNITIVE PERFORMANCE	COGNITIVE HEALTH	COGNITIVE RECOVERY
- NALT (N-acetyl-L-tyrosine) - ALCAR (Acetyl-L-carnosine) - Taurine - Alpha-GPC - Methylcobalamin (B12) - Caffeine - Theacrine (TeaCrine) - Vinpocetine - Noopept - Adaptogens: Rhodiola, Ashwagandha, Panax Ginseng, Lion's Mane, Cordyceps Mushroom Smart Drugs*: Provigil, Nuvigil, Adrafinil	- Curcumin - Zeaxanthin - Lutein - Coffee Berry - Vinpocetine - Alpha-GPC - Bacopa - Rhodiola - Ginkgo Biloba - Ashwagandha - Methylcobalamin (B12) - Antioxidants (resveratrol, pterostilbene, EGCD) - Microdose LSD* - Microdose Psilocybin* * Under a doctors supervision	- Exogenous ketones - Lutein - Zeaxanthin - High DHA omega 3 - Creatine

Graphic 50 – Categories of Nootropics

Just like you should with any new nutritional strategies, talk to your doctor before trying nootropics. Also do your research and if something doesn't feel right once you've started taking it, discontinue its use.

Remember: what works for one person may not work for you, and vice versa. Because the medical community is so risk-averse, they tend to shun self-experimentation—but as you get to know your body better, you will be better able to tell what ingredients bring clarity, energy and enhanced health to your life.

Formulator's Corner
Nootropic Stacks

Basics: Nootropics often work best when they are "stacked" together. A stack is two or more cognitive-enhancing supplements that, when combined, work synergistically to produce even better results than either would on its own. One person's stack may give them clarity and focus while the same combination would give someone else anxiety, which is why it's crucial to experiment in order to determine your desired stack for your specific goal.

Useful Nootropic Stacks:

L-Theanine + Caffeine: This is probably the most common stack, as L-theanine tends to balance out the less desirable effects of caffeine (e.g., nervousness, anxiety and heart rate). The result is usually a calmer sense of heightened energy and focus.

Racetam + Choline: One of the racetams (e.g., piracetam, aniracetam, phenylpiracetam and noopept) is typically combined with choline (alpha-GPC, CDP) because the racetams all affect choline and acetylcholine use in your brain in some way. In general, racetams inhibit the breakdown of acetylcholine (an excitatory neurotransmitter), of which choline is a building block.

TeaCrine + Dynamine: These two methylxanthines, which come from the same family as caffeine and theobromine, have become popular with energy and nootropic stacks. They each have different half-lives (meaning how long they stay in the body and have an effect). Stacking caffeine with these two works for some. TeaCrine and Dynamine do not have the adaptation effect of caffeine, which doesn't work as well with chronic use. Studies have also shown they have fewer side effects like sleep disturbance. Both also stack well with a choline source.

MCT

Anyone who has even a bit of knowledge about the world of keto has likely heard of MCTs. Though not as popular as CBD, this other three-letter supplement has been known to decrease appetite, improve alertness and increase energy.

As the dietary pendulum has swung from low-fat to high-fat in recent years, it is becoming increasingly accepted that dietary fat isn't inherently bad, and that eating it doesn't necessarily put you on the fast track for getting fat. With this paradigm shift, there's been an increased importance on identifying what types of fats—and more importantly, which foods—are best. After all, not all dietary fat is created equal.

Most naturally-occurring fats—both in the foods we eat and the ones made in our bodies—contain 14-18 carbon atoms and are considered long-chain fatty acids. Fats with more than 20 carbon atoms are called very-long-chain fatty acids (such as the omega-3, DHA), while short-chain fatty acids consist of 1-6 carbons (for example, butyrate, which has four carbons and is referred to as C4).

UNDERSTANDING MCTs

CAPRYLIC ACID, C8

CAPRIC ACID, C10

CAPRIC ACID, C12

MEDIUM-CHAIN FATTY ACIDS (MCFA)

GLYCEROL BACKBONE

CAPRYLIC ACID, C8

A MEDIUM-CHAIN TRIGLYCERIDE (MCT)

Graphic 51 – Medium-Chain Triglyceride
vs Medium Chain Fatty Acids

Medium-chain fatty acids, more commonly called medium-chain triglycerides (MCTs), are fats with 6-10 carbons. The main foods containing MCTs are coconut oil, palm kernel oil, butter, milk, yogurt and cheese. For example, about 13-15 percent of the fat in coconut oil comes from the MCTs C8 and C10. Meanwhile, about 7-9 percent of the fat in butter comes from these very same MCTs.

As science has increasingly shown, MCTs can promote ketosis along with a wide range of additional health benefits:

Increased energy levels. Because of their shorter length, MCTs are metabolized and transported differently in the body than the more common long-chain fatty acids. They are easily digested and rapidly absorbed, after which they are transported directly to the liver, where they can be burned quickly and efficiently for energy.[105]

Less likely to be stored as fat. MCTs are transported directly to the liver and bypass adipose (fat) tissue, which makes them less susceptible to being stored there. What's more, while dietary fat typically provides nine calories per gram, MCTs have a lower amount of usable energy, providing only seven calories per gram. This also makes them more likely to be burned rather than stored.[106]

Increased metabolic rate. Compared to long-chain fats, MCTs have been shown to increase metabolic rate and total daily caloric expenditure. In one study, researchers found that participants who added 15-30 grams of MCTs to their diet experienced a five percent increase in metabolic rate without any other changes to diet or exercise.[107]

Enhanced satiety and appetite management. Several studies have shown that MCTs may increase satiety, reduce appetite and decrease total caloric intake. MCTs may also trigger the release of key satiety and appetite-suppressing hormones (to a greater degree than other types of fats). Also, as plenty of research seems to show, sometimes eating the right fats can actually help keep you lean.[108]

Improved weight management. Considering that MCTs may both increase metabolic rate and help manage food intake (calories out and calories in, respectively),[109] it stands to reason that supplementing and replacing normal dietary fat with MCTs can help support weight management. For metabolism, appetite and weight management benefits associated with MCTs, studies suggest a range of between 18-24 grams is best.

Increased ketone bodies. One of the most outstanding benefits of MCTs is that they readily convert to ketone bodies, an important clean-burning source of fuel that also plays a significant role as a signaling molecule. Ketones fuel the brain, but they are also used by the heart, skeletal muscles and other tissues. In addition to being a critical "alternative" energy source, ketones are also the most energy-efficient fuel and yield more usable energy than glucose or fat. Consuming MCTs is one way to boost levels of ketones, though keep in mind that fasting, ketogenic diets and intense exercise can also increase your levels of ketone bodies.

TOP 6 BENEFITS OF MCTS

- INCREASED METABOLIC RATE
- LESS LIKELY TO BE STORED AS FAT
- INCREASED ENERGY
- BETTER SATIETY (FULLNESS)
- WEIGHT MANAGEMENT
- KETONE PRODUCTION

Graphic 52 – Top Benefits of MCTs

Over the last several years, MCTs have been called the brain-activating drug, as they help to increase brain energy, treat depression, optimize intestinal flora and treat everything from autism to Alzheimer's. They are a cornerstone of a keto diet, but they can also be the cornerstone of your mental health and growth.

Formulator's Corner
MCTs

Know Your MCTs:

C6 MCT (less than 0.5 percent of coconut oil)**:** Converts quickly to ketones, but in its natural form has high GI discomfort and smells and tastes very bad, so it is often extracted out of MCT products.

C8 MCT (about 7 percent of coconut oil)**:** This is the best form of MCTs for supplementing the ketogenic diet, as it elicits the highest level of ketones in the blood at the most rapid rate compared to C10 and C12.

C10 MCT (about 7 percent of coconut oil)**:** Gets converted to ketones quickly but slightly slower than C8 MCTs.

C12 MCT (about 49 percent of coconut oil)**:** This does not get treated like an MCT by the body as it bypasses the liver to be digested, making it less effective at producing ketones than C8 and C10. It does have some antimicrobial effects, however.

C8 MCT + BHB Salts: This is a potent ketogenic energy booster, eliciting higher levels of ketones in the blood than MCT alone. My favorite combo is these plus dihydroberberine.

MCT Oil vs. Powder: Powder appears to have fewer digestive side effects than oil. It is also more versatile and easier for mixing into drinks and foods.

Blend MCTs Into Coffee or Morning Smoothies. This can boost ketone levels for energy and better cognition. This can also help with intermittent fasting, as MCT will not cause insulin levels to rise and can suppress hunger for a few more hours. You can use MCT when transitioning to a ketogenic diet since it helps to upregulate specific transport proteins that move ketones into the cells to be used for energy. MCT oil is a great base for salad dressings and an ideal way to increase fat intake on a keto diet.

CBD

If I had said 10 years ago that there would be a CBD section in the local grocery store, you would have laughed. Cannabinoids are now being hailed as the cure for nearly everything. While they aren't in fact a cure-all, they are an incredibly potent healing, anti-inflammatory and mood-enhancing supplement.

Cannabis, also known as marijuana, is the herbal source of cannabinoids and while it's been around for thousands of years, we are just beginning to understand its full range of properties and uses. Hemp is another source of cannabis, which is higher in CBD (20 percent or more) and lower in THC (less than 0.3 percent), while cannabis is lower in CBD (10 percent or more) and higher in THC (greater than 20 percent).

To understand the complex and overwhelming impact cannabinoids have on human biology, we need to better understand the system behind them.

THE ENDOCANNABINOID SYSTEM

While most people are familiar with the main systems of the human body—the nervous system, circulatory system and endocrine system, for example—there's one system that was just recently discovered: the Endocannabinoid System (ECS). It has been called the "universal" or "master" regulator. "Endo" means "in the body," so endocannabinoids are compounds our body naturally makes.[110] Still, sometimes this system, like the others, can fall out of balance: if we don't make enough endocannabinoids, we don't have the right compounds at the right time or enough receptors to receive them.

First identified in the 1990s, the ECS is the primary homeostatic regulatory system of the body. In other words, the ECS helps promote and restore balance and can be viewed as the body's natural adaptogen system, constantly working to maintain equilibrium. The ECS's salient homeostatic roles have been summarized as "relax, eat, sleep, forget and protect."[111]

The ECS helps regulate everything from the nervous system to mood and memory. One of the major effects of endocannabinoids produced by the ECS is to regulate the release of neurotransmitters like serotonin and dopamine. In addition, our ECS affects how we respond to stress and pain, impacts our digestive system and regulates our appetite and metabolism. It also influences immune function and inflammatory response. As if that wasn't enough, it even plays a role in our sleep, skin, bone health, thermoregulation and fertility.

Unlike other systems of the body (such as the nervous or circulatory systems), the ECS has receptors broadly distributed throughout the body in nearly every organ. There are two primary receptors:

- Cannabinoid receptor 1 (CB1), which is prominent throughout the central nervous system and is also found in adipose, hepatic, testicular, ocular, vascular endothelial, splenic and musculoskeletal tissues.

- Cannabinoid receptor 2 (CB2), which is primarily found in cells involved in immune function, as well as scattered through the central and peripheral nervous systems where they are associated with inflammation and addiction.[112]

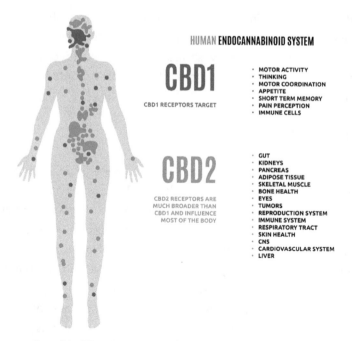

Graphic 53 – Human Endocannabinoid System[113]

The ECS plays a tremendous and pervasive body-balancing role and is one of the most important bodily systems involved in establishing and maintaining human health. With its complex actions throughout the immune system, nervous system and virtually all the body's organs, it's no surprise that the ECS and endocannabinoids have been dubbed "a bridge between body and mind."[114]

In fact, emerging research suggests that suboptimal function of the ECS (such as endocannabinoid deficiency or overactive CB1 activity) may be to blame for many physical, psychological and emotional problems that folks are facing today, including issues related to mood, stress, fear, sleep, metabolism, physical discomfort, digestive distress and more.

"Two eminent scientists at the NIH [National Institutes of Health] said that the endocannabinoid system is involved in essentially all human disease," said Raphael Mechoulam, the scientist responsible for elucidating the structures and stereochemistry of CBD and THC in the 1960s.[115]

Practically speaking, if you are the type of person who has "tried everything" to address nagging health issues but haven't given the ECS the attention it deserves, you really haven't tried everything. Addressing your ECS may be one of the most important steps you can take.

VARIETIES OF CBD

Although the ECS was only recently discovered, CBD was first isolated in 1940—more than 20 years before THC, which has historically dominated cannabis research—and was characterized structurally in 1963. While THC has well-known psychoactive properties (it is the compound responsible for producing the "high" associated with marijuana), CBD is a non-psychoactive cannabinoid. CBD accounts for up to 40 percent of the cannabis plant's extract.[116]

Phytocannabinoids, which you can think of simply as cannabinoids made by plants, have similar activity to endocannabinoids made by the body. In other words, phytocannabinoids nourish the ECS, and in doing so, they support overall wellness and help the body maintain good health. The most common example of where these compounds are found, of course, is cannabis—which was first reportedly used back in 2,600 BC in China, where it was called "the drug that takes away the mind." Two of the most noteworthy phytocannabinoids are tetrahydrocannabinol (THC) and cannabidiol (CBD). There are several other known sources of naturally-occurring phytocannabinoids—namely black pepper, clove, echinacea, green tea, panax ginseng, hops and rosemary.

While THC and CBD are by far the most studied phytocanna-binoids and get all the love, cannabis contains more than 100 phytocannabinoid compounds which act on the ECS. As an added bonus, cannabis also contains terpenes, flavonoids and over 200 ter-penoids, which give cannabis its weedy smell and are thought to influence the effects of the phytocannabinoids. This occurs via the "entourage effect," a term scientists initially coined when they dis-covered the endocannabinoid system and its combination of "active" and "inactive" synergists (in the 1990s, for example, they found "in-active" compounds enhanced the effects of the "active" endocannabinoids, AEA and 2-AG).[117]

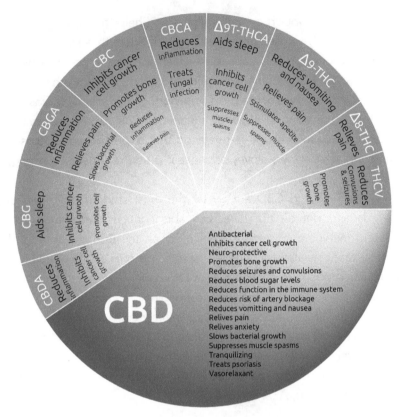

Graphic 54 – Benefits of CBD

While there is much debate about which type of CBD is better, there doesn't seem to be a clear "best" or "most effective" option at this stage. Many people point to a 2015 study published in the journal *Pharmacology & Pharmacy*, which suggested that whole-plant CBD-rich extracts (i.e., full-spectrum) showed superior therapeutic properties compared to single-molecule CBDs (i.e., CBD isolate).[118]

Having said all that, there's a dearth of research in general examining the impacts of CBD supplementation, particularly in comparison to its commercial popularity and the outstanding claims surrounding it. This is because almost all completed studies have looked exclusively at healthy volunteers using purified CBD extracts rather than full-spectrum compounds.

As the science of CBD evolves, so too will our understanding of its optimal form and dosing (which may also shift on an intra-individual basis over the course of a lifetime as the body's physiology changes). At the end of the day, it is about listening to your body, giving it what it needs and finding what works best for you.

Formulator's Corner
CBD

CBD Isolate: This is the purest form of CBD from a natural source and it benefits from the "entourage effect" of cannabinoids, terpenes and other phytocannabinoids. Synthetic CBD is fully pure and could be the safest thing to take if you are tested or concerned about even trace cannabinoids like THC. It does not have the entourage effect but is also the most predictable for that reason.

CBD + THC: These work better on pain in tandem, and CBD lowers the effective dose for the psychoactive THC. (Of note: THC is illegal in most states and many countries and you may require a prescription to buy it legally.)

CBD + Curcumin: These are two effective anti-inflammatory compounds that might work on complementary mechanisms of action.

CBD + MCTs: These can work well together since CBD may be more effective with coadministration of fats, especially ones that are uniquely metabolized and yield energy in the form of ketones.

THE GROWTH MINDSET

When discussing growth, it's crucial to never forget that it always begins with the mind.

In 2007, Carol Dweck, a professor of psychology at Stanford, authored a book called *Mindset*. In it, she described the difference between the growth mindset and the fixed mindset. The fixed mindset refers to the belief that elements of our identity such as character, intelligence and creative abilities are genetically inherent and "fixed," and are thus unchangeable. A growth mindset, however, is the belief that you can grow and improve. You can change and evolve.

As it turns out, there's far more about who we are that actually *is* changeable and adaptable over time compared to what isn't—but only if we believe it.

Since much of our success in life is dependent on the way we think, here are some tips to developing a growth mindset:

"Start with your why." As Simon Sinek's amazing book *Start with Why* explains, knowing your "why" is the best place to start. While those with a growth mindset do have a sense of purpose, it's important not to be so fixed on it that you can't change your course if new opportunities arise.

Once you have clarity on your *why*, everything becomes much simpler. Almost every decision in life can be made by asking, "Is this serving my *why* or not serving my *why*? Am I moving closer to my goal or away from it? Is this giving me positive or negative energy?"

In Japan, there is a concept called Ikigai (pronounced ee-key-guy), which translates to "a reason for being," or more simply, "a reason to jump out of bed in the morning." Ikigai has been dubbed "the Japanese formula for happiness" and "the Japanese secret to a long and happy life." The overarching idea is quite simple: When you discover your Ikigai, you unlock the secret to living a long, happy and meaningful life. Perhaps the beauty of Ikigai is that once you "find" it, you can simplify your life tremendously. In other words, you can stop chasing rabbits and start pursuing what sparks joy for you.

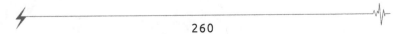

Graphic 55 – The Definition of Ikigai[119]

It is about the journey, not just the destination. Life is all about the process. The outcomes we want will happen naturally if we emphasize the right behaviors. Being immersed in the process allows us to learn, to grow and to experience things. As with every journey, there are going to be ups and downs—but by being present, we get to remain engaged, learn lessons and appreciate the process.

The beautiful is in the "broken." No one is perfect, and most people have a hard time relating to perfection anyhow. Growth requires being honest about our flaws. Making excuses can quickly turn into a bad habit. We are all imperfect, but there is beauty in our imperfections because they make us unique. All traits and personalities are advantageous in certain situations and disadvantageous in others. As a result, sometimes your strengths are your weaknesses, and vice-versa, so our smartest move is to own our imperfections. I may have been called "thunder thighs" growing up but reframing my experiences allows me to see my big legs as a source of power: I excel at volleyball, basketball and squats. I am unique. I am strong. I am proud. I own it. And so should you, whatever your uniqueness is.

Fear of failure is much worse than failure itself. The fear of failure can leave us paralyzed and terrified to try new things. But the last thing you want to do is live with regrets for not having tried. As Bruce Lee famously said, "Don't fear failure. Not failure, but low aim, is the crime. In great attempts, it is glorious even to fail." Discard the word "failure," because there is no such thing. Successful people view everything as an experiment: you either hit the jackpot or you realize, "Nope, that wasn't it." As Nelson Mandela said, "I never lose. I either win or learn." The point is not that you will never fail but that failure is a powerful teacher. As long you are out there trying, accept the results and move on to the next experiment. It is a beautiful process, so don't beat yourself up.

When you fail—*and you will when you actually try*—recognize the dramatic difference between the statements "I failed" and "I am a failure." As Zig Ziglar says, "Failure is an event, not a person. Yesterday ended last night."

As an experimenter, you must be bold and willing to try—which means you're willing to fail. When you do, you will see great rewards for your courage. President Theodore Roosevelt may have said it best in his "The Man in the Arena" speech:

"It is not the critic who counts; not the man who points out how the strong man stumbles, or where the doer of deeds could have done them better. The credit belongs to the man who is actually in the arena, whose face is marred by dust and sweat and blood; who strives valiantly; who errs, who comes short again and again, because there is no effort without error and shortcoming; but who does actually strive to do the deeds; who knows great enthusiasms, the great devotions; who spends himself in a worthy cause; who at the best knows in the end the triumph of high achievement, and who at the worst, if he fails, at least fails while daring greatly, so that his place shall never be with those cold and timid souls who neither know victory nor defeat."

Adversity is an opportunity for growth. The obstacle is the way. Getting out of our comfort zone is how we evolve and become stronger, smarter, faster, better. To get into that flow of purpose and improvement, you must be clear on your *why*. Once you can see your *why*, you'll be able to see where and how things are falling into place to make that *why* happen— and you won't have to push as hard. It can also mean people coming into your life to help you achieve that *why* because they're drawn towards your energy and sense of purpose. When you make the time to pursue your purpose and are willing to face adversity to do it, your head turns up, you get the energy you need and you pay more attention to the world. As you'll discover, sometimes the right things have been in your life all along, but you were too overwhelmed to notice them.

> **You cannot live with intent if you don't know what your own intentions are.**

Reframing is powerful. Developing a growth mindset means challenging the thought patterns you have developed over time. Instead of thinking, "What if I fail at this?" think, "Even if I fail, I will still have learned something. I won't be the only person to have ever failed at something." Become mindful of the language you use and examine your patterns of behavior. Ask yourself, "If others spoke to me the way I speak to myself, would I keep them around?" Probably not! So, identify and challenge those thought patterns.

The word "yet." Our lives become fuller when we refuse to place limits on the things we haven't done. If you add the word "yet" to your vocabulary, you can start transforming your language to believe that when it serves you and you have the time and energy, you can achieve all of your goals. You may not be focused on a specific thing right *now*, but it is possible. It is something you have not achieved ...*yet.*

You need feedback to improve. Feedback is crucial to growth; there is no way around it. Whether you give it to yourself or accept it from someone else, being in the right mindset is everything. This involves taking stock of what you tried to accomplish and why it did or did not work. While not everyone has your best interests in mind, try to take feedback mostly from those who do and then make sure their feedback is honest and constructive. Ask yourself: if you were someone else and this advice was given to you, would it make sense? If you pull your personal connection out of it, does it still make sense? Then, let it be what it is.

Celebrate your wins. We do not celebrate our wins often enough. If you're going to stay in a growth mindset and continue to grow, you need to celebrate your growth, step-by-step. If the way to achieve growth is through steps forward, then celebrate each step and take time to say, "Yes, I learned and I won." It is not just "the things that did not serve me were lessons" or "the things that did serve me were wins." It is both.

Have gratitude for where you are now. Success begets more wins and successes. When you get a big feather in your cap, it is worth celebrating with anyone who helped you along the way. Be thankful for where you have made it thus far along the journey! You are amazing. You are powerful. You can keep going. Look at all you went through to get *here*, to this exact moment in time! If you want to be a leader, a role model or someone people look to, you must believe in yourself. You must be proud of yourself. You must love yourself. If you don't love and believe in yourself, it's going to be hard for others to love and believe in you.

FOREVER YOUNG

It has been said that a body in motion stays in motion. Motion generates energy, and having, giving and receiving energy is what will keep you going for a lifetime. Aging is all about growth, but ultimately, the final destination of growth is death. As we age, we require more enhancements in order to improve not just our lifespan, but our healthspan as well.

Healthy aging is not necessarily just for those that are in their 50s, 60s, 70s, 80s and beyond; it is really for everyone. It is about making lifestyle changes that you stick with rather than radical changes that you may not be able to sustain. The great irony is that by growing mentally, physically and spiritually over time, we are able to stay young.

Are you ready to go back to the future? No, this does not involve a time-traveling DeLorean. Instead, we are going to be talking about how you can *turn back the clock on your body age.* Growth is not just about enhancing the quality of your life today; it's about how those enhancements are going to ensure you have a more energized future. I am talking about younger-looking skin and a leaner, stronger, more mobile and functional body. Are you looking for greater ease and comfort? More stamina, endurance and freedom to do the things you enjoy? I know it sounds a bit like an infomercial, but I promise it's not; this is as close to the fountain of youth as any of us are going to get.

When it comes to body age, one of the most used scientific terms thrown out is **telomeres**, which are considered a biomarker of aging. To understand telomeres, we have to start by understanding chromosomes. Chromosomes are threadlike structures within the nuclei of our cells, and each one is packed with DNA that contains all of our genetic information. Telomeres are the outermost sections of our chromosomes that serve as a kind of "cap"—kind of like the plastic tips on the end of your shoelaces. If there were no telomeres, all the genetic information contained in our chromosomes could spill into other genetic material, becoming entangled or recombined and essentially confusing our body's genetic instructions (or even causing mutations).

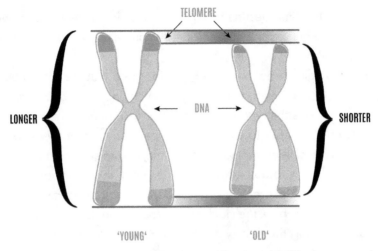

Graphic 56 - Telomeres and Aging[120]

Telomeres allow chromosomes to be replicated properly during cell division. Every time a cell divides, its telomeres get shorter. In other words, *telomere length shortens with age*. If you can test the length of your telomeres (by using TeloYears or Viome, for example), you can determine your biological age. Famed biohackers like Dave Asprey and Ben Greenfield have shown that by using many anti-aging hacks like peptides, hyperbaric chambers and IV NAD (to name a few), their biological ages are lower than their actual chronological ages. This is proof that we can slow down the aging process by influencing our biology through biohacking. While cell division and telomere shortening are normal processes of aging, certain lifestyle factors can affect the rate of telomere shortening as well—including smoking, lack of physical activity, obesity, stress, exposure to pollution and more.

If you really want to turn back the clock on your body age, there is another critical component of your cells that we need to talk about: mitochondria. Remember those? Just to jog your memory, mitochondria are the components of our cells that are responsible for providing energy in the form of a molecule called ATP. In fact, the mitochondria produce about 95 percent of the body's energy. In the absence of a dense network of efficient mitochondria, our ability to live, breathe, move, be energetic and live life to the fullest becomes severely compromised.

The truth is that the traditional view of mitochondria as "power plants" is incomplete. In fact, mitochondrial health and function may very well be the "missing link" to keeping our youthful energy throughout our entire lifespan. As it turns out, *mitochondrial dysfunction* is linked to nearly every age-related human health issue and can make your golden years far less golden.

For the most part, the way we can stay youthful is really no secret: move more, move often and move in a variety of ways. Eat primarily real food, ditch the junk and experiment with going longer periods *without* eating. Get outside and connect with nature. Spend time with those you care about—like-minded people who have similar interests and push you to be your best. Practice stress management techniques but also step outside your comfort zone (particularly when it comes to physical temperatures!) to foster growth. And if you are like Ben Greenfield or Dave Asprey, you might be injecting peptides, ozonating blood, applying serums and more (I am exploring many of these modalities right now as well).

The key is seeking inner peace, loving yourself and owning your truth, but also recklessly protecting that truth so you are always working towards a self-realized life. It's about putting more life in your years, not just more years in your life.

GROWTH AND IMMUNITY

One of the books that was fundamental to my own growth mindset was *The Four Agreements*. In it, Don Miguel Ruiz offers four absolutes by which to live a happy life: Be impeccable with your word. Don't take anything personally. Don't make assumptions. Always do your best. I challenge you as soon as you are done with this book to pick that one up. It was an inspiration for me, and I believe it will be for you as well.

I have found that the first agreement, "be impeccable with your word," is especially powerful. It's arguably the most powerful tool you have as a human; it's a tool of magic. But like a double-edged sword, your word can create the most beautiful dream or it can destroy everything around you.

I'm not just talking about how and what you say to *others*. More critical is how we talk to and describe ourselves. As the poet Hafiz is credited with saying, "The words you speak become the house you live in." Along those lines, "I am" are the two most powerful words in the world, and the words that follow them follow us in our lives. Too often, we beat ourselves down with negative self-talk and become life-long victims of negativity and self-criticism programmed by others and ourselves. Instead, you need to create patterns of self-love and self-acceptance. You need to reprogram your thoughts and self-talk and speak yourself into your power, your truth and manifest your best life.

> **"I am" are the two most powerful words in the world, and the words that follow them follow us in our lives.**

Just as Ruiz's guide suggests, an energized life starts with a series of simple steps. You don't need to be a rocket scientist or a billionaire or a supermodel to live it. You just have to make clear and conscious choices about the type of life you want to live and how you will support it.

When we find the ways to enhance our lives today—whether through establishing a growth mindset, finding the supplements that increase our vitality and slow down the aging process or just challenging ourselves to grow every day—we will discover that we are not only increasing our healthspan but are also more engaged in life.

I encourage you to challenge yourself. We all get to choose our happiness, and we can do that wherever we are right now. Even if we're not happy with our job, the number on the scale or our marriage, we can still choose at this moment to shift our perspective. We are going to find the positives in our journey and accept that it is all part of our great story. It is all a part of growth.

Immunity and resilience have been common themes throughout the book—and for good reason. Resilience is the path to a robust, renewable supply of vibrant energy. One of the silver linings of COVID-19 is that it's shifted immunity to center stage, as we acknowledge that taking steps to support a healthy immune system shouldn't be an afterthought or part-of-the-year type of thing, but rather an all-the-time priority if we want our body's defenses at their peak potential while protecting us from foreign invaders.

As an advocate of preventative as opposed to reactive healthcare, I'm happy to see that people are taking their health more seriously. From elders all the way down to the youngest kiddos, everyone is paying better attention to personal hygiene and there has never been, to my knowledge, more accessible information about germs and prevention (though whether it's accurate is a different story for a different day).

One of the most hopeful aspects that has emerged from the rise in preventative measures is a greater understanding and appreciation for the immune system. Unmatched in complexity, the immune system is an intricate network of specialized tissues, organs, cells and chemicals designed to protect *you* from toxins and pathogens.

Like virtually everything else in the body, it's not about more, more, more—or more appropriately, boost, boost, boost—when it comes to supporting the immune system. Rather, a healthy, robust and properly functioning immune system is one that's balanced and maintained within a normal, healthy state.

Of course, I strongly believe in using an array of supplements to help optimize the immune system to support a robust and proper immune response. Before we get to my top immune-support supplements (see the Formulator's Corner), let's talk about some "big guns" that can really go

It's about putting more life in your years, not just more years in your life.

a *long* way in keeping you healthy. These are lifestyle and prevention strategies that can help optimize immune function—or more simply, lower your chances of having to fend off bad bugs in the first place.

Move your body, but don't overdo it. Regular exercise is a powerful tool to strengthen the immune system. But too much heavy exercise—like soul-crushing workouts—is just as bad as being sedentary. Both can increase your odds of getting sick. Stick to 30-60 minutes of exercise per day at a moderate level most of the time when you're not doing HIIT.

Chill out. While short-term stress can enhance the immune system, it suppresses the immune system when it's chronic and persistent. Studies show that psychological stress increases the risk of illnesses like the common cold in a dose-dependent manner. In other words, the more stressed you are, the more likely you are to get sick.

Make sure you're effectively managing stress by doing things like meditating 10-30 minutes a day, practicing yoga, partaking in daily prayer and practicing gratitude. Something as simple as taking three slow and deep breaths every hour while thinking of something you're grateful for can lower stress hormones and improve immunity.

Get your beauty rest. If you want to increase your odds of getting infected with a virus like coronavirus, don't get enough sleep. Sleeping fewer than seven hours can make you *three times* more likely to get sick. Like stress, a lack of sleep suppresses the immune system by reducing natural killer cell activity, amongst other things. Make sure you're getting seven to nine hours of quality sleep per night. You can increase the quality of your sleep by making sure your bedroom is dark, cool and quiet (though using a white noise machine or fan really helps).

Clean up your diet. This means eating healthful foods *and* ditching the junk food. For starters, load up on immune-boosting nutrients from foods, like vitamins A (sweet potatoes and liver), C (citrus fruits and cruciferous veggies), D (eggs and mushrooms) and E (dark leafy greens), as well as zinc (beef and pumpkin seeds) and selenium (Brazil nuts and sardines).

This is the perfect time to weed out refined carbohydrates (like added sugar and refined grains) and highly-refined vegetable oils (like soybean, canola, corn, cottonseed, safflower and sunflower oils), which contribute to persistent, unhealthy inflammation and impair the body's natural immune response. It is also a good idea to limit (or better yet, avoid) alcohol and, of course, to avoid smoking.

Stay connected. This can be challenging, especially during dire times that call for you to stay home and limit public gatherings. But loneliness and social isolation are serious threats to immunity, lowering internal defenses and making you more prone to getting sick. For example, research published in the *Proceedings of the National Academy of Sciences* shows that loneliness can alter immune system cells in a way that increases vulnerability to illness.

Strong connections and social support, on the other hand, nourish, protect and support the immune system—perhaps through their potent stress-relieving properties. Challenging as it may be, make every effort to stay connected with those you care about—even if it's just through phone calls and virtual meetings. While you're at it, be a good neighbor; check in with the members of your tribe to see how you can help.

Get outdoors. Distancing yourself from others and limiting your trips to public places does not mean you need to be holed up inside; this is in fact arguably one of the worst things you can do for your well-being and immune system. According to the Environmental Protection Agency (EPA), the levels of indoor air pollutants are often two to five times higher than outdoor levels (and in some cases, can exceed 100 times that of outdoor levels). In other words, the air inside is often more harmful than the air outside.

Beyond that, spending time outdoors can boost mood, lower feelings of stress and anxiousness, boost energy levels and work wonders for the immune system. For example, studies have shown that spending time in nature increases activity of natural killer cells (NK), which are critical components of the innate immune system. Scientists think that breathing in phytoncides—antimicrobial compounds released into the air by trees and other plants—increases levels of NK and their associated virus-killing compounds.

I live on a lake and love to jump in, even in the winter. I work from home and I walk around the lake every morning and take 30-minute sunshine breaks at least twice while I am working during the day. My autonomic nervous system thrives on it. My friend and fellow biohacker Kayla Osterhoff says it best: "I got 99 problems and 87 of them are cured by standing outside, barefoot in the sunshine." Boom.

GROWTH SUMMARY

- Growth is about enhancement. It is about recognizing the gap between our bio-individuality and the demands of the modern world and finding the formulas to close the gap and launch us into the future. With the right time and attention, anyone can develop their highest potential and create a lifestyle tailored to their individual biology. But you can't discover what works until you've done the deep self-work and experimented a bit. Instead of pretending you're someone else, the greatest biohack of all is to become confident in your own skin, grant yourself grace and own who you authentically are!

- One of the greatest biohacks to growing physically, mentally and spiritually is intermittent fasting (IF), which results in your body being in a post-absorptive state where it can focus on maintenance and recovery instead of digesting and building.

- Diet and exercise can take us incredibly far in our health journey, but supplements help us transcend the barriers that diet and exercise can't. Nootropics can boost focus, concentration and perceived feelings of energy. When used carefully, they can acutely enhance cognitive function and protect and repair the brain. The second core supplement is MCTs, which promote ketosis, as well as a wide range of health benefits including treatment of depression and everything from autism to Alzheimer's. The third is CBD, which can be an incredibly potent healing, anti-inflammatory and mood-enhancing supplement.

- The endocannabinoid system can be viewed as the body's natural adaptogen system, constantly working to maintain equilibrium and helping to regulate everything from the nervous system to mood and memory. The ECS's outstanding homeostatic roles have been summarized as "relax, eat, sleep, forget and protect."

If you've always felt "something off" about you, addressing your ECS may be one of the most important steps you can take.

- Ikigai is the Japanese concept meaning "a reason for being," or more simply, "a reason to jump out of bed in the morning." Research shows that people with a growth mindset have a sense of purpose. It is important to keep the big picture in mind, but not be so fixed on it that you can't change your course should an opportunity arise. In order to live energized lives, we must discover what works for our individual biology. We must reject the one-size-fits-all approach and create a diet and regimen that works for our specific needs, challenges and schedules.

- If you want others to believe in you and see you as a leader and role model, you must believe in yourself. Developing a growth mindset means challenging your thoughts and the thought patterns you have developed over time. As we age, we require more enhancements in order to not only improve our lifespan, but also our healthspan.

Resource Hacks

Growth

Pay Attention to Your Words and Thoughts: Replace negative thoughts with more positive ones. Watch your thoughts and become your own guide. Intend to think more positive thoughts and hold yourself to it.

5-Minute Journal: Plan your day with the 5-Minute Journal (through the app or book) to be more effective, then take a few minutes in the evening to look back on your day. This can calm the mind.

Create a Vision Board:

Think about your goals, dreams and hopes.

Divide them into categories such as: relationships, finance, personal growth, mental, physical and spiritual.

Write down what you hope to achieve in each area.

Use a free Canva.com account to create a template for your board.

Use Pinterest, Google or personal photos to find images that correspond to your dreams.

Create your vision board. Save the digital version to your phone and computer so that you see it daily.

Remind yourself of your goals and look at them daily to start seeing them come to life.

*For live links, updated content, bonus graphics
and a hidden chapter, go to
EnergyFormulaBook.com*

YOUR TRIBE SURVEY

Do you feel you have a strong support system of family and friends around you?		
Yes, I have a strong support system of people around me who believe in me and encourage me.	(3)	
I have some family and friends who support me but also have a few close to me who are not supportive.	(2)	
No, I am missing this element of support from friends and family in my life.	(1)	
If you took on the traits of the five people closest to you, would you be happy with the result?		
Yes! I purposely surround myself with people who are actively working towards improvement in their life.	(3)	
Mostly. Of the five people closest to me, most live lives I would be proud to emulate.	(2)	
Sadly, no. The traits of the five people closest to me are not traits I want to share.	(1)	
How would you rate the quality of your current relationships?		
Excellent. I have quality relationships with family and friends and feel satisfied with the people I surround myself with	(3)	
My relationships could be better, but I do have several close relationships that I value.	(2)	
The relationships I have right now are struggling and need improvement.	(1)	
Is community something you prioritize within your relationships and environment?		
Yes. I value and prioritize community; it is important to me on many different levels.	(3)	
I value community but do not often put myself out there to make it happen on a regular basis.	(2)	
Community is not something that has been a priority in my life and I am not sure how to make it happen.	(1)	

Do you have someone in your life who is actively mentoring you, and is there someone you are also doing the same thing for?		
Yes. I am involved in a mentoring relationship where I both receive and give counsel on a regular basis.	(3)	
I have been mentored before in the past but am not currently in this type of relationship.	(2)	
No, I do not have a mentor and have never had this kind of relationship.	(1)	
Do you feel connected to those around you and enjoy strong bonds of friendship and community in your life, or are you going it alone?		
I feel very connected to those around me and enjoy strong relationships and community—together these make me a better person!	(3)	
I am somewhat connected to others but still feel alone at times and have a desire for stronger relationships.	(2)	
I often feel alone and disconnected from others. I need and want better relationships so that I feel more supported in life.	(1)	
Are you ready to begin biohacking your life and improving it for the better?		
Yes! I am ready to do this! I have already taken steps to begin biohacking my life and am ready to explore other avenues of self-improvement for the benefit of myself and others.	(3)	
I think I'm ready, but I'm still a little unsure. I want to improve my life but need some guidance to get there.	(2)	
I want to get there but am hesitant to begin. My life needs a complete overhaul!	(1)	
YOUR TOTAL		

7-11 points: You have got some work to do! This book is a great place to start!

12-16 points: You are heading in the right direction! Keep at it!

17-21 points: You are really on the ball! Only small tweaks are needed to be your best self!

Chapter 6: Your Tribe: Cultivating Deep and Meaningful Connections

"And it turns out that tribes—not money, not factories— can change our world, can change politics, can align large numbers of people. Not because you force them to do something against their will, but because they wanted to connect."

—Seth Godin

In 2018, Harvard University released an incredible study conducted over the course of 75 years reviewing a subset of men and women working and living in and outside of Boston. The participants came from varied ethnic, racial, socioeconomic and religious backgrounds. The goal of the study was to examine the best determinants for quality and longevity of life. Was it the color of your skin? How much money you made or where you came from? Where you lived or what you did for a living?

What they discovered was that none of these superficial traits mattered. Money, race and occupation were irrelevant. The single factor for healthy aging was the quality of people's relationships. The bottom line is that how happy we are in our relationships can have a tremendous impact on both how well and how long we live. This Harvard Study of Adult Development found that the people who were most satisfied in their relationships—people who leaned into relationships with family, with friends and with community—at age 50 were the healthiest at age 80, and they lived longer, happier lives (up to 8 years longer, according to this study).[121]

Scientists have identified a similar trend in what is referred to as Blue Zones. Blue Zones are areas across the world where there are significant populations of centenarians—people who have lived to be over 100 years old. What they found was that though diet, exercise and not smoking were common variables, the biggest effect on longevity in these areas was the shape and quality of the community's relationships.[122]

A few years back, my wife and I had the chance to host an exchange student in our home. Our neighbors typically hosted one student a year, but that year, they were accidentally assigned two students of the same nationality. They asked if we could take one of them so that both students could still come to America. We agreed and were lucky enough to host a young woman from Sardinia: Claudia. She was going to a local high school, but during her year with us, we had the opportunity to meet her Italian boyfriend and her family. The next year, we traveled to Sardinia to stay with them. She is now like a daughter to me, and her family is truly my family.

Ironically, what I learned from the visit was the same lesson I experienced from saying yes to my neighbors' request: when we open our home to new people and build tribes within our communities, our lives become immeasurably richer.

By going out into the world and inviting people into our homes and hearts, we learn more about the world—and about ourselves. We celebrate our identities by taking part in and building communities that best reflect our ideals and principles. Though much has been made of the Blue Zone diet, what I experienced in Sardinia was that it wasn't just about the food the people were eating; it was about the tribe and routines surrounding them.

Through those bonds, they lead happier, more productive lives. They approach each day with the type of calm, focused energy that so many Americans lack. In Sardinia, people wake up and appreciate their morning before starting the day. They work and are incredibly productive, but there is a flow to their labor. They do not see work as their primary purpose, but rather as a means to support their lives and families. In the evening, they sit down for dinner, usually with a large group of extended family, enjoying fresh, local wine and food and deeply connecting with the company around them.

They will usually sit for two or three hours and have a communal fellowship where they really enjoy each other. It is so much more than just eating or drinking wine. It is about having a support structure that you can look forward to every day. This creates real accountability between community members, as they are each other's therapists in a way, too—they open up over the table. Yes, they talk and laugh, but they also really listen to each other, which leads to rich and reliable daily connections. There are also no cell phones to be found anywhere. No distractions. They are just present—with the food and the wine, but most importantly, with each other in that moment.

Though they eat pasta and bread, everything is made with whole foods, with *real* and unadulterated ingredients that are fresh and local …and nine times of 10, the people make their meals themselves in their houses. As a result of being so involved in the process, they truly know every ingredient.

Formulator's Corner
Anti-Aging Polyphenol Supplements (and their Respective Foods)

Polyphenols are plant-derived compounds with a variety of biological and health properties. They are best known for being the most abundant antioxidants found in food. More than 500 different polyphenols have been identified in foods. Most polyphenols have antioxidant and anti-inflammatory properties, and they may have protective effects on mitochondrial functioning.

Certain polyphenols may enhance mitochondrial efficiency and stimulate mitochondrial biogenesis—which is science-speak for increasing the size and number of mitochondria. They stimulate autophagy (otherwise known as cellular detoxification) and promote mitophagy (which refers to "cleaning out" the mitochondria).

Here are some of the most noteworthy polyphenols and the foods in which you can find them. You can also add supplements—and for anti-aging effects, that may be the most appropriate route to take, as you would need considerably higher amounts of them than you could normally get from eating the foods considered "high" in polyphenols.

Anti-Aging Polyphenol Supplements
(and their Respective Foods - continuation)

Resveratrol: Japanese knotweed can be taken as a supplement, along with peanuts, raspberries, blueberries and grape skins (red wine).

Many people drink a small amount of dry red wine like Cabernet Sauvignon every other day, and I think that's a perfectly acceptable thing to do. Although that will provide some resveratrol, the amount is going to be much lower than what would be needed to promote anti-aging effects.

EGCG: Green tea, cocoa and blackberries.

Pterostilbene: Blueberries and pterocarpus marsupium.

Quercetin: Onions, apples, oranges, bell peppers, tea and green vegetables.

Chlorogenic Acid: Coffee.

Kaempferol: Parsley, kiwifruit, oranges, potatoes, apples, strawberries, grapes, watermelon and onions.

Fisetin: Strawberries, apples, persimmons and onions.

Anthocyanins: Berries, apples, cherries, grapes, plums, red cabbage, red onions and radishes.

Polyphenomenal: Bulletproof makes one of my favorite supplements that combines many of these polyphenols, called Polyphenomenal.

Finding people who I could count on but who I also knew would hold me accountable has been key in my journey. I didn't need people telling me how great I was all the time or breaking me down constantly, either. I needed people who could tell me when I was lit up and pursuing my truth but who could also let me know when I was being inauthentic and losing my way.

The goal is to find an authentic circle of people you know and trust —people that challenge you to grow but who are also there for and support you. Though social media is amazing for building and strengthening connections, it can also lead to a lot of unsolicited advice and opinions from people who aren't entirely qualified to give it. If we allow them in, those opinions can have a profound and powerful influence on our thoughts, behaviors and actions. The good news, though, is that the choice is yours. As Les Brown says: "Someone's opinion of you does not have to become your reality."

Many of those people don't actually know your life; they know *their* life and they are projecting it onto you. Beware of who you are listening to when you're being given advice, criticism or even support. Ninety percent of these social media comments can be positive, but there is always that 10 percent who will project their insecurities (and will sometimes attach extrapolated and misunderstood science or "facts" as support) to make you feel insecure.

I am reminded of the South African concept "Ubuntu," which is best described as "I am because of who we all are." In other words, Ubuntu places emphasis on solidarity, compassion, respect, human dignity and collective unity. Ubuntu focuses on reciprocity, humanity and morality in the interest of building and maintaining community with mutual caring. According to anti-apartheid and human rights activist Desmond Tutu, a person with Ubuntu is one with self-assurance who is open and available to others and affirms them. Perhaps the spirit of Ubuntu can best be illustrated by those who have propelled the world toward oneness: Martin Luther King, Jr., Mahatma Gandhi, Mother Theresa and Nelson Mandela.

There is nothing more important than the relationships we have, which is why we must be conscious about the people we choose to have in our lives. Legendary motivational speaker Les Brown, who I quoted just a few paragraphs ago, has been very influential to me in this particular area. He's known for coining the acronym (and hashtag) OQP, which stands for "only quality people." This means that if you want success, fulfillment, energy and so on, you should surround yourself with OQP. As Brown says, "Align yourself with people you can learn from, people who want more out of life, people who are stretching and searching and seeking some higher ground in life."

There's also the flow approach, which dictates that if you live your truth with purpose and passion, your tribe will find you. It will happen authentically, without too much effort on your part. As renowned psychologist Carl Jung is quoted as saying, "An old alchemist gave the following consolation to one of his disciples: 'No matter how isolated you are and how lonely you feel, if you do your work truly and conscientiously, unknown friends will come and seek you.'"

We cannot understand the world by reading and watching filtered media on our phones. As Dr. Amy Shah says, "We are a sad generation with happy pictures." Think about that for a second. We must put down our cell phones and connect for real with each other. We need to look people in the eye and deeply, truly see them. This is more important than ever, as these days we are often trapped behind masks, unable to connect in the way that has been so natural to us for millennia. We need to go out of our way to make simple human connections—and see how quickly we can make a difference in so many lives (even seemingly "random" ones) by doing so.

There is nothing more important than the relationships we have, which is why we have to be conscious about the people we choose to have in our lives.

We are in a rare moment where we can reset everything if we want to. We can reevaluate our work, our relationships, our priorities and our routines to determine who and what really reflects our purpose and passion.

If the number one determinant of longevity is the quality of your relationships, it might be time to make the conscious choice you've been applying to experimentation, nutrition, exercise, routines and growth to the people and communities you allow into your life. Into your inner circle. Into your tribe.

FIND YOUR TRIBE

Over the last several years, I've discovered a community of people who were tired of living in the chaos—people who refer to themselves as biohackers. I know "biohacking" can sound a little intimidating and I will admit, there are some people in the community who are. Some members are interested in putting sensors and hardwire in their bodies to measure vital signs and performance, which can make some people gulp. In a way, the marketing around biohacking is extreme and perhaps overly masculine—and to be honest, it may be part of the reason why I was initially drawn to it! After all, if you're a man who feels like you're not strong enough, smart enough or high-performing enough, wouldn't you go to extreme lengths to feel strong, smart and powerful?

While the biohackers (many of whom are now close friends and confidants) *do* have plenty of proven methods and techniques to make your biology work better for you, I realized that many of the people I'd idolized in the community had deep human problems of their own that weren't obvious from the outside—and, much like me, they weren't advertising them very openly. The more time I spent in the community, the more I realized that what it was really about was different than what was advertised.

In 2019, I had the chance to go on a two-week retreat with some biohackers in Iceland. I was there with a number of other growth-minded people committed to a more attuned and healthy way of life, and together we shared amazing fresh and healthy meals as well as mind and body workout sessions. We went for polar

I learned from an early age that anyone is capable of huge and transformative change, at any time. I know because I achieved it myself.

dips and toured the hot springs, but more than anything, we engaged in deep and intimate conversations with one another. We developed ideas, built plans and created friendships that will last the rest of my life (Kayla, Kristen, Eugenia, Elena, Nic, Pavel, and so many more).

In Iceland, every night at dinner we would share something about ourselves and something we were grateful for. The friendships we formed not only made the two weeks a special retreat from daily life, but also reinvigorated the lives we were choosing to lead. There is just something so low-key and device-minimal about Iceland that is almost otherworldly. We all felt transported and absolutely transformed.

I saw clearly during that time that I'm different from the most hardcore members of the biohacking community because I've always been far more interested in our *software* than our hardware. I learned from an early age that anyone is capable of huge and transformative change, at any time. I know because I achieved it myself.

As a biohacker, I've learned the power that can be created when people rally together as a group and say we will not accept the myths that have been force-fed to us by those that stand to profit from them, whether it comes from outdated medical wisdom, distortions from the pharmaceutical industry or wherever else. The scientific discoveries the community has pushed forward are huge, but the key is that it came from a group of people coming together to make the world a better place. Most importantly, they were making it a better place for their community first—and that part is easy to overlook.

I love the science of biohacking, but I also love the creativity of it. I love the fact that we get to be designers of our own fates, our bodies, our relationships and our lives, and I especially love the idea that to change the world, we need to create the change within. Even as we look forward to what technology, supplements and advancements in health and medicine can bring us, part of what biohackers have helped the world to realize is that we need to put more faith in the human spirit and in human traditions …because they have worked for us since the beginning of history. We must see what parts of modern life are blocking us from our traditions and more natural ways of being so we can tap into our truest selves, integrating the past and the future to take us all the way there. When we look to the past, we can see that one of the biggest changes has been our relationships with one another.

YOUR **PAST**   **YOU**   YOUR **FUTURE**

\>\>\>\>\>\>\>\>\>\>\>\>\>\>\>   <<<<<<<<<<<<<<<<<<

METHODS FROM THE PAST, THAT WE'VE KNOWN FOR YEARS:

'BIOHACKS' USED BY **ATHLETES, MILLIONAIRES AND ENTREPRENEURS** TO ACHIEVE A BETTER LIFE:

MEDITATION/PRAYER
e.g. prayer, quiet time, reflection

GRATITUDE
e.g. affirmations, gratitude journal

JOURNALING
e.g. creative writing, day planning, goal setting

DANCING
e.g. salsa, club, home sunbathing

SUNBATHING
e.g. laying out, taking a walk

WHOLE FOOD
e.g. paleo, non-processed food

PLANT MEDICINE
e.g. microdosing, journeying with medical/therapy support

MINDSET
e.g. Mindful Meditation, Journaling

TECHNOLOGY
e.g. Devices that track your health, DNA analysis, microbiome test

SLEEP
e.g. Blue Light Blockers, Red Light, ChiliPad

EXERCISE
e.g. Blood Flow Restriction, HIIT

SUPPLEMENTATION
e.g. Nootropics, Peptides, Exogenous ketones

NUTRITION
e.g. The Ketogenic Diet, Intermittent fasting, Paleo

PHARMACEUTICALS
e.g. Microdosing LSD, other drugs

Graphic 57 – Blending Methods of Ancestral Wisdom with Modern Day Tools and Technology

My time in Iceland made me think about how we end up turning into the five people with whom we surround ourselves (shout out to my "Spirit Birds" Kayla, Kirsten, Eugenia and Elena). We tune into their energies and personalities and usually end up sharing both their good and bad attributes. I look at five of my closest friends who each bring out a different quality in my own life and the traits that they epitomize:

Resilience. My friend Todd is a businessman. Sure, he is successful, but that is not the point. What makes Todd so special is that he is resilient. He has been through so much tragedy and maybe because of that, he recognizes that success is fleeting. He focuses on becoming a better person rather than a richer one. When he speaks to you, you can tell that he is not thinking about anything but the conversation you're having. You feel truly present in his presence and it is a quality I have tried to emulate.

Integrity. My friend Keith (who is equally matched by his amazing wife, Michelle) is a successful entrepreneur and knows everyone in the keto, paleo, biohacking and consciousness space, but he does not really even seem to notice. He does not do much social media and shies away from any type of self-promotion. When he goes to conferences, he acts like any other participant, attending guest lectures and asking questions, even if the conference is his own. He takes the time to be with people.

More importantly, he has seen the pain and sadness I carry (as well as my joy), and he has been a guide and a resource throughout my transformation. He "holds space"—quiet, powerful, still, unwavering. He is there for me and for others in his life. So present. His work, while incredible and important, isn't his business. His work is *us*—me, you and himself. He is the real deal and a reminder that while many of us can get caught up in the hype of the work and achievement, growth and connection are our real reason for being here. He is a monument to that vision.

Kindness. Every other week, my friend John and his wife Carol host a full day of volleyball games at their house. They invite everyone over, cook and spend a lot of money on beer, bottled water and amazing food to grill, even though they are not overly wealthy. When I saw guests take all the leftovers home, I asked John about it. "Hey, if they need it more than me, it's theirs," was his response. But John and Carol are more than amazing hosts; they have also built a community of people who love volleyball and have become better friends through that shared activity. John does not even play that much anymore, but he has no plans of stopping the get togethers. As he said, he is not in it for the game but for the friendships.

Brilliance. My friend Jakob is *that* guy. The one who could solve a crime in 24 hours. He has an Elon Musk brain which allows him to compute inputs like a master. He also happens to be a great guy, so he can not only offer an intellectual answer to your quandary, but also do it with heart and humor. He is also the kindest and most patient father of two beautiful girls who are like nieces to me. What I have realized is that having knowledge is not enough; it is how you communicate that knowledge that ultimately defines your impact. I have learned from Jakob that being the smartest guy in the room is not enough—in fact, it can be lonely. I need to also have humility and humor to develop the life and relationships that bring me joy and not isolation.

Loyalty. I would say this trait could apply to all my friends because I deeply value loyalty, but my business partner Kylin and I have been through a lot together. Whenever you are entangled financially with another person there is always cause for concern, but with Kylin, I know that we both have each other's backs and we recognize that every business we have together is a little like having a child. We share a special entity that's more than just a business, and we want to keep it safe and help it succeed. That means we need to be honest and on the same page with each other. Together, we are better able to support and promote one another's dreams.

Accountability. A key yet often overlooked or underappreciated member of your tribe is your coach. You *have* to have a coach, or what Craig Ballantyne refers to as "professional accountability." Research shows that when you are accountable to a professional, you are going to get expert advice

> **If we build a tribe of like-minded people, we never have to be alone again. But it's more than that; together, and I actually mean this, we can change the world.**

and you are going to do the work.[123] It can't be friend or a buddy; what you need is somebody to draw the hard line and hold you accountable. A coach is someone who understands where you have been *and* where you want to be so he or she can guide you along the way. Ideally, you would have a life coach, a business coach, a fitness coach, and a mental health coach. Start with what you can afford and if you can't afford much, get someone who's at least one step in front of you and willing to trade with you in mentorship (meaning they mentor you in a skill and hold you accountable and you, in turn, reciprocate and provide them value back).

Dr. Rob Wildman took me under his wing at Dymatize and helped me become one of the leading figures in my industry. I worked extremely hard for Rob in return and would go to (and through) the wall for him. He taught me to always use the word "we" not "me" when referring to any work we did...even if I did it alone. We were stronger together, more unified, and it lifted all of us up. He wasn't just teaching me about the supplement industry, but how to be a good executive and leader. I have also found that being involved with various masterminds provides many mentors, teachers and people who challenge me and my self-limiting beliefs in the best way.

Surrounding yourself with OQP provides a powerful layer of social support, accountability and inspiration. It pushes you, in a good way, to level up. As the saying goes, if you want to get far, you're going to do it standing on the shoulders of giants—not alone, and not by yourself. For real evolution, you need mentors and coaches; in other words, you need a personal positive growth team from like-driven (but not necessarily like-minded) peers.

As you level up, remember to pay it forward—just like those who have helped you. My greatest hope is that after reading this book, you will enjoy so much radiant energy, vibrant health and wild success that you will share your story, encouragement and inspiration with others—and that together, our reach might contagiously and infinitely expand like concentric ripples of water from a stone we dropped in the pond together.

We create the tribe who can help us self-realize, but more importantly, who we can help to do the same. If we are hustling and grinding, we are not truly seeing or listening to other people around us.

People out there are hurting. People need us. There are people out there who are potential game-changers for us, who can radically change our lives. If we're just keeping our heads down, trying to get through the day, we'll miss them. We are often in the "right place at the right time," but we aren't always in the right frame of mind to recognize those opportunities.

Finding the time to be with our tribe is critical not only for our well-being but also to support our life choices. Though our families can be wonderful support systems—and my wife Shelley is at the top of that list—those who aren't related to us by blood or by marriage but share a similar mindset and principles can be the ideal unobjective touchstone for us and our work. They can help us create the kind of fellowship that can not only extend our lifespan, but also immensely enhance it.

If we build a tribe of like-minded people, we never have to be alone again. But it's more than that; together, and I actually mean this, we can change the world.

BIOHACKTIVISM

Being a biohacker means optimizing yourself and being out in front of where "scientific consensus" is. Unfortunately, biohacking has become so focused on the "N of 1" that we have forgotten how important the tribe is to our journey. The "quantified-self" of biohacking can become a very lonely and self-absorbed world, leading people to get obsessive and addicted to self-experimenting. That is not how we make real change in the world.

After a few years of being deeply involved in the biohacking communities, I began to realize that it was time to go beyond biohacking. It was time to take that message out into the world and build bigger and better communities around it. I realized that we need to become more than biohackers; we had to become biohacktivists.

Biohacktivism is about hacking your biology not just for your own betterment, but for the world around you. When your head is up and you're living an energized life, you can pay more attention to that world. You can have more empathy, establish deeper connections and help others do the same. By engaging in a community and a tribe that shares the same beliefs—not to mention resources, suggestions and support —we can draw more energy from the world around us and be motivated and inspired by our peers who are leading the way. After all, transformation demands to be shared.

Being a biohacker means optimizing yourself and being out in front of where "scientific consensus" is.

Once we're more conscious of the choices we're making, once we've taken control of our routines and life, once we have more energy and joy, we naturally want to share ourselves and our discoveries with other people. They say misery loves company, but I don't think that's true—it's more like misery hates company (at least, it hates real, *quality* company). If misery hates company, joy is the host of the party. When you're living in joy, you're finally empowered to be your true self.

We complain so much about what's going on outside of ourselves, but we fail to see where we have the power to change it. Gandhi was right: we should be the change we wish to see in the world.[124]

Through that change, we realize we can start helping others make similar changes. Energy is contagious, and once you begin to increase your own, you will find people beginning to naturally gravitate toward you. They will want what you have, and it will become your responsibility to show them how they can get it.

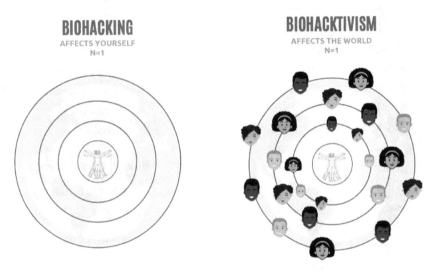

Graphic 58 – Biohacking vs. Biohacktivism

As I said at the beginning of this book, the world feels increasingly overwhelming. It seems like we are being inundated with crisis after crisis—mass shootings, potential pandemics, global warming. It is amazing any of us get out of bed in the morning.

If misery hates company, joy is the host of the party.

We have two choices: we can either put our heads down as we become paralyzed with fear and wait for it to be over, or we can become empowered to change ourselves, our communities and ultimately, the world! We can create a world that looks for the best in the future while still honoring the past—and in the end, we can bring everyone into the dash.

SPREAD THE LOVE

My wife and I don't have children, but we recognize that taking care of something is an important part of community building. No matter who you are or how much money you have (or do not have), there is no better feeling than walking through the door to find someone who is excited to see you.

In our family, we have a dog and cat, Maya and Shinobi respectively, that we love like children (our "fur babies"). Not only do they bring us immeasurable love, but they also require that we show up for them. Whether we feed them, walk with them, play with them or take them to the park, animals help connect you to the world outside yourself.

Our human relationships are deeply valuable, but they are complicated. Pets make your house feel like a home. They can be critical members of your tribe (or pack!)

Formulator's Corner
Mood Boosting Supplements

SAMe: A methylator that stimulates the synthesis of key neurotransmitters, exerting an antidepressant effect.

Zembrin: Enhances cognitive function and inhibits serotonin breakdown for a little lift. Works well with 5-HTP.

5-HTP: Supports positive mood and is a precursor to serotonin. Works well with Zembrin.

High DHA Fish Oil: Helps with phospholipids in the brain and is effective in reducing symptoms of depression.

Saffron: May exert antidepressant effects by balancing levels of dopamine, norepinephrine and serotonin.

Vitamin D3: Low levels of vitamin D have been associated with depression. Both the sun and supplements can help.

Magnesium: Helps promote calmness and ease tension, allowing better sleep.

Vitamin B6 (P5P): Supports neuronal health and nerve conduction and helps your body make serotonin.

Vitamin B12: (methylcobalamin): Plays a role in synthesizing and metabolizing serotonin.

GABA (PharmaGABA is my favorite version): Helps relieve stress and promotes emotional well-being.

When I think about change, I am often reminded of the story about the starfish: One day, a father and daughter are walking along a beach covered in starfish. The father begins to pick up the starfish and throw them back into the sea, explaining to his daughter that they will die if they stay on the beach. But even after throwing many into the ocean, many more remain on the sand.

The daughter stops and says, "Dad, look how many more starfish there are. How will that ever make a difference?"

The father picks up one more starfish, tosses it into the water and says, "It made a difference to that one."

Not everyone is ready for, willing or able to change. This is just as true for the people in your home as it is for work colleagues—but that doesn't mean you shouldn't keep trying to make a difference. Being a change-maker is hard, and it can feel like your efforts are often for naught. But all it takes is one person to make a meaningful difference. As Theodore Roosevelt said, "Start where you are. Use what you have. Do what you can. It will be enough."

Work is the one place people typically think love does not belong. The fact is that we spend so much of our time at work that we often grow to know, respect and appreciate our colleagues and business partners. The old way of doing business was to keep everything impersonal and austere so people wouldn't get their feelings hurt. That not only turned the 10+ hour workday into an endurance slog, but also led to an economic system with very little heart.

I spend so much time working that I want to love the people I work with. I might get burned sometimes, but I have found business partners who are my best friends (like Kylin, Martin and Ralf). I want to work with friends who have the same principles and guiding values as I do.

Through authentic, inspiring relationships, we motivate each other. We don't get bogged down in complaining or listening to other people's complaints; we lift each other up and inspire one another forward.

There are so many ways to show people you love them—and that includes strangers. Giving your time, money or items you don't use anymore are important parts of being in your community, but more importantly, the act of giving teaches us how far our love can go. The people I know with the fullest lives—with friends and families and colleagues who adore and support them—are also the most generous people. They give from a place of love, and in return, they receive so much.

Often one of the best things we can give someone is our experience, which is why there are few relationships as intimate and transformative as the teacher-student relationship. As we mentor others, we are often learning from the process as well.

At the base of Maslow's pyramid are base-level needs of reproduction, food, water and sleep. At the top of the pyramid, the highest need is self-actualization. I believe that is our purpose—to become who we were always meant to be. From there, our greatest responsibility is to help others self-actualize. We can do that as employers, as colleagues, as parents, as friends, as siblings and as children. I think our purpose is to give, to mentor, to teach and to pass on. Evolution is not about individual learning, but rather the things we pass on that become those ripples in the pond.

Being a "go-giver" rather than just a "go-getter" is key—my friend JJ Virgin taught me this. Yes, it is great to be a go-getter. Go-getters are people who take action. Rather than waiting around for the perfect set of circumstances (which rarely ever happens), go-getters make things happen. As great as it is to be a go-getter, being a go-giver is even better. Being a go-giver means you add value to others in a way that helps them while at the same time increases your own sense of joy, fulfillment, purpose and energy. Moving from go-getter to go-giver means shifting your focus from getting to giving —and constantly and consistently adding value to the lives of others.

When you give, you are fulfilling what you are supposed to be and do, and in the process, you are helping someone else reach their fulfillment. This will help energize you on the days you don't have the physical energy!

INVEST IN YOUR NETWORK

Relationships are just like any other investment in your life: you put something in to receive something in return. I'm not talking about any sort of quid pro quo arrangement; this isn't about giving to others for the sole purpose of what you're going to get. This is about believing enough in the people and relationships in your life that you are willing to invest time, money, energy and love to make them as real and rich as they deserve to be.

The best way I know to show someone I care is simply to show up for them. That could be through the simple act of picking them up at the airport or picking up the tab at dinner—or it could be by reaching out to them when they need it most.

I remember a few years back, I was struggling with some health problems and mentioned it to an acquaintance. We knew each other from the keto world, so he understood what my diet and lifestyle looked like. After our meeting, I told him I was beat and was going to go to my room and crash.

I woke up around 6 pm to someone knocking on my door. That business acquaintance had ordered a healthy, delicious keto meal and had it delivered to my door—and it was still hot! From that day forward, this acquaintance became a good friend. He wasn't trying to get anything from me, and what he had done had formed a powerful friendship and real empathy.

So many people wonder what they can get out of relationships — something we see way too much across social media. Everyone is trying to build their brand or career off of someone else's. It's all about piggybacking and leverage and "What can you do for me?" But really, the question should be, "What can I do for you?" The more you invest your time and abilities in someone else, the more you will find that you are creating genuine relationships.

We will gladly spend hundreds of thousands of dollars on college in order to advance our professional careers, but then we see the $2,000 price tag on a conference that could connect us to a tribe and forever transform our lives and think: *There's no way I can afford that!*

Building your network in real and transformative ways will help you do more than advance your personal goals; it will also help you find a tribe of people who not only share your entrepreneurial and professional vision but also your entire life vision! You will find people who can inspire you when you've had a long day and you're wondering whether it's all worth it. They are the ones who are willing to send along a hot meal that says, "You're not alone."

Formulator's Corner
Immune Health Supplements

Vitamin C: To borrow a line from Forrest Gump, vitamin C and the immune system go together like peas and carrots. That's because vitamin C contributes to immune defense by supporting various aspects of both adaptive and innate immunity. Of course, it also protects against oxidative stress and epithelial barrier function. On top of that, levels of vitamin C drop sharply during periods of stress. It's no wonder that vitamin C supplementation has been shown to help reduce the incidence and severity of viral infections like the common cold! I prefer liposomal vitamin C and a dose of 1-2 grams is good for preventive measures. During times when immune challenges are particularly prominent, IV vitamin C is the way to go.

Vitamin D: There are vitamin D receptors located throughout the body, including the various cells of the immune system. Vitamin D insufficiency is common and is associated with increased susceptibility to viral infections. A recently published study found that vitamin

Immune Health Supplements (continuation)

Magnesium: Not usually recognized for its immune prowess, magnesium plays essential roles in both the innate (non-specific) and adaptive (specific) branches of the immune responses. A healthy magnesium intake is important to promote both healthy levels of inflammation and a healthy stress response, both of which tie into a healthy and properly functioning immune system. Magnesium recommendations can vary based on diet, exercise and other factors, but 300-400 mg a day is usually a good spot. I like a highly absorbable chelated form of magnesium such as magnesium bisglycinate.

Medicinal Mushrooms: An array of mushroom extracts have been shown to provide significant immune support. For example, they may boost the activity of various components of the immune system such as macrophages and natural killer (NK) cells, as well as increase phagocytosis and the production of immune compounds that are necessary for a healthy immune response. The proteoglycans and polysaccharides—such as beta-glucan—in mushrooms may be largely responsible for these immune-support properties. Some of my favorite mushrooms for immunity are **reishi, cordyceps** and **chaga.**

D deficiency was associated with a significantly increased risk for COVID-19, but a brand-new randomized controlled trial sounds encouraging—it showed that supplementation with vitamin D drastically reduced the severity of symptoms associated with COVID-19, reducing the rate of admission to the ICU from 50 percent (no vitamin D supplementation) to 2 percent (vitamin D supplementation). I find that supplementation is best tailored to one's vitamin D status. I like to test vitamin D levels instead of making broad-stroke recommendations. Some people may need to supplement with as much as 250-500 mcg (or 10,000-20,000 IU).

Immune Health Supplements (continuation)

Zinc: Although it doesn't get quite as much love as vitamin C, zinc is on the very same level when it comes to immune support, as it's involved in hundreds of metabolic reactions, including the body's immune responses. Like vitamin C, supplementation with zinc has been shown to help reduce the incidence and severity of viral infections like the common cold. On the flip side, insufficient zinc intake decreases immune function and is a sure-fire recipe to catch a bug. Another cool aspect of zinc is that it's antiviral and can reduce the replication of viruses. Up to 75 mg of zinc can be taken daily for short periods to provide support for immune challenges. When I feel something coming on, I reach for my bottle of zinc acetate lozenges (Life Extension), which seem to work very well for me and others.

Lysine: Lysine is an essential amino acid that promotes immune function. It is important for both antibody responses and cell-mediated immune responses. This is a fairly inexpensive and underrated immune support nutrient, and I usually recommend 1-5 g a day depending on how immunocompromised you are.

Quercetin: A powerful antioxidant bioflavonoid, quercetin can favorably modulate the immune system. It seems to be particularly helpful in regulating the body's immune response during environmental exposures (e.g., seasonal allergies). It may assist in supporting healthy levels of inflammation and stabilizing mast cells (which store and release histamine) and basophils. Recent research also shows that quercetin is a potent inhibitor for angiotensin-converting enzyme 2 (ACE2), which is a receptor for SARS-CoV-2, the coronavirus that causes COVID-19. Along those lines, quercetin may provide antiviral support for COVID-19.[125] I like quercetin phytosome, which has improved oral absorption, and a dose of 250-500 mg is generally a good recommendation.

Immune Health Supplements (continuation)

N-Acetylcysteine (NAC): NAC is a rising star when it comes to immune support. It's a potent antioxidant and a precursor to glutathione, and it is particularly well known for supporting optimal respiratory health. For example, it helps support normal mucus levels in the sinuses and respiratory system. It has also been shown to help promote healthy levels of a variety of immune compounds (e.g., lymphocytes, neutrophils and cytokines). A dose of 600-1200 mg is usually a good place to be.

Glutathione: Glutathione is known as the body's "master antioxidant." It's one of the body's most important antioxidant and detoxification factors. Normal levels of glutathione are critical for a robust immune system. Glutathione can increase levels of natural killer (NK) cells, which play a fundamental role in the body's immune response. I recommend liposomal glutathione from Quicksilver Scientific.

AHCC: AHCC is a standardized extract of cultured shiitake or Lentinula edodes mycelia (ECLM), which contains a mixture of nutrients including oligosaccharides, amino acids, and minerals. AHCC has been shown to modulate the numbers and functions of immune cells, including natural killer (NK) and T cells, which play important roles in host defense. Supplementation with AHCC can help protect against infections and it's one of the first things I reach for if I feel something coming on.

Ergothioneine: L-Ergothioneine, which is found most prominently in mushrooms, is a powerful antioxidant that has become known as the "longevity vitamin." Recent research has shown that ergothioneine has immune-enhancing properties. It can help promote healthy cytokine expression and signaling. Look for MitoPrime, the branded version of this next-level antioxidant.

COMMUNITY AND THE IMMUNE SYSTEM

The most interesting part of this pandemic is the social price we are having to pay in order to stay physically well. People do not stay healthy in isolation. As with the Blue Zones, lifespan and healthspan are best predicted by the state and strength of our relationships. We don't thrive when we're away from community —and the same is true for our immune systems.

Recent studies have shown that loneliness and social isolation lead to poorer health because they lead to inflammatory issues, with increased levels of two inflammatory chemicals: C-reactive protein and fibrinogen. When people have long-term increased levels of these inflammatory markers, it can lead to an increased risk of poorer health over time. What is particularly interesting is that COVID-19 accelerates inflammatory responses, which can act as a perfect storm for people already struggling with auto-immune and inflammatory disorders.

Now more than ever, we need to find ways to develop and strengthen community by creating safe and healthy ways to connect with other humans. Even as the pandemic fades, we need to rebuild our society to better honor and inspire human connections.

As I hope I've made clear, building a tribe is not just about finding people who can help you but about finding a group of people who want to join you in helping the world. Much like the Avengers, there is power in numbers. I always think back to that first *Iron Man* movie. Sure, Tony Stark (played by Robert Downey, Jr.) was funny and sarcastic and the action was great, but the movie didn't make you feel *involved*.

By the time *Avengers: Endgame* came out, when all the characters were working together, you would think people knew the superheroes personally. Whether it's in Marvel comics, at the Super Bowl or just with your team at the office, having a group of people come together around shared ideals is the most energizing experience in the world.

I don't think of biohacktivism in terms of creating a revolution. It is about building a community. When we're not focused on hustling and grinding, we can be in the flow of life, manifesting our tribe. We can make conscious and empowered choices about people and how we want to interact with them. We are no longer afraid to express our emotions or appreciation. We are connected with the world around us and we are meeting our highest need as our highest selves. We are living our lives to their fullest potential, and are helping others to do the same.

YOUR TRIBE SUMMARY

- A major 75-year study done by Harvard University showed that the single biggest factor for healthy aging was the quality of one's relationships. When you are living in joy, you are finally empowered to live your true self, which is why it is so critical to find an authentic circle of people you know and trust who can also provide accountability. There is nothing more important than the relationships we have, which is why we must be conscious about the people we choose to have in our lives.

- We are who we surround ourselves with. Look at your five closest friends and colleagues. How do they add value to your life? What lessons are they teaching you through their own relationships? How can you either strengthen those relationships or find a group which better matches your "manifested" life and vision?

- "Biohacktivism" is about hacking your biology not just for your own betterment and longevity, but also for the world around you. If we are hustling and grinding, we are not seeing other people or listening to them. We are just getting through the day. Our purpose should be to become who we are meant to be—and after that, to help others self-actualize.

- Often one of the best things we can give someone is our experience; when you give, you are fulfilling what you are supposed to do and who you are supposed to be. You are helping others reach their fulfillment. This will energize you even on days where you are feeling low.

- Now more than ever, we need to find ways to develop and strengthen community, creating safe and healthy ways to connect with other humans. One of the best ways to show someone you care is simply to show up for them.

- "Ubuntu" is an African philosophy that may best be described by the phrase "I am because of who we all are." Ubuntu places emphasis on solidarity, compassion, respect, human dignity and collective unity, and focuses on reciprocity, humanity and morality in the interest of building and maintaining community with mutual caring.

Resource Hacks

Your Tribe

Put Your Cell Phone Down: A critical part of connecting to people and food is putting away whatever prevents that. A phone on the table is a signal that you are not fully engaged. Even a cell phone buzzing in your pocket sends a distracting signal. A great rule at a restaurant is if you pull the phone out, you pay for dinner.

Give Your Undivided Attention to Your Loved Ones at Dinner: This is often the only time of day you get to spend time with your family.

Take Note of the People You Surround Yourself With: Are they making you a better human or are they draining you and holding you back? Write down what you can change in the next three months.

Send a Message or a Letter: Writing someone you care for or appreciate when you don't need something from them is powerful. Wouldn't you like that?

Think About How You Can Reach Out or Help Someone: You can do this without focusing on getting anything in return. Be the change you want to see in the world.

Share Your Knowledge and Skills With the People Around You So That They Can Benefit: Expect nothing in return from all the above. Do good things simply because it feels good to do so.

For live links, updated content, bonus graphics
and a hidden chapter, go to
EnergyFormulaBook.com

The ENERGY Formula: Putting it All Together

"We shall not cease from exploration and the end of all our exploring will be to arrive where we started and know the place for the first time."

—T.S. Eliot

Before we became an agrarian society, we lived in tribes. It is not so hard to imagine. Cultures all over the world—from Africa to Sardinia, from South America to Scandinavia—still participate in tribal life. In these communities, the members are deeply networked, life moves slower and people come together to celebrate life and rituals no matter their economic standing. They recognize that if the tribe is together, they are stronger for it.

We are not going to reverse our industrialized society overnight, but the fact is, we have one of the greatest opportunities in human history to restructure how we move through this world. As we move towards an ever-challenging future, it is clear that we have more to learn from our past than we have realized.

When people ask me, "Where do we go from here?" I often tell them, "We go back."

We can't ignore the modern age and there are certainly great technologies worth embracing, but we can see where our tribal ancestors were right about how we eat, how we use our bodies, how we prioritize what matters and how we engage with one another.

For a while now, we've been living in fight or flight and then wondering why we don't react well to life.

Living a life with intention and purpose means slowing down enough to make the right choices. We can analyze the situation and are able to engage our logic and reasoning to decide on the healthiest response.

Do we grab the bag of Doritos or do we seek out whole foods? Do we stay in a bad relationship or do we believe in ourselves enough to know that we can make it on our own—and maybe even find a better person? Do we get resentful at our colleague for getting the promotion we believed was ours, or do we start to take a serious look at why we are not succeeding the way we believe we should? Do we learn how to take joy in someone else's well-earned achievement?

When you take control of your life, you will truly own it. You will see that you are on your path, looking through your own lens—and it's a different path and lens than anyone else's. Walking that path with intent, looking in the mirror, facing yourself and doing deep self-work is key. It's about changing what we say after "I am"—saying "beautiful," "smart," "thriving," "energetic," "compassionate," "purpose-filled" and "amazing" …all things we believed when we came into this world and somehow unlearned along the way. It's embracing all sides of you, believing in yourself and truly taking ownership so you can see how much influence you really have over your choices, your reactions, your life and your world. After that, we can reframe our role in all of it. We begin to see that what makes us different makes us beautiful.

Through this process, we stop holding back our uniqueness and instead learn to manifest in the flow. We stop grinding, trying to be something we're not and going after things we do not need. Instead, we own our passion and purpose and begin to notice that things come our way with serendipity, sometimes even effortlessly, because we just *flow*. It's the creative state we are in between the zone and the Zen, when we express our gifts with ease, fearlessly. We are vibrant. We are energetic. The world will take notice. Growth, tribe, connection and longevity are just by-products of this. So, if you do one thing, make it this: be unabashedly you, and grant yourself some grace along the way (one of my best lessons in life).

A quote I love by Oscar Wilde is: "Be yourself…everyone else is taken." So, own it. I feel wholeheartedly that you will find real magic and unmistakable synergy in The ENERGY Formula when you put the pieces together. You will begin to see the difference not only in your life, but also in the lives of the world around you.

Formulator's Corner
Shawn's Top Supplements for EVERYONE

Vitamin D3 + K2

Dihydroberberine/Berberine

Collagen

Magnesium (High Bioavailability)

Ashwagandha & Rhodiola

High-Quality Multivitamin with Active B Vitamins
(Methylcobalamin, P5P, 5-MTHF, etc.)

L-Ergothioneine

Alpha-GPC

Creatine

Curcumin (High Bioavailability)

High DHA Fish Oil

Prebiotics, Probiotics and Postbiotics (Synbiotics)

I know what it's like to live wired and tired, and I still occasionally have some rough days where I want to just give up (we all do). Even so, I know I don't want to be there for long—and I have a way forward now. I have new patterns, new routines and a new mindset to pull me out. Here is the thing: no supplement on the planet can supplement your mindset—trust me, there are a number of psychoactive or nootropic substances I've tried!

We own our passion and purpose and begin to notice that things come our way with serendipity, sometimes even effortlessly, because we just *flow*. It's the creative state we are in between the zone and the Zen, when we express our gifts with ease, fearlessly. We are vibrant. We are *energetic*.

Perception is *your* reality. As you begin to Experiment, transform your Nutrition and Exercise, establish your Routine, Grow past your comfort zone and finally build Your tribe, you will find that your reality shifts as well. You are no longer surviving in the sympathetic grind; you are thriving in the parasympathetic flow!

To me, success is not about dollars and cents or job title or fame. Success is simply how much joy you have in your life.

I always like examining humanity's evolution to see what has driven us to become the stewards of this civilization and this time in history. I believe if you look at what makes humans unique, it is not just about the survival of the individual. Sure, we protect our lives first and foremost, but what drives our supremacy is that the survival of our species actually supersedes survival of the individual. That is why it feels so good to help others: because we are actually protecting our species. We are helping it survive.

That is where, deep down in our DNA, we find our purpose, where we feel actualized and where we tap into our greatest joy. When we are truly giving to another person, in ways big and small, we experience a joy that is immeasurable. We find ourselves happier, but we also start making better choices for our lives. We become energized.

At the end of the day, that is really the goal of all biohacktivism—we are trying to find ways to live joyful, happier, healthier and longer lives so we can help others to do the same.

As the writer Paul Bowles once remarked, "Death is always on the way. But the fact that you don't know when it will arrive seems to take away from the finiteness of life. It's that terrible precision that we hate so much. Because we don't know, we get to think of life as an inexhaustible well. Yet everything happens a certain number of times and a very small number really. How many more times will you remember a certain afternoon of your childhood? Some afternoon that's so deeply a part of your being that you can't even conceive of your life without it. Perhaps four or five times more; perhaps not even. How many more times will you watch the full moon rise? Perhaps 20 and yet it all seems limitless." And in a way, it is.

Perception is *your* reality. As you begin to Experiment, transform your Nutrition and Exercise, establish your Routine, Grow past your comfort zone and finally build Your tribe, you will find that your reality shifts as well. You are no longer surviving in the sympathetic grind; you are thriving in the parasympathetic flow!

Though COVID-19 has brought tragedy to many, it has also been a great wake-up call. It has forced us to take a step back and decide, is this the life I want to lead? We know that time is fleeting, we can see our mortality closer up than ever before and at the same time, life has slowed down just enough for us to get a better view of what we want.

Since the pandemic began, I have been able to ask myself about the "return on investment" for my life choices—not just financially, but for my body and my soul. Instead of travelling 300 days a year, I have been able to re-center at home and focus on what I genuinely care about.

I would imagine the same is true for you. How have you been forced to slow down since COVID-19 began? How have you had to re-prioritize your life or better understand your priorities?

Instead of getting caught up in the *busyness* of business, this time has forced us all to ask the deep questions about what is working and what is not. What truly lights you up? What gives you that creative spark, that joy for living? What are you going to start doing differently? What makes you passionate? Where is your flow? If you could choose your ultimate life, what would it look like? Start taking steps towards it. I am committing to that. I want more life in my years and not just more years in my life.

I've started doing therapy (as *any* growth-minded person should) and exploring plant medicine (which may become my next book!). I began connecting more deeply with friends and family and, since I couldn't go to the gym, I started going into nature more and connecting to the earth. I started spending more time in the sun and breathing fresh air.

I have been playing volleyball, walking, biking and hiking almost every day. As a result, I have never been more productive in my life. It is easy to get caught up in the fear—to live in the fight-or-flight of COVID-19, politics or anything else—but there is also a flow to this new time. A practice in patience, consciousness and *purpose*.

There is no way I could have made any of this happen myself. None of us have the power to shut it all down, but with the pandemic shutting our *normal* lives down, we have found we do have the power to reset. We can create new systems and schedules. We can develop new formulas and traditions. We can decide which relationships are important, where we want to go now on this new path and how we want to establish better-energized lives to truly embrace those new-found priorities.

Like being on keto, you don't want to eat the cheap processed stuff that's so not worth it—you want to wait for the really decadent cake. I don't want to travel anymore unless it's to some place or event where I'll be really inspired. I want to be inspired by that great slice of cake in all areas of my life.

We are all biohacktivists. We are looking up and connecting with the world around us. We are paying attention. We are more present than ever before because we have slowed down enough to see what is happening. We are not "heads down" anymore.

We are now living The ENERGY Formula. Experiment, Nutrition, Exercise, Routines, Growth and Your tribe are now a part of your daily life to optimize and thrive. We can be more present, more mindful, more creative and more in the *flow*.

Life is not limitless. Life *is* fleeting, and that has never felt more true or relevant as it has in this last year. For all we know, we only have one chance to live passionately and purposefully. We have one life— one *dash* in which to live.

Let's start truly *living* now! Together.

Resource Hacks

Shawn's Top 12 Hacks from the Book

Sleep Hygiene: Go to bed at the same time and get up at the same time every day. Make a sleep fortress and eat during the daylight hours.

Create a Strong Morning Routine: Breathing, gratitude, walking, exercise, podcasts, planning, sungazing, grounding, etc.

Batch Tasks: Like putting calls together, focus on one big task for the day but take breaks—for your eyes, circulation, breathing, de-stressing and greater productivity.

Hot and Cold: Take hot and cold showers and go into saunas and cold plunges to build resilience.

Experiment with One Thing at a Time: Embrace your bio-individuality; don't use a "shotgun" approach.

Exercise Regularly: Find things you enjoy, but also use HIIT, BFR and intra-set stretching to get results.

Paleo: In the simplest terms, eating whole foods without allergenic triggers is the most foundational diet.

Keto: If you're metabolically dysfunctional (overweight, glucose intolerant, etc.), this may be a way to lose weight and gain energy.

Shawn's Top 12 Hacks from the Book (continuation)

Get Metrics: This includes bloodwork, mental health tests, wearable HRV and sleep data, glucose and ketones, gut microbiome, genetics. Use all of this data to determine what is working and what is not.

Surround Yourself with a Dream Team: Build a team of mentors: find the right voices to build you, challenge you and support you and be that voice for yourself (even if only through books and podcasts).

Develop Deep Relationships: Be both a great listener and the change you want to see in the world.

Adversity Builds Strength: Look at challenges as opportunities to build strength; the truly successful are experts at reframing…they win or they learn.

BONUS (and Most Important): Love yourself so you can show up for others in the best way—self-care is critical, as is positive self-talk.

Where to Find MORE from Shawn Wells!

Get Connected:

Instagram: https://www.instagram.com/shawnwells/
YouTube: http://www.youtube.com/c/shawnwells
Facebook: https://www.facebook.com/Ingredientologist
LinkedIn: https://www.linkedin.com/in/ingredientologist/
Twitter: https://twitter.com/Ingredientology
Pinterest: https://www.pinterest.com/Ingredientologist/

More on the Book:

Book Home Page: http://www.energyformula.com
Book Bonuses: http://www.energyformulabook.com

Downloadable Guides, Blogs and Newsletter:

Biohacking, Supplements, Keto & more: https://shawnwells.com/

Hire Me:

Formulations and Novel ingredient Design: https://zonehalo.com/

End Notes

CHAPTER 1: EXPERIMENT

[1] Joana Araújo, Jianwen Cai, June Stevens. Prevalence of Optimal Metabolic Health in American Adults: National Health and Nutrition Examination Survey 2009–2016. Metabolic Syndrome and Related Disorders, 2018; DOI: 10.1089/met.2018.0105

[2] How Does Caring for and Optimizing the Health of the Mitochondria, influence One's Own Health and Well-Being? (2016, July 26). https://livinglovecommunity.com/2016/07/20/mitochondria/

[3] Bonkowski, Michael S., and David A. Sinclair. "Slowing ageing by design: the rise of NAD+ and sirtuin-activating compounds." *Nature reviews Molecular cell biology* 17, no. 11 (2016): 679.

[4] Covarrubias, A.J., Kale, A., Perrone, R. et al. Senescent cells promote tissue NAD+ decline during ageing via the activation of CD38+ macrophages. Nat Metab 2, 1265–1283 (2020).

https://doi.org/10.1038/s42255-020-00305-3

[5] Camacho-Pereira, Juliana, Mariana G. Tarragó, Claudia CS Chini, Veronica Nin, Carlos Escande, Gina M. Warner, Amrutesh S. Puranik et al. "CD38 dictates age-related NAD decline and mitochondrial dysfunction through an SIRT3-dependent mechanism." *Cell metabolism* 23, no. 6 (2016): 1127-1139.

[6] Antonio, Leen, Marian Dejaeger, Roger Bouillon, Frederick Wu, Terence O'Neill, Stephen Pye, Ilpo Huhtaniemi et al. "Free 25-hydroxyvitamin D, but not free 1.25-dihydroxyvitamin D, predicts all-cause mortality in ageing men." In 22nd European Congress of Endocrinology, vol. 70. BioScientifica, 2020.

[7] Ltd, I. (n.d.). How Many Productive Hours in a Work Day? Just 2 Hours, 23 Minutes... https://www.vouchercloud.com/resources/office-worker-productivity

[8] I4cp: The COVID-19 Hit on Productivity is Accelerating in Most Companies - i4cp. (n.d.). https://www.i4cp.com/coronaviri/i4cp-the-covid-19-hit-on-productivity-is-accelerating-in-most-companies

[9] Thomas, T. (n.d.). Parasympathetic & Sympathetic Nervous System. https://happyhealthyyou.com.au/blogs/articles/parasympathetic-sympathetic-nervous-system

[10] Csikszentmihalyi, M. (2008). *Flow: The psychology of optimal experience*. New York: Harper Perennial Modern Classics.

[11] Faller, Josef, Jennifer Cummings, Sameer Saproo, and Paul Sajda. "Regulation of arousal via online neurofeedback improves human performance in a demanding sensory-motor task." *Proceedings of the National Academy of Sciences* 116, no. 13 (2019): 6482-6490.

[12] The Mind Tools Content Team By the Mind Tools Content Team, Team, T., Wrote, B., Wrote, A., & Wrote, M. (n.d.). The Inverted-U Theory: Balancing Performance and Pressure With the Yerkes-Dodson Law. https://www.mindtools.com/pages/article/inverted-u.htm

CHAPTER 2: NUTRITION

[13] Li, Yanping, An Pan, Dong D. Wang, Xiaoran Liu, Klodian Dhana, Oscar H. Franco, Stephen Kaptoge et al. "Impact of healthy lifestyle factors on life expectancies in the US population." *Circulation* 138, no. 4 (2018): 345-355.

[14] How it's made: Cholesterol production in your body. https://www.health.harvard.edu/heart-health/how-its-made-cholesterol-production-in-your-body

[15] Diehl, H., D.H.Sc., MPH, Esselstyn, C., Jr., M.D., Folsom, A. R., M.D., MPH, Grundy, S., M.D., Ph.D., Jacobson, M. F., Ph.D., Kuller, L., M.D., Dr.PH, …Stamler, J., MD. (2015, May 8). Scientists' Comment on Dietary Cholesterol.
https://cspinet.org/sites/default/files/dietary-cholesterol-comments.pdf

[16] Nelson, Robert H. "Hyperlipidemia as a risk factor for cardiovascular disease." *Primary Care: Clinics in Office Practice* 40, no. 1 (2013): 195-211.

[17] Hu, Tian, Katherine T. Mills, Lu Yao, Kathryn Demanelis, Mohamed Eloustaz, William S. Yancy Jr, Tanika N. Kelly, Jiang He, and Lydia A. Bazzano. "Effects of low-carbohydrate diets versus low-fat diets on metabolic risk factors: a meta-analysis of randomized controlled clinical trials." *American journal of epidemiology* 176, no. suppl_7 (2012): S44-S54.

[18] Gardner, Christopher D., Alexandre Kiazand, Sofiya Alhassan, Soowon Kim, Randall S. Stafford, Raymond R. Balise, Helena C. Kraemer, and Abby C. King. "Comparison of the Atkins, Zone, Ornish, and LEARN diets for change in weight and related risk factors among overweight premenopausal women: the A TO Z Weight Loss Study: a randomized trial." *Jama* 297, no. 9 (2007): 969-977.

[19] Gardner, Christopher D., John F. Trepanowski, Liana C. Del Gobbo, Michelle E. Hauser, Joseph Rigdon, John PA Ioannidis, Manisha Desai, and Abby C. King. "Effect of low-fat vs low-carbohydrate diet on 12-month weight loss in overweight adults and the association with genotype pattern or insulin secretion: the DIETFITS randomized clinical trial." *Jama* 319, no. 7 (2018): 667-679.

[20] Schulze, Matthias B., Miguel A. Martínez-González, Teresa T. Fung, Alice H. Lichtenstein, and Nita G. Forouhi. "Food based dietary patterns and chronic disease prevention." *Bmj* 361 (2018).

21 Sacks, Frank M., George A. Bray, Vincent J. Carey, Steven R. Smith, Donna H. Ryan, Stephen D. Anton, Katherine McManus et al. "Comparison of weight-loss diets with different compositions of fat, protein, and carbohydrates." *New England Journal of Medicine* 360, no. 9 (2009): 859-873.

22 Paleo diet: Eat like a cave man and lose weight? (2020, August 25). https://www.mayoclinic.org/healthy-lifestyle/nutrition-and-healthy-eating/in-depth/paleo-diet/art-20111182

23 Suzanne, M., and Ming Tong. "Brain metabolic dysfunction at the core of Alzheimer's disease." *Biochemical pharmacology* 88, no. 4 (2014): 548-559.

24 Moss, Michael. Salt, sugar, fat: How the food giants hooked us. Random House, 2013.

25 Fortuna, Jeffrey L. "The obesity epidemic and food addiction: clinical similarities to drug dependence." *Journal of psychoactive drugs* 44, no. 1 (2012): 56-63.

26 Coccurello, Roberto, and Mauro Maccarrone. "Hedonic eating and the "delicious circle": from lipid-derived mediators to brain dopamine and back." *Frontiers in neuroscience* 12 (2018): 271.

27 da Mata Gonçalves, Renata Fiche, Danyela de Almeida Barreto, Pâmela Ione Monteiro, Márcio Gilberto Zangeronimo, Paula Midori Castelo, Andries van der Bilt, and Luciano José Pereira. "Smartphone use while eating increases caloric ingestion." *Physiology & behavior* 204 (2019): 93-99.

28 Robinson, Eric, Paul Aveyard, Amanda Daley, Kate Jolly, Amanda Lewis, Deborah Lycett, and Suzanne Higgs. "Eating attentively: a systematic review and meta-analysis of the effect of food intake memory and awareness on eating." *The American journal of clinical nutrition* 97, no. 4 (2013): 728-742.

29 Nelson, Joseph B. "Mindful eating: the art of presence while you eat." *Diabetes Spectrum* 30, no. 3 (2017): 171-174.

[30] Cherpak, Christine E., and Sherryl Van Lare. "Mindful Eating: A Review Of How The Stress-Digestion-Mindfulness Triad May Modulate And Improve Gastrointestinal And Digestive Function." *Integrative Medicine: A Clinician's Journal* 18, no. 4 (2019).

[31] Magiorkinis, Emmanouil, Aristidis Diamantis, Kalliopi Sidiropoulou, and Christos Panteliadis. "Highights in the history of epilepsy: the last 200 years." *Epilepsy research and treatment* 2014 (2014).

[32] Preiato, D. (2019, October 31). Low Carb vs. Keto: What's the Difference? https://www.healthline.com/nutrition/low-carb-vs-keto

[33] Puchalska, Patrycja, and Peter A. Crawford. "Multi-dimensional roles of ketone bodies in fuel metabolism, signaling, and therapeutics." *Cell metabolism* 25, no. 2 (2017): 262-284.

[34] Deemer, Sarah E et al. "Impact of ketosis on appetite regulation-a review." Nutrition research (New York, N.Y.) vol. 77 (2020): 1-11.

[35] Goldberg, Emily L., Ryan D. Molony, Eriko Kudo, Sviatoslav Sidorov, Yong Kong, Vishwa Deep Dixit, and Akiko Iwasaki. "Ketogenic diet activates protective γδ T cell responses against influenza virus infection." Science immunology 4, no. 41 (2019).

[36] Ketogenic diet: Role in seizure control. (2009, April 24). https://gardenrain.wordpress.com/2009/04/23/ketogenic-diet-role-in-seizure-control/

[37] Najt, Charles P., Salmaan A. Khan, Timothy D. Heden, Bruce A. Witthuhn, Minervo Perez, Jason L. Heier, Linnea E. Mead et al. "Lipid droplet-derived monounsaturated fatty acids traffic via PLIN5 to allosterically activate SIRT1." Molecular Cell 77, no. 4 (2020): 810-824.

[38] Simopoulos, Artemis P. "Overview of evolutionary aspects of w3 fatty acids in the diet." *World review of nutrition and dietetics* 83 (1998): 1-11.

[39] Patterson, Elaine, Rebecca Wall, G. F. Fitzgerald, R. P. Ross, and C. Stanton. "Health implications of high dietary omega-6 polyunsaturated fatty acids." *Journal of nutrition and metabolism* 2012 (2012).

[40] Yan, Fang, and D. B. Polk. "Probiotics and immune health." *Current opinion in gastroenterology* 27, no. 6 (2011): 496.

[41] Yessenkyzy, Assylzhan, Timur Saliev, Marina Zhanaliyeva, Abdul-Razak Masoud, Bauyrzhan Umbayev, Shynggys Sergazy, Elena Krivykh, Alexander Gulyayev, and Talgat Nurgozhin. "Polyphenols as Caloric-Restriction Mimetics and Autophagy Inducers in Aging Research." *Nutrients* 12, no. 5 (2020): 1344.

[42] Paganini-Hill, Annlia, Claudia H. Kawas, and Maria M. Corrada. "Lifestyle factors and dementia in the oldest-old: the 90+ study." *Alzheimer disease and associated disorders* 30, no. 1 (2016): 21.

[43] O'Keefe, James H., Salman K. Bhatti, Ata Bajwa, James J. DiNicolantonio, and Carl J. Lavie. "Alcohol and cardiovascular health: the dose makes the poison… or the remedy." In *Mayo Clinic Proceedings*, vol. 89, no. 3, pp. 382-393. Elsevier, 2014.

[44] The 3 Ketogenic Diets Explained: SKD, CKD & TKD. (2020, February 03). https://www.ruled.me/3-ketogenic-diets-skd-ckd-tk

[45] Kubala, J. (n.d.). The Keto Flu: Symptoms and How to Get Rid of It. **https://www.healthline.com/nutrition/keto-flu-symptoms**

[46] Guerrera, Mary P., Stella Lucia Volpe, and Jun James Mao. "Therapeutic uses of magnesium." *American family physician* 80, no. 2 (2009): 157-162.

[47] Eaton, S. Boyd, and Melvin Konner. "Paleolithic nutrition: a consideration of its nature and current implications." *New England Journal of Medicine* 312, no. 5 (1985): 283-289.

[48] Konner, Melvin, and S. Boyd Eaton. "Paleolithic nutrition: twenty-five years later." *Nutrition in Clinical Practice* 25, no. 6 (2010): 594-602.

[49] Alcock, Joe, Carlo C. Maley, and C. Athena Aktipis. "Is eating behavior manipulated by the gastrointestinal microbiota? Evolutionary pressures and potential mechanisms." *Bioessays* 36, no. 10 (2014): 940-949.

[50] Bian, Xiaoming, Liang Chi, Bei Gao, Pengcheng Tu, Hongyu Ru, and Kun Lu. "Gut microbiome response to sucralose and its potential role in inducing liver inflammation in mice." *Frontiers in physiology* 8 (2017): 487.

[51] Keto Sweetener Guide: Best & Worst [Sucrolose, Stevia, Erythritol]. (2019, September 30).

[52] Arnold, L. Eugene, Nicholas Lofthouse, and Elizabeth Hurt. "Artificial food colors and attention-deficit/hyperactivity symptoms: conclusions to dye for." *Neurotherapeutics* 9, no. 3 (2012): 599-609.

[53] Costantini, Lara, Romina Molinari, Barbara Farinon, and Nicolò Merendino. "Impact of omega-3 fatty acids on the gut microbiota." *International journal of molecular sciences* 18, no. 12 (2017): 2645.

[54] Queipo-Ortuño, María Isabel, María Boto-Ordóñez, Mora Murri, Juan Miguel Gomez-Zumaquero, Mercedes Clemente-Postigo, Ramon Estruch, Fernando Cardona Diaz, Cristina Andrés-Lacueva, and Francisco J. Tinahones. "Influence of red wine polyphenols and ethanol on the gut microbiota ecology and biochemical biomarkers." *The American journal of clinical nutrition* 95, no. 6 (2012): 1323-1334.

[55] Yao, Juan, Baoxin Zhang, Chunpo Ge, Shoujiao Peng, and Jianguo Fang. "Xanthohumol, a polyphenol chalcone present in hops, activating Nrf2 enzymes to confer protection against oxidative damage in PC12 cells." *Journal of agricultural and food chemistry* 63, no. 5 (2015): 1521-1531.

[56] The low FODMAP diet: Does it work for IBS? (n.d.). https://www.medicalnewstoday.com/articles/319722

[57] Leeming, Emily R., Abigail J. Johnson, Tim D. Spector, and Caroline I. Le Roy. "Effect of diet on the gut microbiota: Rethinking intervention duration." *Nutrients* 11, no. 12 (2019): 2862.

CHAPTER 2: EXERCISE

[58] Ruiz, Jonatan R., Xuemei Sui, Felipe Lobelo, James R. Morrow, Allen W. Jackson, Michael Sjöström, and Steven N. Blair. "Association between muscular strength and mortality in men: prospective cohort study." *Bmj* 337 (2008): a439.

[59] Li, Ran, Jin Xia, X. I. Zhang, Wambui Grace Gathirua-Mwangi, Jianjun Guo, Yufeng Li, Steve McKenzie, and Yiqing Song. "Associations of muscle mass and strength with all-cause mortality among US older adults." *Medicine and science* in *sports and exercise* 50, no. 3 (2018): 458.

[60] Bohannon, Richard W. "Grip strength: an indispensable biomarker for older adults." *Clinical interventions in aging* 14 (2019): 1681.

[61] Seals, Douglas R., and Simon Melov. "Translational geroscience: emphasizing function to achieve optimal longevity." *Aging (Albany NY)* 6, no. 9 (2014): 718.

[62] Seals, Douglas R., Jamie N. Justice, and Thomas J. LaRocca. "Physiological geroscience: targeting function to increase healthspan and achieve optimal longevity." *The Journal of physiology* 594, no. 8 (2016): 2001-2024.

[63] Church, David D., Jay R. Hoffman, Gerald T. Mangine, Adam R. Jajtner, Jeremy R. Townsend, Kyle S. Beyer, Ran Wang, Michael B. La Monica, David H. Fukuda, and Jeffrey R. Stout. "Comparison of high-intensity vs. high-volume resistance training on the BDNF response to exercise." *Journal of Applied Physiology* (2016).

[64] Marston, Kieran J., Michael J. Newton, Belinda M. Brown, Stephanie R. Rainey-Smith, Sabine Bird, Ralph N. Martins, and Jeremiah J. Peiffer. "Intense resistance exercise increases peripheral brain-derived neurotrophic factor." *Journal of science and medicine in sport* 20, no. 10 (2017): 899-903.

[65] Gordon, Brett R., Cillian P. McDowell, Mats Hallgren, Jacob D. Meyer, Mark Lyons, and Matthew P. Herring. "Association of efficacy of resistance exercise training with depressive symptoms: meta-analysis and meta-regression analysis of randomized clinical trials." *Jama Psychiatry* 75, no. 6 (2018): 566-576.

[66] Lauersen, Jeppe Bo, Ditte Marie Bertelsen, and Lars Bo Andersen. "The effectiveness of exercise interventions to prevent sports injuries: a systematic review and meta-analysis of randomised controlled trials." *British journal of sports medicine* 48, no. 11 (2014): 871-877.

[67] Volpi, Elena et al. "Muscle tissue changes with aging." *Current opinion in clinical nutrition and metabolic care* vol. 7,4 (2004): 405-10.

[68] Rodio, M. (2018, May 21). Low Weight High Reps = More Strength. https://www.mensjournal.com/health-fitness/if-you-want-build-muscle-and-gain-strength-lift-lighter-weights-more-reps/

[69] Feito, Yuri et al. "High-Intensity Functional Training (HIFT): Definition and Research Implications for Improved Fitness." *Sports (Basel, Switzerland)* vol. 6,3 76. 7 Aug. 2018,

[70] Garber, Carol Ewing et al. "American College of Sports Medicine position stand. Quantity and quality of exercise for developing and maintaining cardiorespiratory, musculoskeletal, and neuromotor fitness in apparently healthy adults: guidance for prescribing exercise." *Medicine and science in sports and exercise* vol. 43,7 (2011): 1334-59.

[71] Gillen, Jenna B et al. "Twelve Weeks of Sprint Interval Training Improves Indices of Cardiometabolic Health Similar to Traditional Endurance Training despite a Five-Fold Lower Exercise Volume and Time Commitment." *PloS one* vol. 11,4 e0154075. 26 Apr. 2016.

[72] Broom, David R et al. "Acute effect of exercise intensity and duration on acylated ghrelin and hunger in men." *The Journal of endocrinology* vol. 232,3 (2017): 411-422.

[73] Stensvold, Dorthe et al. "Effect of exercise training for five years on all cause mortality in older adults-the Generation 100 study: randomised controlled trial." *BMJ (Clinical research ed.)* vol. 371 m3485. 7 Oct. 2020.

[74] Franz, Marion J et al. "Weight-loss outcomes: a systematic review and meta-analysis of weight-loss clinical trials with a minimum 1-year follow-up." *Journal of the American Dietetic Association* vol. 107,10 (2007): 1755-67.

[75] DiPietro, Loretta et al. "Three 15-min bouts of moderate postmeal walking significantly improves 24-h glycemic control in older people at risk for impaired glucose tolerance." *Diabetes care* vol. 36,10 (2013): 3262-8.

[76] Hanssen, Mark J W et al. "Short-term cold acclimation improves insulin sensitivity in patients with type 2 diabetes mellitus." *Nature medicine* vol. 21,8 (2015): 863-5.

[77] Hubbard, Tricia J, and Craig R Denegar. "Does Cryotherapy Improve Outcomes With Soft Tissue Injury?." *Journal of athletic training* vol. 39,3 (2004): 278-279.

[78] Rymaszewska, Joanna et al. "Whole-body cryotherapy as adjunct treatment of depressive and anxiety disorders." *Archivum immunologiae et therapiae experimentalis* vol. 56,1 (2008): 63-8.

[79] Mäkinen, Tiina M et al. "Autonomic nervous function during whole-body cold exposure before and after cold acclimation." *Aviation, space, and environmental medicine* vol. 79,9 (2008): 875-82.

[80] Campbell, John P, and James E Turner. "Debunking the Myth of Exercise-Induced Immune Suppression: Redefining the Impact of Exercise on Immunological Health Across the Lifespan." *Frontiers in immunology* vol. 9 648. 16 Apr. 2018.

CHAPTER 4: ROUTINE

[81] LeGates, Tara A et al. "Light as a central modulator of circadian rhythms, sleep and affect." *Nature reviews. Neuroscience* vol. 15,7 (2014): 443-54.

[82] Singh, H. (2020, April 18). How to Biohack Sleep Cycle, Learn impact on immunity, Weight and Mind. https://dobiohacking.com/what-is-circadian-rhythm-how-to-fix-the-sleep-cycle/

[83] Schroeder, Analyne M, and Christopher S Colwell. "How to fix a broken clock." *Trends in pharmacological sciences* vol. 34,11 (2013): 605-19.

[84] Osman, Amal M et al. "Obstructive sleep apnea: current perspectives." *Nature and science of sleep* vol. 10 21-34. 23 Jan. 2018.

[85] Stepanski, Edward J, and James K Wyatt. "Use of sleep hygiene in the treatment of insomnia." *Sleep medicine reviews* vol. 7,3 (2003): 215-25.

[86] Tosini, Gianluca et al. "Effects of blue light on the circadian system and eye physiology." *Molecular vision* vol. 22 61-72. 24 Jan. 2016

[87] Schroeder, Analyne M, and Christopher S Colwell. "How to fix a broken clock." *Trends in pharmacological sciences* vol. 34,11 (2013): 605-19.

[88] Colrain, Ian M et al. "Alcohol and the sleeping brain." *Handbook of clinical neurology* vol. 125 (2014): 415-31.

[89] Cirillo, F. (2006). The pomodoro technique (the pomodoro). *Agile Processes in Software Engineering and, 54*(2), 35.

[90] Sutton, E. F., Beyl, R., Early, K. S., Cefalu, W. T., Ravussin, E., & Peterson, C. M. (2018). Early time-restricted feeding improves insulin sensitivity, blood pressure, and oxidative stress even without weight loss in men with prediabetes. Cell metabolism, 27(6), 1212-1221.

[91] Yamanaka, Y., Honma, K. I., Hashimoto, S., Takasu, N., Miyazaki, T., & Honma, S. (2006). Effects of physical exercise on human circadian rhythms. Sleep and Biological Rhythms, 4(3), 199-206.

[92] Does Too Much Blue Light Make You Anxious, Stressed and Depressed? https://www.blockbluelight.com.au/blogs/news/blue-light-and-depression-and-stress

[93] Sinatra, S. T., Oschman, J. L., Chevalier, G., & Sinatra, D. (2017). Electric nutrition: The surprising health and healing benefits of biological grounding (Earthing). Altern Ther Health Med, 23(5), 8-16.

[94] What Athletes And Weekend Warriors Need To Know About Heart Rate Variability. https://www.sporttechie.com/need-know-heart-rate-variability/

[95] Sleep in American Poll 2020. https://www.sleepfoundation.org/wp-content/uploads/2020/03/SIA-2020-Q1-Report.pdf?x39478

CHAPTER 5: GROWTH

[96] Hachmo, Y., Hadanny, A., Hamed, R. A., Daniel-Kotovsky, M., Catalogna, M., Fishlev, G., ... & Zemel, Y. (2020). Hyperbaric oxygen therapy increases telomere length and decreases immunosenescence in isolated blood cells: a prospective trial. Aging, 12.

[97] Weber, D. D., Aminazdeh-Gohari, S., & Kofler, B. (2018). Ketogenic diet in cancer therapy. Aging (Albany NY), 10(2), 164.

[98] Nauman, G., Gray, J. C., Parkinson, R., Levine, M., & Paller, C. J. (2018). Systematic review of intravenous ascorbate in cancer clinical trials. Antioxidants, 7(7), 89.

[99] Antunes, F., Erustes, A. G., Costa, A. J., Nascimento, A. C., Bincoletto, C., Ureshino, R. P., ... & Smaili, S. S. (2018). Autophagy and intermittent fasting: the connection for cancer therapy?. Clinics, 73.

[100] Bodén, S., Myte, R., Wennberg, M., Harlid, S., Johansson, I., Shivappa, N., ... & Nilsson, L. M. (2019). The inflammatory potential of diet in determining cancer risk; A prospective investigation of two dietary pattern scores. PloS one, 14(4), e0214551.

[101] Anton, S. D., Moehl, K., Donahoo, W. T., Marosi, K., Lee, S. A., Mainous III, A. G., ... & Mattson, M. P. (2018). Flipping the metabolic switch: understanding and applying the health benefits of fasting. *Obesity, 26*(2), 254-268.

[102] Austech, & Austech. (2019, August 27). Research-based Health Benefits of Intermittent Fasting. http://blogs.uwa.edu.au/futurehealth/2018/01/05/research-based-health-benefits-of-intermittent-fasting/

[103] Giurgea, C. (2005, April 25). The nootropic concept and its prospective implications. Retrieved from Giurgea, C. (1973). The "nootropic" approach to the pharmacology of the integrative activity of the brain 1, 2. Conditional reflex: a Pavlovian journal of research & therapy, 8(2), 108-115.

[104] Julson, E. (n.d.). The 14 Best Nootropics and Smart Drugs Reviewed. Retrieved from Hoffman, J. R., Ratamess, N. A., Gonzalez, A., Beller, N. A., Hoffman, M. W., Olson, M., ... & Jäger, R. (2010). The effects of acute and prolonged CRAM supplementation on reaction time and subjective measures of focus and alertness in healthy college students. Journal of the International Society of Sports Nutrition, 7(1), 1-8.

[105] St-Onge M-P. Dietary fats, teas, dairyand nuts: potential functional foods for weight control? Am J Clin Nutr. 2005 Jan;81(1):7–15.

[106] St-Onge, M. P. (2005). Dietary fats, teas, dairy, and nuts: potential functional foods for weight control?. The American journal of clinical nutrition, 81(1), 7-15.

[107] St-Onge M-P, Ross R, Parsons WD, Jones PJH. Medium-chain triglycerides increase energy expenditure and decrease adiposity in overweight men. Obes Res. 2003 Mar;11(3):395–402.

[108] Stubbs, R. J., & Harbron, C. G. (1996). Covert manipulation of the ratio of medium-to long-chain triglycerides in isoenergetically dense diets: effect on food intake in ad libitum feeding men. International journal of obesity and related metabolic disorders: journal of the International Association for the Study of Obesity, 20(5), 435-444.

[109] St-Onge, M. P., & Bosarge, A. (2008). Weight-loss diet that includes consumption of medium-chain triacylglycerol oil leads to a greater rate of weight and fat mass loss than does olive oil. The American journal of clinical nutrition, 87(3), 621-626.

[110] Sallaberry, C. A., & Astern, L. (2018). The endocannabinoid system, our universal regulator. Journal of Young Investigators, 34(6).

[111] McPartland, J. M., Guy, G. W., & Di Marzo, V. (2014). Care and feeding of the endocannabinoid system: a systematic review of potential clinical interventions that upregulate the endocannabinoid system. PloS one, 9(3), e89566.

[112] Yang, Peng et al. "Latest advances in novel cannabinoid CB(2) ligands for drug abuse and their therapeutic potential." *Future medicinal chemistry* vol. 4,2 (2012): 187-204.

[113] CBD Benefits: The Endocannabinoid System and Appetite. (2020, September 22). https://www.amsterdamgenetics.com/cbd-benefits-the-endocannabinoid-system-and-appetite/

114 Alger, B. E. (2013, November). Getting high on the endocannabinoid system. In Cerebrum: the Dana forum on brain science (Vol. 2013). Dana Foundation.

115 "The Discovery of the Endocannabinoid System: Centuries in the Making." NeuroscienceNews. NeuroscienceNews, 28 January 2019 https://neurosciencenews.com/endocannabinoid-system-10651/

116 Maroon, J., & Bost, J. (2018). Review of the neurological benefits of phytocannabinoids. Surgical neurology international, 9.

117 Russo, E. B. (2019). The case for the entourage effect and conventional breeding of clinical cannabis: no "strain," no gain. Frontiers in plant science, 9, 1969.

118 Gallily, R., Yekhtin, Z., & Hanuš, L. O. (2015). Overcoming the bell-shaped dose-response of cannabidiol by using cannabis extract enriched in cannabidiol. Pharmacology & Pharmacy, 6(02), 75.

119 Myers, C. (2018, February 23). How To Find Your Ikigai And Transform Your Outlook On Life And Business. https://www.forbes.com/sites/chrismyers/2018/02/23/how-to-find-your-ikigai-and-transform-your-outlook-on-life-and-business/

120 How to Lengthen Telomeres and Delay Telomere Shortening. (2020, September 16). https://www.parsleyhealth.com/blog/telomeres-stay-young-aging/

CHAPTER 6: YOUR TRIBE

121 Mineo, L. (2017). Good genes are nice, but joy is better: Harvard study, almost 80 years old, has proved that embracing community helps us live longer, and be happier. Harvard Gazette.

122 Mishra, B. N. (2009). Secret of eternal youth; Teaching from the centenarian hot spots ("blue zones"). Indian Journal of Community Medicine: Official Publication of Indian Association of Preventive & Social Medicine, 34(4), 273.

123 Mohr, D., Cuijpers, P., & Lehman, K. (2011). Supportive accountability: a model for providing human support to enhance adherence to eHealth interventions. Journal of medical Internet research, 13(1), e30.

124 Nanda, B. (2020, January 26). Mahatma Gandhi. https://www.britannica.com/biography/Mahatma-Gandhi

125 Liu, X., Raghuvanshi, R., Ceylan, F. D., & Bolling, B. W. (2020). Quercetin and Its Metabolites Inhibit Recombinant Human Angiotensin-Converting Enzyme 2 (ACE2) Activity. Journal of Agricultural and Food Chemistry.

CPSIA information can be obtained
at www.ICGtesting.com
Printed in the USA
LVHW081921100522
718418LV00003B/20